UNDERSTANDING CONSUMER DECISION MAKING

The Means–End Approach to Marketing and Advertising Strategy

UNDERSTANDING CONSUMER DECISION MAKING

The Means–End Approach to Marketing and Advertising Strategy

Edited by

Thomas J. Reynolds
LifeGoals, LLC

Jerry C. Olson
Pennsylvania State University

LEA LAWRENCE ERLBAUM ASSOCIATES, PUBLISHERS
2001   Mahwah, New Jersey   London

Lawrence Erlbaum Associates, Inc., Publishers
10 Industrial Avenue
Mahwah, New Jersey 07430

Cover design by Kathryn Houghtaling Lacey

Library of Congress Cataloging-in-Publication Data

Understanding consumer decision making : the means-end approach to marketing
and advertising strategy / Thomas J. Reynolds and Jerry C. Olson, editors.
    p. cm.
Includes bibliographical references and index.
   ISBN 0-8058-1730-1 (cloth : alk. paper) — ISBN 0-8058-1731-X (pbk. : alk. paper)
    1. Consumer behavior. 2. Marketing—Management. I. Reynolds, Thomas J.
(Thomas John), 1947– II. Olson, Jerry C. (Jerry Corrie), 1944–
HF5415.32.U53 2001
658.8'342—dc21   99-047703
                                                                 CIP

Books published by Lawrence Erlbaum Associates are printed on acid-free paper,
and their bindings are chosen for strength and durability.

Printed in the United States of America
10 9 8 7 6 5 4 3 2

*We dedicate this book to our teachers–Norman Cliff
and Ara Parseghian (TJR) and Jacob Jacoby (JCO)–
who, by their example and direction,
helped us to question, learn, and grow*

Contents

**V.   THEORETICAL PERSPECTIVES
       FOR MEANS–END RESEARCH**

Foreword

John A. Howard
George E. Warren
Columbia University

Many, perhaps most of the ideas introduced in academic marketing since the 1950s or so have originated in other disciplines, especially economics, psychology, and sociology. One interesting aspect of the means–end approach is that it is largely home-grown in that most of its development has occurred within the marketing discipline. I was one of the first to discuss how a means–end perspective to consumers could be useful in marketing. The means–end approach was a theme I included in several books, including my 1963, *Marketing: Executive and Buyer Behavior*, my 1969 collaboration with Jagdish Sheth, *The Theory of Buyer Behavior*, and more recently my textbook, *Consumer Behavior in Marketing Strategy* (1989), and the revised second edition of *Buyer Behavior in Marketing Strategy* (1994).

In the mid–1970s, Tom Reynolds and Jon Gutman became interested in means–end ideas. They were intrigued with the idea that people think at different levels of abstraction, and therefore, consumers do not always think about products in terms of physical attributes. This focus on product attributes was common in the ubiquitous research on multi-attribute attitude models in vogue at the time. In contrast, the means–end approach suggested that consumers think about and make purchase choices at more abstract levels such as the consequences (benefits or risks) that the product provides. In some cases, consumers might even consider the personal values the product could help them achieve.

Reynolds and Gutman developed their ideas about means–end chains in an impressive stream of publications. In their vision, a means–end

chain was a cognitive structure of meaning that connects product attributes to the consequences of product use. They felt these chains of meaning were critical to understanding both how and why consumers make
purchase decisions. Thus, the means–end approach represents a more
personalized, more emotional, more personal, more idiosyncratic vision
of how consumers think and make decisions about which products to buy
to satisfy their needs.

By the mid- to late–1980s, other researchers had become interested in
the means–end approach and were publishing papers about it, some of
which were critical. Several of these authors — Chuck Gengler, Klaus
Grunert, and Jerry Olson — are represented in this volume. More recently,
other researchers also represented in this volume began doing means–end
research — Hans Baumgartner, Suzanne Beekman, Joel Cohen, Rik Pieters,
John Rossiter, Piet Vanden Abeele, Beth Walker, Luk Warlop, and Steve
Westberg.

Another interesting aspect of the means–end approach, at least to me, is
how practical issues of application seem to have spurred its development.
I suspect that much of Reynolds and Gutman's early thinking about the
means–end approach was influenced by their use of the means–end approach in a variety of commercial applications to real business problems.
Being forced to deal with the myriad of issues that arise in a practical application seems to have spurred fairly rapid progress on both conceptual
and methodological fronts. A downside of the focus on business applications was the relatively few publications about many of these ideas and
developments. More recently, however, the publication rate increased
considerably in the 1990s as more researchers became interested in
means–end chains from a scholarly perspective.

Despite its practical bent, the means–end approach does have strong
roots in various theoretical concepts, mostly in psychology. Some founda-
tional areas include Kelley's Personal Construct Theory, Rokeach's value
theory, and associative network theory from cognitive psychology. As
sources of inspiration, ideas, and methods, these areas have nourished the
means–end approach and contributed to its development. The influence
of these basic theoretical areas is reflected throughout this volume. However, despite the progress since the 1970s, the means–end theory remains
to be fully and formally explicated. This book does not accomplish that
goal, but it moves us a long way toward a theory of means–end chains.

To conclude, I am pleased to see how the means–end approach has developed from its intuitive beginnings and its increasing use by assorted
researchers in corporations and universities. Still, even though the means–
end approach is some 30 or 40 years old, many people are unfamiliar with
means–end concepts and how to use them. This volume takes a large step
toward rectifying that situation. I believe this book will be valuable to a

wide range of academic and business researchers and marketing managers. The appropriate audiences include both the novice who may wish to read the book cover to cover as well as the seasoned means–end veteran who is likely to sample selectively from the book. All will find new ideas and inspiration here. I recommend it to your attention.

Preface

Although many marketing researchers and some academic scholars are familiar with the means–end approach to understanding consumers, only a few regularly incorporate the means–end approach into their research programs. Many others are unfamiliar with this useful perspective. Thus, more than 20 years after its introduction, many people do not understand the means–end approach or appreciate its advantages. Our goals in editing this book are to help business managers and academic researchers understand the means–end perspective and the methods by which it is operationalized and to demonstrate how to use the means–end approach to develop better marketing and advertising strategy.

There are several possible reasons for the rather slow growth of interest in means–end theory and its applications, many of which are addressed by the authors of these chapters.

1. Essentially, the means–end approach is a qualitative method, although it is more structured than many qualitative methods. Most market researchers are comfortable with quantitative methods, but fewer researchers feel comfortable using qualitative methods. In particular, some researchers are uncomfortable with the high amounts of subjective interpretation they must perform in using the means–end approach.

2. The means–end approach requires in-depth, one-on-one interviews with consumers, which can last from 1 to 2 hours. Analysis of the interview data requires extensive effort in coding (summarizing and categoriz-

ing) and interpreting the meaning of the results. Perhaps the high amount of effort in data collection and analysis explains the reluctance of some to use the means–end approach.

3. To date, it has been rather difficult for researchers to learn about the means–end approach. Many details concerning the rather involved methods have not been discussed in print. The theoretical foundations of the means–end approach have not been well articulated, either. Moreover, many of the articles about the means–end approach are published in a variety of scattered, somewhat obscure journals and books. Thus, the fragmented and somewhat inaccessible research literature concerning the means–end approach contributes to its relative obscurity.

4. Some researchers question the reliability and validity of laddering interviews in producing useful data. In particular, the repeated question probes used in laddering ("Why is that important to you?") seem too aggressive or too leading to some researchers.

5. Another problem concerns a lack of clarity about the theoretical foundations of the means–end approach. Because few researchers have dealt with theoretical issues and because much of the published work on means–end chains has an applied tone, many researchers feel the approach is merely an application technique with little or no theoretical value. Thus, the theoretical underpinnings of the means–end approach remain somewhat obscure.

6. Finally, managers have not always been able to see how they can use the customer insights gained from the means–end approach to solve particular marketing problems.

In this book, we seek to address each of the above mentioned problems with the means–end approach. The authors of the various chapters discuss methodological issues regarding interviewing and coding, present applications of the means–end approach to marketing and advertising problems, and describe the conceptual foundations of the means–end approach. The book contains a mix of original and previously published articles in roughly a 65:35 ratio. We included several previously published articles because we want the book to serve as a single, convenient source of information about the means–end approach.

The book is divided into five parts:

I.   Introduction
II. Using Laddering Methods to Identify Means–End Chains
III. Developing and Assessing Advertising Strategy
IV. The Means–End Approach to Developing Marketing Strategy
V.   Theoretical Perspectives for Means–End Research

The target audience for this book includes academic researchers in marketing and related fields, graduate students in business, marketing research professionals, and business managers. The book is intended as a reference book containing ideas about the means–end approach and its applications; however, it could be used as a textbook supplement for MBA or PhD courses on consumer behavior, advertising, or marketing strategy.

We sincerely hope that managers, researchers in business and academia, and students will find the means–end approach discussed here to be interesting and useful in their work.

ACKNOWLEDGMENTS

This book was a long time in coming, and we are indebted to the many individuals who helped make it possible. Most importantly, we thank the authors who produced excellent chapters for this book and then waited patiently for them to appear in print. We appreciate their creative thinking and good humor. In the same spirit, we thank our editors, Ray O'Connell and Anne Duffy at Lawrence Erlbaum Associates, for their encouragement and helpful suggestions. Jerry thanks his graduate students, Michael Mulvey, Torsten Ringberg, and Glenn Christensen, for their valuable help. Finally, each of us (Tom and Jerry) thanks the other for the good ideas, hard work, and friendship we have shared since the 1970s.

— *Tom Reynolds and Jerry Olson*

I

INTRODUCTION

The Means–End Approach to Understanding Consumer Decision Making

Jerry C. Olson
Penn State University

Thomas J. Reynolds
Richmont Partners

ABSTRACT

The purpose of this introductory chapter is to introduce the means–end approach to those readers who are not familiar with the approach and to refresh the memory of those with greater experience. To those ends, the means–end approach and its conceptual foundations are described and how managers can use the means–end approach to understand consumer decision-making is discussed. Specific chapters in the book cover all these issues in greater detail.

INTRODUCTION

The title for this book reveals the main goals. The chapters in this book describe the means–end approach to understanding consumer decision making and show how such understanding can inspire and guide managers' decisions about marketing and advertising strategy. The fundamental idea underlying the means–end approach is that decision makers choose courses of action (including behaviors such as the purchase of particular brands) that seem most likely to achieve important outcomes. The "means–end approach" is an umbrella term that refers to a set of methods for interviewing consumers about the reasons for their decision choice and interpreting consumers' responses in terms of linkages between outcomes.

The chapters in this book emphasize understanding consumer decision making, in contrast to merely predicting the choice outcomes of decision making. The latter type of research usually bases predictions of a decision choice on consumers' ratings of the importance of many potentially salient decision criteria. Unfortunately, being able to accurately predict choices offers relatively little strategic direction to the manager because this approach provides little or no understanding of why these criteria are important to the consumer. In contrast, means–end research concerned with understanding consumer decision making not only identifies which choice criteria are salient to the consumer, but digs deeper to explain *why* those factors are important to a decision maker. Many of the chapters in this volume illustrate how such deep understanding can powerfully guide and inspire managers' strategic thinking.

In this chapter we begin by describing how marketing managers should think about consumer decision making. Then we briefly review the conceptual foundations of the means–end approach or model and describe the basic means–end model. Finally, we discuss how this approach can help both business and academic researchers understand the most fundamental aspects of consumer decision making. The various chapters in this volume cover each of these issues in much greater detail.

WHAT DO MARKETERS NEED TO KNOW ABOUT CONSUMER DECISION MAKING?

Marketers face many difficult issues in their work: What value (meaning or equity) does my brand have? How can I induce consumers to adopt a new brand? How can I position a brand without cannibalizing my current brands? For decades, marketing researchers have studied consumer decision making in an attempt to provide answers to such questions. Unfortunately, much of that work fails to provide a deep understanding of how consumers make decisions.

Understanding consumer decision making is a two-step process. First, the marketing problem of concern must be framed as a specific decision made by consumers. Second, managers need to understand precisely how consumers go about making that decision. Both steps are reviewed in this section. First, we identify four fundamental issues that managers must address in order to frame the consumer decision—consumers, decision focus, decision context, and choice alternatives. As seen in the following, these four issues can be posed as formal questions that managers and researchers should answer. Doing so frames the marketing problem as a specific consumer decision and thus focuses the researcher on the most relevant aspects of decision making. Second, we identify the two key issues that underlie an understanding of that decision: (1) What are the salient choice criteria that consumers consider in evaluating alternatives, and (2) Why are those factors important to the consumer?

Who Are the Relevant Consumers

Consumers, of course, are vital to all types of business organizations. A common and succinct description of a business emphasizes the importance of consumers (customers or buyers): The purpose of a business is to create and keep a customer. In most for-profit business organizations, marketing has the major responsibility of developing strategies that will create customers (by inducing people to buy a product for the first time) and keep customers (by influencing people to buy the product multiple times).

Developing effective marketing strategies requires identifying which consumers are most relevant to the marketing problem and thus are the key decision makers. Although this issue can be straightforward, answering this question can be challenging and complex (see chaps. 11 and 12, this volume).

Decisions About What?

Consumers make decisions about many things, of course. It is important to recognize that all decisions involve choices among alternative behaviors or courses of action. That is, a choice decision always involves the selection of one possible behavior or action from a set of at least two alternative behaviors (Peter & Olson, 1999). Strictly speaking, people do not choose product A or brand B. Instead, they choose to buy, consume, recommend, sell, or return brand A rather than brand B. That is, one decides whether to buy a Coke or a Pepsi, shop at Giant or Safeway supermarket, or drink the last beer or save it until tomorrow. This means that consumer decision making is about evaluating and selecting alternative behaviors or actions.

Focusing on behaviors as choice alternatives rather than the typical marketing research focus on physical products, brands, or stores may seem a minor or subtle point, but it has important ramifications for both researchers and managers. By recognizing that consumers chose among behaviors, not objects, decision-making research is placed in context because behaviors always occur in an environmental context. A heightened behavior perspective also reveals that all marketing strategies are actions taken by the marketer that are intended to influence certain actions of consumers.

Although much decision-making research is narrowly focused on brand purchase behavior, consumers actually make decisions about many types of behaviors. These decisions include such issues as what information sources to consult, when to shop, where to park, what stores to patronize, what alternatives to even consider, and how to pay for a purchase. Some of these decisions may be trivial to the success of a marketing program (Where should I park?), whereas other (nonpurchase) decisions may be just as important as brand choice and, therefore, could be the focus of research and marketing strategy. For instance, in order to buy certain products, consumers must make a series of decisions about a sequence of behaviors. Researchers should identify the key decision (behaviors) in the sequence. For instance, to buy an exclusive brand of women's clothing, one must first decide to shop in a specialty store that carries this line. Thus, the store choice decision has a critical influence on consumers' decision to purchase a particular brand of dress.

In sum, it is critical that managers identify which consumer behaviors are most relevant for the marketing problem of interest. Developing a valid answer to this apparently easy question can be quite challenging (for an example, see chap. 11, this volume).

What Is the Decision Context?

Understanding consumers' decision making requires careful attention to the context in which the decision occurs. Context can be understood at micro (immediate) and macrolevels. All behaviors occur in some specific context, which includes the immediate physical environment and the social environment (presence and influence of other people, including friends, relatives, and sales people). Specific behaviors are also influenced by broader contextual factors, such as one's economic situation, cultural influences, and social roles. Marketers should attempt to understand the most powerful contextual influences on the consumer (see chap. 11, this volume, for a good example).

What Are the Choice Alternatives?

Once researchers know the consumer group of interest, the behaviors of greatest relevance, and the context in which those behaviors (and the decisions) occur, they can then address the fourth issue — identifying the relevant choice alternatives. To study decision making as it naturally occurs, researchers need to know the specific choice alternatives that consumers actively consider in making their choice decisions? Typically, a consumer considers only a limited number of choice alternatives at any one time — perhaps only two or three. These two or three choice alternatives create a microcontext for the decision-making process that constrains the choice criteria consumers consider in the decision and influences the relative salience or importance of those criteria.

Framing the Marketing Problem as a Consumer Decision

To use the means–end approach most effectively in solving marketing problems, managers should frame each marketing problem as a consumer decision (or as a series of decisions for complex problems). Each of the issues previously discussed is a step in the framing process. The process of framing the marketing issue or problem as a consumer decision can be formalized by requiring the researcher or manager to answer four questions:

1. Who are the relevant consumers or customers whose decisions I need to understand?
2. For those consumers, what particular behaviors or actions (shopping, brand choice, or consumption decisions) are most relevant to my marketing problem?
3. What are the social and physical contexts in which those behaviors or actions occur?
4. What choice alternatives does the consumer consider when making the key decisions in those situations?

Developing answers to these questions refocuses the managers attention by framing the marketing problems as one or more consumer decisions. Once the consumer decisions of major interest are known, the means–end approach can be used most effectively in understanding the two main issues in decision making: (a) What choice criteria do consumers use to evaluate the choice alternatives and choose among them?; and (b) Why do consumers find these particular choice criteria to be personally relevant (salient or important)?

In summary, answering the four framing questions clearly identifies one or more consumer decisions. Although the framing questions are not necessarily easy to answer, it is critical that they can be answered in as much precision and detail as possible. Often, dealing with these four questions requires deep thinking by managers and possibly some preliminary research and analysis. Several of the chapters in section IV of this volume illustrate this reframing process and its power (e.g., see chaps. 11, 12, and 13, this volume).

UNDERSTANDING THE DECISION-MAKING PROCESS

To understand consumer decision-making managers must address two issues: (a) What choice criteria do consumers use to evaluate the choice alternatives and choose among them?; and (b) Why are those particular choice criteria personally relevant to the consumers?

What Are the Salient Choice Criteria?

Eliciting the salient choice criteria is fairly straightforward. One can simply ask consumers to tell you what they are. Most elicitation methods are variations on such a direct inquiry. The key to success in identifying the actual choice criteria consumers use in decision-making is to insure that the decision context is activated in the consumer's mind when the elicitation question is asked. This requires a detailed understanding of the decision context, including the immediate physical and social environment in which the decision occurs as well as broader and less tangible contextual factors, such as consumers' lifestyle, socioeconomic variables, and broad historio-cultural factors. Finally, the set of considered choice alternatives provides yet another contextual influence on the choice criteria that consumers use to make a decision choice.

To elicit the choice criteria consumers actually use in a decision, researchers must activate the appropriate contextual basis for the decision. They can do so by establishing the key contextual factors in their questioning. For instance, one might ask the direct question: "When you are choosing among brands A, B, and C of cola soft drinks for an afternoon work break (or for a drink after exercise, etc.), what factors do you consider in making your decision?" It is quite possible that the salient choice criteria, or at least some of them, will vary from one set of considered choice alternatives to another. That is, a consumer is likely to use different choice criteria when choosing between a 4-wheel drive pickup truck and a small Mercedes Benz sedan than when selecting between a Mercedes Benz sedan and a BMW sedan.

Why Are These Choice Criteria Personally Relevant?

Personal relevance is the cornerstone to understanding consumer decision-making, and understanding personal relevance is the main advantage of the means–end approach. It seems obvious that consumers' purchase decisions are heavily influenced by the perceived personal relevance of the choice alternatives. That is, consumers are likely to select those choice alternatives that are seen as more useful for their needs (relevant for achieving goals and values). To understand personal relevance, marketing researchers have examined a variety of concepts such as involvement, product importance, attitude, interest, value, commitment, and even brand loyalty, but personal relevance remains an elusive concept. Most marketing research is content to measure the extent of personal relevance by identifying the specific concepts consumers use to evaluate alternative products or brands in a decision choice and having consumers rate their importance. Embarrassingly, little research has focused on un-

derstanding why these particular concepts are seen as salient choice criteria — that is, why do consumers perceive these concepts to be personally
relevant for their needs. Understanding the reasons *why* a concept is a salient factor in the decision-making process is critically important for understanding consumer decision making. Because the means–end approach is well suited to address issues of "the why of personal relevance,"
it is particularly useful for understanding consumer decision making.

THE MEANS–END CHAIN APPROACH

In this section, we briefly review the means–end approach, giving special
attention to the basic assumptions underlying its conceptual foundations.
We also present a brief historical overview of the development of the
means–end approach. Finally, we describe the component parts of the
means–end model. These issues also are treated in the various chapters in
this volume.

Foundational Assumptions

The conceptual foundation for the means–end approach rests on a few
simple, yet powerful assumptions or ideas. Although most of these ideas
are probably familiar to most marketers, they have not been integrated to
form a coherent perspective on consumer decision making. The means–
end approach constitutes a major step toward that goal.

• *Problem Orientation:* Because consumers experience many problems
in their daily lives, consumer decision making may be framed as problem
solving, which focuses on needs or goals (desired states) or deficiencies
(discrepancies between what one wants and what one has). A problem-solving orientation emphasizes that consumers try to solve their
problems by deciding to engage in various actions intended to achieve
their goals (or reduce deficiencies). Some of these actions may include the
purchase of products and services. Chapters 17 and 18 concern the relation between the means–end model and consumers' motivations and
goals, respectively.

• *Focus on Consequences:* The means–end approach emphasizes the
consequences or outcomes of a decision — as experienced by the consumer. The basic assumption is that when people buy a product, they actually are buying one or more experiences (consequences). Those outcome
experiences could be achieving the goal, or they might be a subgoal related to some larger, overall goal. The means–end approach explicitly as-

sumes that these desirable experienced consequences are the most salient considerations in decision making.

• *Positive and Negative Consequences:* Many salient consequences are positive experiences that consumers want to experience. However, other consequences are negative or aversive experiences that consumers are seeking to avoid or minimize. In chapters 12, 13, and 15, Reynolds describes these positive and negative consequences as *equities* and *disequities*, respectively. The overarching means–end principle in decision making is that consumers seek personally relevant alternatives that provide positive consequences (benefits) or avoid negative outcomes (risks).

• *Types of Consequences:* The means–end approach distinguishes between two major classes or types of consequences, whether positive or negative. Many salient consequences are rather tangible and direct experiences that are likely to occur immediately after a decision, usually during or soon after product consumption—"I wasn't hungry after eating that candy bar." In means–end terminology, these are called *functional consequences*. In contrast, other self-relevant consequences are more emotional, personal experiences. Some of these experiences can occur long after the purchase decision—"I still feel good wearing this dress," or, "People continue to notice my five-year-old car." These psychological and social consequences, respectively, are termed *psychological consequences* in the means–end approach.

• *Linkages or Connections:* The means–end approach focuses the greatest attention on the linkages between components—attributes, functional consequences, psychosocial consequences, and values. The linkages are critical because they carry the majority of the meaning.

• *Personal Relevance:* The functional and psychosocial consequences that are most instrumental or central to a person's major life goals and core values are the most personally relevant to that person. Because the means–end approach identifies which consequences are most strongly connected to important end goals and values, it helps in understanding the basis for personal relevance.

• *Intentional, Conscious Decision Making:* Finally, the means–end approach implicitly assumes that consumers' goal-directed purchase behaviors are *voluntary* and *conscious*. That is, we assume purchase decision making requires a conscious choice among at least two alternatives (buy brand X or buy brand Y, or buy the medium size or the giant size). Although the purchase process may eventually become habitual, largely automatic and unconscious, it is assumed that a conscious decision-making process did occur at some time in the past. If so, the basis for that decision can be modeled with the means–end approach. Consumer decision making may be influenced by many emotional and symbolic factors, some of which are tacit and unconscious. The means–end approach does not address how such factors may affect decision making, although it may provide hints about such influences.

To summarize, the means–end approach assumes that consumers decide which products and services to buy based on the anticipated consequences (experienced outcomes, need satisfaction, goal or value achievement) associated with each considered alternative. Typically, these consequences derive from consumers' actions involved with owning and using the alternative brands in question. The means–end approach claims that the most important choice criteria in a decision are the *anticipated experiences or consequences* associated with the various choice alternatives. Stated differently, consequences (not attributes) are the consumers' focal concern.

The means–end approach recognizes that consumers are concerned with both positive and negative experiences (benefits to be sought or risks to be avoided). Thus, consumers evaluate choice alternatives in terms of both the positive and negative consequences that are most personally relevant to them. As a general principle, therefore, consumers are likely to select the alternative that maximizes the positive outcomes and minimizes the negative ones.

In conclusion, the means–end approach provides a conceptual framework for understanding how consumers use choice criteria in the decision process and a methodology (laddering interviews) for identifying those factors. Essentially, the means–end approach treats consumers' choice criteria as means–end chains of linked consequences at different levels of abstraction. Thus, the means–end approach can identify what choice criteria are used by consumers to evaluate and select among choice alternatives and also explain why those particular choice criteria are salient or self-relevant to consumers. In this sense, then, researchers can use the means–end approach not only to describe consumer decision making but also to understand it.

A (Very) Brief History

The conceptual and measurement (laddering) basis for the means–end approach was developed over the past two decades through the efforts of Tom Reynolds and Jonathan Gutman. In marketing, the current interest in the means–end approach began with the seminal work of Gutman and Reynolds in the late 1970s (cf. Gutman, 1978, 1982; Gutman & Reynolds, 1979). The roots of the means–end approach, however, extend back much further to early economists' visions of consumers who calculate expected utility by considering the value of the consequences of their actions and to earlier work in marketing.

Various marketing scholars have explored aspects of a means–end approach, although no one has yet developed a complete and formalized means–end theory. Among the earliest of these was John Howard (1963, 1977) whose several books and general model of buyer behavior (Howard & Sheth, 1969) included many means–end ideas. In the early 1970s, Grey Advertising developed an interesting benefit chain model (Young & Feigen, 1975) that generated considerable interest. Myers' (1976) benefit structure analysis added to that interest. A flurry of means–end flurry of activity occurred later in the 1970s with an early means–end chain proposed by Geistfeld, Sproles, and Badenhop (1977), Cohen (1979), and Hirschman (1979). All of these discussions shared several common characteristics and assumptions that reveal their means–end nature. Each author recognized that consumers' product-related knowledge exists at different levels of abstraction and that these levels are hierarchically related. Although each model portrayed these levels a bit differently, most included the concrete level of actual, physical product attributes as well as a more abstract and personal level containing emotions, goals, and values.

Other important theoretical ideas and measurement techniques that contributed to the development of the means–end approach include the personal construct theory of George Kelly (1955) and the important marketing concept of benefit segmentation (Haley, 1968). With the ubiquitous multiattribute work of the 1970s, researchers became used to measuring product attributes, functional benefits, and consumers' values (Rokeach, 1973; Vinson, Scott, & Lamont, 1978). In the late 1970s and early 1980s, researchers began to combine these early intellectual elements with ideas from cognitive psychology about associative networks and levels of abstraction to form what is now called the means–end approach (cf. Gutman, 1982, 1984; Olson & Reynolds, 1983). Despite initial interest in the means–end approach, relatively few researchers worked with means–end approach during the 1980s. Reynolds and Gutman (cf. Gutman & Reynolds, 1979; Reynolds & Gutman, 1984, 1988) were the primary proponents of the means–end approach during this period. More recently, researchers have attempted to refine and clarify the conceptual foundations of the means–end approach (Gutman, 1990, 1991; Walker & Olson, 1991), although that process is by no means complete. Several chapters in this volume contribute to a clearer theoretical exposition of means–end approach (especially see Section V, this volume), but additional work is necessary to complete this project.

As is typical in other domains, means–end researchers devoted most of their attention to methodological issues, including developing measures and refining the analysis procedures. In particular, researchers worked to develop the personal interviewing procedures called laddering. In 1988, Reynolds and Gutman published an important paper on laddering techniques, which is reprinted here as chapter 2. (In addition, this volume contains two chapters on laddering methods: chap. 3 presents a critical commentary on laddering problems with laddering, and chap. 4 discusses further advancements in laddering techniques). The methodological focus also addressed data coding and data analysis, including computer-assisted data analysis (Gengler & Reynolds, 1995); alternative ways of modeling means–end data (Aurifeille & Vallette-Florence, 1995; Vallette-Florence & Rapacchi, 1991), and alternative graphic presentations of means–end maps (Gengler, Klenosky, & Mulvey, 1995).

To summarize, the published research to date has increased our knowledge about the means–end approach, its techniques, and its applications. Unfortunately, most means–end research is proprietary, consulting applications to practical marketing problems. However, several of the projects that have been released to be made public are represented in this volume (see Sections III and IV, this volume).

The Basic Means–End Model

In the most general means–end formulation, consumers have three levels of product-related knowledge — product attributes, the consequences or outcomes of using a product, and the broad goals or values that may be satisfied by use of that product (cf. chap. 4 in Peter & Olson, 1999). These three levels of consumer knowledge are combined to form a simple, hierarchical chain of associations:

$$\text{Attributes} \rightarrow \text{Consequences} \rightarrow \text{Values}$$

This set of associations is called a means–end chain because consumers see the product and its attributes as a means to an end. The desired *end* involves satisfaction of self-relevant consequences and values. The *chain* is the set of connections or linkages between attributes, consequences, and values. These linkages or associations have a hierarchical quality in that they connect concepts at a more concrete level of meaning (product attributes) to concepts at a more abstract level (values).

The means–end approach implies that product attributes, per se, have little or no importance or relevance to consumers. Instead, attributes have meaning and value for consumers largely in terms of the consequences they are perceived to bring about. The end consequence in a means–end chain is often a personal goal or a life value the consumer is striving to achieve.

The simplest means–end chain model links attributes to consequences to values. Some researchers have proposed more complex means–end chains that distinguish finer gradations of attributes and consequences. Consider the six-level model described by Olson and Reynolds (1983).

Concrete Attributes → Abstract Attributes → Functional Outcomes →
Psychosocial Outcomes → Instrumental Values → Terminal Values

This means–end model connects the tangible, concrete attributes of a
product to highly abstract and intangible personal and emotional values
(goals or needs) through a chain of increasingly relevant abstract outcomes that also become increasingly personal, emotional, motivating, and
self-relevant. Most researchers agree that this rather complex, six-level
model is not necessary for most business applications or even for most
theoretical purposes. Thus, a four-level model has eventually become the
"standard" (most common) means–end chain.

Attributes → Functional Consequences → Psychosocial
Consequences → Values or Goals

To summarize, the means–end approach first identifies which choice
consumers consider in evaluating alternative actions and selecting a chosen alternative. These personally relevant factors are the basis for consumers' preferences and are likely to be the most powerful components of an
effective positioning strategy. Second, the means–end approach provides
the critical understanding of why these factors are salient in the decision-making process by identifying the personally relevant consequences
of the choice criteria, as seen by consumers. These consequences can exist
at different levels of abstraction, from immediate functional outcomes to
more personally psychological consequences to highly personal and subjective life goals or values.

Importance of Consequences

Understanding consequences is key to understanding the means–end approach. Although consequences can be modeled at varying levels of abstraction (cf. Gutman, 1982; Olson & Reynolds, 1983), two levels of consequences are sufficient for most marketing analyses. During consumption,
product features or attributes produce immediate and tangible consequences that are experienced directly by consumers. (A laundry detergent
"gets stains out.") These outcomes are called *functional consequences*. In
turn, functional consequences can lead to higher level, more personal consequences that are more affective or emotional. These outcomes can be of
two types—*psychological consequences* (I feel like a good homemaker) and
social consequences (Others will notice my clean clothes). We combine both
types of outcomes into psychosocial consequences.
    The means–end approach emphasizes that the connections, links, or as-
sociations between concepts at different levels of abstraction carry or cre-

ate the meaning of any one concept. The meaning of any one concept is given by the other concepts to which it is connected. Stated differently, the reasons why each attribute is salient (or personally relevant) are given by the chains of consequences each attribute produces or leads to. Thus, means–end chains of linked consequences are the basis for the evaluation of the attribute (Is this attribute a good thing or a bad thing [for me]? How good or bad is it [for me]?).

A related implication of a focus on consequences or outcomes is the accompanying focus on behavior. Most of the consequences associated with the attributes of a product occur, either directly or indirectly, as a function of behaviors performed by consumers. This simple point is very important. By themselves, attributes can not have direct consequences. Rather, consumers must perform behaviors, particularly product usage behaviors, that then generate those consequences. This simple point is so obvious that one can miss its importance. Attributes, taken alone, have no consequences, and thus have no relevance. Consequences occur only when the consumer buys and consumes (or uses) the product and thereby experiences the consequences of use. For example, to experience the consequences of pleasurable taste and hunger reduction of a candy bar, one must first buy the candy bar, open the wrapper, and eat the candy bar. If the consumer does not perform these behaviors, the consequences will not occur. Note that the consequences the consumer experiences are partly due to the product attributes and partly due to the consumption behaviors of the consumer (eating very fast produces a different experience than slowly eating and savoring the candy bar). Of course, marketers might also be interested in other types of consequences associated with candy-bar consumption, such as littering, in which case they would be interested in other behaviors, such as discarding the wrapper.

APPLICATIONS OF MEANS–END THEORY TO CONSUMER DECISION MAKING

The essence of the means–end view of consumer decision-making is that consumers make decisions to solve problems (obtain desired consequences), and those consequences are relevant considerations in decision making because of their perceived relation with the goals or values that are salient in that decision context. Thus, in making decisions about which products or brands to buy, consumers necessarily focus on consequences (outcomes or experiences), rather than attributes. Stated differently, products or product attributes, per se, are not inherently important to consumers. Rather, consumers think about likely solutions to their problems when making purchase decisions.

Once a marketing problem has been clearly framed as a distinct consumer decision, the means–end approach (laddering interviews and data analysis) is used to address two key issues concerning consumer decision-making: What choice criteria do consumers use to evaluate and choose among the choice alternatives? Why are these choice criteria personally relevant to these consumers?

To dig deeper in consumers' decision-making process, it is especially critical to identify the choice alternatives that each consumer considers in the focal decision of interest. The specific choice criteria and their particular relevance (meaning) to the consumer are highly constrained by the unique contextual details of the choice situation. The decision context includes the choice set of alternatives that the consumer considers. For example, the researcher might ask: "Over the past year, what brands of soft drinks did you buy?" Thus, a buyer of cola soft drinks might identify three brands that he or she sometimes buys—Coke, Pepsi, and Dr. Pepper. These brands constitute the *consideration set* of choice alternatives the consumer might consider on any given choice occasion. This consideration set of choice alternatives has a critically important contextual influence on the choice criteria.

Eliciting Choice Criteria

There are various ways of eliciting choice criteria. (Several chapters in this volume provide detailed examples). As one example, the researcher might first establish the relative portion of a consumer's purchase choices devoted to each alternative by simply asking: "Over the past year, what percentage of your purchases would you say go to each brand?" The consumer might respond: "Coke 60%, Pepsi 30%, and Dr. Pepper 10%." With this context, established, the interviewer can then elicit choice criteria for each choice decision comparison: "When choosing between Coke and Pepsi, what factors do you consider?"

Identifying Equities

Alternatively, the researcher could ask a more direct question designed to address a deeper aspect of the decision-making process: "Why do you buy Coke more often than Pepsi?" Also, "Why do you buy Pepsi more often than Dr. Pepper?" Such questioning is designed to elicit the positive factors that attract the consumer to one brand, relative to another, in a very specific choice context. If those positive factors are strongly connected with a particular brand by many consumers, they can be considered equities by the marketing company. *Equities* are the positive factors that attract consumers to the brand. In a real sense, these equities are the basis for *brand equity*, as they provide much of the financial value of a brand. These various equities about the brand are really a set of mental representations (perceptual orientations or meanings) in the minds of a group of consumers.

Identifying Disequities

Likewise, the negative factors that influence consumers' decision making (choice criteria that repel consumers from a brand) also must be identified and understood. These negative factors, if associated with a particular brand by many consumers, might be considered disequities. *Disequities* are the aversive factors that keep consumers from buying a brand or from buying it more often. These unfavorable meanings in consumers' minds reduce or limit the financial value of the brand — they reduce brand equity.

Disequities can be elicited in a similar fashion to equities. Continuing the soft drink example, the researcher could ask: "Why don't you buy Coke more often (or, all the time)? Why don't you buy Pepsi more often than Coke? Why don't you purchase Dr. Pepper more frequently?" This line of questioning will elicit negative choice criteria that are specific to each brand.

Understanding Personal Relevance

Once the four framing issues have established the context of a clearly defined decision, including specific choice alternatives (e.g., buying Coke vs. Pepsi vs. Dr. Pepper), the means–end interviewing can proceed to determine the reasons why the choice criteria are personally relevant to the consumer. This requires laddering interviewing methods (Reynolds & Gutman, 1984, 1988). The interviewer then can ask laddering questions ("why is _____ important to you?") to establish the reasons why these choice criteria are important (salient, or self-relevant) in the consumers' decision-making process. (See Section II of this volume.) The elicitation methods for identifying choice criteria and the subsequent laddering interview will vary depending on the decision history of each consumer. For instance, if one consumer buys only Coke, all laddering would focus on the reasons for that preference (potential equities) and perhaps reasons why other brands are unacceptable (disequities for other brands).

Grounding in Context

Much of the past decision-making research treats brand choice decisions in general terms; context is not considered at all or only in a shallow manner. Thus, researchers usually take a more general approach to eliciting choice criteria. "When you think about buying soft drinks, what factors do you consider in your decision?" Now we can recognize that this approach mostly elicits positive reasons for buying one or more of the brands, but these choice criteria are not linked to particular brands. Thus an analysis of brand equities and disequities at the brand level is not possible. This then severely restricts the decision-making insights that can yield useful marketing strategies at the brand level. Many of the chapters in this volume provide excellent examples of the importance of context.

SUMMARY

The means–end approach is a powerful tool for business and academic researchers. The means–end approach is particularly effective in helping researchers and managers understand consumer decision making about virtually anything, including purchase choices at the brand or product category levels. The means–end approach is capable of providing detailed understanding of very specific aspects of consumer decision making (as illustrated in several chapters of this volume). Managers then can use these insights to develop highly focused marketing and communication strategies that are intended to influence those decision processes (see chap. 9, this volume). The insights into consumer decision making provided by the means–end approach also are relevant for academic consumer researchers interested in developing deep understandings of the processes by which consumers actually make decisions.

The chapters in this book illustrate all the aspects of the means–end approach discussed here. We hope you enjoy reading them.

REFERENCES

Aurifeille, J.-M., & Valette-Florence, P. (1995). Determination of the dominant means–end chains: A constrained clustering approach. *International Journal of Research in Marketing, 12,* 267–278.

Cohen, J. B. (1979). The structure of product attributes: Defining attribute dimensions for planning and evaluation. In A. D. Shocker (Ed.), *Analytic approaches to product and market planning* (pp. 54–86). Cambridge, MA: Marketing Science Institute.

Geistfeld, L. V., Sproles, G. B., & Badenhop, S. B. (1977). The concept and measurement of a hierarchy of product characteristics. In H. K. Hunt (Ed.), *Advances in consumer research*, Vol. 5 (pp. 302–307). Ann Arbor, MI: Association for Consumer Research.

Gengler, C. E., Klenosky, D. B., & Mulvey, M. S. (1995). Improving the graphic representation of means–end results. *International Journal of Research in Marketing, 12,* 245–256.

Gengler, C. E., & Reynolds, T. R. (1995). Consumer understanding and advertising strategy: Analysis and strategic translation of laddering data. *Journal of Advertising Research, 35,* 19–33.

Gutman, J. (1978). Uncovering the distinctions people make versus the use of multi-attribute models: Do a number of little truths make wisdom? In *Proceedings of the 20th Annual Con-*

ference of the Advertising Research Foundation. New York: Advertising Research Foundation, 71–76.

Gutman, J. (1982). A means-end chain model based on consumer categorization processes. *Journal of Marketing, 46,* 60–72.

Gutman, J. (1984). Analyzing consumer orientation toward beverages through means–end analysis. *Psychology and Marketing, 1*(3/4), 23–43.

Gutman, J. (1990). Adding meaning to values by directly assessing value-benefit relationships. *Journal of Business Research, 20,* 153–160.

Gutman, J. (1991). Exploring the linkages between consequences and values. *Journal of Business Research, 22,* 143–149.

Gutman, J., & Alden, S. (1984). Adolescents' cognitive structures of retail stores and fashion consumption: A means–end analysis. In J. Jacoby & J. Olson (Eds.), *Perceived quality of products, services, and stores* (pp. 115–138). Lexington, MA: Lexington Books.

Gutman, J., & Reynolds, T. J. (1978). An investigation of the levels of cognitive abstraction utilized by consumers in product differentiation. In J. Eighmy (Ed.), *Attitude research under the sun* (pp. 128–152). Chicago: American Marketing Association.

Gutman, J., & Reynolds, T. J. (1979). An investigation of the levels of cognitive abstraction utilized by consumers in product differentiation. In J. Eighmy (Ed.), *Attitude research under the sun* (pp. 128–152). Chicago: American Marketing Association.

Gutman, J., & Reynolds, T. (1982). Segmentation of complex markets: Identification of perceptual points of view. In A. A. Mitchell (Ed.), *Advances in consumer research,* Vol. 9 (pp. 392–397). Ann Arbor, MI: Association for Consumer Research.

Gutman, J., & Reynolds, T. J. (1987). Coordinating assessment to strategy development: An advertising assessment paradigm based on the MECCAS model. In J. Olson & K. Sentis (Eds.), *Advertising and consumer psychology,* Vol. 3 (pp. 242–258). New York: Praeger.

Haley, R. I. (1968). Benefit segmentation: A decision oriented research tool. *Journal of Marketing, 32,* 30–35.

Hirschman, E. C. (1979). Attributes of attributes and layers of meaning. In J. C. Olson (Ed.), *Advances in consumer research,* Vol. 7 (pp. 7–12). Ann Arbor, MI: Association for Consumer Research.

Hirschman, E. C. (1980). Attributes of attributes and layers of meaning. In J. C. Olson (Ed.), *Advances in consumer research* (pp. 7–12). Ann Arbor, MI: Association for Consumer Research.

Howard, J. A. (1977). *Consumer behavior: Application and theory.* New York: McGraw-Hill.

Howard, J. A., & Sheth, J. N. (1969). *The theory of buyer behavior.* New York: Wiley.

Kelly, G. (1955). *The psychology of personal constructs.* Vols. I and II. New York: W. W. Norton.

Myers, J. M. (1976). Benefit structure analysis: A new tool for product planning. *Journal of Marketing, 40,* 23–32.

Olson, J. C., & Reynolds, T. J. (1983). Understanding consumers' cognitive structures: Implications for advertising strategy. In L. Percy & A. Woodside (Eds.), *Advertising and consumer psychology* (pp. 77–90). Lexington, MA: Lexington Books.

Peter, J. P., & Olson, J. C. (1999). Consumers' product knowledge and involvement. In *Consumer behavior and marketing strategy,* 3rd Edition (pp. 63–91). Homewood, IL: R. D. Irwin.

Reynolds, T. J., & Gutman, J. (1984). Laddering: Extending the repertory grid methodology to construct attribute-consequence-value hierarchies. In R. E. Pitts, Jr. & A. G. Woodside (Eds.), *Personal values and consumer psychology* (pp. 155–167). Lexington, MA: Lexington Books.

Reynolds, T. R., & Gutman, J. (1988). Laddering theory, method, analysis and interpretation. *Journal of Advertising Research, 28,* 11–31.

Reynolds, T. J., Gutman, J., & Fiedler, J. A. (1985). Understanding consumers' cognitive structures: The relationship of levels of abstraction to judgments of psychological distance and preference. In L. F. Alwitt & A. A. Mitchell (Eds.), *Psychological processes and advertising effects* (pp.). Lawrence Erlbaum Associates.

Rokeach, M. (1973). *The nature of human values*. New York: Free Press.

Vallette-Florence, P., & Rapacchi, B. (1991). Improvements in means–end chain analysis using graph theory and correspondence analysis. *Journal of Advertising Research, 31,* 30–45.

Vinson, D. E., Scott, J. E., & Lamont, L. M. (1977, April). The role of personal values in marketing and consumer behavior. *Journal of Marketing, 41,* 44–50.

Walker, B. A., & Olson, J. C. (1991). Means-end chains: Connecting products with self. *Journal of Business Research, 22,* 111–118.

Young, S., & Feigen, B. (1975). Using the benefit chain for improved strategy formulation. *Journal of Marketing, 39,* 72–74.

II

USING LADDERING METHODS TO IDENTIFY MEANS–END CHAINS

SECTION OVERVIEW

The laddering interview is the preferred method for identifying consumers' means–end chains. Basically, *laddering* is a semistructured qualitative method in which respondents describe, freely in their own words, why something is important to them. The qualitative nature of laddering derives from the open-ended response format, the freedom of respondents to respond to questions in their own words, and of course, the necessity for researchers to interpret the meaning of those responses. Unlike some qualitative methods, however, the laddering interview has a definite structure that derives from the ordering of the questions and the use of standard probing questions to gain additional responses. Interviewers have a definite agenda to follow and the questioning flows similarly for each interview. In these senses, then, laddering is considered a structured qualitative method.

The basic laddering interview has two key steps or processes. First, the interviewer must identify the key choice criteria that consumers claim to use in making a purchase choice from among a considered set of alternatives (perhaps several different brands). Second, the interviewer seeks to learn why those choice criteria are important, salient, or relevant to the consumer. This is done by asking a series of simple "why" questions ("Why is it important to you that your bank is located on the way to work?").

21

The means–end approach assumes that consumers value certain product attributes because those attributes are seen as instrumental in producing (or leading to) important (self-relevant) outcomes or consequences. The laddering interviewer continues to probe for higher ordered, more abstract reasons for salience or importance by asking why each mentioned consequence is important to the consumer ("Why is it important to you that your bank be conveniently located?"). Nearly always, a consequence is important because it leads to another, more abstract consequence ("A convenient location gives me more time with my family"). Some laddering interviews reach the level of personal values — a type of very abstract consequence ("Spending more time with my family makes me feel like a good parent"). Most laddering interviews stop at the basic value level — the "end" of a means–end chain — because the value has no higher level consequences to which it is seen as leading.

As with most qualitative methods, the interviewer is the key instrument in laddering. Laddering data are as good as the interviewers who collect them. Although seemingly simple and easy, laddering interviews actually are rather complex. Good laddering interviews demand intelligent and experienced interviewers. Interviewers should understand the conceptual basis for the means–end approach. They should understand the logic of the laddering interview and know why certain things are to be probed and emphasized. Interviewers must be able to quickly determine which concepts are important and which are not, in order to determine which concepts and comments to follow up and which to ignore.

Conducting actual interviews under the supervision of a skilled interviewer is the ideal way to gain the requisite knowledge about laddering. To some extent, however, interviewers can learn useful information through reading about laddering techniques. This section contains reprints of two of the best published papers about doing laddering interviews. Each chapter describes several interviewing techniques to use in conducting a laddering interview. This section also includes two original papers, one of which is critical of aspects of laddering, and the other of which offers new ideas for improving laddering interviews. Together, these four chapters review the basic laddering approach, identify problem areas in laddering interviews, offer criticisms of laddering methods, and present a wealth of ideas for conducting laddering interviews.

• Chapter 2 by Reynolds and Gutman is the now-classic exposition of the methods used in a laddering interview. The authors describe a variety of techniques and various "tricks of the trade" for solving many of the problems that arise during laddering interviews. Their chapter is a must read for less-experienced laddering interviewers, but even laddering experts can benefit from a rereading of this important chapter.

- In chapter 3, Grunert, Beekman, and Sorensen take a critical look at laddering. The authors identify what they see as the critical conceptual underpinnings of laddering, and they use that perspective to discuss the problems and shortcomings of the traditional laddering interview. The authors make an interesting distinction between two types or levels of laddering rigor — they contrast the typical hard laddering approach (following a fairly rigid sequence of questioning) with a looser, soft approach. Chapter 3 helps explicate the usually implicit assumptions underlying the means–end approach. Perhaps it will stimulate researchers to develop alternative laddering methods that are consistent with those theoretical assumptions.

- In chapter 4, Reynolds, Dethloff, and Westberg present a number of newer methods and techniques for conducting laddering interviews. Many of these ideas have not appeared previously in print. This chapter is an excellent instruction guide in "advanced laddering techniques."

- In chapter 5, Gengler and Reynolds focus on the analysis of laddering data. They present a detailed example of how laddering data is analyzed to provide deep understanding of consumer decision making. The authors also show how the Consumer Decision Map (CDM) can be used to guide managers' thinking about appropriate advertising strategy.

Taken together, these four chapters provide an excellent overview of laddering methods, conceptual foundations of laddering, and applications of laddering results. Novice interviewers will learn a great deal about how to collect means–end data using laddering interviews. Armed with this knowledge and sufficient practice, most people can become competent laddering interviewers. Even experienced laddering interviewers will find useful hints and techniques to incorporate in their toolbox of laddering methods. We hope these chapters encourage researchers to undertake research that will contribute to further developments of laddering methodology.

2

Laddering Theory, Method, Analysis, and Interpretation

Thomas J. Reynolds
Strategic Research, Development and Assessment

Jonathan Gutman
University of New Hampshire

Personal values research in marketing has recently received a substantial amount of attention from both academics and practitioners. This more in-depth profiling of the consumer and his or her relationship to products offers potential not only for understanding the "cognitive" positionings of current products but also permits the development of positioning strategies for new products. Endorsing this more psychological view of the marketplace, Sheth (1983) suggested that to be competitive in marketing products in the 1980s, both researchers and management are going to have to, if they have not already, adopt this consumer-based orientation rather than one that merely focuses on product characteristics.

The application of the personal values perspective to the marketing of consumer products can be classified into two theoretically grounded perspectives, macro representing sociology and micro representing psychology (Reynolds, 1985). The *macro approach* refers to standard survey research methodology combined with a classification scheme to categorize respondents into predetermined clusters or groups (e.g., VALS methodology of the Stanford Research Institute). Products and their positioning strategies are then directed to appeal to these general target groups, such as the Merrill Lynch solitary bull appealing to the "achiever" orientation whose desire is to stand out and "get ahead of the pack" (Plummer, 1985).

Reynolds (1985) noted, although strong on face validity, these rather general classifications fail to provide an understanding, specifically, of how the concrete aspects of the product fit into the consumer's life. As such, the macro survey approach only gives part of the answer, namely, the overall value orientation of target segments within the marketplace. Missing are the key defining components of a positioning strategy – the linkages between the product and the personally relevant role it has in the life of the consumer.

The more psychological perspective offered by the micro approach, based on means–end theory (Gutman, 1982), specifically focused on the linkages between the attributes that exist in products (the means), the consequences for the consumer provided by the attributes, and the personal values (the "ends") the consequences reinforce. The means–end perspective closely parallels the origin of attitude research represented by Expectancy-Value Theory (Rosenberg, 1956), which posited that consumer actions produce consequences and that consumers learn to associate particular consequences with particular product attributes they have reinforced through their buying behavior. The common premise, then, is that consumers learn to choose products containing attributes that are instrumental to achieving their desired consequences. Means–End Theory simply specifies the rationale underlying why consequences are important, namely, personal values.

The focus of this chapter is on detailing the specifics of the in-depth interviewing and analysis methodology, termed "laddering" (Gutman & Reynolds, 1979; Reynolds & Gutman, 1984a), for uncovering means–end hierarchies defined by these key elements and their linkages or connections. The combination of connected elements, or ladder, represents the linkage between the product and the perceptual process of consumers, which as pointed out previously, yields a more direct and thus more useful understanding of the consumer.

LADDERING

Laddering refers to an in-depth, one-on-one interviewing technique used to develop an understanding of how consumers translate the attributes of products into meaningful associations with respect to self, following Means–End Theory (Gutman, 1982). Laddering involves a tailored interviewing format using primarily a series of directed probes, typified by the "Why is that important to you?" question, with the express goal of determining sets of linkages between the key perceptual elements across the range of attributes (A), consequences (C), and values (V). These association networks, or ladders, referred to as perceptual orientations, represent combinations of elements that serve as the basis for distinguishing between and among products in a given product class.

It is these higher order knowledge structures that we use to process information relative to solving problems (Abelson, 1981), which, in the consumer context, is represented by choice. Basically, distinctions at the different levels of abstraction, represented by the A-C-Vs, provide the consumer with more personally relevant ways in which products are grouped and categorized. Thus, the detailing and subsequent understanding of these higher level distinctions provides a perspective on how the product information is processed from what could be called a motivational perspective, in that the underlying reasons why an attribute or a consequence is important can be uncovered.

For example, the following ladder, starting with a basic distinction between types of snack chips, represents part of the data collection from a single subject in a salty-snack study:

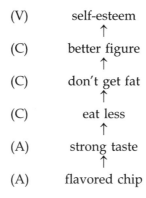

(V)	self-esteem
(C)	better figure
(C)	don't get fat
(C)	eat less
(A)	strong taste
(A)	flavored chip

These elements were sequentially elicited from the respondent as a function of the laddering technique's ability to cause the respondent to think critically about the connections between the product's attributes and, in this case, her personal motivations.

The analysis of laddering data such as this across respondents first involves summarizing the key elements by standard content-analysis procedures (Kassarjian, 1977), although bearing in mind the levels of abstraction, A-C-V, conceptualization. Then a summary table can be constructed representing the number of connections between the elements. From this summary table dominant connections can then be graphically represented in a tree diagram, termed a hierarchical value map (HVM). (This type of cognitive map, unlike those output from traditional factor analysis or multidimensional scaling methods, is structural in nature and represents the linkages or associations across levels of abstraction [attributes-consequences-values] without reference to specific brands.) Unfortunately, although basically accurate, this general description of the analysis process has not been specific enough to permit first-time analysts (or their su-

periors) to feel comfortable with dealing with all the vagaries of qualitative data of this type. Thus, a step-by-step procedure, including both the
analysis and the assessment of the resulting map, will be detailed by way
of example later.

Interpretation of this type of qualitative, in-depth information permits
an understanding of consumers' underlying personal motivations with
respect to a given product class. Each unique pathway from an attribute to
a value represents a possible perceptual orientation with respect to viewing the product category. Herein lies the opportunity to differentiate a
specific brand, not by focusing on a product attribute, but rather by communicating how it delivers higher level consequences and ultimately how
it is personally relevant, essentially creating an "image positioning." This
understanding typically serves as the basis for the development of advertising strategies, each representing a distinct "cognitive" positioning,
which reinforces the various levels of abstraction for a given perceptual
orientation (Olson & Reynolds, 1983; Reynolds & Gutman, 1984b).

In sum, the express purpose of the interviewing process is to elicit attribute-consequence-value associations consumers have with respect to a
product or service class. The general notion is to get the respondent to respond and then to react to that response. Thus, laddering consists of a series of directed probes based on mentioned distinctions initially obtained
from perceived differences between and among specific brands of products or services. Again, after the initial distinction obtained by contrasting
brands is elicited, all subsequent higher level elements are not brand specific. The laddering results can be used to create an HVM summarizing all
interviews across consumers, which is interpreted as representing dominant perceptual orientations, or "ways of thinking," with respect to the
product or service category.

OBJECTIVES

Since the introduction of the laddering methodology into the consumer
research domain, numerous applications, both applied and academic,
have been executed (Gutman, 1984; Gutman & Alden, 1984; Gutman,
Reynolds, & Fiedler, 1984; Olson & Reynolds, 1983; Reynolds & Gutman,
1984a, 1984b; Reynolds & Jamieson, 1984). Again, the primary application
has been to develop a cognitive hierarchical value map indicating the interrelation of the attributes, consequences, and personal values for a given
product or service category.

Unfortunately, the term laddering in the marketing community has become a somewhat generic term representing merely a qualitative, in-

depth interviewing process (Morgan, 1984), without reference to either its theoretical underpinnings (Gutman, 1982) or the rather critical distinction between the interviewing process and analytical methods used to derive meaning from the resulting data (Durgee, 1985). Not only have these critical distinctions been overlooked, but even the standard definition of laddering as an interviewing methodology, to date, has not been addressed in the academic literature. Given the value of this type of in-depth understanding of the consumer, in particular, the potential with respect to the specification of more accurate and appropriate positioning strategies, a comprehensive documentation of this research approach is needed.

Thus, it is the primary objective of this article to detail the interviewing techniques that pertain to laddering in order to provide a foundation for both its application as well as subsequent method evaluation. A secondary objective is to provide a detailed description of how the analysis of this specific type of qualitative data is performed. The third and final objective is to demonstrate how the laddering results are interpreted with respect to developing and understanding perceptual orientations and product positionings.

INTERVIEW ENVIRONMENT

General Considerations

An interviewing environment must be created such that the respondents are not threatened and are thus willing to be introspective and look inside themselves for the underlying motivations behind their perceptions of a given product class. This process can be enhanced by suggesting in the introductory comments that there are no right or wrong answers, thus relaxing the respondent, and further reinforcing the notion that the entire purpose of the interview is simply to understand the ways in which the respondent sees this particular set of consumer products. Put simply, the respondent is positioned as the expert. The goal of the questioning is to understand the way in which the respondent sees the world, where the world is the product domain comprised of relevant actors, behaviors, and contexts. The approaches and techniques discussed in this article are designed to assist the respondent in critically examining the assumptions underlying their everyday commonplace behaviors. Wicker (1985) discussed how researchers might use some of these same devices in breaking out of their traditional modes of thinking.

Importantly, interviewers must position themselves as merely trained facilitators of this discovery process. In addition, due to the rather personal nature of the later probing process, it is advisable to create a slight sense of vulnerability on the part of the interviewer. This can be accomplished by initially stating that many of the questions may seem somewhat obvious and possibly even stupid, associating this predicament with the interviewing process, which requires the interviewer to follow certain specific guidelines.

Obviously, as with all qualitative research, the interviewer must maintain control of the interview, which is somewhat more difficult in this context due to the more abstract concepts that are the focus of the discussion. This can be best accomplished by minimizing the response options, in essence being as direct as possible with the questioning, while still following what appears to be an unstructured format. By continually asking the "Why is that important to you?" question, the interviewer reinforces the perception of being genuinely interested and thus tends to command the respect and control of the dialogue.

By creating a sense of involvement and caring in the interview, the interviewer is able to get below the respondent's surface reasons and rationalizations to discover the more fundamental reasons underlying the respondent's perceptions and behavior. Understanding the respondent involves putting aside all internal references and biases and putting oneself in the respondent's place. It is critical that rapport be established before the actual in-depth probing is initiated as well as maintained during the course of the interview. Basically, the interviewer must instill confidence in the respondent so the opinions expressed are perceived as simply being recorded rather than judged.

Also critical to the interviewing process is the ability of the interviewer to identify the elements brought forth by the respondent in terms of the level of abstraction framework. Thus, a thorough familiarity with the means–end theory is essential.

Sensitive areas will frequently produce superficial responses created by the respondent to avoid introspection about the real reasons underlying the respondent's behavior. A clinical sensitivity is further required of the interviewer to both identify and deal with these frequent and potentially most informative types of dialogue.

As in all interview situations, because the respondents will react directly in accordance with the interviewer's reactions—both verbal and nonverbal—it is vital to make the respondent feel at ease. One should carefully avoid potentially antagonistic or aggressive actions. Moreover, to avoid any interview-demand characteristics, nonverbal cues such as approval, disapproval, surprise or hostility, or implying rejection should be avoided. Put simply, the interviewer should be perceived as a very interested yet neutral recorder of information.

LADDERING METHODS

Eliciting Distinctions

Laddering probes begin with distinctions made by the individual respondent concerning perceived, meaningful differences between brands of products. Having made a distinction the interviewer first makes sure it is bipolar, requiring the respondent to specify each pole. The respondent is then asked which pole of the distinction is preferred. The preferred pole then serves as the basis for asking some version of the "Why is that important to you?" question. The following overviews three general methods of eliciting distinctions that have proven satisfactory. The interview outline generally includes at least two distinct methods of eliciting distinctions to make sure no key element is overlooked.

Triadic Sorting (Kelly, 1955)

Providing the respondent with sets of three products as in the Repertory Grid procedure is one way to elicit responses from a respondent. Following are instructions for a wine cooler study which used triads to elicit initial distinctions.

Instructions for Triads

You will be presented with five groups of three different wine coolers. For each group of three you will have the opportunity to tell me how you think about the differences among the coolers. For example, if you were given a group of three cars: Lincoln Continental, Mustang, and Cadillac you might say "car maker" as a way of thinking about them. Two are made by Ford and one is made by General Motors. Another way to think about them is size—big versus small. Of course, there are many different ways that you could think about the cars, for example:

- high styling versus ordinary styling
- economy versus luxury
- sporty versus traditional

There are no right or wrong answers. As I present you with each group, take a moment to think about the three wine coolers.

Specifically, I want you to tell me some important way in which two of the three wine coolers mentioned are the same and thereby different from the third. Again, when I show you the names of the three wine coolers, think of some overall way in which two of the coolers are the same and yet different from the third. If your response for one group of wine coolers is the same as for a previous group, try to think of another way in which they differ.

Preference-Consumption Differences

Preference differences can also be a useful device for eliciting distinctions. Respondents, after providing a preference order for, say, brands of coolers, might be asked to tell why they prefer their most preferred brand to their second most preferred brand, or more simply to say why one particular brand is their most preferred (or second most preferred, least preferred, etc.) brand.

To illustrate:

> You said your most preferred brand is California Cooler and your second most was Bartles and Jaymes. What is it, specifically, that makes California Cooler more desirable?

Along these same lines, one might ask about preference and usage and query instances where liked brands are used infrequently or less well-liked brands are used more frequently. This device worked well in a proprietary study of snack chips. Differences between what people like and what they actually used opened up the discussion to include strategies to limit or control the consumption of snacks.

Differences by Occasion

In most cases it is desirable to present the respondent with a personally meaningful context within which to make the distinctions. This contributes to more important distinctions being elicited as respondents' distinctions are being examined in the context of the setting in which they naturally occur (Barker, 1968; Runkel & McGrath, 1972). Attention to the context of consumer behavior provides a more meaningful context for laddering to proceed. People do not use or consume products in general; they do so in particular contexts. A study done in the convenience restaurant category (Gutman, Reynolds, & Fiedler, 1984) used triads between various convenience restaurants as a starting point. It was soon discovered that the distinctions elicited represented such obvious physical characteristics of the places compared (namely, hamburgers vs. chicken) that they did not permit movement to higher, more personally meaningful areas from this starting point.

Respondents were then questioned about their usage of various convenience restaurants and the occasion (day-part, who with, concomitant activities) in which they frequented them. Using this information to provide a relevant context relating to frequent usage of the category, respondents were given the same triads but with a context for making a comparison. For example, it might be suggested to a mother with young children that she has been out shopping with her children, and it being lunch time, she wants to stop for lunch on the way home. Three convenience restaurants could be compared for their suitability with respect to this usage situation. Respondents could respond to triads using their two or three most frequent usage occasions as a context for responding.

What is important is to provide a meaningful basis for the respondent to keep in mind when thinking about differences among the stimuli. In this manner their distinctions are more likely to lead to a meaningful consideration of outcomes accruing to the respondent, which relate to making distinctions among the products.

Selecting Key Distinctions to Ladder

Typically, a respondent can only mention 10 to 12 different distinctions for a given product category. Once a satisfactory number of distinctions have been mentioned, the interviewer has basically two options on how to select which ones will serve as the basis for building ladders. Either the interviewer can judgmentally select which distinctions are to be used on the basis of prior knowledge of the category or with respect to the specific research issue at hand. Or, the interviewer can present a card with all the mentioned distinctions on it and have the respondent rate the relative importance of each, then select those with the highest ratings.

The Two Basic Problems of Laddering

Prior to the detailing of the specific interviewing techniques, two of the most common problems encountered in laddering and the general type of tactics required to counter the situation are reviewed. An understanding of these basic issues will provide a necessary basis for learning the more detailed techniques to be presented later in the article.

The Respondent Really Does Not "Know" the Answer. When asked why a particular attribute or consequence is important to them, the respondent often cannot articulate a "ready" reason. This lack of previous thinking of the reason underlying why the lower level construct is important can be dealt with by asking what would happen if the attribute or consequence was not delivered. Essentially this is negative laddering. The "nonconscious" reason (preferred in the Mean–End approach to the psychoanalytic "subconscious") is then typically discovered by the respondent imagining the negative, resulting from the absence of the given construct, and then relating that back to what must be delivered if that negative is to be avoided.

Another general class of probing to avoid blocks on the part of the respondent is to change or rephrase the question in a situational context, much like the more concrete method illustrated earlier for initially eliciting distinctions. By discussing the issue in this manner, an answer is typically "discovered" due to the ability to concretize the issue at hand and deal with specific circumstances.

Issues That Become Too Sensitive. As the respondent is taken through the laddering process, that is, moved upward through the levels of abstraction, the dynamics of the interview become more and more personal. Reaction to the continued probing "Why is that important to you?" question about sensitive issues can vary from "waffling" (redefining the question at an equal or lower level) to stating "I don't know," silence, or even formulating extraneous arguments as an attempt to talk around the issue. Also, the respondent can manifest avoidance behavior by attaching negative or adverse characteristics to the interviewing process or to the interviewer.

Basically, three techniques can be employed to deal with respondent blocks due to sensitive issues. The first involves moving the conversation into a third-person format, creating a role-playing exercise. The second, and most dangerous option, is for the interviewer to reveal a relevant personal fact (typically fabricated) about himself or herself that makes the respondent feel less inhibited by comparison. The third, and most common, is to make a note of the problem area and come back to the issue when other relevant information is uncovered later in the interview.

Techniques

Each of the following techniques is illustrated by using one common-product class, wine coolers, for purposes of simplicity. A short definition of each technique is presented. Then verbatim transcriptions are shown to give a more complete example of the laddering process. Summary ladders are detailed to illustrate the content classification by level of abstraction (A/C/V). Note that each ladder is contained within the HVM depicted in Fig. 2.1.

1. Evoking the Situational Context (*). Laddering works best when respondents are providing associations while thinking of a realistic occasion in which they would use the product. It is the person that is the focus of study, not the product. Therefore, it is essential to elicit from respondents the most relevant occasions for product consumption and to use these as the focus of the interview.

Interviewer: You indicated that you would be more likely to drink a wine cooler at a party on the weekend with friends, why is that?

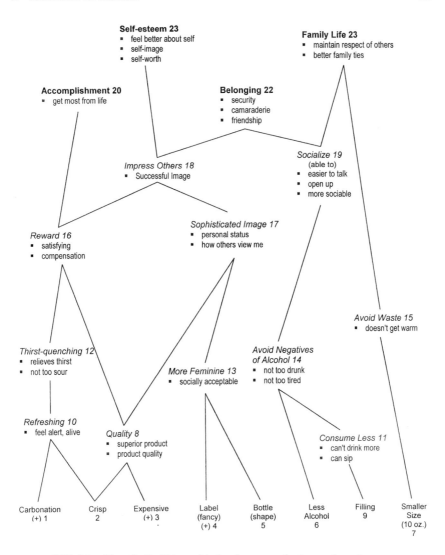

FIG. 2.1.   Hypothetical hierarchical value map of wine cooler category.

Respondent: Well, wine coolers have *less alcohol* than a mixed drink and because they are so *filling* I tend to drink fewer and more slowly.

Interviewer: What is the benefit of having less alcohol when you are around your friends?

Respondent: I never really have thought about it. I don't know.

Interviewer: Try to think about it in relation to the party situation. (*) When was the last time you had a wine cooler in this party with friends situation?

Respondent: Last weekend.

Interviewer: Okay, why coolers last weekend?

Respondent: Well, I knew I would be drinking a long time and I *didn't want to get wasted*.

Interviewer: Why was it important to not get wasted at the party last weekend?

Respondent: When I'm at a party I like to *socialize*, talk to my friends, and hopefully make some new friends. If I get wasted I'm afraid I'd make an ass of myself and people won't invite me next time. It's important for me to be *part of the group*.

The summary ladder for (1) is:

$$
\begin{array}{cl}
\text{V} & \text{sense of belonging} \\
 & \text{(part of the group)} \\
 & | \\
\text{C} & \text{socialize} \\
 & | \\
\text{C} & \text{avoid getting drunk} \\
 & \text{(wasted)} \\
 & | \\
\text{A} & \text{less alcohol/filling}
\end{array}
$$

2. Postulating the Absence of an Object or a State of Being (*). One way of "unblocking" respondents when they cannot move beyond a certain level is to encourage them to consider what it would be like to lack an object or to not feel a certain way. This device often enables respondents to verbalize meaningful associations.

Interviewer: You said you prefer a cooler when you get home after work because of the *full-bodied taste*. What's so good about a full-bodied taste after work?

Respondent: I just like it. I worked hard and it feels good to drink something satisfying.

Interviewer: Why is a satisfying drink important to you after work?

Respondent: Because it is. I just enjoy it.

Interviewer: What would you drink if you didn't have a cooler available to you? (*)

Respondent: Probably a light beer.

Interviewer: What's better about a wine cooler as opposed to a light beer when you get home after work?

Respondent: Well, if I start drinking beer, I have a hard time stopping. I just continue on into the night. But with coolers I get *filled up* and it's *easy to stop*. Plus, I tend to not eat as much dinner.

Interviewer: So why is continuing to drink into the evening something you don't want to do?

Respondent: Well, if I keep drinking I generally *fall asleep* pretty early and I don't get a chance to *talk to my wife* after the kids go to bed. She works hard with the house and the kids all day — and it's really important that I talk to her so we can keep our good relationship, our *family life*, going.

The summary ladder for (2) is:

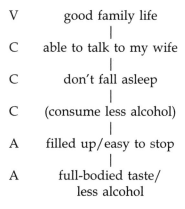

3. *Negative Laddering (*).* For the most part, the laddering procedure proceeds by probing the things respondents do and the way respondents feel. However, much can be learned by inquiring into the reasons why respondents do not do certain things or do not want to feel certain ways. This technique is particularly relevant when respondents cannot articulate why they do the things they do. Exploring hidden assumptions in this manner and using the device of making the opposite assumption have proven to be useful devices in making respondents aware of implications of common behaviors (Davis, 1971).

Interviewer: You indicated a distinction between 12 ounce and 16 ounce bottles. What size bottle do you prefer?

Respondent: I always buy a 12 ounce bottle.

Interviewer: What's the benefit of buying a 12 ounce bottle?

Respondent: I just buy it out of habit.

Interviewer: Why wouldn't you buy a 16 ounce? (*)

Respondent: It's *too much* for me *to drink* and it *gets warm* before I can finish it all. Then I have to *throw it away*.

Interviewer: So how do you feel when you have to throw it away?

Respondent: It makes me mad because I'm *wasting my money*.

Interviewer: What's the importance of money to you?

Respondent: I'm in charge of the family budget, so it's my *responsibility* to make sure it's spent right.

The summary ladder for (3) is:

```
V     responsibility to family
                |
C          waste money
                |
C          throw it away
        (don't drink all of it)
                |
C            gets warm
                |
C       too much to drink
                |
A           larger size
```

4. *Age-Regression Contrast Probe* (*).   Moving respondents backward in time is another effective device for encouraging respondents to think critically about and be able to verbalize their feelings and behavior.

Interviewer: You said you most often drink coolers at the bar. Why is that?

Respondent: I've never really thought about it. I just order them.

Interviewer: Is there a difference in your drinking habits compared to a couple of years ago? (*)

Respondent: Yes, I drink different types of drinks now.

Interviewer: Why is that?

Respondent: Well, before I used to be in college, and the only thing around seemed to be beer.

Interviewer: So why do you drink coolers now?

Respondent: Well, now I have a career and when I do go out I go with coworkers. Drinking a wine cooler looks better than drinking a beer.

Interviewer: Why is that?

Respondent: The *bottle shape* and the *fancy label* look *more feminine* than drinking a beer.

Interviewer: Why is that important to you?

Respondent: It's important to me to have a *sophisticated image* now that I'm in the work force. I want to be just *like my coworkers*.

The summary ladder for (4) is:

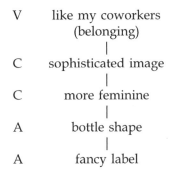

```
V       like my coworkers
            (belonging)
                |
C       sophisticated image
                |
C          more feminine
                |
A           bottle shape
                |
A            fancy label
```

5. Third-person Probe (*). Another device for eliciting responses from respondents when they find it difficult to identify their own motives or to articulate them is to ask how others they know might feel in similar circumstances.

Interviewer: You mentioned you drink wine coolers at parties at your friend's house. Why do you drink them there?

Respondent: Just because they have them.

Interviewer: Why not drink something else?

Respondent: I just like drinking coolers.

Interviewer: Why do you think your friends have them at parties? (*)

Respondent: I guess they want to *impress* us because wine coolers are *expensive*. They relate quality to how *expensive* it is.

Interviewer: Why do they want to impress others?

Respondent: Since coolers are new, they are almost like a *status symbol*.

Interviewer: So what is the value to them of having a status symbol?

Respondent: My friends always like to do one better than anyone else. It's probably related to their *self-esteem*.

The summary ladder for (5) is:

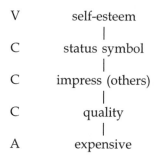

V	self-esteem
C	status symbol
C	impress (others)
C	quality
A	expensive

6. Redirecting Techniques: Silence (*)/Communication Check (**). Silence on the part of the interviewer can be used to make the respondent keep trying to look for a more appropriate or definite answer when either the respondent is not willing to think critically about the question asked or when the respondent feels uncomfortable with what he or she is learning about themselves.

A communication check simply refers to repeating back what the respondent has said and asking for clarification, essentially asking for a more precise expression of the concept.

Interviewer: You mentioned you like the carbonation in a cooler. What's the benefit of it?

Respondent: I don't think there's any benefit to carbonation.

Interviewer: Why do you like it in a cooler?

Respondent: No particular reason.

Interviewer: (silence) (*)

Respondent: Come to think of it, carbonation makes it *crisp* and *refreshing*.

Interviewer: Why is that important?

Respondent: It makes it *thirst quenching*, especially after mowing the lawn and is a pick-me-up.

Interviewer: Let me see if I understand what you're saying. (**) What do you mean by saying a pick-me-up?

Respondent: I mean after I finish it's like a *reward* for *completing a chore* I dislike.

The summary ladder for (6) is:

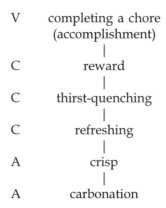

Summary

The reader will no doubt notice the similarity of these techniques to other qualitative interviewing approaches. The purpose here has been to demonstrate their use in laddering and to show how the ladders per se emerge from the interviewer-respondent interaction.

After spending a fair amount of time on one ladder without closure to a higher level, it becomes necessary to either terminate further discussion or proceed on to another ladder and circle back later. If one attribute or consequence ceases to become mobile, it is of no benefit to continue the laddering process with it because time is limited. The more familiar the interviewer becomes with the techniques and procedures, the better the interviewer is able to judge if an outcome can be reached in the line of questioning. By moving on to another subject, the respondent is given time to think more about the issue. The respondent may have a block and the shift can sometimes resolve the problem.

The central idea is to keep the focus of the discussion on the person rather than on the product or service. This is not an easy task because typically at some point the respondent realizes that the product seems to have disappeared from the conversation. Unfortunately, there are situations where techniques and procedures are unable to produce a means–ends chain. The respondent may be inarticulate or simply unwilling to answer. It also takes a length of time for the interviewer to test all the techniques and develop a personal style that can produce ladders. As with any qualitative technique experience becomes the key.

Typically, two or three ladders can be obtained from roughly three fourths of the respondents interviewed. Approximately one fourth of the respondents, depending on the level of involvement in the product class, cannot go beyond one ladder. The time required from distinctions to final ladders varies substantially, of course, but 60 to 75 minutes represents a typical standard.

ANALYSIS

Content Analysis

As overviewed earlier, the initial task of the analysis is to content-analyze all of the elements from the ladders. The first step is to record the entire set of ladders across respondents on a separate coding form. Having inspected them for completeness and having developed an overall sense of the types of elements elicited, the next step is to develop a set of summary codes that reflect everything that was mentioned. This is done by first classifying all responses into the three basic A/C/V levels and then further breaking down all responses into individual summary codes (see Table 2.1 for wine-cooler codes).

Obviously, one wants to achieve broad enough categories of meaning to get replications of more than one respondent saying one element leads to another. Yet, if the coding is too broad, too much meaning is lost. The key to producing consistency in this stage, as in all content analysis, is reliability checks across multiple coders.

Importantly, the goal at this level of the analysis is to focus on meanings central to the purpose of the study, remembering that it is the relationships between the elements that are the focus of interest, not the elements themselves. For example, "avoids the negatives of alcohol" in Fig. 2.1 is a summarization of several more detailed elements (namely, not too tired, not too drunk, don't say dumb things, and don't get numb). If all those separate elements were given separate codes it is likely that none of the relations between them and other elements would have very high frequencies, and they would not appear in HVM.

Once the master codes are finalized, numbers are assigned to each. These numbers are then used to score each element in each ladder producing a matrix with rows representing an individual respondent's ladder (one respondent can have multiple ladders and thus multiple rows), with the sequential elements within the ladder corresponding to the consecutive column designations. Thus the number of columns in the matrix corresponds to the number of elements in the longest ladder plus any identification or demographic codes. (See the Appendix for the hypothetical score matrix representing one ladder for 67 respondents from which the HVM in Fig. 2.1 was constructed.)

TABLE 2.1
Summary Content Codes for Hypothetical Wine Cooler Example

Values

(20) Accomplishment
(21) Family
(22) Belonging
(23) Self-esteem

Consequences

(8) Quality
(9) Filling
(10) Refreshing
(11) Consume less
(12) Thirst-quenching
(13) More feminine
(14) Avoid negatives
(15) Avoid waste
(16) Reward
(17) Sophisticated
(18) Impress others
(19) Socialize

Attributes

(1) Carbonation
(2) Crisp
(3) Expensive
(4) Late
(5) Bottle shape
(6) Less alcohol
(7) Smaller

It is this "crossing over" from the qualitative nature of the interviews to the quantitative way of dealing with the information obtained that is one of the *unique* aspects of laddering and clearly the one that sets it apart from other qualitative methods. This summary score matrix, then, serves as the basis for determining the dominant pathways or connections between the key elements as well as providing the ability to summarize by subgroup (e.g., men only).

The Implication Matrix

Two research issues remain: constructing hierarchical maps to represent respondents' ladders in the aggregate and determining the dominant perceptual segments represented in the overall map of aggregate relations. To accomplish this, the next step is the straightforward one of constructing a matrix that displays the number of times each element leads to each other element (operationally defined at this level as which elements in a given row precede other elements in the same row). Such a matrix will be a square matrix with a size reflecting the number of elements one is trying to map, usually between 30 and 50. Two types of relations may be represented in this matrix: direct relations and indirect relations.

Direct relations refer to implicative relations among adjacent elements. The designations of (A) through (E) for the elements refer simply to the sequential order within the ladder. That is, given our wine cooler example:

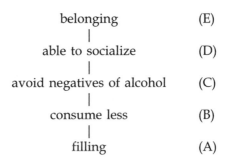

The A-B ("filling–consume less" relation is a direct one as is B-C, C-D, and D-E. However, within any given ladder there are many more indirect relations, A-C, A-D, A-E, B-D, and so forth. It is useful to examine both types of relations in determining what paths are dominant in an aggregate map of relations among elements. Without examining indirect relations, a situation might exist where there are many paths by which two elements may be indirectly connected but where none of the paths are represented enough times to represent a significant connection. For example, there may be other paths by which "avoids negatives of alcohol" leads to "belonging." Nevertheless, it is helpful to keep track of the number of times "avoids negatives of alcohol" ultimately leads to "belonging" when examining the strength of ladders as derived from the aggregate matrix of relations.

Another option in constructing the overall matrix of relations among elements is whether to count each mention of a relationship among elements that an individual respondent makes or to count a relation only once for each respondent, no matter how many times each respondent mentions it. Given the previous ladder as an example, if "filling–consume less" leads to several higher level associations for a given individual, do you count that indirect relation as many times as it occurs, or just once per respondent? The significance of an element is in part a function of the number of connections it has with other elements, which argues for counting all mentions, but it does distort the construction of the map where there are surprisingly few (to those not familiar with this research) connections between elements in the overall matrix. Often, of all the cells having any relations, only one-half will be mentioned by as many as three respondents.

Table 2.2 presents the row-column frequency matrix indicating the number of times directly and indirectly all row elements lead to all column elements. The numbers are expressed in fractional form with direct relations to the left of the decimal and indirect relations to the right of the decimal. Thus "carbonation" (element 1) leads to "thirst-quenching" (element 12) four times directly and six times indirectly. More precisely, this means that four respondents said carbonation directly leads to thirst-quenching, whereas two respondents sequentially related the two elements with another element in between.

Constructing the Hierarchical Value Map

In filling in the implication matrix, individual respondent's ladders are decomposed into their direct and indirect components (see Table 2.2). In constructing the HVM, "chains" have to be reconstructed from the aggregate data. To avoid confusion, the term "ladders" will refer to the elicitations from individual respondents; the term "chains" will be used in reference to sequences of elements which emerge from the aggregate implication matrix.

To construct a HVM from the matrix of aggregate relations, one begins by considering adjacent relations, that is, if A → B and B → C and C → D, then a chain A-B-C-D is formed. There doesn't necessarily have to be an individual with an A-B-C-D ladder for an A-B-C-D chain to emerge from the analysis. A HVM is gradually built up by connecting all the chains that are formed by considering the linkages in the large matrix of relations among elements.

The most typical approach is to try to map all relations above several different cutoff levels (usually from 3 to 5 relations, given a sample of 50 to 60 individuals). The use of multiple cutoffs permits the researcher to evaluate several solutions, choosing the one that appears to be the most informative and most stable set of relations. It is typical that a cutoff of 4 relations with 50 respondents and 125 ladders will account for as many as two thirds of all relations among elements. Indeed, the number of relations mapped in relation to the number of relations in the square implication matrix can be used as an index of the ability of the map to express the aggregate relationships. There are (naturally enough) a tremendous number of empty cells and quite a few relations that are mentioned only once. Again, in establishing a cutoff level, one may count only the direct linkages in any cell, or one may count the total number of linkages, direct or indirect.

To actually construct a HVM from the series of connected pairs, one must literally build up the map from the chains extracted from the matrix

TABLE 2.2
Summary Implication Matrix

	8	9	10	11	12	13	14	15	16	17	18	19	20	21	22	23
1 Carbonation	1.00		10.00		4.06			.01	.14		.04		.06			.04
2 Crisp	3.00		4.00		.04				.04	.03	.04	.01			.07	.05
3 Expensive	12.00								2.04	1.01	1.09		1.06		.05	.03
4 Label	2.00					2.02				2.04	.02		.01		.02	.03
5 Bottle shape	1.00		1.00			2.02	5.00			1.03					.02	.03
6 Less alcohol			1.00		1.00		.01		.01		.01	1.01			.01	
7 Smaller				1.00				3.00				.01		.04	.01	
8 Quality						3.00		1.00	4.00	4.03	4.04	.01	3.02	.02	.09	.04
9 Filling				4.00			.04						1.03		.03	.02
10 Refreshing					10.00	1.00			5.10	.01	.06	.04	.04		.05	.02
11 Consume less							5.00							.02	.03	
12 Thirst-quenching									14.00		.08		.06		.04	.04
13 More feminine										7.00	.02				1.03	.04
14 Avoid negative											1.00			4.01	.04	
15 Avoid waste												5.00		2.00		
16 Reward											11.00		8.00		.06	1.05
17 Sophisticated											4.00	1.00	1.00		4.02	5.03
18 Impress													1.00		10.00	9.00
19 Socialize														3.00	5.00	
20 Accomplishment																
21 Family																
22 Belonging																
23 Self-esteem																

Note. No relations exist between the attribute elements.

of implicative relations. Considerable ingenuity is needed for this task, with the only guideline being that one should try at all costs to avoid crossing lines. This discipline provides a coherence to the map and adds considerably to its interpretability. The criteria for evaluating the ability of the overall map to represent the data is to assess the percentage of all relations among elements accounted for by the mapped elements. The reader will note that Fig. 2.1 also contains both the significant direct and indirect relations among adjacent elements.

Before constructing the HVM from the data in Table 2.2, it is necessary to point out the types of relations that might exist among elements. Five types of relations are of note:

A-D   Elements mapped as *adjacent* that have a high number of *direct* relations.

N-D   Elements mapped as *nonadjacent* that have a high number of *direct* relations.

A-I   *Adjacent* elements that have a high number of *indirect* relations but a low number of direct relations.

N-I   *Nonadjacent* elements that have a low, nonzero number of direct relations but a high number of *indirect* relations.

N-O   *Nonadjacent* elements that have a low (or *zero*) number of indirect relations.

An illustration of these five types will help make clear the consideration process required in the construction of the map.

The first type of relationship, A-D, is the most common and represents the standard basis typically used in constructing the map. However, even when only the strong pairwise linkages are summarized, a certain degree of simplification can be gained from folding in consistent elements. For example, 10 respondents directly associated "carbonation" (1) with "refreshing" (10) producing a strong linkage. And, "carbonation" (1) and "thirst-quenching" (12) have four direct relations and six indirect relations producing a separate yet related linkage. In this case, one option would be to map two lines, 1-10 and 1-12. Another option that permits essentially the same interpretation is to map 1-10-12 in which both are embedded. In effect the "carbonation-thirst-quenching" (1-12) relation is a "N-D" type as described previously, because these elements are mapped nonadjacently even though they have a high number of direct relations.

The possibility exists that some relations would not be considered to be positioned adjacently because of a low number of direct relations, yet because of a high number of indirect relations this positioning appears reasonable (A-I). To illustrate, "fancy label" (4) and "bottle shape" (5) are each linked directly to "more feminine" (13) twice, which is below the cutoff value chosen to construct the HVM. However, both elements have two indirect relations with "more feminine" in addition to their two direct relations. It would seem reasonable to position both elements adjacently to "more feminine," omitting the element or elements that come between them and "more feminine." In the case where there are a number of diffuse paths between two elements such that no path is dominant, as was rather simply demonstrated here, it is often useful to omit the minor relations and just map the dominant path.

If a chain is representative of several individuals' ladders, the elements in that chain will be characterized by a high number of indirect relations among nonadjacent relations—although such nonadjacent elements will not necessarily have any direct relations (the "N-I" relation). This is the type of relationship that characterizes a Guttman scale. For example, "reward" (16) leads to "self-esteem" (23) one time directly, but five times indirectly. If "reward" did not ultimately lead to "self-esteem," even though it does lead to "impress others" (18), and "impress others" leads to "self-esteem," we would certainly not characterize the "reward-impress others-self-esteem" chain (16-18-23) as a strong one. Thus, the "N-I" relations, even though they are not plotted, are important determinants of the quality of the chains depicted in the HVM.

The last category of relations, nonadjacent relations that have low or no indirect or direct relations (N-O), deserves careful consideration because of an artifact in the way the HVM is constructed. As an example, "crisp" (2) does not appear in any respondent's ladder with either "accomplishment" (2) or "self-esteem" (23); however, it does have seven indirect linkages with "belonging" (22). The common aspects of the "carbonation" (1) path and the "crisp" path account for the HVM being drawn in this manner.

In constructing the HVM in Fig. 2.1 from the data in Table 2.2, the most efficient way is to start in the first row for which there is a value at or above the arbitrary cutoff level you have chosen. Using a cutoff of 4, the first significant value is "carbonation—refreshing" (1, 10) with a value of 10.00 indicating 10 direct relations and 0 indirect relations between these two elements. Next, one would move to the tenth row to find the first value at or exceeding the cutoff value. It can be seen in Table 2.2 that "thirst-quenching" (column 12) is the first significant value. Thus, the chain has grown to "1-10-12." Continuing in the same manner the chain would next extend to "reward" (1-10-12-16), then to include "impress others" (1-10-12-16-18), and, lastly, to include "belonging" (1-10-12-16-18-22).

Having reached the end of the chain, one goes back to the beginning to see if there are other significant relations in the same rows of the matrix that already have been inspected. For example, inspecting the first row indicates that "carbonation" is connected to "thirst-quenching," "reward," and "impress others"—all elements that are already included in the chain.

In addition, "carbonation" is linked to "accomplishment" and "self-esteem" (20 and 23). A similar pattern will be observed when links with "thirst-quenching" (12) are inspected.

However, when "reward" (16) is inspected, it should be noted that moving across to column 20 in row 16, another significant relation is found. Thus another chain with common links to the original chain is plotted (1-10-12-16-20). And, "impress others" (18) also is linked to "self-esteem" (23), producing the family of chains shown in the following:

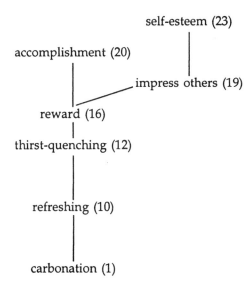

The next step is to move to the second row and start the process over again. It will be seen that "crisp" has one set of connections that are identical to "carbonation" and thus could be plotted (and is so plotted in Fig. 2.1) next to "carbonation." "Crisp" also has connections to "quality" (8), and thus a new chain is started. It can be seen by inspecting Table 2.2 that "expensive" (3) has 12 direct connections with "quality." Starting with a "3-8" chain, "quality" (8) is connected to "reward" (16) four times so we can include a line between "quality" and "reward," thus yielding a "3-8-16" chain. "Quality" also leads to "sophisticated image" (17) four times directly and four times indirectly for a total of eight connections; therefore, we can connect these two elements in the HVM. In scanning row 17 of Table 2.2 it can be seen that "sophisticated image" has 11 direct linkages with "impress others," so that these two elements can be connected in the HVM.

In a similar fashion, "fancy label" and "bottle shape" (4 and 5) have two direct and two indirect linkages with "more feminine" (13), and that "more feminine" has seven direct linkages with "sophisticated image"

(17). Examination of rows 6, 7, 9, 11, and 14 (less alcohol, smaller size, filling, consume less, and avoid negatives of alcohol) have linkages only with
"able to socialize" (element 19). Thus in Fig. 2.1, it is only "able to socialize" that links up with any elements on the left side of the HVM. It is only
at the values level, "belonging," that the right side of the map is connected
to the elements of the left side.

The goal of mapping these hierarchical relations is to interconnect all
the meaningful chains in a map in which all relations are plotted with no
crossing lines (which in almost all studies is possible). This results in a
map that includes all relevant relations and yet is easy to read and interpret. The HVM in Fig. 2.1 accounts for 94.5% of all the direct and indirect
relations contained in the 67 ladders from which it was developed.

Having plotted all relations, it is desirable to look at all elements in the
map in terms of the numbers of direct and indirect relations they have
with other elements, both in terms of other elements leading into them
and in terms of their connections to higher order elements. Table 2.3 presents the sums of the direct and indirect relations for each element. For ex-

TABLE 2.3
Summary of Direct (XX) and Indirect (YY) Relations
for Each Element (XX.YY)

Code	To	From
1	15.35	0.00
2	7.23	0.00
3	17.30	0.00
4	6.14	0.00
5	5.10	0.00
6	6.60	0.00
7	4.05	0.00
8	19.23	19.00
9	5.12	0.00
10	16.26	16.00
11	5.09	5.00
12	14.22	15.00
13	6.09	6.04
14	10.05	10.05
15	2.00	4.01
16	20.11	25.33
17	15.05	15.15
18	20.00	21.40
19	8.00	8.11
20	0.00	14.25
21	0.00	9.12
22	0.00	20.56
23	0.00	15.37

ample, "belonging" (22), at the values level, is the element that has the most elements leading to it. Thus, it might be seen as the core value in terms of importance to the product class. In addition, three other elements are noteworthy for having a high frequency of elements leading from them as well as into them, namely, "reward" (16), "impress others" (18), and "quality" (8). Indeed, the quality → reward → impress others → belonging chain can be seen to have a high number of relations among its respective elements.

Determining Dominant Perceptual Orientations

Once a hierarchical value map is constructed, one typically considers any pathway from bottom to top as a potential chain representing a perceptual orientation. For example, in Fig. 2.1 the total number of unique pathways between elements at the attribute level and elements at the values level is 23, any or all of which warrant consideration. To more fully understand the strength of the chains, the intrachain relations can be summarized and evaluated. The partitions within Table 2.4 demonstrate this process. Table 2.4 includes detailing of the relations for four chains within Figure 2.1 in an easier-to-read format than tracking them down in the row-column frequency matrix in Table 2.2. Part A of Table 2.4 shows the direct and indirect relations linking "carbonation" with "accomplishment." It can be seen by inspection that all elements are linked directly or indirectly to all other elements in the chain. "Carbonation" has six indirect linkages with "accomplishment," meaning that these two elements are included in six respondents' ladders. "Refreshing" and "thirst-quenching" have four and six indirect linkages, respectively, and "reward" has eight direct linkages with "accomplishment." In all, the chain accounts for 51 direct relations among elements and 46 indirect relations.

Part B of Table 2.4 shows the "carbonation–self-esteem" chain. This chain accounts for more direct relations than does the chain in Part A of Table 2.4. It is also longer, having more elements in it. In general, the linkages among elements at the bottom of this chain have fewer linkages with the elements at the top of the chain. "Refreshing" has only two indirect linkages with "self-esteem."

In Part C of Table 2.4, a chain is shown that has fewer elements and accounts for far fewer relations. It can also be seen that "less alcohol" is not strongly associated with "socialize" or "belonging." Such a weakness, as indicated by the lack of associations respondents are making between these elements, might represent an opportunity for a campaign to strengthen this tie (in the beer category this indeed is what the L.A. brand has done in its advertising in the low-alcohol segment of that category).

TABLE 2.4
Partitions of Chains by Relations

Part A "Carbonation–Accomplishment" Chain						
0	2	10	12	16	20	0
2	0.00	4.00	0.04	0.04	0.00	4.06
10	0.00	0.00	10.00	5.10	0.04	15.14
12	0.00	0.00	0.00	14.00	0.06	14.06
16	0.00	0.00	0.00	0.00	8.00	8.00
20	0.00	0.00	0.00	0.00	0.00	0.00
0	0.00	0.00	0.00	0.00	0.00	41.28

Part B "Carbonation–Self-Esteem" Chain							
0	1	10	12	16	18	23	0
1	0.00	10.00	4.06	0.14	0.04	0.04	14.26
10	0.00	0.00	10.00	5.10	0.06	0.02	15.18
12	0.00	0.00	0.00	14.00	0.08	0.04	14.12
16	0.00	0.00	0.00	0.00	11.00	1.05	12.05
18	0.00	0.00	0.00	0.00	0.00	9.00	9.00
23	0.00	0.00	0.00	0.00	0.00	0.00	0.00
0	0.00	0.00	0.00	0.00	0.00	0.00	64.63

Part C "Less Alcohol–Belonging" Chain					
0	6	14	19	22	0
6	0.00	5.00	1.01	0.01	6.02
14	0.00	0.00	5.00	0.04	5.04
19	0.00	0.00	0.00	5.00	5.00
22	0.00	0.00	0.00	0.00	0.00
0	0.00	0.00	0.00	0.00	16.06

Part D "Bottle Shape–Self-Esteem" Chain						
0	5	13	17	18	23	0
5	0.00	2.02	1.03	0.00	0.03	3.08
13	0.00	0.00	7.00	0.02	0.04	7.06
17	0.00	0.00	0.00	4.00	5.03	9.03
18	0.00	0.00	0.00	0.00	9.00	9.00
23	0.00	0.00	0.00	0.00	0.00	0.00
0	0.00	0.00	0.00	0.00	0.00	28.17

Part D of Table 2.4 shows that, whereas "bottle shape" and "more feminine" are linked to "sophisticated image," there is not a strong association with "impress others." This may suggest more of an internal orientation whereas the "expensive–quality" association with "impress others" is quite strong and may be reflective of an external orientation.

APPLICATIONS

Accordingly, consideration can now be made of the options available to the researcher who uses the laddering approach and is faced with the challenge of applying the results to the solution of some marketing problem. The HVM obtained through the laddering procedure offers several particularly valuable types of information. It can serve as a basis for: (a) segmenting consumers with respect to their values orientations for a product class or brand; (b) for assessing brands or products in a fashion similar to the use of more traditional ratings; (c) evaluating competitive advertising; and (d) as a basis for developing advertising strategies.

Segmentation

The goal of segmentation schemes is to classify respondents with respect to some aspect of their behavior, attitudes, or dispositions in a way that helps us understand them as consumers. The values orientations in a person's ladder may serve as the basis for classification, or the researcher may group these values at a still higher level. It is also possible to include attribute-value connections in the segmentation scheme. Once a segmentation scheme has been developed, respondents' brand-consumption behavior or reactions to advertising may be assessed.

Table 2.5 includes a summary by attribute and value for respondents whose ladders extended to the values level. "Belonging" was included in the most ladders, with "self-esteem," "accomplishment," and "family life" following in decreasing order of frequency (nine ladders did not reach the values level and thus are omitted from this analysis). The values

TABLE 2.5
Ladder Frequencies for Attribute-Value Linkages

	Achievement			Social		
	Accomplishment (14)	Self-esteem (15)	Total (29)	Belonging (20)	Family life (9)	Total (29)
Physical attributes	6	4	10	10	7	17
Carbonation	6	4	10	0	0	0
Crisp	0	0	0	7	0	7
Less alcohol	0	0	0	1	4	5
Filling	0	0	0	2	3	5
Price	7	5	12	5	0	5
Packaging	1	6	7	5	2	7
Label	1	3	4	2	0	2
Shape	0	3	3	2	0	2
Size	0	0	0	1	2	3

can be grouped at a higher level using "achievement" and "social" as higher level value orientations. An equal number of subjects fall into each of these two values-level orientations.

One could also include the attribute-value connections in the segmentation scheme, assessing them at the levels used in the HVM or in grouping them as shown in Table 2.5 into marketing-mix components. In this example, the attributes "less alcohol" and "filling" are linked to social values, whereas "price" is tied more closely to achievement values. "Packaging" attributes are equally divided, although "size" is identified with social values, not achievement values.

Respondent segments could be studied for brand-consumption differences and preferences and advertising reactions evaluated. These segmentation bases could be translated into larger scale research on brand usage and preference and advertising theme evaluation. That is, the findings from this research could become the basis for more traditional paper-and-pencil methods that more readily lend themselves to large-scale data collection.

Product–Brand Assessment

Evaluation of a product or brand is another important marketing question for which the results of laddering research may be of use. It is advantageous to allow respondents to use their own frame of reference when providing their evaluations of a brand rather than some researcher-supplied attributes that may not be the subject's own. For many product categories or subclasses of categories, respondents are much more likely to make preference judgments at the consequence and values levels than at the attribute level (Reynolds, Gutman, & Fiedler, 1984; Reynolds & Jamieson, 1984).

A statistical approach, Cognitive Differentiation Analysis (CDA), was developed (Reynolds, 1983; Reynolds & Sutrick, 1986) to enable researchers to determine the level of abstraction (attribute, consequence, or value) at which preference judgments are being made by consumers. This approach provides indices indicating the discrimination power of each of the descriptors with respect to a set of pairwise discrimination between stimuli. To collect data for this type of analysis, respondents are asked to sort or rate pairwise combinations of brands in the relevant product class according to their respective preference distance. Respondents are also asked to provide information on the extent to which the brands possess or satisfy the elements at each level of abstraction in their ladders. One appealing feature of this analytical method is that it only requires ordinal data — no interval scale properties are necessary.

This information not only allows a determination of the levels within a respondent's ladder at which preference is determined, but the overall index of the ladder allows the researcher to determine each respondent's optimal ladder. Results from CDA analyses have shown that people are not particularly good at recognizing their own most discriminating way of evaluating the brands within a product class, nor do they recognize the level of abstraction at which their judgments are being made (see Reynolds [1985] for a detailed summary of the method and the results). This suggests that researchers ought to be suspicious of self-report rating systems inherent in many attitude models and consumer surveys.

The output from laddering, coupled with the unique analytical procedures it allows, provides researchers with a better understanding of the basis on which consumers make distinctions between competing brands. Further, it provides a basis for developing a product space that is truly aligned with preference, as such spatial maps may be obtained using different levels of abstraction as a frame of reference. Too often product-planning decisions are based on discrimination differences and not preference differences. Consumers, given the means–end framework, are assumed to have multiple orientations that are triggered by a given occasional context (i.e., combination of situation and actors). Thus, if the means–end perspective is valid, preference would in most cases be multidimensional in nature. Therefore, the laddering approach provides a unique opportunity to understand the product class in the consumer's own context. This would seem to provide a good start for making decisions about products and brands.

Assessing Advertising

Another important use for the results obtained through laddering research is to uncover respondents' evaluations of advertising. Advertising is viewed differently when perceived in the context of different levels of abstraction (attribute, consequence, and value). To accomplish this, after laddering, when respondents are sensitized to the complete range of their internal feelings about a product class, they are shown a series of ads and asked to rate them on the extent to which the ad communicates at each level and to provide some comment on why it does or does not communicate at that level.

Analysis of these comments leads to the construction of a series of statements reflecting their content. To further broaden the coverage of these statements, a model depicting an advertising research paradigm can be used (see Fig. 2.2). This model indicates the components of an ad in relation to levels of involvement the consumer may have with the ad. Fifty to sixty statements can be developed covering the advertising's message elements, executional frameworks, perceptions of the advertisers' strategy and involvement with the ad, involvement of the ad with the respondent's

FIG. 2.2. Advertising research paradigm based on means–end chain model and hierarchical value structure analysis.

personal life, and the extent to which the ad taps into values at a personal level.

These statements can then be used to assess the relative communication at the various levels. This can be accomplished, after a sensitizing laddering procedure, by showing ads and asking "if the following statement applies" to each respective ad. This process can be operationalized by a game-board approach (Gutman & Reynolds, 1987) where a triangle is provided to the respondent with each vertex representing a separate ad. The use of three ads is suggested as an attempt to avoid the respondent from becoming too much of an advertising expert. As each statement is read the respondent can record the applicability to one ad (recording the statement code at the respective vertex), or two ads (recording on the connecting line), or all three (recording in the middle of the triangle). If the statement does not apply to any of the three ads, a "not applicable" response alternative is also provided.

The resulting percentage endorsement of each statement for each advertisement provides a good indication of how the ad is viewed and the level at which the ad communicates. That is, some ads may communicate well at the attribute level but not at the consequence or values level. Conversely, other ads may communicate well at the values level but be weak at the attribute level. An effective ad in this context is defined as one that communicates across all levels, linking attributes to benefits and to personal values which often drive consumer decision-making.

Developing Advertising Strategy

Perhaps the major benefit of laddering is the insight it provides to advertising strategists. A definition of advertising communications that will permit advertising strategies to be developed from the HVM is briefly discussed (see Reynolds & Gutman [1984] for a fuller discussion and illustration). The levels of abstraction framework, which underlie the formation of means–end chains, provide a basis for coordinating the results of laddering to advertising strategy development. That is, the perceptual constructs depicted in the HVM can be used as the basis for developing a strategy that will appeal to consumers with that particular orientation toward the product class.

Figure 2.3 shows the Means–Ends Conceptualization of Components of Advertising Strategy (MECCAS) in terms of five broad characteristics that correspond to the levels of abstraction conceptualization (Olson & Reynolds, 1983; Reynolds & Gutman, 1984). "Driving force," "consumer benefit," and "message elements" are directly coordinated to the values, consequences, and attributes levels of the means-end model. The executional framework relates to the scenario for the advertisement—the "vehicle" by which the value orientation is to be communicated. The specification of this tone for the advertisement is a critical aspect of strategy specification. It comes from an overall understanding of the way of perceiving the product class as indicated by a particular means-end path. As is apparent with this specification, added guidance can be given to creatives without infringing on their creativity.

The remaining and key aspect of advertising strategy specification is the concept of "leverage point." Having all the other elements in mind, it is finally necessary to specify the manner by which the values-level focus will be activated for the advertisement, that is, how the values consider-

Driving Force
The value orientation of the strategy; the end-level to be focused on in the advertising.

Leverage Point
The manner by which the advertising will "tap into," reach, or activate the value or end-level of focus; the specific key way in which the value is linked to the specific features of the advertising.

Executional Framework
The overall scenario or action plot, plus the details of the advertising execution. The executional framework provides the "vehicle" by which the value orientation is communicated; especially the gestalt of the advertisement; its overall tone and style.

Consumer Benefit
The major positive consequences for the consumer that are explicitly communicated, verbally or visually, in the advertising.

Message Elements
The specific attributes, consequences, or features about the product that are communicated verbally or visually.

FIG. 2.3. Means–Ends Conceptualization of Components of Advertising Strategy.

ations in the advertisement are connected to the specific features of the advertisement. (Examples of advertising strategy specifications are not provided — the references cited previously provide ample illustrations.)

Nonetheless, the advantages of being able to specify advertising strategy for all relevant parties — management, creatives, and researchers — can be reviewed. The strategy statement itself becomes a concrete way of specifying advertising strategy alternatives. These alternatives are linked to the chains that underlie them, and thus a direct connection exists between the strategy and the perceptual orientation of the consumer. Furthermore, the MECCAS model coupled with the results from the HVM facilitate the development of several (truly different) strategies for comparison and review. Lastly, when a strategy has been selected for execution, the MECCAS model provides for a better common understanding of what the final product should be. This obviously leads to the use of the MECCAS specification as the basis for evaluating the effectiveness of the advertisement.

SUMMARY

This chapter reviews and illustrates the technique of laddering both as an interviewing process and through subsequent analysis. It demonstrates the technique's usefulness in developing an understanding of how consumers translate the attributes of products into meaningful associations with respect to self-defining attitudes and values. The underlying theory behind the method, means–end theory, is discussed, as well as the elements of the means–end chains representing the cognitive levels of abstraction: attributes, consequences, and values.

The interview environment necessary for laddering to take place is given special attention along with the particular probing techniques employed in the qualitative process of laddering. Basically, the respondent has to feel as if on a voyage of self-discovery and that the object of the trip is to revisit everyday, commonplace experiences and examine the assumptions and desires driving seemingly simple choice behavior.

Several specific interviewing devices are described for eliciting product distinctions from respondents that serve to initiate the laddering process, among them the use of triads, exploring preference-consumption differences, and examining how consumption differs by occasion. The value of the occasional context, providing a concrete frame of reference to generate meaningful distinctions, is emphasized. Other techniques for moving the laddering interview upward when blocking occurs are also discussed and illustrated.

The analysis of laddering data is detailed noting the critical difference between this methodology and more traditional qualitative research, namely, the primary output being (structurally) quantitative in nature in the form of a hierarchical value map (HVM). In this vein, the content analysis of ladder elements is positioned as an important step in this "crossing over" from the qualitative to quantitative.

Detailed attention is paid to the construction of the HVM from the implication matrix, which represents the number of direct and indirect linkages between the qualitative concepts elicited during the laddering process. Five types of relations among elements are discussed, and their respective implications for constructing a HVM are illustrated.

Having the HVM to work with, the next step in transforming the output of laddering into useful information for marketing decision-making is to determine the dominant perceptual orientations. That is, all potential pathways (connections among elements) must be examined to determine their relative strength of association. Two primary considerations are specified with examples, namely, the number of relations among elements within the chain and the extent to which all elements are interconnected.

Lastly, the issue of applications is discussed referencing the key research problems of perceptual segmentation, determining the importance weights of the various components of the ladders, and the development and subsequent assessment of advertising from this value perspective. All of the application areas have in common that they depend on laddering's ability to draw out from the respondent the true basis for any meaningful connection they have to the product class.

ACKNOWLEDGMENTS

We would like to express our appreciation to Monique Vrinds and Gregory Bunker of the Institute for Consumer Research for both their technical and practical illustrations of the laddering process.

REFERENCES

Abelson, R. (1981). The psychological status of the script concept. *American Psychologist, 36*, 715–729.

Barker, R. G. (1968). *Ecological psychology: Concepts and methods for studying the environment of human behavior*. Stanford, CA: Stanford University Press.

Davis, M. S. (1971). That's interesting: Toward a phenomenology of sociology and a sociology or phenomenology. *Philosophy of the Social Sciences, 1*, 309–314.

Durgee, J. F. (1985). Depth-interview techniques for creative advertising. *Journal of Advertising Research, 25*, 6, 29–37.

Gutman, J. (1982). A means–end chain model based on consumer categorization processes. *Journal of Marketing, 46*, 2, 60–72.

Gutman, J. (1984). Analyzing consumer orientations toward beverages through means–end chain analysis. *Psychology and Marketing, 1*, 3/4, 23–43.

Gutman, J., & Alden, S. (1984). Adolescents' cognitive structures of retail stores and fashion consumption: A means–end analysis. In J. Jacoby & J. Olson (Eds.), *Perceived quality of products, services and stores* (pp. 99–114). Lexington, MA: Lexington Books.

Gutman, J., & Reynolds, T. J. (1979). An investigation at the levels of cognitive abstraction utilized by the consumers in product differentiation. In J. Eighmey (Ed.), *Attitude research under the sun* (pp. 128–150). Chicago: American Marketing Association.

Gutman, J., & Reynolds, T. J. (1987). Coordinating assessment to strategy development: An advertising assessment paradigm based on the MECCAS approach. In J. Olson & K. Sentis (Eds.), *Advertising and consumer psychology* (pp. 242–258). Praeger.

Gutman, J., Reynolds, T. J., & Fielder, J. (1984). A new analytic framework for family decision-making. In M. L. Roberts & L. Woertzel (Eds.), *The changing household: Its nature and consequences.* Cambridge, MA: Ballinger Publishing.

Kassarjian, H. (1977). Content analysis in consumer research. *Journal of Consumer Research, 4,* 1, 8–18.

Kelly, G. A. (1955). *The psychology of personal constructs.* New York: W. W. Norton.

Morgan, A. (1984). Point of view: Magic town revisited. *Journal of Advertising Research, 24,* 4, 49–51.

Olson, J. C., & Reynolds, T. J. (1983). Understanding consumers cognitive structures: Implications for advertising strategy. In L. Percy & A. Woodside (Eds.), *Advertising and consumer psychology.* Lexington, MA: Lexington Books.

Plummer, J. (1995, February). Upfront research and emotional strategies. Speech given at Northwestern University School of Business, Evanston, Illinois.

Reynolds, T. J. (1983). A nonmetric approach to determine the differentiation power of attribute ratings with respect to pairwise similarity judgements [sic]. In proceedings of American Marketing Association Educator's Conference on Research Methods and Causal Modeling. Chicago: American Marketing Association.

Reynolds, T. J. (1985). Implications for value research: A micro vs. macro perspective. *Psychology and Marketing, 2,* 4, 297–305.

Reynolds, T. J., & Gutman, J. (1984a). Laddering: Extending the repertory grid methodology to construct attribute-consequence-value hierarchies. In R. Pitts & A. Woodside (Eds.), *Personal values and consumer psychology,* Vol. II. Lexington, MA: Lexington Books.

Reynolds, T. J., & Gutman, J. (1984b). Advertising is image management. *Journal of Advertising Research, 24,* 1, 27–36.

Reynolds, T. J., Gutman, J., & Fiedler, J. (1984). Understanding consumers' cognitive structures: The relationship of levels of abstraction to judgements [sic] of psychological distance and preference. In A. Mitchell & L. Alwitt (Eds.), *Psychological Processes of Advertising Effects: Theory, Research and Application* (pp. 27–36). Hillsdale, NJ: Lawrence Erlbaum Associates.

Reynolds, T. J., & Jamieson, L. (1984). Image representations: An analytical framework. In J. Jacoby & J. Olson (Eds.), *Perceived quality of products, services and stores* (pp. 115–138). Lexington, MA: Lexington Books.

Reynolds, T. J., & Sutrick, K. (1986). Assessing the correspondence of one or more vectors to a symmetric matrix using ordinal regression. *Psychometrika, 51,* 1, 101–112.

Reynolds, T. J., & Trivedi, M. (1989). An investigation of the relationship between the MECCAs model and advertising affect. In A. Tybout & P. Cafferata (Eds.), *Advertising and consumer psychology,* Vol. IV (pp. 373–390). Lexington, MA: Lexington Books.

Rosenberg, M. J. (1956). Cognitive structure and attitudinal affect. *Journal of Abnormal and Social Psychology, 53,* 367–372.

Runkel, P. J., & McGrath, J. E. (1972). *Research on human behavior: A systematic guide to method.* New York: Holt, Rinehart & Winston.

Sheth, J. (1983). Marketing megatrends. *Journal of Consumer Marketing, 1,* 5–13.

Wicker, A. (1985). Getting out of our conceptual ruts. *American Psychologist, 40,* 1094–1103.

APPENDIX
Raw Data From Hypothetical Wine Cooler Data

Respondent number			Content codes			
1	1	10	12	16	20	0
2	1	10	16	0	0	0
3	1	10	12	16	16	23
4	3	6	20	0	0	0
5	4	17	20	0	0	0
6	2	10	12	16	18	22
7	1	12	16	20	0	0
8	3	8	20	0	0	0
9	1	12	16	18	23	0
10	1	10	16	0	0	0
11	3	8	20	0	0	0
12	2	10	12	16	18	22
13	1	12	16	20	0	0
14	1	12	16	18	23	0
15	1	10	12	16	20	0
16	3	16	20	0	0	0
17	1	10	12	16	20	0
18	2	10	12	16	18	22
19	1	10	12	16	18	23
20	1	10	16	0	0	0
21	2	10	12	16	18	22
22	3	20	0	0	0	0
23	1	10	12	16	20	0
24		1	10	16	0	0
25	3	6	16	20	0	0
26	3	6	16	18	23	0
27	3	8	18	20	0	0
28	3	18	23	0	0	0
29	3	16	23	0	0	0
30	3	8	18	22	0	0
31	3	8	17	18	23	0
32	3	17	18	23	0	0
33	4	13	17	18	23	0
34	4	13	17	18	22	0
35	5	13	17	23	0	0
36	5	17	23	0	0	0
37	4	17	23	0	0	0
38	5	13	22	0	0	0
39	6	14	18	22	0	0
40	6	14	21	0	0	0

(Continued)

Respondent number	Content codes					
41	6	14	18	0	0	0
42	6	14	21	0	0	0
43	6	14	21	0	0	0
44	9	11	14	19	22	0
45	9	11	14	19	21	0
46	9	11	14	21	0	0
47	9	1	14	19	22	0
48	7	15	21	0	0	0
49	7	15	21	0	0	0
50	7	15	0	0	0	0
51	3	8	16	18	22	0
52	3	8	18	22	0	0
53	2	8	17	22	0	0
54	3	8	16	18	22	0
55	3	8	18	22	0	0
56	2	8	17	22	0	0
57	2	8	17	19	22	0
58	1	8	15	0	0	0
59	6	10	16	0	0	0
60	6	12	0	0	0	0
61	6	19	21	0	0	0
62	7	11	14	19	22	0
63	4	8	13	17	23	0
64	4	8	13	17	22	0
65	5	8	13	17	23	0
66	5	10	13	17	22	0
67	9	19	21	0	0	0

3

Means–End Chains and Laddering: An Inventory of Problems and an Agenda for Research

Klaus G. Grunert
The Aarhus School of Business

Suzanne C. Beckmann
Copenhagen Business School

Elin Sørensen
University of Southern Denmark

INTRODUCTION

Laddering and means–end chains are one of the most promising developments in consumer research since the 1980s. It is an approach that takes consumers' individuality seriously but, nevertheless, comes up with quantitative results. It is rooted in a cognitive approach, and allows for emotional and unconscious (or, at least, semiconscious) factors. It is intuitively appealing to the practitioner but has, likewise, attracted academic research.

Increased acceptance and use of a new approach inevitably leads to the detection of unresolved issues and problems. Many of these unresolved issues are related to the collection and analysis of laddering data. However, many of these also point at problems of a more theoretical nature. In this chapter presented are some of the issues regarded as unresolved and suggested research that could help in solving these problems. The major part of this chapter deals with methodological problems of the interview technique called laddering, of coding laddering data, and of analysing the coded data. However, also shown, methodological and theoretical issues are partly interlinked: Resolutions of methodological problems may require theoretical progress or at least a clarification of some theoretical issues. We therefore start with a discussion of some unresolved theoretical issues.

MEANS–END CHAIN THEORY

A discussion of means–end chain theory is made difficult by the fact that the epistemological status of means–end chains (MEC) is not completely clear. MEC have been used and discussed from the viewpoint of various research traditions, ranging from an interpretivist phenomenological view to a neo-positivist nomological view. For the sake of simplicity, however, two basic views are distinguished (Grunert & Grunert, 1995). They are the motivational and the cognitive structure view.

The *motivational view* is that laddering and MEC are concerned with obtaining insight into consumers' buying motives (i.e., in the way basic motives are linked to shopping behavior). Laddering and MEC are then a modern variant of motivation research in the Dichter (1960) tradition. Laddering can give valuable insight by prompting consumers to reflect on their buying motives in a way not typical for daily shopping behavior. Such insight is bound to be qualitative in its character, and the kind of structures derived are situationally constructed meanings. A theory in this context is a set of categories useful for structuring laddering response data in such a way that the researcher's understanding of the consumer is improved.

The *cognitive structure view* is that MEC are a model of consumers' consumption-relevant cognitive structure (i.e., of the way consumption-relevant knowledge is stored and organised in human memory). MEC would then be an element in a more complete cognitive theory of the consumer based on the general cognitive view of human beings, as depicted in Fig. 3.1. According to the cognitive view, people analyze information obtained from the environment by relating it to information already stored in memory, and use that information to direct behavior toward the attainment of goals (Grunert, 1994; Simon, 1990). MEC are then a model of how consumption-relevant information is stored in memory (i.e., about consumption-relevant cognitive structure). When supplemented with theories or assumptions about the analysis of input from the environment, activating and adding to cognitive structure and with theories or assumptions about the formulation of output, based on cognitive structure, MEC become part of a theory with the aim of explaining and predicting consumer behavior.

The literature on MEC does not take a clear stand on which of these two views are being endorsed. The Grey Benefit Chain (Young, 1975), one of the early approaches, seems to be most in the motivation research tradition. Asselbergs (1989), while adapting schema theory and therefore a cognitive perspective, regarded MEC generated by laddering not as measures of cognitive structure, but as a reconstruction of relevant informa-

environment   **human being**

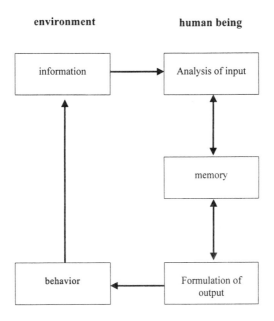

FIG. 3.1.   The cognitive view of human beings.

tion, which also tends toward the first view. Gutman, Olson, and Reynolds (Gutman, 1982; Olson, 1989; Olson & Reynolds, 1983; Peter & Olson,
1993; Reynolds & Gutman, 1988) adopted a cognitive structure perspective, saying that the hierarchical value map derived from laddering data is
"an aggregate map of cognitive structure" (Olson & Reynolds, 1983, p. 85).

These two views are related to different general views on scientific
analysis in consumer research, as previously indicated. If one adopts the
interpretivist phenomenological view that all measurements are context
dependent, the notion of measuring a situation-invariant cognitive structure does not make much sense. If one, on the other hand, adopts a
neo-positivist nomological perspective, as would be typical for most of
cognitive psychology, measuring only meaning that is dependent on the
interview situation—which may include stimuli prompting the respondent to recall during the interview consumption situations—would appear unsatisfactory because such measurements could not be taken as empirical estimates of constructs that can enter nomological propositions.

We only deal with the second view in the following. It raises two questions: Why are MEC expected to be a better model of consumers' cognitive
structures than other possible models of cognitive structure? How can
MEC be integrated to a more complete cognitive theory in such a way that
it becomes possible to explain and predict behavior?

Means–End Chains Versus Other Models
of Cognitive Structure

The literature on cognitive psychology is replete with models of cognitive structure. Most of them are variants of a basic network model,[1] that is, a model consisting of two types of elements: *concepts*, also called cognitive categories or nodes and their *associations*, also called links. They can be categorised on the following dimensions.

- *Positional versus distributional* (Anderson, 1983; Johnson-Laird, 1984; McClelland, 1985): Is a particular piece of information stored at any one place in cognitive structure, or is every piece of information distributed across the whole structure?
- *Episodic versus semantic* (Tulving, 1972, 1985): Is the cognitive structure a store of general, semantic information, or is it a store of information about events with a time-and-place tag?
- *Verbal versus imagery* (Paivio, 1986; Ruge, 1988): Is the information structured in verbal form or in such a way that it can at least be converted to verbal information by a lexicon, or is the information in images?
- *Declarative versus procedural* (Cowan, 1988) Is it information about facts, information which can be verbalised and explained? Or is it information about doing things, mental programs which can be performed, but not necessarily verbalised?
- *Hierarchical versus nonhierarchical* (Chang, 1986): Are cognitive categories organized in the cognitive structure on a concreteness-abstractness dimension, or not?
- *Types of associations* (Grunert, 1982a; Norman & Rumelhart, 1975): Does the cognitive structure distinguish between different types of associations—like set membership, causality, or type—and is there any syntax on what may be associated in which way?

It is not difficult to place MEC on these dimensions. First of all, MEC are in the family of network models because they consist of nodes and links. They are positional because a node refers to a specific concept. They are semantic because they depict general knowledge on products, their attributes and consequences, and not knowledge about individual usage events. They are verbal because language is used both in measurement and in presenting the resulting models of cognitive structure. They refer

---

[1]Of course, there are alternatives to network models: Schemas, frames, and scripts are some of the nonnetwork constructs that have been used to model cognitive structures. Discussing their relative merits and deficiencies is, however, far beyond the scope of this chapter.

to declarative knowledge because they only involve knowledge about states that can be verbalized and not procedural knowledge. They are hierarchical because the cognitive categories in a MEC are ordered by abstractness. And finally, they restrict associations to a particular type, namely associations expressing causality: An attribute leads to a consequence and a consequence to a value.

It is more difficult to find arguments that MECs are the most appropriate model of cognitive structure in the context of consumer behavior. MECs do have face validity, but it is unproblematic to find arguments for other types of cognitive structure as well.

There is ample evidence that consumer behavior is influenced by *episodic information*. Critical incidences (i.e., previous key experiences with products and services that are clearly linked to a specific time and space) do influence intentions to repeat a behavior, even when this information has not necessarily been converted to semantic information. A single quarrel with a hotel clerk, remembered clearly with regard to time and place, may lead to the decision never to visit the hotel again. A spectacular airline crash makes people seek other airlines or avoid flying altogether (for some time). Generosity of an outlet manager in exchanging a defective item may reinforce the decision to shop at this outlet again. A clearly remembered salmonella infection after eating chicken may lead people to avoid chicken in the future. These are all instances of episodic information influencing consumer behavior.

Nonverbal imagery has been shown to be a major component in how consumers store information. Visual information enhances both encoding and recall, and, although the issue is far from settled, much empirical evidence seems to suggest that not all visual information is turned to a propositional form in memory but is stored separately as mental imagery (Kosslyn, 1975; Pylshyn, 1973). Some consumer researchers have therefore advocated the use of pictorial stimuli in researching consumers' cognitive structures (Phillips, Olson, & Baumgartner, 1995; Ruge, 1988; Zaltman & Higie, 1993).

Consumer behavior clearly draws on *procedural knowledge*. The way one reaches to the shelf for obtaining an item that has been bought many times, the route driven and the outlet visited in daily shopping, what one asks for at the butcher's counter may all be aspects of consumer behavior that have, to a large degree, become automated and hence procedural. If one looks beyond shopping activities, procedural knowledge abounds in the use of the goods purchased in the home: Preparing meals, cleaning the house, getting rid of waste and garbage are all activities where procedural knowledge plays a large role.

Research on semantic memory has shown that knowledge may be organized in a *nonhierarchical* way (Chang, 1986). In the context of means–

end chains, this would imply that in addition to A-C-V chains, A-V-A-C chains or chains with redundant links would be allowed. This issue is potentially accessible by reaction time experiments: The classical means–end chain would predict that the verification of a statement about a link between an attribute and a value would take longer than the verification of a statement about a link between an attribute and a consequence. Contradicting results would be evidence of a nonhierarchical structure.

Finally, associations beyond subjective causality (e.g., supplementarity or substitutability of products, that is set membership associations) may be added. One can even ask whether causality as a central guiding principle for organizing experience may be culture-specific, that is, mostly applicable to the Western civilizations.

MEC are therefore clearly not a *complete* model of consumers' cognitive structure. They can be regarded as an excerpt of consumers' cognitive structure, concentrating on aspects of it that are regarded as relevant from a specific angle. The problem is that this angle has not been made very explicit in the literature. Theoretical research, placing MEC in the broader context of models of cognitive structure, would therefore be welcome. Such research should specify the theoretical choices made in MEC theory and provide arguments founded in the literature on cognitive psychology, under which circumstances the specific aspects of cognitive structure captured by MEC are the most appropriate. Theoretical research resulting in propositions on how MEC could be broadened to include other forms of knowledge would likewise be helpful.

MEC and the Explanation/Prediction of Behavior

As Fig. 3.1 shows, a model of cognitive structure by itself cannot explain or predict behavior; it has to be supplemented by assumptions about cognitive processes (this argument is presented in more detail in Grunert & Grunert, 1995). MEC have not yet been integrated into a theory that includes such assumptions and, therefore, it has been difficult to evaluate the usefulness of MEC as a tool to explain or predict consumer behavior. If, however, MEC are to develop into a theoretical tool within the nomological research tradition, it is important that such a theory be developed.

There is, of course, no lack of theories on consumer behavior with a cognitive orientation. If MEC are to be developed into a more full-scale theory, it is necessary to specify which range of behavior the theory is supposed to explain, and why and how the theory is different from existing theories. Theory development is not the purpose of this chapter, but we suggest that the kind of behaviors to be explained is the choice between alternative courses of action, especially actions involving the purchase or use of products and services. We also suggest that the *theory of reasoned ac-*

tion, aimed at explaining similar kinds of behavior, can serve as a useful point of departure and of comparison. In the theory of reasoned action,[2] the cognitive structure relevant for predicting behavior is assumed to consist of sets of *beliefs*, which are pairs of cognitive categories linked by an association. In one set of beliefs, courses of action are linked to consequences of those actions, and in another set relevant others are linked to reactions to these courses of action. The link between these two sets of beliefs and behaviors is explained by the well-known formula

$$B \sim BI = w_1 \Sigma b_i\, a_i\ + w_2 \Sigma nb_i\, mc_i$$

The theory of reasoned action thus takes two sets of factors as externally given: (1) the *excerpt of cognitive structure*, which is relevant for explaining and predicting the behavior in question, that means the two sets of beliefs and their strengths (b_i, nb_i), and (2) the motivation associated with the beliefs (a_i, mc_i) are assumed to be known and to be stable across the range of behaviors to be explained.

Given that these factors are known, the theory says that the intention to perform a particular course of action will vary with the sum of the motivations weighted with the strengths of the beliefs. The theory of reasoned action is not very explicit about which type of cognitive processes actually could bring this about, but it has been shown that a spreading activation process in a semantic network can bring about results that correspond to this specific variant of a linear model (Grunert, 1982b).

Relating back to the overall cognitive framework in Fig. 3.1, the theory of reasoned action thus has two components: a model of cognitive structure and a model of output formulation. The theory does not say why certain beliefs become relevant (or salient) in the context of a particular choice of courses of action, and it does not explain how the motivations determining the impact of the beliefs on behavioral intention come about. In the description of the theory, it is explicitly acknowledged, however (Ajzen & Fishbein, 1980; Fishbein & Ajzen, 1975), that characteristics of the choice situation determine both which beliefs become salient and which motivations determine behavior. The process in which the individual analyses the situation and activates a subset of beliefs from his or her cognitive structure is just not part of the theory. In the terms of Fig. 3.1, the theory of reasoned action has the overall structure:

BEHAVIOR = f [MEMORY, FORMULATION
OF OUTPUT | ANALYSIS OF INPUT]

---

[2]We refer to the more well-known theory of reasoned action and not to its successor, the theory of planned behavior, for reasons of simplicity of expositon only. (See Ajzen, 1985; Ajzen & Madden, 1986.)

In MEC theory, neither the relevant excerpt from the cognitive structure nor the motivation is given. Rather, by measuring MEC one uncovers a broader excerpt from cognitive structure that is relevant across a large range of situations, and, in any particular situation, only a subset of it may become behaviorally relevant. Likewise, motivation is not assumed to be stable, but different values and consequences may be more or less motivating in different situations. A theory relating MEC to behavior thus would not only have to specify the formulation of output leading to behavioral intention once the relevant excerpt from cognitive structure and motivation is known but also the analysis of input explaining how, in a given situation and under given motivational constraints, certain parts of cognitive structure become relevant. If both types of processes would be specified, it would become possible to predict behavior contingent on the situation and the motivational state of the individual. We would then obtain a more complete cognitive theory, which also explains those factors that are taken for given in the theory of reasoned action:

BEHAVIOR = f [ANALYSIS OF INPUT,
MEMORY, FORMULATION OF OUTPUT]

A few building blocks in constructing such a theory are already available. Reynolds (Reynolds & Perkins, 1987) developed Cognitive Differentiation Analysis, where respondents' ratings of how well a product fits with the various steps in a ladder are used to explain product preference or product perception. In a similar vein, Bagozzi (Bagozzi & Dabholkar, 1994) used regression analysis to relate the presence of certain links in respondents' ladders to their past behavior and to the two summary constructs of the theory of reasoned action, that is, attitude toward the act and subjective norm. Both are more pragmatic solutions for a problem of analysis rather than attempts at real theory building, but they can be interpreted as attempts to formalize the formulation of output (like behavioral intention or preference) based on excerpts from cognitive structure that follow a means–end structure. Reynolds and Perkins (1987), in addition, suggested a principle for the analysis of input as well: Their results from Cognitive Differentiation Analysis suggest that preference tasks activate the more abstract sections of MEC, whereas perceptual tasks seem to activate the more concrete sections.

In sum, the theoretical problem addressed in this section is the lack of a theory that links MEC to consumer behavior. We propose that such a theory should both specify cognitive processes determining how situational factors lead to the activation of subsets of cognitive structure, and how these subsets then lead to the formation of behavioral intentions. Theoretical research proposing or testing such theories, possibly as an extension of the theory of reasoned action, would make an important contribution.

COLLECTING LADDERING DATA

Addressed here are four problems in regard to the execution of laddering interviews: elicitation techniques and product stimuli, situational specificity, forked answers, and the decision of when to stop probing.

Elicitation Techniques and Product Stimuli

The first step in a laddering interview is to determine the product attributes that are to be the point of departure for the probing process. Depending on which attributes are elicited, the resulting ladders will differ.

The kinds of attributes elicited from respondents depend on the retrieval cues provided to the respondent in the interview situation. Four major types of cues have been used. In a free elicitation situation, the respondent is provided only with the general product class as a retrieval cue, possibly supplemented by a usage situation (Olson & Muderrisoglu, 1979). In *triadic sorting*, usually concrete products are presented to the respondent as cues (Reynolds & Gutman, 1988). In *free sorting*, respondents are provided with a larger number of products, typically on a set of cards (Peter & Olson, 1993). In *attribute selection tasks*, the respondent is provided with a list of possible attributes as cues. This raises two questions. Will the set of attributes finally selected as the starting point for ladders differ depending on which elicitation method is used? And, if yes, which set of attributes is the right one?

The answer to the last question obviously depends on one's aim with the study as such. If retained as an overall aim of laddering studies to measure excerpts from cognitive structure that, in the context of a larger theory, would be able to predict consumer behavior, especially choice behavior when choosing between various alternative purchases, then the right set of attributes is the one that comprises those attributes that tend to be used in making decisions between alternative products or services. Such attributes may be both intrinsic and extrinsic and may have varying levels of concreteness. They may not be attributes of the product at all. Consumers may feel a lack of competence in making choices and leave the choice of product to an agent (e.g., as when buying tires for a car). Consumers may decide not to buy a product because it is only available at an outlet that is not on their usual shopping route. In both cases the relevant set of attributes would be attributes of an agent or retailer, not of the products themselves. Also, consumers may base decisions on attributes of the production process that are not mirrored in the final product, as when buying ethical food.

A triadic-sorting task, with an emphasis on visible differences between products, favors concrete intrinsic at the expense of extrinsic or less concrete attributes and may therefore lead to the generation of irrelevant attributes (e.g., about the size or color of products), which may then result in short and irrelevant ladders. A free elicitation task may face the opposite problem: The respondent may generate abstract product attributes or even consequences, necessitating backward laddering in order to obtain complete chains. Also, in a free elicitation task, when the respondent is unable to generate attributes spontaneously, he or she will aid their retrieval process by framing the problem at hand, for example by imagining a certain choice situation or a certain usage situation. Because this framing is not necessarily communicated to the interviewer, a set of respondents may generate various sets of attributes referring to different situations, without the possibility of taking in consideration these differences in the subsequent analysis of the data.

With regard to elicitation techniques in a laddering interview the problem thus is that different techniques may lead to different sets of attributes being generated, leading to the measurement of different excerpts from cognitive structure with no a priori way of knowing which technique will lead to the right result. It would be helpful to see research looking at how the elicitation method affects the resulting set of attributes and how different elicitation methods fare with regard to the relevance of the attributes generated, where relevance should be linked to which extent the attributes are actually used in choice situations. Interesting first attempts to look at these issues are reported by Bech-Larsen and Nielsen (1999) and Steenkamp and van Trijp (1997).

Situational Specificity

One of the strengths of a cognitive structure approach as compared to a multiattribute approach is that the situational dependency of attribute importance is explicitly acknowledged and is explained by the way in which attributes are linked to consequences and values. This can have two possible consequences for the way the laddering interview is conducted. Either one is interested in the cognitive structure with respect to a certain usage situation only; then it should be assured that this is the situation respondents have in mind during the laddering interview, or one is interested in cognitive structure broadly, covering the main usage situations relevant for the product category in question. In this case, it becomes important that the interviews cover a variety of usage situations. Depending on the main purpose of the study, the treatment of situational specificity in the interview should therefore differ. In the first case, the situation should be explicitly explained to the respondent, and it would be the interviewer's task to ensure that the respondent sticks to this situation throughout the interview. In the latter case, it may be appropriate to start with an elicitation of situations before even starting to elicit attributes (which may be situationally dependent, as previously explained). It may even be advisable to distinguish real from ideal situations, in cases where consumers have a preference for a product but usually abstain from buying it due to social influences or perceived lack of control (Ajzen & Madden, 1986).

The problem discussed here is that much of the information generated during a laddering interview depends on the usage situations the respondents have in mind, and the interview technique, in its standard form, provides no means of handling this situational specificity. It would be helpful to have research investigating how different framing, in terms of situations, leads to different results of laddering studies. Based on such results, one could come up with suggestions on how to make usage situations an integral part of the laddering interview.

Forked Answers

In a laddering interview, it is assumed that respondents' answers can be structured according to a linear sequence of cognitive categories of increasing levels of abstraction. This is unproblematic as long as, at every step in the probing process, the respondent retrieves only one cognitive category from his or her memory that appears to be a suitable answer. However, when the respondent has a quite elaborate cognitive structure with regard to the product in question, the retrieval process may result in the retrieval of several cognitive categories at the same level of abstraction. As an example, the probe "why is good taste important to you?" may lead to the retrieval of three answers: (a) "it makes me feel relaxed and joyful," (b) "my family will be pleased," and (c) "it shows that I am a good housekeeper." The interviewer has various ways of handling this. When the interview is conducted in a flexible way, the interviewer may record the various answers and continue to ladder from each answer one after the other. If the interviewer insists on pursuing one ladder and urges the respondent to concentrate on one answer, the additional categories retrieved may linger in working memory and interfere with later answers to further probes, leading to deviations from the ideal of producing a stream of cognitive categories with increasing levels of abstraction. The further probe "why is it important for you to please your family" may then result in an answer like "my family likes it when I am a good housekeeper," which may be regarded as an attempt, from the respondent's side, to pick up some loose ends in his or her working memory and, at the same time, to come up with an answer that suits the interviewer.

The problem discussed here is that respondents, in a laddering interview, may feel a natural tendency to come up with more than one answer to any particular probe. Although this phenomenon undoubtedly exists, little is known about how frequent it is, which consequences it has for the results, and how various ways of conducting laddering interviews could affect it. Any research shedding light on these matters would be useful. In addition, suggestions for new techniques allowing forked answers and making use of them would be welcome as well, especially because the sequence in which answers at a given level of abstraction are given and their interresponse times may contain important additional information on association strengths in cognitive structure.

When to Stop, When to Go On

When should an interviewer stop probing? When the respondent has reached the level of terminal values, it seems natural to stop probing. But what if a respondent has difficulties in finding further answers already at the level of consequences or even abstract attributes—and keeps saying, for example "I simply like tastiness?". How far should the interviewer press the respondent for additional answers? Interviewers in laddering studies have mentioned this as one of the most difficult aspects of conducting laddering (Grunert & Grunert, 1995).

When the cognitive structure is especially weak—there are few and weak associations between cognitive categories—the respondent may soon be unable to retrieve additional categories in answering questions that probe for more abstract categories. There is ample research demonstrating what happens in situations when a respondent has difficulties in retrieving more answers to a question but is pressed to do so nevertheless (Gruenewald & Lockhead, 1980; Strube, 1984). The respondent will make a new attempt at retrieval by using a different strategic perspective. An example will make this clear. When a respondent has given "being healthier" as a consequence of eating a food product, and the interviewer asks "why is it important to you to be healthier?", there may be no immediate answer. In trying to find an answer, the respondent can use different strategic perspectives. The respondent may have gone through recent illnesses and what life would have been like without them. The respondent can consider, whether she or he actually wants to be healthier and how health may compete with other higher order values. The respondent can try to imagine future life situations when good health would be especially important, like going on a skiing holiday or getting through a week of stressful worklife. In each case, quite different cognitive categories may be retrieved.

The stronger the impact of strategic perspectives on the answers given by the respondent or, put another way, the more the task changes from a retrieval task to a problem-solving task, the more doubtful it becomes whether the interview will lead to some kind of measurement of the respondent's cognitive structure. At best, the measurement will be affected by unknown strategic perspectives. At worst, the respondent may actually construct new links between cognitive categories; that is the respondent's cognitive structure will be changed during the interview.

One could argue that these associations existed before but had not been retrieved in consciousness before the laddering interview. That is, the laddering procedure was successful in making explicit associations that seldom become conscious. This interpretation is impossible to refute. If we accept, however, that learning associations always requires conscious awareness of the pair of elements to be learned (a view that is widely accepted, see the review by Hoffmann, 1994), then retrieval of a pre-existing association should be accompanied by a feeling of recognition and not of surprise.

The problem addressed here is whether hard probing increases or decreases the validity of the results of laddering. To some extent, this problem is also amenable to research. Change of strategic perspectives or construction of new associations will be noticeable to the attentive interviewer as pauses, breaks, unfinished sentences, and so forth and can also be detected after the interview by analysing tapes. By reanalyzing laddering data, omitting answers that the respondent gave only after considerable deliberation of that kind, one could, first of all, gain some insight on how hard probing affects the results. When the results of a laddering study are used in the context of a theory to predict behavior, one could additionally check the predictive validity of the additional information provided by hard probes.

Hard Versus Soft Laddering

Most of the problems discussed in this section, namely the possible elicitation of irrelevant attributes, unclear situational dependence of the answers given by the respondent, forked answers, and answers that have come about only by putting heavy pressure on the respondent, could be detected and possibly circumvented by a trained interviewer if the interviews are conducted in a way that encourages a natural and redundant flow of speech, based on which the interviewer reconstructs ladders only after the interview. This type of interview may be designated, where the natural flow of speech of the respondent is restricted as little as possible, as soft laddering. In contrast, hard laddering refers to interviews and data collection techniques where the respondent is forced to produce ladders one by one and to give answers in such a way that the sequence of the answers reflects increasing levels of abstraction. Data-collection techniques that do not involve personal interviews at all, like self-administered questionnaires (Pieters, Baumgartner, & Stad, 1994; Walker & Olson, 1991; Young & Feigin, 1975) and computerized data-collection devices are all examples of hard laddering.

Although the soft approach is potentially better in handling the types of problems discussed in this section, at the same time it leads to increased degrees of freedom for the interviewer, which may introduce new biases. The interviewer must try to make sense of the answers and relate them to the means–end model. This requires interpretation and, often, generalization by the interviewer. For example, people may retrieve episodic instead of semantic information, which usually means that they start telling little stories ("last time I bought this, I noticed . . ."). People may give an answer and immediately start elaborating it ("I like bread with wrinkles. Not wrinkles generally, but, you know, the type which . . ."). People may jump back and forth between the levels of abstraction. All of this requires cognitive processing on the interviewer side in order to distil ladders: generalize from the episodic to the semantic, simplify the elaborate, and sort out levels of abstraction. The more this occurs, the more influence the interviewer has on the results. Hard laddering is an attempt to avoid this.

It would be interesting to see more research comparing the results of hard and soft laddering. In cases where a test of convergent validity establishes that both hard and soft laddering lead to largely similar results (Botschen & Thelen, 1998), one could safely conclude that hard laddering is a preferable technique because it is easier to administer and less costly. When the results differ however, then an investigation of predictive validity, in the context of a larger theory as sketched earlier in this chapter, would be called for. It would be highly useful to have research that can pin down under which circumstances it may be safe to perform hard laddering, and when it appears necessary to employ soft laddering.

CODING OF LADDERING DATA

Two problem areas in coding are discussed: the distinction between attributes, consequences, and values; and the problem of finding the right levels of abstraction. This leads us to the general problem of increasing transparency and reliability in the coding of laddering data.

Distinction Between Attributes, Consequences, and Values

The distinction between attributes, consequences, and values should, of course, be based on a conceptual definition of these terms. The laddering literature is surprisingly void of such definitions. In practice, many borderline cases turn up. When the respondent says "healthy"—is this an attribute or a consequence? "The bread is healthy" probably designates an (abstract) attribute. "I will be healthy when I eat this bread" seems to be a consequence. But, is health not a value? Making such categorizations in a uniform way is heavily dependent on the availability of context information (i.e., on the extent to which a term like *healthy* is embedded in a redundant flow of natural speech). How much context information is available will, again, depend on the way the laddering interview is executed. Laddering done by self-administered questionnaires or by computer (the hard form) usually provides very little context information. In laddering tasks where the interviewer records the answers as notes in ladder schemes, the context information is available to the interviewer only and not in subsequent coding. Only when the interviews are taped and transcribed is the full context available in coding.

It would be helpful in any laddering study to obtain information on the reliability of classifying answers as attributes, consequences, or values. It would be even more helpful to see research showing how this reliability may depend on the way the laddering interview was conducted.

Finding the 'Right' Level of Abstraction

The difference between two answers is rarely purely lexical. To define them as synonyms and group them in the same category, the category has to be at a more abstract level than the answers themselves. For example, 'excellent taste' and 'pretty good taste' may both be sorted into 'good taste'. 'Good taste' and 'bad taste' may both be sorted into 'taste'. 'No chemicals' and 'no preservatives' may be sorted into 'only natural ingredients'. Such codings appear intuitively unproblematic, although they obviously lead to a loss of information.

If the coding stops at that level, the resulting number of categories will usually still be large (easily 40–50 concepts). The implication matrix will be correspondingly large, the cell frequencies will be low, and it will not be possible to compute and draw a hierarchical value map, destroying the most appealing device of the laddering technique. Thus, a more radical coding is typically required to reduce the data (Gutman, 1991). This usually means that the level of abstraction for each category has to be raised considerably. 'No artificial colors', 'no preservatives', 'more minerals', 'better ingredients', and 'freshly milled flour' all become 'ingredients'. Many may still find this uncontroversial. It is at the consequences and value levels that the real difficulties start. Can 'joy' and 'not being depressed' both be coded into 'well-being'? Or can 'have experiences' and 'curiosity' be coded into 'variation'? Such rather broad categories usually have to be created, if a technically manageable implication matrix shall result.

The problem, not specific to the coding of laddering data but common to many forms of content analysis, is the lack of transparency of the coding process, leading to a low degree of intersubjectivity.

Increasing Transparency and Reliability
in the Coding of Laddering Data

It is obvious that coding is a complicated process that gives a lot of latitude to the researcher, and much more attention should be paid to it in the typical methodology discussion than has been the case until now. In particular, the process should be made more intersubjectively accessible. Having parallel coders is of course the most common recourse used in research practice. But with laddering-type data parallel coders may be a mixed blessing. The raw data used for the coding, usually laddering schemes or interviewer notes, already involves a loss of information compared to the original interview. Context information, which may be helpful or important when coding the data, has already been lost. The interviewer, who has conducted the interview to be coded, will be the best possible coder because she or he will remember part of the context information (and also better be able to clarify matters by referring back to a tape). A second coder, who does not have this background information, may perform the coding in a different way due to this lack of implicit context information. We would then observe a low-intercoder reliability, the reason being a difference in the context information available to the two coders.

The need for context to attach meaning to an answer refers to the general problem qualitative researchers call *indexicality*: For the researcher, it is possible to understand, or make sense of a respondent's answer only by relating it to that respondent's individual background. Answers must be interpreted relatively to the respondent's background, experience, career, her or his interpretation of the data collection situation, and so forth (Gutman, 1991; Hoffmann-Riem, 1980; Hopf, 1978; Küchler, 1981; Schütze, Meinefeld, Springer, & Weymann, 1973). The less one knows in advance about how respondents think about the topic to be researched (i.e., the less one knows about the product attributes, consequences, and values likely to be used by them to attach meaning to a certain product category) the more serious the indexicality problem. And the more context information available, the easier this process of assigning meaning will be. Although this argument is raised mostly from an interpretivist phenomenological perspective, the general issue of a valid assignment of meaning to data is relevant also from a nomological perspective.

Therefore, there may be good reason to have the interviewers code the data themselves and to avoid parallel coders; however, this makes it all the more important to devise instruments that can make the coding process more transparent and reliable. Some of the experience and tools developed within the realm of computer-assisted content analysis (Grunert & Bader, 1986; Züll & Mohler, 1992) concerned with finding more intersubjective ways of coding text data, may be helpful here. The basic idea developed is that of *iterative coding*. This means that a first coding is performed, and the implications of this coding are made transparent by aids like keyword-in-context lists, leftover lists, and insertion of codes in the text database. Based on these aids, the coding is revised, and the implications of the revised coding are analyzed in the same way. This procedure continues until the coding appears satisfactory. Of course, the decision about what can be regarded as satisfactory, to a large extent, still rests on face validity considerations and, therefore, on the judgement of the individual researcher. However, such procedures provide documentation for how the coding has proceeded thus increasing the intersubjectivity of the process.

Applied to laddering data, one could imagine a windows-based software aid with three parallel windows: one in which the raw text or the interview notes appear (for soft laddering only), one in which the ladders appear, and one in which synonyms are defined (i.e., where categories are formed). Both the step from raw text to ladders and from ladders to categories can be performed mouse-based, so that consequences of a particular coding step become immediately visible in the context of all previously performed codings. The software could assemble all entries into a particular category with their text or ladder contexts for perusal and could prompt for coding at the discretion of the researcher. The presently available software for coding laddering data is rather cumbersome, and work leading to improved tools for this important step is called for.

ANALYSIS

The major tool in the analysis of laddering data has been the derivation of a hierarchical value map. Discussed is the phenomenological status of hierarchical value maps and then several technical problems in their derivation. It should also be noted that alternatives to hierarchical value maps have been presented as well: Both multidimensional scaling (Aurifeille, 1991) and multiple correspondence analysis (Valette-Florence & Rapacchi, 1991) have been suggested as alternatives. These techniques result in a representation where the cognitive categories are not linked in a network but placed in a multidimensional space where distances are used to express association. These alternative techniques are not further discussed because we believe that a network representation is more adequate to data based on a theoretical background where cognitive structures are assumed to be modeled as networks.

What Is a Hierarchical Value Map?

The *hierarchical value map* (HVM), the main output from a laddering analysis, is a characterization of a group of respondents. There are two possible views (one modest, one ambitious) of HVMs. The modest view is that a

HVM is a device that allows us to see the major results from a laddering study of a group of respondents without having to go through all the individual ladders. The more ambitious view is that the HVM is an estimate of cognitive structure for that group of respondents. Whereas the laddering literature does not take a clear stand on which view one should adopt, the more ambitious view would be in line with much previous research on estimating cognitive structures, especially within the word association paradigm (Deese, 1965; Szalay & Deese, 1978). The argument for the more ambitious view runs as follows: at the individual level, our data are not rich enough to estimate a respondent's cognitive structure. In a laddering study, the 2-3 ladders typically obtained from an individual respondent reveal some aspects of his or her cognitive structure, but they are not an estimate of the cognitive structure itself because the cognitive structure is not a collection of single chains but an interrelated net of associations. However, when we obtain ladders from a group of *homogeneous* respondents, the set of ladders obtained from them, taken together and analyzed by an appropriate algorithm, yields an estimate of this group's cognitive structure.

The view taken should determine which operations are regarded as admissible when aggregating laddering data. In the following discussion, we assume the more ambitious view. However, the problems discussed will affect the interpretability of hierarchical value maps also when only the modest view is adopted.

Determination of Cutoff Level

In principle, based on the implication matrix, one could draw a map that shows all the cognitive categories that resulted from the coding process and in which two cognitive categories are linked whenever the corresponding cell in the implication matrix has a nonzero entry. In practice, this is seldom possible or desirable because of the large number of nonzero entries in the typical implication matrix (many times several hundreds). In practice, one tries to find a HVM that includes the most important links. This is achieved by specifying a *cutoff level*.

The cutoff level gives the minimum cell entry in the implication matrix necessary to be represented as a link in the map. Because the distribution of the cell entries is usually heavily skewed—many cell entries are very low, and only a few are high—the cutoff level is a powerful device for reducing the complexity of the map. The problem is that there are no theoretical or statistical criteria to guide the selection of the cutoff level. Thus, usually a compromise is attempted between retaining information on the one hand and creating a manageable map on the other hand.

Pieters, Baumgartner, and Stad (Pieters, et al., 1994) suggested that the cutoff level to be selected where the *concentration index* is highest. The concentration index is defined as the percentage of all links in a given implication matrix that are retained at a given cutoff level, divided by the percentage of cells in the implication matrix retained. A hierarchical value map based on a cutoff level with the highest concentration index represents the highest possible number of links in the data with the lowest possible number of categories. This is intuitively appealing, but it should be noted that the outcome of such a procedure is heavily dependent on how rigorous the coding of the data has been performed. A coding procedure that retains many categories and thus a smaller loss of information during coding will lead to a cutoff level with only a small percentage of active cells and of links that are retained resulting in considerable information loss when constructing the hierarchical value map. A coding procedure that results in only few categories, with a large loss of information in coding, will lead to a cutoff level where, comparatively, many active cells and links enter the HVM, which then represents most of the information in the implication matrix.

There is thus a trade-off between information loss during coding and information loss due to the use of a cutoff level in constructing the HVM. These relations are only poorly understood, and the choice of cutoff levels rests mainly on rules of thumb. It would therefore be desirable to see research coming up with more rigorous methods for determining cutoff levels, possibly based on a quantification of several dimensions of information loss involved.

Homogeneity of Respondents

An interpretation of the hierarchical value map as an estimate of the cognitive structure of a group of respondents presupposes that the group of respondents is homogeneous, or, more precisely, that their cognitive structure can be regarded as homogeneous with regard to the excerpt we want to measure. Ideally, one should test this assumption, before attempting interpretations of the hierarchical value map. Such tests could be conducted on the raw data before deriving the HVM, or they could be conducted on the HVM itself.

There is only very limited methodological research giving advice on how that can be done, and we can only point to a number of issues. The mere fact that the individual ladders differ does not, of course, constitute evidence for a lack of homogeneity if we assume a measurement model in which the production of ladders in the interviews is guided by a stochastic process. What we would need is a statistical test on whether the differences between individual sets of ladders would be compatible with such a random process. Not having such a test, a more pragmatic solution would be to perform a cluster analysis on the existence of links in the ladders of individual respondents. If we obtain clusters with clearly distinct sets of links, it becomes intuitively less likely that the respondents are homogeneous, and we may take that as a face validity test of the homogeneity assumption.

Roehrich and Valette-Florence (1991) reported an example in which laddering data served as input to a cluster analysis. Their clustering was based on the existence of links between categories, and the unit of analysis (i.e., the units to be clustered) were ladders, not respondents. Every respondent may then be a member of more than one cluster, so that, interpreted on the basis of respondents and not ladders, a set of overlapping clusters results. However, it should be possible to conduct a similar procedure with respondents instead of ladders as the unit of analysis.

Looking not at the raw data, but at the HVM, the mere fact that a certain path is based only on a subset of the respondents does not by itself constitute evidence of a homogeneity problem, for the same reason as previously discussed. If, however, one would find that the hierarchical value map can be divided into submaps, such that the paths in subset A would be based on answers from subgroup I of the respondents and the paths in subset B on answers from subgroup II, then this would indicate a homogeneity problem. The conceptual consistency index developed by Roehrich and Valette-Florence (1991) may be used as a diagnostic device in this context. For any path in a hierarchical value map, the index is the difference between the highest frequency of any direct link in the path and the frequency of indirect links between the start and the end node of the path. A high index indicates that only few or no respondents had ladders including the whole path, which hence has come about mainly by aggregating respondents with different ladders. A low or zero index indicates that the whole path mirrors ladders as voiced by the respondents. The fictive HVM in Fig. 3.2 serves to illustrate how the index could be used to shed light on the homogeneity issue. If the index is high for paths A1-C1-V1, A2-C1-V1, and A3-C2-V2 but low for paths A1-C1-V2 and A2-C1-V2 then this seems to indicate that the HVM merges two distinct groups of respondents, one characterized by the paths A1-C1-V1 and A2-C1-V1 and the other characterized by the path A3-C2-V2.

The problem discussed in this section is the lack of clear criteria for whether a hierarchical value map may be taken as an estimate of cognitive structure for a homogeneous group of respondents or not. A few suggestions for applying clustering techniques to shed light on group differences between respondents have been made, but clearly rigorous methodological research on the clustering of laddering data is called for. The foundation that is really missing however, is a stochastic measurement theory linking the production of ladders in the interview to an underlying cogni-

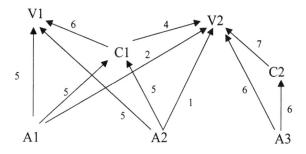

Conceptual consistency index:

A1-C1-V1=6-5=1

A2-C1-V1=6-5=1

A3-C1-V1=7-6=1

A1-C1-V2=5-2=3

A2-C1-V2=5-1=4

FIG. 3.2. Fictive example of hierarchical value map.

tive structure. Based on such a theory, statistical tests could be developed that allow to test the homogeneity assumption.

The Nonredundancy Assumption

The existing algorithms for deriving HVMs favor long chains. This goes for the paper-and-pencil method described by Reynolds and Gutman (1988), the program LADDERMAP by Reynolds and Gengler, and the graph-theoretical method proposed by Valette-Florence and Rapacchi (1991). In terms of cognitive structure theory, favoring long chains is identical with assuming *nonredundancy* of the cognitive structure. Nonredundancy means that, if Category 1 at abstraction level A is linked to Category 2 at abstraction level B, which again is linked to Category 3 at abstraction level C, then there should not be a direct link between Categories 1 and 3 because such a link would be redundant. This assumption, which is also called the *economy-of-storage* assumption, has been debated for a long time in research on semantic memory (see Chang, 1986, for an overview). There is experimental evidence both for and against it. But it is an assumption that is used in many successful models of semantic memory, and using it in the context of means–end chain research may thus be defensible. It only becomes problematic in connection with nonhomogeneity of respondents. If respondent I has a ladder 1-2-3, and respondent II has a ladder 1-3, then both underlying cognitive structures may, at the individual level, conform to the principle of nonredundancy. But when both ladders enter the same HVM, a problem arises: If, at the aggregate level, there is a link 1-2-3 (Categories 1 and 3 are linked indirectly), then there will be no link 1-3, even if such links were observed at the individual level. This can have rather astonishing results (the following example is presented in more detail in Grunert & Grunert, 1995). Imagine that, out of a sample of 30 respondents, 25 have the ladder *good taste–well-being*, and 5 have the ladder *good taste–function better–well-being*. In the aggregate map, the whole group of respondents would then be characterized by *good taste–function better–well-being* because a direct link between *good taste* and *well-being* would be redundant. The map hence communicates the erroneous impression that, for this group of respondents, good taste leads to the personal consequence that they can function better with various marketing implications. Actually, most of the respondents just mentioned that they enjoy a good taste.

The nonredundancy assumption is therefore a problem only when homogeneity is a problem as well. Whenever the homogeneity of the respondents is unclear, the nonredundancy assumption can lead to misleading characteristics of the HVM. It may then be advisable to allow redundant HVMs.

Improved Algorithms for Deriving Hierarchical Value Maps

In trying to develop better algorithms for the analysis of laddering data, the first step should be an explicit stand on what a HVM is supposed to do. If it is meant as an estimate of cognitive structure then the next step would be to spell out clearly the assumptions made about the nature of that structure, especially about nonredundancy/economy-of-storage. The technical problem to be solved then is to aggregate only respondents whose cognitive structures can be regarded as reasonably homogeneous with regard to the product in question. This should be achieved by applying clustering methods to the laddering data before aggregation. If, on the other hand, the more modest view is adopted (i.e., a HVM is only a graphical device for the purpose of summarizing main results from a laddering study) then the nonredundancy assumption should be relaxed, and algorithms should be developed that allow redundant links. This may make the maps a little harder to read, but it may avoid misinterpretations. Improved algorithms living up to these requirements, as well as software implementing them, would be welcome additions to the tool box of laddering researchers.

THE VALIDATION OF RESULTS
FROM A LADDERING STUDY

Laddering, being a qualitative data collection technique, is usually employed with small to medium sample sizes. In many application contexts, the question arises whether the HVM derived can be generalized to a larger population, that is whether the results have external validity. A few attempts have been made to validate results from a laddering study by quantitative data collection techniques.

Valette-Florence (Roehrich & Valette-Florence, 1991; Valette-Florence & Rapacchi, 1990) has used a card-sorting task, in which respondents first were shown a pile of attribute cards and had to select the most important attribute for the product in question. Then they were shown a pile of consequence cards and had to select the most important consequence following from the attribute. Finally they were shown a pile of value cards and had to select the value following from the consequence. The procedure can be repeated with the second-most and third-most important attribute, if desired. It has the advantage that respondents produce ladders just as in a real laddering interview, and the analysis of the data by means of implication matrices and hierarchical value maps can proceed just as in a normal laddering study.

Vanden Abeele (1990) has presented whole chains in verbalised form to respondents (e.g., "Milk is nutritious and full of vitamins and nutrients. It helps keeping in good health, and those having a good health can live a long and rich life"). Respondents had to rate how well they thought the chain fit the product in question. For those chains that were rated as best fitting, the various component links of the chain ("Milk is nutritious and full of vitamins and nutrients", "Eating vitamins and necessary nutrients helps keeping in good health", and "Good health ensures a long and rich life") were then rated for credibility.

Grunert (1997) has employed an extension of conjoint analysis to validate MEC. As in traditional conjoint analysis, respondents are presented product profiles, which are systematically varied with regard to product attributes. These product profiles are then rated, not on a unidimensional preference or purchase intention scale as in traditional conjoint analysis but with regard to those consequences and values that previous qualitative research has shown to be associated with the product attributes. As a result, a covariance matrix of attributes, consequences, and values is obtained, and a HVM can be estimated by structural equation estimation techniques.

Ter Hofstede et al. (1998) have employed the Association Pattern Technique as a quantitative approach to measuring means–end chains. It basically involves presenting respondents with empty A by C and C by V matrices, where respondents have to mark those cells where they think there is an association.

The four examples show a need and some suggestions for a quantitative validation of studies employing the laddering method. Research employing new methods or comparing the virtues of these existing suggestions would be beneficial and important cornerstones when the predictive validity of means–end estimations is to be tested in the context of a broader cognitive theory, as suggested earlier.

A PROGRAM FOR RESEARCH

In this chapter we summarize a number of problems, both theoretical and methodological, which have been identified with regard to means–end chain theory and the laddering method. The problems and the research questions they lead to are summarized in Table 3.1. We conclude with a few general observations.

Firstly, the discussion has clearly shown how theoretical problems and methodological problems are interrelated. Questions like attribute elicitation in the interview or the optimal derivation of the HVM cannot be solved unless the theoretical status of both individual ladders and hierarchical value maps is clarified. The underlying cognitive model of consumer behavior has to be spelled out in more detail, and a stochastic measurement model relating individual cognitive structures, ladders produced in an interview, and the hierarchical value map as an estimate of cognitive structure has to be developed. This would also allow for a more rigorous statistical treatment of many of the matters that are solved in ad-hoc ways now, like the clustering of respondents and the determination of cutoff levels.

Secondly, none of the problems discussed is unresearchable or inherently unsolvable. Some of them can be addressed by straightforward, empirical research, like the comparison of different forms of attribute elicitation, the impact of situational specificity, or the differences between hard and soft laddering. Others require the development or adaptation of statistical techniques or the development or adaptation of cognitive theories. If researchers could be attracted to these issues in sufficient numbers, considerable progress seems possible within a few years.

TABLE 3.1

Problems and Research Topics in Laddering and Means-End Chains

Topic Area	Problem	Research Task
Means-end chain theory	Unclear which excerpt of consumers' cognitive structure is tapped by MEC and why this is important.	Theory development placing MEC into broader model of cognitive structure; specifying under which circumstances MEC cover the most relevant aspects of cognitive structure.
	MEC cannot be used to explain or predict consumer behavior.	Development of theory combining MEC model with model of processes for analysis of situational input and formulation of output.
Collection of laddering data	Choice of elicitation techniques will affect the outcome of a laddering study.	Analysis of impact of type of elicitation task on set of attributes, on relevance of attributes, on resulting ladders; development of new elicitation techniques.
	Usage situation respondents have in mind affects outcome of study but is not controlled.	Analysis of how framing in terms of situations affects results; development of methods to treat situations more systematically in laddering.
	Respondents may give forked answers.	Analysis of frequency of forked answers and their impact on results; effect of various types of laddering on forked answers.
	Unclear when interviewer should stop probing.	Comparison of results based on more and less extensive probing, predictive validity of results.
	Hard versus soft laddering.	Tests of convergent and predictive validity of results obtained by hard and soft laddering.
Coding of laddering data	Distinction between attributes, consequences and values not always clear.	Analysis of reliability of these classifications and how they are affected by different types of laddering.
	Difficult to find right level of abstraction in coding.	Develop methods to increase transparency and reliability of coding process based on techniques of computer-assisted content analysis.
Analysis	Nonhomogeneous respondents may lead to misleading results when integrated into one HVM.	Better methods for clustering respondents based on laddering data; development of stochastic measurement theory for laddering.
	No stringent criteria for choice of cutoff level in construction of HVM.	Development of algorithm for optimization of cutoff level based on information loss functions.
	Algorithms favoring long paths (nonredundancy, economy of storage) may produce misleading results in HVM with nonhomogeneous respondents.	Development of improved algorithms for derivation of HVM including options for nonredundancy.
Validation of results from laddering	External validity of results from qualitative laddering interviews difficult to assess by quantitative surveys.	Comparison of approaches to quantify ladders; development of new approaches for quantitative surveys.

87

Finally, we believe that the area of laddering and MEC, in spite of this catalogue of problems, has the potential for making a very significant contribution to consumer research. It could evolve to the cognitive theory of consumer behavior, with a tool box of measurement devices developed to bridge the gap between construct and reality.

REFERENCES

Ajzen, I. (1985). From intentions to actions: A theory of planned behaviour. In J. Kuhl & J. Beckmann (Eds.), *Action control: From cognition to behavior* (pp. 11–39). Berlin, Germany: Springer.

Ajzen, I., & Fishbein, M. (1980). *Understanding attitudes and predicting behavior*. Englewood Cliffs, NJ: Prentice-Hall.

Ajzen, I., & Madden, T. J. (1986). Prediction of goal-directed behavior: Attitudes, intentions, and perceived behavioral control. *Journal of Experimental Social Psychology, 22,* 453–474.

Anderson, J. R. (1983). *The architecture of cognition*. Cambridge, MA: Harvard University Press.

Asselbergs, P. (1989). *Competitive advertising – New developments in qualitative positioning research: Meaning structure analysis*. Rotterdam, Netherlands: IPM.

Aurifeille, J.-M. (1991). Contribution of 'instrumental values' to means–end chains analysis and to advertising conceptualization. Paper presented at *Workshop on value and lifestyle research in marketing* (pp.). Brussels, Belgium: EIASM.

Bagozzi, R. P., & Dabholkar, P. A. (1994). Consumer recycling goals and their effects on decisions to recycle: A means–end analysis. *Psychology & Marketing, 11,* 1–28.

Bech-Larsen, T., & Nielsen, N. A. (1999). A comparison of five elicitation techniques for elicitation of attributes of low involvement products. *Journal of Economic Psychology, 20,* 315–341.

Botschen, G., & Thelen, E. (1998). Hard versus soft laddering: Implications for appropriate use. In I. Balderjahn, C. Mennicken, & E. Vernette (Eds.), *New developments and approaches in consumer behaviour research* (pp. 321–339). Stuttgart: Schäffer-Poeschel.

Chang, T. M. (1986). Semantic memory: Facts and models. *Psychological Bulletin, 99,* 199–220.

Cowan, N. (1988). Evolving conceptions of memory storage, selective attention, and their mutual constraints within the human information processing system. *Psychological Bulletin, 104,* 163–191.

Deese, J. (1965). *The structure of associations in language and thought*. Baltimore, MD: John Hopkins.

Dichter, E. (1960). *The strategy of desire*. New York: Doubleday.

Fishbein, M., & Ajzen, I. (1975). *Belief, attitude, intention and behavior*. Reading, MA: Addison-Wesley.

Gruenewald, P. J., & Lockhead, G. R. (1980). The free recall of category examples. *Journal of Experimental Psychology: Human learning and memory, 6*(3), 225–240.

Grunert, K. G. (1982a). *Informationsverarbeitungsprozesse bei der Kaufentscheidung: Ein gedächtnispsychologischer Ansatz* [Information processing in purchase decisions: A memory psychology perspective]. Frankfurt, Germany: Lang.

Grunert, K. G. (1982b). Linear processing in a semantic network: An alternative view of consumer product evaluation. *Journal of Business Research, 10,* 31–42.

Grunert, K. G. (1994). Cognition and economic psychology. In H. Brandstätter & W. Güth (Eds.), *Essays in economic psychology* (pp. 91–108). Berlin, Germany: Springer.

Grunert, K. G. (1997). What's in a steak? A cross-cultural study on the quality perception of beef. *Food Quality and Preference, 8,* 157–174.

Grunert, K. G., & Bader, M. (1986). Die Weiterverarbeitung qualitativer Daten durch computerunterstützte Inhaltsanalyse [Processing qualitative data by computer-aided content analysis]. *Marketing - ZFP, 4,* 238–247.

Grunert, K. G., & Grunert, S. C. (1995). Measuring subjective meaning structures by the laddering method: Theoretical considerations and methodological problems. *International Journal of Research in Marketing, 12,* 209–225.

Gutman, J. (1982). A means–end chain model based on consumer categorization processes. *Journal of Marketing, 46*(2), 60–72.

Gutman, J. (1991). Exploring the nature of linkages between consequences and values. *Journal of Business Research, 22*(2), 143–149.

Hoffmann, J. (1994). Unbewußtes Lernen: Gedanken zur weiteren Forschung [Unconscious learning: Thoughts on further research]. *Psychologische Rundschau, 45*(1), 43–46.

Hoffmann-Riem, C. (1980). Die Sozialforschung einer interpretativen Soziologie—Der Datengewinn [Social science and interpretative sociology—data collection]. *Kölner Zeitschrift für Soziologie und Sozialpsychologie, 32,* 339–372.

Hopf, C. (1978). Die Pseudo-Exploration—Überlegungen zur Technik qualitativer Interviews in der Sozialforschung [Pseudo-exploration—thoughts on the methodology of qualitative interviews in social research]. *Zeitschrift für Soziologie, 7,* 97–115.

Johnson-Laird, P. N., Herrmann, D. J., & Chaffin, R. (1984). Only connections: A critique of semantic networks. *Psychological Bulletin, 96,* 292–315.

Kosslyn, S. M. (1975). Information representation in visual images. *Cognitive Psychology, 7,* 341–370.

Küchler, M. (1981). Kontext—Eine vernachlässigte Dimension empirischer Sozialforschung [Context—a neglected dimension in social research]. In J. Matthes (Eds.), *Lebenswelt und soziale Probleme* (pp. 344–354). Frankfurt, Germany: Campus.

McClelland, J. L., & Rumelhart, D. E. (1985). Distributed memory and the representation of general and specific information. *Journal of Experimental Psychology: General, 114,* 159–188.

Norman, D. A., & Rumelhart, D. E. (1975). *Explorations in cognition.* San Francisco, CA: Freeman.

Olson, J. C. (1989). Theoretical foundations of means–end chains. *Werbeforschung & Praxis*(5), 174–178.

Olson, J. C., & Muderrisoglu, A. (1979). The stability of responses obtained by free elicitation: Implications for measuring attribute salience and memory structure. In W. L. Wilkie (Eds.), *Advances in Consumer Research* (pp. 269–275). Ann Arbor, MI: Association for Consumer Research.

Olson, J. C., & Reynolds, T. J. (1983). Understanding consumers cognitive structures: Implications for advertising strategy. In L. Percy & A. G. Woodside (Eds.), *Advertising and consumer psychology* (pp. 77–90). Lexington, MA: Lexington Books.

Paivio, A. (1986). *Mental representations: A dual coding approach.* Oxford, England: Oxford University Press.

Peter, J. P., & Olson, J. C. (1993). *Consumer behavior, 3rd ed.* Homewood, IL: Irwin.

Phillips, D. M., Olson, J. C., & Baumgartner, H. (1995). Consumption visions in consumer decision making. In F. Kardes & M. Sujan (Eds.), *Advances in consumer research,* Vol. 22 (pp. 280–284). Provo, UT: Association for Consumer Research.

Pieters, R., Baumgartners, H., & Stad, H. (1994, May 17–20). Diagnosing means–end structures: The perception of word-processing software and the adaptive-innovative personality of managers. In J. Bloemer, J. Lemmink & H. Kasper (Ed.), *23rd EMAC conference, 2* (pp. 749–763). Maastricht, Netherlands: European Marketing Academy.

Pylshyn, Z. W. (1973). What the mind's eye tells the mind's brain: A critique of mental imagery. *Psychological Bulletin, 80*(1), 1–24.

Reynolds, T. J., & Gutman, J. (1988). Laddering theory, methods, analysis, and interpretation. *Journal of Advertising Research, 2,* 11–31.

Reynolds, T. J., & Perkins, W. S. (1987). Cognitive differentiation analysis: A new methodology for assessing the validity of means–end hierarchies. In M. Wallendorf & P. Anderson (Eds.), *Advances in consumer research* (pp. 109–113). Provo, UT: Association for Consumer Research.

Roehrich, G., & Valette-Florence, P. (1991). A weighted cluster-based analysis of direct and indirect connections in means–end chains: An application to lingerie retail. In K. G. Grunert & P. Valette-Florence (Eds.), *Workshop on values and lifestyle research in marketing,* Brussels, Belgium: EIASM.

Ruge, H.-D. (1988). *Die Messung bildhafter Konsumerlebnisse* [Measuring pictorial consumption experience]. Heidelberg, Germany: Physica.

Schütze, F., Meinefeld, W., Springer, W., & Weymann, A. (1973). Grundlagentheoretische Voraussetzungen methodisch kontrollierten Fremdverstehens [Basic requirements for methodologically controlled external understanding]. In A. B. Soziologen (Eds.), *Alltagswissen, Interaktion und gesellschaftliche Wirklichkeit* (pp. 433–495). Reinbek, Germany: Rowohlt.

Simon, H. A. (1990). Invariants of human behaviour. *Annual Review of Psychology, 41,* 1–19.

Steenkamp, J. B., & van Trijp, H. (1997). Attribute elicitation in marketing research: A comparison of three procedures. *Marketing Letters, 8,* 153–165.

Strube, G. (1984). *Assoziation* [Association]. Heidelberg, Germany: Springer.

Szalay, L. B., & Deese, J. (1978). *Subjective meaning and culture: An assessment through word associations.* Hillsdale, NJ: Lawrence Erlbaum Associates.

ter Hofstede, F., Andenaert, A., Steenkamp, J. B., & Wedel, M. (1998). An investigation into the association pattern technique as a quantitative approach to measuring means–end chains. *International Journal of Research in Marketing, 15,* 37–50.

Tulving, E. (1972). Episodic and semantic memory. In E. Tulving & W. Donaldson (Eds.), *Organization of memory* (pp. 381–403). New York, NY: Academic Press.

Tulving, E. (1985). How many memory systems are there? *American Psychologist, 40,* 385–398.

Valette-Florence, P., & Rapacchi, B. (1990). A cross-cultural means–end chain analysis of perfume purchases. In N. E. Synodinos, C. E. Keown, K. G. Grunert, & T. E. Muller (Eds.), *Proceedings of the third symposium on cross-cultural consumer and business studies* (pp. 161–172). Honolulu, HI: University of Hawaii.

Valette-Florence, P., & Rapacchi, B. (1991). Improving means–end chain analysis using graph theory and correspondence analysis. *Journal of Advertising Research, 31*(1), 30–45.

Vanden Abeele, P. (1990). *A means–end study of dairy consumption motivation.* No. EC Regulation 1000/90-43ST). EC.

Walker, B. A., & Olson, J. C. (1991). Means-end chains: Connecting products with self. *Journal of Business Research, 22*(2), 111–119.

Young, S., & Feigin, B. (1975). Using the benefit chain for improved strategy formulation. *Journal of Marketing, 39*(3), 72–74.

Zaltman, G., & Higie, R. A. (1993). *Seeing the voice of the customer: The Zaltman metaphor elicitation technique* (Working paper No. 93–114). Marketing Science Institute.

Züll, C., & Mohler, P. P. (1992). *Textanalyse* [Text analysis]. Opladen, Germany: Westdeutscher.

4

Advancements in Laddering

Thomas J. Reynolds
Strategic Research, Development and Assessment

Clay Dethloff
Wirthlin Worldwide

Steven J. Westberg
Wirthlin Worldwide

INTRODUCTION

Positioning, a term made popular by Ries and Trout in 1972 with *Positioning: The Battle for Your Mind,* is defined as designing and executing a marketing strategy to form a particular mental representation of a product or brand in the consumer's mind (Peter & Olson, 1993). Because these representations comprise an array of image and characteristic associations, positioning offers marketers the potential to meaningfully differentiate their brand in the marketplace, because it provides consumers with reasons to choose the brand. But identifying the right combination of images and characteristics to associate with a brand is an extremely difficult task given the number of possible variations that exist and the competitive pressures in the marketplace. Consider the automobile industry, for example. Potential positioning classifications include quality, technical sophistication, driving performance, style, luxury, utility, value, and even popularity. Each broad classification contains additional subtypes as numerous as the car models themselves. The critical question for the marketer is which positioning is best? How can a brand be positioned, or repositioned, to motivate more consumers to purchase?

Positioning, above all else, must strive to differentiate a brand as special and superior to the competition. To do this, the position must be based on the same criteria that consumers use when choosing a brand in a given category. This is the most direct path to gaining marketplace success and long-term equity for the brand. Thus, effective positioning begins with understanding the consumer because the position must become an integral part of the consumer's brand choice process.

The means–end approach (Gutman, 1982), as accomplished via laddering interviews (Olson & Reynolds, 1983; Reynolds & Gutman, 1988), enables marketers to look at their brands through the consumer's eyes and see the brand in terms of the consumer's decision-making criteria. Since the 1980s, thousands of laddering interviews have been conducted investigating dozens of product categories around the world. A number of valuable lessons have been learned.

The purpose of this chapter is to expand on previous descriptions of laddering methodology (cf. Reynolds & Gutman, 1988) to provide marketers with current means–end practices based on this wealth of real-world research experience. By using the research designs, interview techniques, and data analysis procedures outlined here, a marketer can better understand consumers' personally relevant decisions that drive their product and brand choices. Then they can use this understanding to position their brands for greater market success.

Means–End Theory Background

Means–end theory reflects a perspective grounded in cognitive psychology. The focus is on the linkages between attributes that exist in products (the means), the consequences for the consumer provided by those attributes, and the personal values (the ends) that the consequences reinforce (Olson & Reynolds, 1983). Attributes are perceived qualities or features of products or services. Attributes can include both physical (5.0-liter engine) and abstract (style) product characteristics. Importantly, attributes provide or lead to consequences, which are personal outcomes or results derived from usage or consumption. For example, a 5.0-liter engine can produce the consequence of fast acceleration, but expensive service can lead to not having money for other things. If the consequence is desired, then the attribute is considered a positive for the brand. For many people, fast acceleration is desired, so a 5.0-liter engine would be a positive attribute. Conversely, if the consequence is undesired, then the attribute is considered a negative. Expensive service would be a negative if it reduced the money left for other things. Alternatively, expensive service might be positive if it meant getting "the best." Consequences can be classified as either functional or psychosocial. Functional consequences are rather immediate, tangible, physical experiences, whereas psychosocial consequences are emotional or social and more symbolic, including how the consumer personally feels or how the consumer feels about interacting with others.

In turn, consequences are important to the extent they satisfy the consumer's personal values or goals. Values are defined as the beliefs that people hold about themselves, and desirable values are goals that represent governing drives and motivations. For example, fast acceleration might provide a boost to one's ego, a positive goal or value. Just as fast acceleration explained why a 5.0-liter engine was important, an ego boost would explain why fast acceleration was desired. In contrast, negative consequences obstruct or prevent a person from obtaining a personal value. Not having money for other things would be undesirable if it prevents a person from obtaining the value represented by peace of mind. Personal values can be classified as instrumental values, which are higher order personal feelings, or terminal values, which are end states or life goals.

Attributes, consequences, and values — also called the *elements of positioning strategy* — delineate three main levels of cognitive abstraction (Gutman & Reynolds, 1979). Attributes are the most tangible or concrete, whereas values are the most abstract, and consequences lie between. Within each level are the additional classifications mentioned before: concrete and abstract for attributes, functional and psycho-social for consequences, and instrumental and terminal for values. Understanding levels of abstraction is important because product choice is based on the combination of different levels, reflected by the ability of a brand's attributes to provide consequences that satisfy values. The means–end framework explains how attributes of products are given their relative importance in the choice process (Reynolds, Cockle, & Rochon, 1990). Also, elements at different levels perform different functions with respect to perceptual differentiation between brands. Perceptual judgments are believed to reflect attribute discriminations, whereas preference differences are thought to reflect higher order value differences (Reynolds, 1988). Therefore, positioning strategies that exclude higher order elements often fail to motivate consumers to choose the brand.

A consumer's sequence of attributes, consequences, and values (A-C-Vs) associated with a product or brand is called a *means–end chain* and represents a perceptual orientation of decision criteria. The dominant perceptual orientation among all consumers of a brand is known as the brand's positioning. However, just as brands can have multiple attributes and multiple usage occasions, consumers can have multiple chains of decision criteria for a given category and even for a single brand. Uncovering these perceptual orientations, including the most dominant one, is accomplished by an interviewing process called laddering. A laddering interview moves a respondent from a discriminating attribute up the levels of abstraction by asking a form of the question: "Why is that important to you?"

Prior to commencing laddering research, however, four fundamental research design questions should be answered. The answers to these questions serve to frame the laddering interviews and ensure that the research addresses all of the brand's positioning problems. These questions management should answer are: Who are the relevant customers? What are the customers' relevant behaviors? What are the relevant contexts of the behavior? And, what are the competitive choice alternatives?

LADDERING RESEARCH DESIGN:
FRAMING THE PROBLEM

The first design question that should be answered is: Who are the relevant customers to be interviewed? The answer to this question becomes the criterion for selecting the research sample. For developing positioning strategies for products and brands, relevant customers are people whose beliefs are critical to fully understanding the competitive set of brands in the market. Laddering involves detailed probing about consumers' brand beliefs, so respondents must have knowledge about specific brands in the category. In most cases, brand usage is the key criteria because it ensures that respondents are conversant about a brand. One of the best ways to classify brand users is by frequency of use and relative brand loyalty. For brands that product purchase involves someone other than the user, the sample might include purchasers as well as users.

Frequency of category use classifications can include heavy users, light users, and non-users. Heavy users frequently have the greatest level of knowledge and the most extreme views about the category, so they often can provide the most detailed information. They also can represent the greatest volume and profit, although this is not always the case. Light users are usually greater in number than heavy users, and they tend to have less extreme views. They also can represent the greatest potential for brand growth, particularly in mature markets. Finally, nonusers sometimes have little or no category knowledge and cannot offer much insight, but they often can tell why they are not in the category. For relatively new and developing categories, converting nonusers to users is essential for brand growth, so their beliefs must be understood.

There are two types of loyalty classifications — loyal to a brand and not loyal. One way to define loyalty is the consumer's individual brand consumption frequency or volume divided by the individual's total category consumption. For example, a loyal user of brand A can be defined as someone who consumes brand A at least 75% of the time. Non-loyal users, or brand switchers, can be defined as consumers with no more than 50% of their total category consumption being any one brand. Other loyalty classification schemes are last brand purchased (e.g., for automobile buyers), intended brand of purchase (e.g., for first time computer buyers), and brand-family usage (e.g., for line extension or umbrella-branding research).

A combination of usage and loyalty can be specified to ensure that the dominant discriminating beliefs are represented in the sample and that sample groups include consumers who represent future increased sales for the brand. For example, in a frequently purchased consumer goods category where most people are in the category, key sample groups might be heavy loyal consumers, heavy nonloyal consumers, and light consumers. These groups would allow comparison of perceptual orientations that represent (a) why some people consume a lot of one brand, (b) why others consume a lot of several brands, and (c) why some do not consume more of a brand. These comparisons are relevant to management if research goals include (a) maintaining the current core consumer group, (b) increasing switching among other frequent users, and (c) increasing volume from current light users. Once usage groups are determined, demographic criteria can be specified for the sample if there is reason to believe that consumer perceptions will differ by demographics. Gender, age, and geographic location are three variables that often reflect differences in beliefs and attitudes. Other demographic variables such as socioeconomic status, ethnic background, or education might discriminate for some categories.

Because laddering is often used to compare perceptual orientations between groups of consumers, groups can be defined so that distinct gaps exist between the defining group characteristics. For example, using age as a sampling criteria, one group might include 18- to 24-year-olds, whereas the other group might be 30- to 38-year-olds. Leaving a 5-year gap between groups ensures that perceptual differences by age, if any exist, are not obscured. Brand usage and loyalty criteria and other demographic criteria can be specified in this manner as well.

Minimum sample size for laddering research is a function of sample criteria. As a general rule of thumb, a minimum of 20 respondents should be included in any single subgroup. Because each respondent provides at least five ladders for the brands in the category and ladders include, on average, five elements, ladders from 20 respondents can include a minimum of 500 data points. Thus, a relatively small sample size can provide considerable insight about consumer choice and brand distinctions. Also, 20 respondents can provide the full range of attributes, consequences, and values associated with the key brands in the category, when the respondents are carefully specified and screened.

Laddering is not limited to solving products- or brand-positioning problems. Laddering research applications have included such issues as increasing church enrollment, changing public opinion about a social issue, selling a political candidate to voters, increasing sales force recruitment and retention for a direct sales organization, identifying effective sponsorship opportunities, and creating a new corporate identity. In all cases, the general guidelines for determining who are the relevant customers still apply, although customers might need to be reinterpreted as specific church members, ideological belief groups, voter constituencies, sales force or employee groups, and corporate stakeholders who not only customers, but investors, analysts, distributors, employees, and government regulators.

The second design question that should be answered is: What are the customers' relevant behaviors? *Relevant behaviors* are defined as those behaviors that the marketer wishes to understand and then encourage, reinforce, or change. Relevant behaviors are often associated with brand or product usage, so this question is frequently answered when defining relevant consumers. For some product categories, product purchase occurs at the end of a multistep decision-behavior process; then relevant behaviors might include the different actions taken during the process. The sample might then contain different groups based on the primary variables in the decision-behavior process; alternatively, steps in the decision behavior process might be incorporated in the research instrument to frame questioning. For example, people buying a home computer might be classified as those who researched their purchase through multiple sources (magazine reviews and advice from other people), and those who relied exclusively on in-store sales personnel and information displays. For nonproduct or service positioning applications, relevant behaviors are again those consumer actions the marketer would like to reinforce or change. For example, relevant behaviors for a sales force include becoming a sales person, remaining a sales person, quitting as a sales person, and increasing or decreasing sales productivity. Corporate investors' relevant behaviors include buying stock and holding on the stock even during periods of decline.

The third research design question is: What are the relevant contexts of the behavior? The decision-making process people use when selecting a brand or exhibiting some other relevant behavior does not happen in a vacuum. The person will assign different relevance and importance to decision criteria as influenced by the situation or relevant context. For example, a beer consumer may drink Miller Lite at home with friends but will choose Heineken in a restaurant with business associates.

Context includes influential characteristics that, in part, determine the relevant behavior, so context can be defined in several ways. If the relevant behavior is brand choice and usage, then context refers to the physical or psychological occasions of purchase or usage or consumption. Physical occasions of usage or consumption are often described by time, place, activity, and presence of other people. Psychological occasions can be described by influential cultural, social, or personal factors such as the need to please guests at a party or the need to perform well in a business meeting. Context might also include personal life or lifestyle situations that influence the relevant behavior (e.g., fulfilling a parental role might be a contextual characteristic that influences a facet of behavior). Contextual variables in laddering can be represented in the sample selection criteria, or they can be included in the research instrument, either as prespecified scenarios or as elicited from respondents during the interview.

The fourth design question is: What are the competitive choice alternatives? Competitive alternatives are the entire range of options considered by the relevant customers. For example, before settling on a Heineken, our beer drinker may have considered several different beers, along with a glass of wine, a soda, and even an imported mineral water. This example illustrates that competition is best identified on the basis of consumer choice criteria, which include the elements of means–end chains — attributes, consequences, and values. Because elements that determine choice occur at all levels of cognitive abstraction, competition can be classified based on specific elements at different levels. In-kind competitors are products with similar attributes and are usually in the same category. Functional competitors are products with different attributes but similar lower level consequences. Ego-emotive competitors are products that do not provide similar attributes or functional consequences but are still in the choice set, often competing at the psychosocial consequence or value level.

An important result of a laddering study can be identification of primary competitors from the customer's perspective. For positioning research concerning nonproducts or services, other competitors might include opposing candidates (for voters), other work opportunities (for employees), other ideological points of view (for social issue advocates), and other financial opportunities (for investors). Identification of competitors prior to conducting laddering research usually is necessary for specifying the sample. Users of in-kind competitive brands are frequently included in sample designs because these competitors are often the biggest threat, and their customers represent potential sales. However, most categories also face significant competition from one or more functional or ego-emotive competitors, so these should not be overlooked.

Competition can also be defined relative to levels of competition, such as megacategory, category, subcategory and specific product. For example, the megacategory of medicinal drugs includes both over-the-counter (OTC) drugs and prescription drugs. The different subcategories of OTC drugs include cold, flu, allergy, analgesic, stomach and intestinal, topical, and many others. Forms of OTC medications include capsules, caplets, liquids, tablets, ointments, and sprays, which often operate both within and across subcategories. Brands operate both within and across subcategories. Because individual products are unique combinations of layers, studying the attributes and benefits that are associated with each layer can be an efficient way to understand specific products.

Answering the four research-framing questions discussed here — Who is the relevant customer? What are the customers' relevant behaviors? What are the relevant contexts of the behaviors? What are the competitive choice alternatives? — might involve simply putting on paper what is already known, or it might require preliminary research. If additional research is used, the four questions usually can be answered by collecting a detailed consumer diary across a broad sample. For many packaged goods, the diary would focus on brand purchase and use by time of day, day of the week, activities, other people present, intended purpose for the product, considered alternatives (both in-category and others), and other occasion or situation details considered relevant. For durables, the diary might begin with questions about current brand and product usage, then require respondents to describe the steps taken during need recognition, information search and the final product (brand) choice decision. Frequency of use and brand loyalty sample criteria can be determined based on these diaries, along with the behaviors, contexts, and alternatives associated with each sample group.

Preliminary research can be done apart from the laddering research by using a separate sample, or it can immediately precede each laddering interview to provide a tailored, personal basis for the interview questioning. For example, a respondent could be asked to complete a diary during the week or month prior to a laddering interview, and then answer questions based on the diary during the interview. Answering the four framing questions is important to laddering research, because they focus interview questions on the specific bases for brand choice during most product decision occasions. Without proper framing, laddering research might not provide accurate information that can lead, in turn, to an effective positioning strategy.

Once the framing questions have been answered, the research sample can be specified, the research instrument can be created, and pilot interviews can be conducted. Pilot interviews identify questions that respondents might not understand and provide a dress rehearsal for interviewers. During and after completion of pilot interviews, the research instrument can be revised as needed. Then, the sample can be recruited and the actual interviews conducted.

THE LADDERING INTERVIEW

A *laddering interview* is an in-depth, one-on-one process that elicits the means–end chains of attributes, consequences, and values associated with a particular brand, product, or category. The interview should take place in a room free of distractions, with an interviewer who has been trained in laddering methods. Laddering interviews are structured to last anywhere from 45 minutes to 2 hours, so it is recommended that they be tape recorded to ensure that no respondent nuances are missed during the interview. The length of the interview is a function of the complexity of the positioning problem and the need to focus the respondent on their reasons for brand choice during the interview. Brands with a complex decision-behavior process, many different relevant contextual variables, or several strong competitors will require a longer interview to elicit means–end chains associated with the multiple differentiating criteria. Such would be the case for OTC medications, automobiles, and restaurants, to name a few.

Focusing respondents to reveal their true beliefs, feelings and goals requires warm-up questioning to put them at ease with the interviewer and to force them to think about the brands of interest. Warm-up questions also provide an opportunity to elicit nonladdering information that can provide valuable insight into the brand-positioning problem. If not already known, detailed preference and behavior information can be collected, consumer knowledge about competitive brands and perceived availability can be assessed, and price-quality issues can be addressed.

The laddering method differs from typical qualitative research in that laddering is structured to uncover more abstract but personally motivating reasons behind brand choice, in addition to attribute and functional consequence (benefit) reasons for usage. To this end, laddering must begin by identifying the most important distinguishing characteristics of the brand for a given context; then laddering seeks to move the respondent up the levels of abstraction. Moving up levels is done by asking a form of the question: "Why is that important to you?" Said another way, the qualitative results from a laddering structure are deep and focused while a typical qualitative structure are shallow and broad. When done well, laddering allows little room for error because the initial distinctions must be important to the respondent's choice process, the entire ladder is likely to be important to the participant and, therefore, relatively easy to articulate.

ADVANTAGES OF LADDERING

After a series of warm-up questions lasting between 5 and 15 minutes, the interview moves to laddering. Laddering probes begin with the distinctions made by the respondent about perceived differences between brands or products (Reynolds & Gutman, 1988). Distinctions made with respect to different choice situations and specific sets of competitive alternatives provide the best results for laddering because they allow the respondent to examine the choice process in its naturally occurring contexts.

By eliciting consumer beliefs and attitudes within the context of behavior, laddering overcomes a major pitfall of most attitude research. If research is not framed by the appropriate context of choice behavior, respondents are likely to bring out distinctions not necessarily connected with choice. Such a procedure potentially mixes important choice criteria with less meaningful distinctions. Perhaps this explains why attitudes toward an object do not often predict brand choice, but attitudes toward choice behavior concerning the object frequently do.

In order to understand the multiple distinctions that are the basis for purchase and use decisions made by a consumer, different elicitation techniques are required.

METHODS TO ELICIT DISTINCTIONS

Laddering research must be designed to uncover the reasons underlying purchase or consumption decisions, made with respect to competing products and brands across different choice occasions. Both the positive reasons for choosing a brand and the negative reasons for rejecting a brand should be determined. Simply asking what is good about brand A is not enough. The marketer needs to understand how brand A is perceived to be better than, and worse than, the competition. The relative balance of positive and negative associations can provide substantial guidance for positioning strategy development during analysis of the laddering data. Therefore, questions for eliciting distinctions should give each respondent the opportunity to mention positives and negatives.

Following are several methods for eliciting distinctions between brands. Each of these methods can be used in conjunction with defined consumption occasions. For example, frozen waffle distinctions might focus exclusively on breakfast occasions with other breakfast foods as competition. Also, methods can be combined to focus the respondent in a more tightly defined context. Breakfast might be further defined as hurried or leisurely. We can classify the three primary elicitation methods for brand distinctions as: (1) unconstrained general brand relationships, (2) brand relations constrained by current usage differences, and (3) brand relations constrained by potential usage differences. Figure 4.1 summarizes the three primary classifications and shows specific techniques for each.

ELICITATION METHODS: UNCONSTRAINED
GENERAL BRAND RELATIONS

Distinctions based on unconstrained general relations between brands can provide broad category analysis, although they often must be augmented with other methods that focus more on brand preference and

---

Laddering Methods:
Eliciting Distinctions

◆ **Unconstrained General Brand Relationships**

  • **Top-of-Mind Imaging**
  • **Grouping Similar Brands**

◆ **Brand Relationships Constrained By Current Usage Differences**

  • **Contextual Environment**
  • **Preference, Usage and Preference-Usage Differences**
  • **Timing of Purchase or Consumption**

◆ **Brand Relationships Constrained By Potential usage Differences**

  • **Usage Trends**
  • **Product or Brand Substitution**
  • **Alternative Usage Occasions**

FIG. 4.1.   Laddering methods: Eliciting distinctions.

choice. Two specific research designs to elicit brand relation distinctions include Top-Of-Mind Imaging and Grouping Similar Brands. A third method, the Repertory Grid, was discussed by Reynolds and Gutman (1988), although in practice it is seldom used because it requires many comparisons that take a lot of time. Each method relies on preidentified competitive brands for analysis.

Top of Mind Imaging

The respondent is asked to give one or more first-thought associations for each of several brands or product types. The respondent states the polarity (positive or negative?) for each association. Then, the respondent is asked why the characteristic is a positive or negative, and those responses are further probed to uncover the ladder. Top-Of-Mind Imaging identifies the most conspicuous characteristics of a brand but not always the characteristics that differentiate it from close competitors. For example, both Mustangs and Camaros might be identified as performance cars, yet one might be preferred over the other. This technique is used primarily to distinguish between brands in different subcategories, such as juices versus carbonated soft drinks.

Grouping Similar Brands

This method uncovers respondents' top-of-mind product groupings and reasons for groupings. In Grouping Similar Brands, respondents are asked to group brands and products in like categories based on perceived similarity. Then, the primary reason for forming a group, either a positive or negative characteristic, can be elicited and laddered. Additionally, the respondent can be asked to identify the brand or product that best represents the group. Important traits and trait performance for the most representative brand can be elicited and laddered as well.

Two potential problems must be considered when using this technique. First, groups are often based on attribute level distinctions, whereas the brands in the group might provide vastly different consequences. Therefore, brand groupings might not provide insight into actual brand preference or choice criteria. Second, the grouped brands may or may not be in the respondent's consideration set. For example, a respondent might combine Minute Maid orange juice and Minute Maid fruit punch in the same group, even though fruit punch is never considered for purchase.

ELICITATION METHODS: BRAND RELATIONS
CONSTRAINED BY CURRENT USAGE

Brand relations unconstrained by current usage differences are a second type of method for eliciting brand distinctions. Focusing the respondents on their perceived behavior allows the researcher to directly probe the reasons for the behavior. This makes brand comparisons and distinctions relatively easy for the respondent. Questions in the research instrument can be crafted so that distinctions are recorded based on reported behavioral differences, on rank order or scale methods, or on constant sum-allocation methods. Three of the methods used in this design are contextual environment; preference, usage, and preference-usage differences; and timing of purchase or consumption (also discussed by Reynolds & Gutman, 1988).

Contextual Environment

The contextual environment includes predetermined physical or psychological occasions of brand purchase or use. Physical occasions are generally described by the time, place, and people when usage occurs. A psychological occasion is a mental need or inner desire that can span many physical occasions. Psychological occasions are also called need states. As an example, a need for higher level fulfillment, such as social acceptance, can occur across many different physical occasions including work, home with family, or an activity with friends. Other psychological need states include relaxing, rejuvenating, building relationships, reducing stress, and saving time. All brand purchase and usage occurs within physical and psychological occasions. Oftentimes, the researcher has hypotheses about consumer perceptions during specific occasions, so this design allows these perceptions to be investigated. For example, during a laddering interview, brand questioning would be prefaced with a predefined need state or occasion, such as, "Think about those times when you wanted to impress someone" or "Imagine that you have just completed a tough job or accomplished something that was important to you."

Preference, Usage, and Preference-Usage Differences

Comparing consumer's reported brand preferences and usage is one of the most direct and commonly used methods for eliciting brand distinctions. Brands can be ranked or scaled on both preference and usage frequency. Then, brands can be directly compared against each other based on these scales using questions such as: "Why did you give brand A a higher preference rating than brand B?" and "Why do you use brand A more often than brand B?" Investigating the disparity between preference and usage evaluations is another useful technique. For example, a consumer might give brand A a higher preference rating yet use brand B more often. The interviewer might then ask why. When using this technique, selecting the appropriate set of considered brands to include is an important step to avoid overemphasis on price criteria. For example, it may not be helpful to match a Porsche 911 with a Honda Prelude.

Timing of Purchase or Consumption

Timing issues can affect product choice and usage for some products. This technique is similar to that described by Contextual Environment except that time is the primary criteria that determines the occasion. For example, a consumer might be asked, "Why do you use brand A during the initial stage of a flu, but you use brand B during the full-blown stage?" or "Why do you use brand A only in the morning, but you use brand B at any time of the day or night?" Of course, using this technique, as well as the previous two, assumes the researcher has a good understanding of the step-by-step behaviors associated with product purchase and consumption.

ELICITATION METHODS: BRAND RELATIONS CONSTRAINED BY POTENTIAL USAGE DIFFERENCES

Brand relations constrained by potential usage is a third type of method for eliciting distinctions. Distinctions elicited in this manner can be helpful in identifying future brand growth opportunities based on current brand perceptions. These methods can highlight directions to proceed and potential barriers for growth. Elicited distinctions can also help the marketer understand the goals and aspirations of the consumer, resulting in positioning the brand as a part of the desired lifestyle, by tapping into major value trends in society. The methods used in this approach are usage trends, brand or product substitution, and alternative usage occasions.

Usage Trends

Respondents are asked to quantify their beliefs about both past and future brand usage. These beliefs can be based on brands currently used or on new or unused brands. Reasons for past- and future-perceived brand usage trends are then identified and laddered. If the trend is toward increased usage, the ladder will be positive. If it is toward decreased usage the ladder will be negative. Although not meant to provide quantitative measures or predictions about future brand use, this technique provides important insight regarding current purchasing or consumption patterns that consumers see in themselves but that do not match their ideals.

Product or Brand Substitution

Distinctions between brands can be directly assessed based on the ability of one brand to be substituted for another. The brand to be substituted can be a brand currently used by the respondent, if a goal of the research is to increase consumption, or it can be a brand not currently used, if a goal is to increase trial. For an unfamiliar brand, the respondent first can sample or be given a description of the brand. Follow-up questioning might include "How likely would you be to substitute this new brand for your current brand for this occasion? Why (or why not)?"

Alternative Usage Occasions

A third technique to elicit potential usage distinctions involves altering or adding new usage occasions for the respondent to consider. Alternate occasions can be either predetermined or provided by the respondent. For example, the respondent might be asked, "Think of a new situation or occasion in which you might use brand A but that you do not currently.

Why would you consider using brand A during this new occasion? What is keeping you from using brand A during this occasion now?" Both positive reasons why a brand fits a new occasion and negative reasons why it does not fit are elicited and laddered. This method can be used without direct brand comparisons, as the example demonstrated, or with explicit comparisons between brands, depending on the goals of the research.

In practice, multiple elicitation methods are frequently used during a laddering interview to capture the full range of meaningful distinctions between a brand and its competitors. For example, a laddering interview might first utilize Top-of-Mind Imaging to understand general category-level beliefs, then include a Contextual-Environment approach to focus on in-kind brand competition. The study might also include Alternative Usage Occasions or Usage Trends to gain insight about expanding the market. We recommend a minimum of 5 to as many as 12 ladders be elicited from a respondent for a given brand or set of competitive brands. The market environment and goals of management will determine the appropriate mix of methods.

LADDERING TECHNIQUES

Once distinctions have been elicited, laddering must move the respondent up and down the chain of abstraction to uncover the salient higher level elements in the decision-making process and the specific cues that communicate important product or service characteristics. Laddering consists of the interviewer asking a series of questions similar to "Why is that important to you?" The specific questions in laddering are based on the respondent's last answer given, which explains why different questions sometimes are used at different levels in a ladder. The ability of the respondent to verbalize his or her thoughts and feelings also influences the form of the questions asked. Some respondents can provide detailed and in-depth answers effortlessly with only minimal probing, whereas others require the interviewer to ask multiple questions for every response. Following are a few examples of questions, summarized in Fig. 4.2, that can be used to elicit functional and psycho-social consequences based on lower level distinctions:

- "Why is that important to you?"
- "How does that help you out?"
- "What do you get from that?"
- "Why do you want that?"
- "What happens to you as a result of that?"

Laddering Methods:
Moving to Higher Levels

◆ **Positive**

- **Why is that important to you?**
- **How does that help you out?**
- **What do you get from that?**
- **Why do you want that?**
- **What happens to you as a result of that?**
- **How does that make you feel?**

◆ **Negative**

- **Why is that a negative to you?**
- **How does that interfere with what you are doing?**
- **What's wrong with that?**

FIG. 4.2. Laddering methods: Moving to higher levels.

Higher level psycho-social consequences and values are most often feelings or personal beliefs. Thus, asking "How does that make you feel?" is appropriate at these levels. However, this question does not work well at lower levels because it forces the respondent to make too great a leap between levels of abstraction.

Negative ladders require, of course, stating the question in negative terms. At the consequence levels, the interviewer may want to ask: "Why do you want to avoid that?" This effectively turns the discussion from negative to positive. Most respondents are better able to discuss feelings about obtaining a value rather than avoiding one, so laddering is facilitated by talking in positive terms before reaching the value level. Examples of negative questioning are:

- "Why is that a negative to you?"
- "How does that interfere with what you are doing?"
- "What's wrong with that?"

During laddering interviews respondents can become blocked at one level and unable to proceed higher. Although the temptation is strong, the interviewer should at no time put words in the respondent's mouth or give examples to the respondent. It is the job of the interviewer to guide the respondent up the ladder and to record responses accurately, not to fit responses into preconceived patterns or to encourage desired responses.

Laddering Methods:
Overcoming Blocking

♦ **Reiteration of Occasion**
♦ **Alternate Scenario**
♦ **Absence of Product**
♦ **Abstraction From Product**
♦ **Negative laddering**
♦ **Age Regression Contrast**
♦ **Third Person Probe**
♦ **Silence**
♦ **Reiteration of A-C-Vs**

FIG. 4.3.   Laddering methods: Overcoming blocking.

Even when the interviewer has successfully put aside preconceptions about the research results, respondents quickly key on what they think the interviewer wants to hear. Suggestions made by the interviewer risk biasing the response.

To avoid biasing an interview, several interviewing techniques, have been identified for overcoming blocking (most of these can be used with nearly any type of qualitative interviewing method). Most of these were discussed by Reynolds and Gutman (1988), but they are sufficiently important to warrant a review. More than one technique can be used during the course of one ladder, as the need might arise to combine techniques. Occasionally these techniques will fail and the interviewer will feel that no further progress can be made on the ladder. Then the interviewer should move on to finish the interview and possibly come back to the incomplete ladder later. These techniques are listed in Fig. 4.3 in no particular order.

Reiteration of Occasion

When the respondent appears to have forgotten or lost track, the interviewer can remind the respondent of the occasion that is the basis for the ladder. To provide a more vivid basis from which to respond, the interviewer might ask the respondent to provide further information about the occasion (With whom? Doing what? Where?)

Alternate Scenario

The interviewer can ask the respondent to think of another situation or scenario, similar to the one currently being discussed, in which the brand is used in a similar way and for similar reasons. This technique might be used after first trying to reiterate the occasion.

Absence of Product

The interviewer can ask the respondent to describe his or her feelings, responses, and the potential consequences assuming that the brand is unavailable in that situation.

Abstraction From Product

Occasionally, respondents will not be able to leave the brand at the attribute level and will wonder how the brand itself can "make me feel good about myself" or can "improve my relationship with my spouse." The interviewer should ask the respondent to ignore the brand and only consider the last consequence that was mentioned. Reiterating the last consequence often helps keep respondents focused.

Negative Laddering

Negative laddering seeks the respondent's reasons why they do not want to do certain things or feel certain ways. The interviewer can ask the respondent what would happen if they were not able to achieve a certain positive consequence.

Age Regression Contrast

The age regression contrast forces the respondent to compare usage or consumption in a previous time period with the current time. For example, the interviewer may ask the respondent if he or she used the product 5 years ago and then ask why or why not. This technique is similar to the trends method of eliciting distinctions, but here it is used during the actual laddering process to overcome a blockage.

Third Person Probe

The third person probe places the respondent in another person's shoes, which may facilitate a response when the respondent might feel threatened or uncomfortable discussing personal reasons behind behavior. For example, the interviewer could ask the respondent how others might feel in similar circumstances. For example, an overweight respondent might feel uncomfortable talking in the first person about why they use a diet product.

Silence

Silence and patient attention can signal to the respondent that the interviewer is awaiting a more thorough or detailed response. Often the respondent will elaborate on a vague or incomplete answer with no further prompting by the interviewer.

Reiteration of A-C-Vs

To help the respondent maintain a complete train of thought during the ladder, the interviewer can reiterate the answers given up to the blocked point. The complete ladder should also be repeated back to the respondent after a value has been reached allowing the respondent the opportunity to verify his chain of thought. In addition, the interviewer can use this technique to refocus a rambling respondent who has strayed from the ladder.

In the course of a laddering interview, the respondent will not always provide whole or complete responses. The interviewer must be able to identify incomplete responses so that additional probes can draw out useful information. These incomplete responses primarily fall into 6 categories, as listed in Fig. 4.4.

Generic Statements

Respondents sometimes provide very generic answers that have no specific meaning. For example, "satisfied" can be either physical (feeling full after a meal) or emotional (feeling content with oneself). Likewise, "happy" can have multiple meanings such as feeling happy about something accomplished and feeling happy for another person, as well as varying intensity, ranging from mild to ecstatic. Slang words are particularly susceptible to multiple meaning. For example, "cool" to one person might

---

Laddering Methods:
Incomplete Responses

- Generic Statements
- Not Brand Specific
- Multiple Responses
- Chutes and Ladders
- Habit
- "I Like It"

FIG. 4.4. Laddering methods: Incomplete responses.

be completely different from "cool" to someone else. The interviewer must identify generic responses and probe for more detail or clarification. Often, simply asking the respondent "What do you mean?" or "Could you describe that feeling?" will lead to a better understanding. Specific details concerning attribute or functional consequence elements are needed for strategy development because they sometimes tell management exactly how to communicate an important element. For example, friendly service can be further described as a smile from the cashier.

Not Brand Specific

Differentiating characteristics should be brand specific and unambiguous. Distinctions that apply to many brands equally well, or even to the entire category, are not useful for positioning. For example, "ice cold" does not distinguish between carbonated soft drinks, although "carbonation" distinguishes quite well when prefaced with a degree of intensity.

Multiple Responses

Respondents may give more than one answer when providing distinctions or during laddering probes. In these cases, the interviewer should ask which characteristic or idea is most important for the given situation and then continue probing from there. It is possible to ladder multiple "branches," although this can confound analysis and takes extra time during the interview. Prior to interviews, the researcher should decide how to handle multiple responses.

Chutes and Ladders

Distinctions are most often product attributes, but respondents may sometimes mention an upper level element as a basis for differentiating one brand from another. The interviewer can "chute down" by asking: "What is it about the brand that makes it that way?" Occasionally, a respondent might ladder directly from an attribute to a value or appear to leave an important element out. Again, the interviewer can ask, "I'm not sure how (lower level element) leads to (upper level element). Is there something about the brand that makes you feel that way?"

Habit

Respondents tend to say "It's a habit" or "I've always done it that way" when they cannot think of a more rational reason for their usage or consumption behavior. The interviewer should try to uncover when and how the habit started, and why they do not change the habit. Answers from these questions can become a basis for other laddering probes.

I Just Like It

Similar to the generic statement, this phrase occurs frequently in laddering and can almost always be handled the same way. The goal of laddering is to understand why, so the interviewer should ask why the respondent likes something or what specifically the respondent likes.

SUMMARY

This review has covered the most common difficulties and problems that occur during a laddering interview. Other problems will arise that require the interviewer to take appropriate action. To best prepare for these contingencies, laddering interviewers should be selected for their ability to empathize and interact with respondents, they should be adequately trained in both the methods and the theory behind laddering, and they should practice with the instrument before fielding the research. At a minimum, interviewers should understand the means–end theory that is the basis for laddering, and they should be familiar with the elicitation and probing techniques mentioned here and by Reynolds and Gutman (1988). Also, the interviewers should be briefed on the research goals for each part of the interview. With this knowledge, they can listen to respondents' answers objectively to ensure that the information provided will answer the positioning questions outlined in the brief. A rule of thumb for interviewers is to ask themselves: "Do I understand all of the personal reasons why this respondent chooses and uses the brand?" and "Is there anything that I do not understand?"

LADDERING ANALYSIS

Once a representative sample of consumers from a product category have been laddered for their means–end chains, the full range of relevant perceptual orientations for the brands in the category can be summarized graphically in a Consumer Decision Map (CDM). Previously, this graphic was termed a Hierarchical Value Map (Olson & Reynolds, 1983), but because it represents how people make decisions rather than just how their thoughts are organized, the term *Consumer Decision Map* more accurately describes the graphic. A CDM includes the most frequently mentioned elements (A-C-Vs) from the means–end chains as well as the most common associations between the elements. The process of analysis for developing a CDM (see Reynolds & Gutman, 1988) includes three main steps: (1) organizing the ideas found in the ladders into summary codes, (2) creating a frequency matrix for associations between codes, and (3) constructing the CDM from the most common pairs of associated codes. These steps can be performed by Laddermap™ software (Gengler & Reynolds, 1995) or by a manual method. Alternatively, Valette-Florence and Rapacchi (1991) suggested a slightly revised procedure for constructing the map based on graph theory.

The first and possibly most important step in the laddering analysis is to develop a set of summary codes for the strategic elements at each level of means–end theory. These elements must accurately reflect all of the key concepts or beliefs that were mentioned in the ladders from the interviews. Respondents' verbatim statements are grouped based on similarity of meaning under code-word headings, which are then identified as attributes, functional consequences, psychosocial consequences, or values. For example, "tingling taste" and "sparkling fizz" might both be categorized under an attribute-level code word of *Carbonation*. Likewise, "able to work harder," "can perform my job better," and "can get more done on the job" might be coded as *Improves Work Performance*, a psychosocial consequence. Care must be taken at this stage to ensure that codes accurately reflect the respondents' reasons for brand choice, while keeping to a manageable number of codes and not losing the language of the consumer. Oftentimes, the coding process requires multiple iterations to yield 5 to 20 codes are retained for each for the four levels. To retain consumer language, researchers should identify key verbatim remarks that best represent the set of consumer ideas included in a code. Often times, these verbatim remarks can be included directly on the CDM so that managers involved in the subsequent strategy development are fully aware of the meaning represented by each code.

The second step is constructing a matrix that displays the number of times each coded element leads to another coded element. Every time an element precedes another element in a ladder, it gets counted. Both direct connections between elements (where one element directly precedes another element with no elements in between the two) and indirect connections (where one element precedes another in a ladder but one or more additional elements are between them) are counted. Direct connections indicate a direct cause–effect relation between concepts, whereas indirect connections reflect a general association between concepts.

To construct a CDM from the set of connected pairs, one must literally build up the map from sequences of connected elements extracted from the frequency matrix. A criteria for evaluating the ability of the overall map to represent the data is to assess the percentage of all relations among elements accounted for by the mapped elements. In general, the map should account for at least 80% of all pairs that exist in the matrix. A completed map will include the most commonly mentioned coded elements and the most common associations between the elements. As such, it provides the foundation for developing a positioning strategy specified in terms of select elements and connections between them.

MEANS–END OUTPUTS FOR DEVELOPING POSITIONING STRATEGY

The CDM is a general perceptual representation; it does not provide competitive analysis or specific positioning guidance. Additional laddering analyses can be used to guide the development of effective positioning strategies, including understanding the perceptual strengths (equities) and weaknesses (disequities) of the key brands in the market and the relative salience of these equities and disequities in terms of brand choice.

Perceptual equities and disequities based on laddering are composites of the positive and negative elements associated with the brand in the market. Because brand distinctions and the associated ladders are elicited from choice comparisons, they are brand specific. Also, elements elicited in laddering can be positive or negative for a brand, depending on whether the elements are desired or undesired. Therefore, one can create a frequency data matrix with strategic elements along one axis and brands with positive and negative poles along the other, as shown in Table 4.1. Transforming the positives and negatives for each brand into ratios, and the frequencies into percentages provides the necessary information. A verbal description of this data is that elements mentioned more often overall in the ladders are considered more important in terms of brand

TABLE 4.1
Frequencies of Elements (%)

Attributes	Brand A		Brand B	
	Positive	Negative	Positive	Negative
Attribute 1	18	5	5	17
Attribute 2	14	9	11	8
Attribute 3	9	9	5	7
Attribute 4	6	4	2	6
Attribute 5	5	8	4	5
Attribute 6	4	2	2	2
Attribute 7	2	2	2	1
Attribute 8	2	1	3	0
	60	40	54	46

choice, and elements that were mentioned more often as positive for a given brand rather than as negative are considered brand strengths or equities. Brand weaknesses or disequities are elements that were mentioned more often as negative than as positive for a brand. A summary analysis of this information, when overlaid on the CDM, provides additional insight into the consumer's brand choice process by highlighting each element according to its role in the choice process. Thus, elements on the map can be classified according to their relative importance and their degree of positiveness for each brand.

The equity analysis provides the rationale for choosing a respondent sample based on differences in relevant behavior. Different sample behavior groups often have different perceptions that, in part, determine their behavior. Separate equity analyses for each sample group enables marketers to compare brand perceptions between groups in a meaningful way. For example, an important attribute to both heavy users and light users of a brand, that is an equity for heavy users and a disequity for light users is likely to be a key perceptual barrier that, to some extent, prevents light users from becoming heavy users. A positioning strategy meant to increase usage among light users must address this barrier element, along with other salient elements at different levels.

THINKING STRATEGICALLY

Laddering output, in particular the CDM, should stimulate strategic thinking and encourage creative solutions to positioning problems. To this end, the CDM offers many alternatives for developing a positioning, including the following:

- Create a new element for the map.
- Increase the importance of an existing element.
- Decrease the importance of an existing element.
- Create a new linkage between elements.
- Eliminate an existing linkage between elements.
- Change a disequity associated with one's own brand into an equity.
- Change an equity associated with a competitive brand into a disequity.
- Strengthen an association between one's own brand and an element.
- Weaken an association between one's own brand and an element.
- Invent new parts of a map, or create an entirely new map.

Every brand faces a unique positioning problem depending on its market share, the number and size of competitors, current perceptions associated with the brand and its competitors, the types of communication tools available to brand marketers, the characteristics of the category, and numerous other factors. The alternatives listed previously can be used singularly or combined as appropriate to achieve management's goals for its brand. Following are three common market situations that demonstrate how positioning strategy might be developed using these tools and options.

Remove a Barrier

The first situation involves dealing with a major barrier to consumer acceptance—for instance, a differentiating attribute of a new brand is strongly associated with a negative consequence that prevents consumers from trying the brand. One option is to discard the attribute, but this might not be possible if it is integral to the brand or is a key point of differentiation. An alternate positioning solution is to reduce the association with this negative consequence by selecting or inventing a positive consequence of the attribute that supplants the negative. This is essentially what Miller Brewing did with Miller Lite. The attribute was *Fewer* Calories, which led to the negative consequence for heavy beer drinkers of *Weight Watching*. The invented consequence that replaced *Weight Watching* was *Less Filling*.

A second market situation involves establishing an important point of differentiation for a new brand in a mature market. A new element can be created and linked to important existing elements, or an entire new ladder can be invented. This positioning strategy is more likely to succeed if the new brand focuses on an area of the map where the primary competitors do not have strong equities. Another Miller brand, Genuine Draft, became a leading beer in America based on a new attribute called *Cold Filtered* that led to the very important consequence of *Great Taste*. Miller's primary competitor at the time, Budweiser, was not closely associated with *Great Taste*, nor was much emphasis given to how Buds beechwood aged process might lead to *Great Taste*. Budweiser's advertising at the time was focused at higher levels, such as high quality.

A third situation involves a brand with equities in relatively unimportant elements. A positioning solution in this case is to guard against competitive reaction by increasing the importance of these elements as well as strengthening the associations between the elements and the brand. During a time when athletic shoes were dominated by Nike hyping technology in their shoes and Reebok focusing on fashion aspects, Converse languished but hung onto market share with such equities as "the official NBA shoe" and nostalgia among middle-age consumers who wore the brand when growing up. Converse was able to increase consumer associations with both of these ideas to gain share.

INFLUENCING THE MANAGERIAL PROCESS

Designing and implementing a comprehensive laddering research study is an important but partial step to effective long-term results. Once the interviews are complete and the data and preliminary conclusions have been prepared, it is critical that all managers with responsibility for the brand get involved in the process. Presenting laddering results that creates managerial involvement is not difficult, but a few relatively sophisticated communication techniques can enhance the richness of the data.

The CDM is the primary tool for management decision making resulting from laddering research, so presentation emphasis should focus on the map. Laddering results are most easily understood when built from the component pieces. The CDM can be presented one piece (area) at a time either by A-C-V level or by major perceptual orientations or pathways on the map. This piecemeal presentation allows decision-makers to understand the map in manageable parts. Second, multiple maps for a category analysis are confusing if the structure changes for each map. Each category should have one overall map that contains all the elements and connections across different analyses. In this way, positions of the elements and their connections do not change between variations of the map, but the relative equities–disequities and importances of the elements can change and not be confusing.

Another graphical tool that can be used to illustrate both the relative importance and the positive ratios of elements is an equity matrix. An equity matrix is a two-dimensional plot with each axis representing the positive ratios of elements for a sample group. Plotting symbol size represents the overall importance of the element. For example, an equity matrix might represent a contrast between the beliefs of heavy users and light users of a brand. The most important elements from the CDM can be plotted on the matrix with each element's coordinates determined by the positive ratios for the two sample groups.

A third presentation technique is to color-code the elements on the map based on equities and disequities for different sample groups or for different brands. If two consumer groups are being compared, different colors can differentiate between elements seen as equities and disequities by each group. For example, blue might identify equities for both groups, green and yellow might differentiate elements as equities for only one of the groups, and red might distinguish disequities for both groups. Similarly, colors can be used to signify the relative importance of elements or connections on the map.

A CDM and equity–disequity analyses presented in this manner provide the basic tools from which to think about the positioning problem and discuss possible solutions. If everyone involved in the process can read the map and interpret its meanings, brand positioning discussions can lead to more actionable conclusions.

SUMMARY

Brand positioning generally requires in-depth understanding of the consumer's decision-making process. Means–end theory through laddering provides a useful tool to fully explore the consumer's psyche in terms of brand choice criteria. But laddering, like any tool, relies on the craftspeople who use it. In this chapter, we provide useful guidance for designing and implementing laddering research that will yield actionable results for management.

We propose that laddering research begin by answering four key questions: Who are the relevant customers or consumers to be interviewed? What are the customers' relevant behaviors? What are the relevant contexts of the behavior? What are the competitive choice alternatives? Answers to these questions frame the research design including selecting methods to elicit distinctions, selecting the sample, and writing and piloting the research instrument. Interviews based on the laddering techniques described here can provide meaningful and accurate ladders and CDMs that, in turn, form the basis for managerial understanding and action. In sum, laddering is a tool that can help managers gain a clearer picture of consumer decision making so they can think more effectively about their brand positioning challenges.

REFERENCES

Gengler, C., & Reynolds, T. J. (1995). Consumer understanding and advertising strategy: Analysis and strategic translation of laddering data. *Journal of Advertising Research, 35,* 19–33.

Gutman, J., & Reynolds, T. J. (1979). An investigation of the levels of cognitive abstraction utilized by consumers in product differentiation. In J. Eighmey (Ed.), *Attitude research under the sun* (pp. 128–152). Chicago: American Marketing Association.

Gutman, J. (1982). A means–end chain model based on consumer categorization processes. *Journal of Marketing, 46*(2), 60–72.

Olson, J. C., & Reynolds, T. J. (1983). Understanding consumer's cognitive structures: Implications for advertising strategy. In L. Percy & A. Woodside (Eds.), *Advertising and consumer psychology, Vol. 1* (pp. 77–90). Lexington, MA: Lexington Books.

Peter, J. P., & Olson, J. C. (1999). *Consumer behavior and marketing strategy.* Burr Ridge, IL: Richard D. Irwin, Inc.

Reynolds, T. J. (1988). The impact of higher order elements on preference: The basic precepts and findings of means–end theory. *Proceedings of American Marketing Educator's Conference,* San Diego, CA.

Reynolds, T. J., & Gutman, J. (1988). Laddering theory, method, analysis, and interpretation. *Journal of Advertising Research, 28*(1), 11–31.

Reynolds, T. J., Cockle, B., & Rochon, J. P. (1990). The strategic imperatives of advertising: Implications of means–end theory and research findings. *Canadian Journal of Marketing Research, 9*, 3–13.

Ries, A., and Trout, J. (1981). *Positioning: The battle for your mind.* New York: McGraw-Hill.

Vallette-Florence, P., & Rapacchi, B. (1991). Improvements in means–end chain analysis using graph theory and correspondence analysis. *Journal of Advertising Research, 31*(1), 30–45.

5

Consumer Understanding and Advertising Strategy: Analysis and Strategic Translation of Laddering Data

Charles E. Gengler
Baruch College

Thomas J. Reynolds
Richmont Partners

Two major obstacles exist to the proliferation of laddering as a management tool. First, the sheer magnitude of tedious work an analyst must perform to complete an analysis adds excessive costs to any study. Second, many who are familiar with the technique still have difficulty bridging from data to strategy to executional design and implications. This chapter addresses both of those issues by describing a newly available software support tool to make the data analysis a more reasonable task and by discussing the issue of strategy development and implementation. An example within the product category of dog food data is used.

An important issue for both industry and academic consumer researchers is the development of an understanding of how consumers derive personally relevant meaning about products. This meaning is the basis consumers use to shape their decision criteria among competitive products and services. In this chapter, discussed is the process by which pragmatic analysis of qualitative data on consumer meaning can be achieved and how this analysis can be used to enhance creative copy development. All too often, the results of qualitative research could have been written before the research was performed, either because the final results are merely the a priori opinion of the researcher involved or because the results are so obvious that the research need never have been performed. The intent here is to suggest a methodological process that will alleviate both of these problems when gathering information on consumer meaning.

Numerous academic studies have addressed this fundamental issue of meaning from the traditional product-attribute perspective (Bass, Pessemier, & Lehmann, 1972; Bass & Talarzyk, 1972; Lehmann, 1971; McAlister, 1982). Under the attribute perspective, product meaning is the observable physical characteristics of the product. This limiting perspective ignores any type of personal meanings of the product attributes.

Recognizing this deficiency, product meaning has been expanded beyond merely attributes to include benefits those attributes symbolize to the consumer. This orientation concentrates primarily on the direct results the product delivers to the consumer through product purchase or consumption (Haley, 1968, 1984; Myers, 1976). More recently, the definition of product meanings has been expanded yet again to include higher levels of abstraction (Gutman & Reynolds, 1979), namely, personal values (Homer & Kahle, 1988; Mitchell, 1983; Vinson, Scott, & Lamont, 1977).

The ever-broadening focus on understanding the consumer meanings that underlie the decision-making process, from attribute to benefit to personal-value perspectives, is primarily driven by the competitive forces in the marketplace. That is, the dramatic increase in the number of competing brands in most product categories forces marketers to look for positionings that are more directly relevant to the decision-making criteria of the consumer. Clearly, understanding the personally relevant meanings that consumers hold for a product, and the new positioning strategies that may stem from these meanings, is invaluable to marketing strategists.

Means–end theory (Gutman, 1982) presents an appealing framework to more comprehensively represent the consumer meanings that underlie product-positioning research. Rather than focus on a particular level of meanings, the means–end framework incorporates all levels into a conceptual model that additionally focuses on the associations (or derived meanings) between the levels. The associations between concepts offer an explanation of how consumers interpret a product attribute as symbolizing associated benefits. Consumers translate product attributes into the benefits (termed consequences) they produce, and benefits are ultimately translated into the consumer's driving value orientation.

For example, a dog food may have an attribute of being "dry and crunchy." To a dog owner, "dry and crunchy" means the dog food will help deliver the consequences (benefits) of "cleaner teeth" and "healthier dog." In turn, these consequences help the dog owner to fulfill a personal value, to feel a sense of "responsibility as a good owner." Put simply, the product, as defined by its discriminating perceptual attributes, is the *means* that satisfies the more personal *ends*, represented by values.

Importantly, the means–end framework adds a much richer understanding of how consumers derive meaning from products. Within this framework, meanings reflect the linear pattern of concepts and associations across levels of meaning, which, taken together, serve to explain the underlying reasons why the consumer considers a given attribute to be salient. The cognitive perspective of means–end theory can be seen to incorporate attribute, consequence, and value research paradigms into a framework encompassing all three models. It is the associational aspect of the means–end model that provides a unique perspective on consumers' personally relevant meaning.

Recently, several aspects of means–end theory are receiving increased attention. Several articles address research methodology (Reynolds & Gutman, 1988; Valette-Florence & Rapacchi, 1991). Others have addressed the application to positioning strategy design (Olson & Reynolds, 1983; Reynolds & Craddock, 1988; Reynolds & Gutman, 1984). Still others apply means–end theory as a conceptual framework for the strategic assessment of advertising (Gengler, 1990; Gengler & Reynolds, 1993; Reynolds & Gengler, 1991; Reynolds & Rochon, 1991). This attention resulted in the broader realization that significant potential lies in using this consumer-based, strategically oriented research framework. However, three major practical problems emerge: (1) the significant time and cost of gathering individual in-depth, means–end (laddering) data; (2) the time and effort required to perform the content analysis of the qualitative responses (steps in the ladders) and the quantitative summaries of the dominant pathways; and (3) the lack of any detailed framework or system to translate strategic options as represented in the summary Hierarchical Value Map into a working format for the agency creative staff.

LADDERING DATA ISSUES

Data Collection

Several researchers recently addressed the first of these problems: the issue of data collection. Gengler (1990) used an interactive computer program to assess strengths of associations between concepts. The concepts were derived a priori in focus groups. Vallette-Florence and Rapacchi (1990) used a card-sorting task to group concepts that were related. Both of these techniques relied heavily on a priori definition of concepts to be associated and are in that respect inferior to the open-ended format of laddering interviews. However, both techniques are quicker and easier to administer than laddering interviews. The main issue is whether or not researchers feel their consumers are homogeneous and predictable enough to use a predetermined set of concepts. Walker and Olson (1991) used a paper-and-pencil technique of data collection. In their technique, a questionnaire was administered to a group of individuals simultaneously. This

technique shows promise but precludes the insightful probing characteristic to laddering. In sum, a number of researchers are attempting to find
more cost-effective and efficient methods of data collection, but each of
these has potential shortcomings when compared with the laddering technique advocated by Reynolds and Gutman (1988). Indeed, it is difficult to
justify any small savings in time or money when compared with the enor-
mous cost of inaccurate or incomplete results.

Analysis of Laddering Data

The second problem offers a better place to increase the efficiency of conducting a means–end study: streamlining and improving the process of
analysis. Analysis of laddering data is a cumbersome task requiring several days of effort by highly skilled analysts for even a medium-sized
study. The basic analysis steps can be summarized as (see Reynolds &
Gutman, 1988, for a detailed description of these tasks):

1. Breaking the raw, conversational data into separate phrases. These
   phrases are the basic elements on which subsequent analysis is
   based. This involves reviewing the verbatim notes or tapes of the
   discussion probes for the elements that best represent the concepts
   expressed by each individual subject.
2. Content analysis of the elements selected in Step 1.
3. Summation of associations between the content codes, resulting in
   a quantitative assessment of all paired relationships, termed *implications*.
4. Construction of a diagram to meaningfully represent the main implications, termed an HVM.

Translation of Means–End Results
into Strategy and Creative Copy

The third problem involves the lack of any detailed framework to translate strategic options from a laddering study into a working format for the
agency creative staff. Although the issue of divining strategy from results
is often discussed (Olson & Reynolds, 1983; Reynolds & Craddock, 1988),
the focus generally concentrates on definition of the strategy and ignores
the issue of translating that strategy into creative, executional concepts for
advertisements. Discussing advertising strategy, Little (1979) stated:
"Good strategy requires imagination and style and always will. At the
same time, strategy emerges best from a foundation of reliable facts and
sound analysis" (p. 630). Integration of creativity and means-end study results to develop a strategy and design creative executions is an art. To be-

come accomplished at any art requires the development of technique. A key issue, then, is the outlining of techniques which can aid creative staff in developing executions from strategies.

PURPOSE OF THIS CHAPTER

The raw means–end data is the key building block from which all subsequent analysis is based. Although other approaches to data collection have been proposed and are being pursued, the costly interviewing process of laddering is often a necessity. The process is not subject to streamlining without sacrificing quality of understanding of the meanings that drive consumer decision-making. Hence, rather than focus on data collection, the dual purpose of this chapter is to deal explicitly with the analysis and strategic implementation of laddering data. The following sections of the chapter deal with a brief background of means–end theory and laddering, a discussion of improvements in laddering analysis, and the use of laddering results to aid in developing potent creative copy.

Specifically, this chapter first details the use of an interactive software tool that expedites the rather cumbersome and time-consuming analytic steps outlined previously (Gengler & Reynolds, 1989). Content analysis is a major portion of qualitative analysis. Although labor intensive and often tedious, great care and skill must be used in the content analysis, as the results are the basis of all subsequent analysis. Often, content analysis is an iterative task in which the analysts may recode data several times, combining categories, splitting categories, eliminating or creating new categories, until they feel they have achieved the optimal solution. This stage of the analysis process is drastically improved by the use of interactive computer software, so that the content analysis can easily be reviewed and modified.

In addition, automating the process allows analysts to develop several separate or aggregate analysis based on demographic segmentation. After a first analysis, each coding change done by hand can result in many hours of recalculation for the next analysis; whereas an automated tool can help the analyst reach the same point in a matter of seconds. Using the system described here, the summation of associations between content codes can be performed almost instantaneously, and analysts can experiment with different HVMs resulting from these summations quickly and easily. This experimentation would require days of repetitive effort by hand. Essentially, the use of an interactive software tool described here moves the analysis of laddering responses from being a rough, one-shot subjective analysis to a thoroughly reviewed and easily revised final analysis that a marketing manager can put confidence in. In this chapter we go through this process to demonstrate how laddering data can best be analyzed.

Secondly, the chapter presents a conceptual approach to translating laddering data into a format for creative ideation sessions. This translation bridges the gap between the abstract understanding of meanings latent in strategy specification to the concrete construction of creative messages. To be useful to creative executives, a laddering study should deliver more than just a few vague terms specifying an overall positioning. It should deliver information on how consumers relate different meanings and a basis for idea and message development—not a dogmatic restriction of exactly what an advertisement should say. It is information to feed the creative process rather than restrictions to suffocate it. Methods for the effective usage of laddering data are discussed in the final section of this chapter.

BACKGROUND

Personal values are theorized to be a basis of attitude and preference (Howard, 1977; Rosenberg, 1956; Vinson, Scott, & Lamont, 1977). Means–end theory (Gutman, 1982) is based on a personal values orientation, in which personal values are the motivating "end-states of existence" that individuals strive for in their lives (Rokeach, 1973, p. 7). Personal values, then, represent individuals' internal, self-relevant, goal states, whereas products are often represented as a bundle of physical product attributes. Means–end theory simply posits that the way in which these physical attributes of products are linked to personal values of individuals defines how products gain personal relevance and meaning. Thus, a physical attribute of a product is important if that attribute, during product consumption, produces a desirable benefit or consequence to the consumer. In turn, the perceived consequence of product purchase and consumption, derives its importance through the extent that this consequence is linked to another higher level consequence and ultimately into an individual's personal value system. A fundamental problem facing consumer researchers is how to ascertain this means–end cognitive structure (attributes to consequences to values) for any particular market.

Laddering (Gutman & Reynolds, 1979; Reynolds & Gutman, 1988) is the standard method for assessing cognitive structure consistent with the means–end paradigm. The laddering process is performed through a series of one-on-one, in-depth, personal interviews. In the process of laddering, subjects are asked to perform a choice or sorting task in order to uncover a preference-based distinction which they use to choose between brands in the market. The interviewer then continues to ask the respondent a series of probing questions to uncover the structural relationships between this distinction and the respondent's personal value system. In other words, the interviewer is trying to elicit the cognitive relationships that give personal relevance to the product preference distinction. These questions are designed in a manner that will not lead the subject to respond in any specific answer but will prompt them to give an answer that reflects, in their own words, their own particular perspective and meaning. Typically, these questions will be short and of a form similar to "Why is this important to you?" A thorough discussion of the laddering interviewing technique can be found in Reynolds and Gutman (1988).

STAGES OF COMPUTER ANALYSIS OF MEANS–END DATA

Analysis of the responses gathered through laddering interviews involves several steps. To illustrate this process, data gathered on consumer choices of food for their canines is used as an example. This data set contains responses from 67 laddering interviews, with one to four ladders produced from each subject. The discussion of analysis is presented in terms of the stages the analyst must go through, the important considerations at each stage, and how these stages can be facilitated using Gengler and Reynolds' (1989) decision-support tool, LADDERMAP.[1]

Stage A: Specifying Elements of a Means–End Chain

First of all, the conversational nature of the raw data from laddering forces the analyst to separate the ladder responses of each individual into chunks of meaning. These chunks correspond to the distinct levels of product meaning identified by the analyst within the ladder. Two important decisions must be made by the analyst at this stage. First, because the interviews are open-ended and conversational in nature, response not germane to the topic must be eliminated. Secondly, specifying what composes a chunk of meaning is extremely important because these units are the basis of all further stages of analysis. For example, an extract from a typical laddering interview may go something like "I prefer brand J (of dog food) because it is dry and crunchy and it cleans my dog's teeth when she eats it." In this statement, the subject is actually stating two different

---

[1]LADDERMAP is a registered trademark of Means–End Software. LADDERMAP software can be obtained through Charles Gengler, Baruch College, City University of New York.

chunks of means–end information, specifically, the attribute "dry and crunchy" and the consequence "cleans my dog's teeth."

The LADDERMAP software is designed to assist in this stage. An interactive data entry feature is provided. Under this feature, analysts can enter multiple ladders per interview subject and up to ten "chunks" of meaning per ladder. As ladders are entered for each respondent, the analyst is prompted for the first stage of content analysis that is classifying each "chunk" as either an attribute, a consequence, or a value. This classification underlies the theoretical basis of the analysis and aids the analyst in discerning what are and are not relevant "chunks" to include from the verbatim responses. An example of the ladder entry screen is shown in Fig. 5.1, with a ladder from the dog food data.

Stage B: Content Analysis of Means–End Data

Next, the "chunks" of meaning must be content analyzed in order to aggregate and generalize across subjects. This process involves two steps. The first step is to define a dictionary of content codes into which classifications can be made. This involves a preliminary review of the data and the development of a comprehensive (and exhaustive) set of categories into which to classify all of the chunks. The second step is the actual assignment of each verbatim to these codes. In a well-defined product category, in which analysts typically have strong insights into consumers' perceptions and motivations, many of the category codes may be defined a priori. More often, however, in laddering data analysis the steps of code

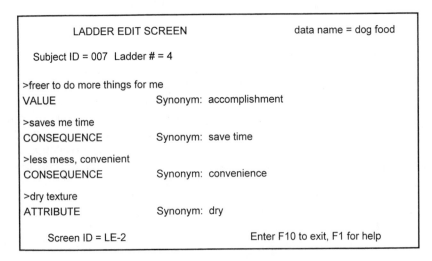

FIG. 5.1. Ladder entry screen from LadderMap software.

definition and classification process are interwoven and the codes essentially evolve during the classification.

To facilitate this highly labor-intensive and recursive task, which inherently requires intensive human judgment and decision-making, the software allows interactive coding in an easy-to-use format. Actual content from the interviews is shown on the screen, grouped under the codes it has been assigned to. An example of the screen is shown in Fig. 5.2, where verbatim responses have been coded under the categories of "Flavor" and "Taste." If, upon inspection, it is found that some concepts are assigned incorrectly, they can be easily corrected and assigned to the proper content code. Also, if the initial coding scheme is very specific, many content codes may have relatively few actual concepts assigned to each. For example, the codes of "Flavor" and "Taste" above could be combined under flavor.

Similar codes can then be easily grouped hierarchically under a larger code, making reassignment an easy task. For example, in Fig. 5.3 all of the items under "Taste" are easily moved under the major heading of "Flavor" by simply assigning "Taste" under "Flavor" in the coding scheme. This enables the analysts to split, combine, or redefine categories quickly and easily on-line. The content analysis task is truly the heart of laddering analysis. It is the step where qualitative data (the raw, verbatim responses from the laddering interviews) are converted into nominal codes that can be quantified. Because codes can be easily combined hierarchically within each other when using the software, we recommend a large number of very specific codes when first analyzing the data and gradually combining and grouping similar meanings until a manageable number of approximately 50 remain. However, if you are performing analysis by hand,

>flavor	n = 5
tastes good, like meat	n = 1
good beefy flavor	n = 1
tastes like real meat	n = 1
variety of flavors	n = 1
meaty flavor	n = 1
>taste	n = 3
tastes better than other brands	n = 1
tastes good	n = 1
my dog likes the taste	n = 1
F2-EDIT SYN F3-Change ACV F4-Track Code F10 EXIT	

FIG. 5.2.   Performing content analysis interactively.

>flavor	n = 5
tastes good, like meat	n = 1
good beefy flavor	n = 1
tastes like real meat	n = 1
variety of flavors	n = 1
meaty flavor	n = 1
taste	n = 3
tastes better than other brands	n = 1
tastes good	n = 1
my dog likes the taste	n = 1

F2-EDIT SYN	F3-Change ACV	F4-Track Code	F10 EXIT

FIG. 5.3.   Combining two categories during content analysis.

we recommend attempting to reduce the number of codes to approximately 50 immediately. Although this may result in a slightly higher misclassification, the combination of categories by hand would be restrictively difficult and tedious, besides being error prone. The lexical listing reports from the software, which report what verbatim responses are categorized under each content code, can be referenced at any future point to see what exactly was collapsed into the final content codes. Any further analysis of the data is only as good as the content analysis. Hence, this task should not be underrated in importance.

Stage C: Defining Connections between Content Codes

Once the laddering data is classified into codes, it can be quantitatively analyzed to produce a diagrammatic representation of the meaning structure. The end product of a laddering data analysis is a graphical representation of means–end structures aggregated across all subjects, the HVM. An HVM consists of the different content codes derived from content analysis arranged on a map and connected with lines. These lines show the common pathways of meanings, representing how product attributes are related to personal values. The main goal of analysis is the construction of the HVM, which is the framework for assessing strategic positionings in the marketplace. This involves two stages: determining what connections should be represented on the HVM, or directed graph, and constructing the HVM in a fashion that is easily readable.

Reynolds and Gutman (1988) presented a straightforward decision rule for determining what associations should be illustrated in an HVM. Each association is compared with a cutoff level. If an association has a strength greater than or equal to that value, then the association or connecting linkage is illustrated on the HVM. The LADDERMAP software implements this decision rule in its HVM construction algorithm.

The algorithm consists of three steps. First, we construct an aggregate implication matrix, which contains the sums of all of the instances where concepts were linked in the laddering interviews. These associations can be counted in two ways—only the direct associations are included, or all the direct plus indirect associations are counted. To illustrate what direct and indirect associations mean, consider a means–end chain of A → B → C. Here, we have direct association from A to B and from B to C and an indirect association from A to C. The sum of direct and indirect associations is an indicator of the strength of a given association. Often, multiple ladders will be gathered from each individual in the course of an interview. The number of ladders elicited from each individual respondent is usually dependent on the respondent's depth of knowledge or involvement in the product category. Also, a respondent may name an association between two concepts several times in different ladders elicited. In this case the association is only counted once per respondent when constructing the implication matrix in order to prevent bias in the aggregate results.

After the implication matrix is constructed, a cutoff value is selected by the analyst to determine which connections should be represented on the HVM. To assist the analyst in making this decision, a bar chart is provided on screen by the software to show how much variance would be explained by different levels of cutoff values (see Fig. 5.4). Typically, this cutoff value is compared against the aggregate of direct plus indirect associations in each cell of the implication matrix. A binary matrix is formed that contains a "1" in each cell for which the corresponding element of the implication matrix is greater than or equal to the cutoff value and a "0" otherwise. These binary flags indicate which associations or connecting linkages should be illustrated on an HVM. However, in the interest of constructing a meaningful uncluttered HVM, not all of the marked associations are actually drawn as individual lines. Some of the connections indicated in the binary matrix are considered redundant and, therefore, do not need to be illustrated. If, for instance, the matrix indicates X → Y, X → Z, and Y → Z, then the direct connection X → Z is redundant because it is captured in the X → Y and Y → Z relationships. Although some may argue that this conceals the X → Z connection, the map would quickly degenerate into an unreadable state if all redundant connections were included. After all of the redundant, "pass through" relations are eliminated, the binary matrix can then be used to draw the final HVM.

The process of summing the implication matrix and determining the connections to be made is a relatively simple task and takes only a few sec-

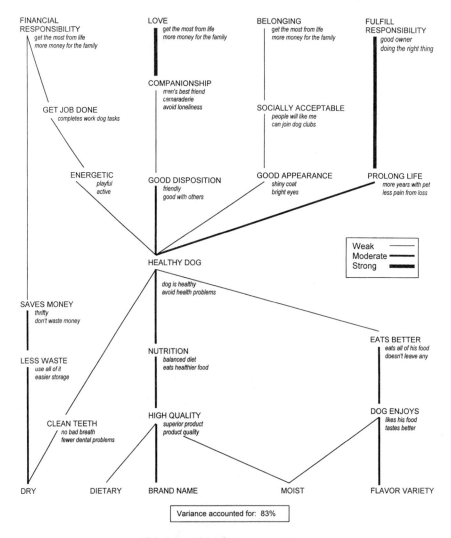

FIG. 5.4.   HVM for canine cuisine.

onds on a microcomputer, whereas it is an extremely long and laborious task by hand. This allows the analyst to go back and make content-analysis-coding changes and subsequent alternate analysis without concern because the quantitative steps can be reproduced rapidly and effortlessly. Furthermore, automation of the task allows the analyst more flexibility and control over the process. This allows for experimentation with different levels of cutoff values and different coding strategies. Interestingly, the total number of 1s accounted for in the HVM that is reported can be considered a measure of the representativeness of the solution. This percentage index serves as a useful summary measure that should be reported in all laddering research.

Stage D: Drawing the Hierarchical Value Map

After the data is analyzed to determine exactly which associations should be illustrated as connections on the HVM, the final stage of producing an HVM must be performed. Two requirements are imposed on the analyst at this stage. First, the finished HVM must represent a significant number of the associations derived from the raw laddering data. From experience in conducting over 100 studies, the minimum threshold value should never be less than 70% with an average number typically in the 75% to 85% range. To represent any smaller percentage can cause valuable insights to be lost. Second, and perhaps more importantly in many business environments, the final HVM must be easily interpretable by management if it is to be a viable tool. Again, this stage involves qualitative judgments made by a skilled analyst to produce an HVM that is both accurate and aesthetically pleasing, hence a tradeoff between validity and parsimony.

The algorithm discussed in Stage C only determines what connections should be made but does not actually indicate where nodes should be placed to draw an intelligible HVM. Gengler and Reynolds (1989) presented a heuristic-based algorithm and interactive editing software that can aid analysts in drawing an HVM derived from the binary matrix. This facility allows the analyst to quickly and easily view several HVMs based on different cutoff points and different coding judgments. Because an aesthetic component of readability affects the interpretability of the HVM, the software provides several interactive capabilities to adjust the map and enhance its readability, such as moving nodes about, cutting and redrawing lines, or renaming nodes to be more representative of the data.

In sum, the construction of an HVM from raw laddering data involves several stages of both quantifiable and nonquantifiable analysis. The major task of bridging from qualitative to quantitative analysis lies in content analysis of the subjects' verbatim responses. Inherently, this is a human judgment task but can be greatly facilitated by the use of interactive computer software. Furthermore, the use of software at this stage facilitates the subsequent quantitative stages of analysis, in particular, summarizing the frequency of the codes by subgroups within the total sample. Although this final stage can be (and is) automated to a great degree by the LADDERMAP software, this is not a task that can be entirely put through a black box to produce useful results. Analyst judgment and decision-making at all stages of the process is a critical component of the analysis.

INTERPRETATION AND STRATEGIC USE
OF HIERARCHICAL VALUE MAPS

The resultant HVM from an analysis of the dog food category is shown in
Fig. 5.4, with verbatim examples nested under each code. (This HVM accounted for 83% of all of the connections or associations in the raw laddering data, which we refer to as a measure of variance.) Again, the HVM
represents the patterns of meaning by which individuals give personal
relevance to product distinctions. The thickness of the lines connecting the
concept nodes similarly represents the varying frequencies of association.

The HVM can be divided into three fairly distinct levels corresponding
to the a/c/v codes. The product attributes (Dry, Dietary, Name Brand,
Moist, and Flavor Variety) are located at the lower part of the map. The
consequences that are basically of two types, functional and psychosocial,
represent the immediate outcomes that the consumer perceives to result
from the corresponding attributes. In other words, the desired consequences or outcomes are the immediate, tangible reasons a consumer attaches importance to the attributes. The Values (Love, Belonging, Fulfill
Responsibility, and Financial Responsibility) placed at the top of the map
represent personally relevant goals or objectives achieved by the lower
level consequences.

The connections between the nodes represent personal meanings.
These links are actually the key to understanding and using an HVM. This
is true for two reasons. First, being able to identify the connections between concepts in the mind of the consumer is essential to understanding
the perceptual basis for decision-making. This represents the cardinal insights offered by an in-depth understanding of the consumer. Second,
once a positioning strategy is determined, the creative task essentially involves developing words, images, and symbols that will create the desired connections in the mind of the consumer. Thus, focusing on the connections between concepts is central to both understanding and using
laddering research.

A common method for interpreting laddering data (Reynolds &
Gutman, 1988) is to consider the unique pathways of meaning from the attribute to the value level as perceptual orientations or perceptual segments. This is useful but also has its shortcoming. As a segmentation
method, this approach is useful only if the analyst takes into account the
method in which the HVM is constructed, namely, that all the concept
nodes in a pathway need not be included in the perceptual orientation.
This is due to the fact that the HVM is constructed to include related "pass
through" nodes through the elimination of redundant connections, minimizing the number of connecting lines required. To avoid this problem,
one must check the implication matrix to make sure the unique pathways

actually represent key defining elements that are significantly interconnected. This method of drawing an HVM assumes that those reading the map will naturally understand that a link from concept A to concept B and from concept B to concept C implies a link from concept A to concept C, even if it is not explicitly drawn. In most cases, drawing in these implicit connections will render a map unreadable due to its complexity and multitude of crossing lines. If one is dealing with a very simplistic knowledge structure or coding scheme or if interviewers failed to elicit full ladders from subjects, a map including all connections may then be feasible.

Alternatively, the implication matrix can be converted to a triangular distance matrix and used as input to a hierarchical clustering algorithm (e.g., see Klenosky, Gengler, & Mulvey, 1993). Different attributes, consequences, and values are grouped together by the analysis. The LADDERMAP program creates a file for this purpose, which can be easily used with any standard statistical applications package. Each of these clusters could be viewed as a perceptual orientation and a basis for a psychographic segment. An issue, then, is to assess which of these is the appropriate target market for a given brand.

MAKING POSITIONING DECISIONS BASED ON MEANS–END PATHWAYS

Each of the perceptual orientations discussed as segments should be evaluated as a potential product positioning. This is accomplished by benchmarking the strengths and weaknesses of the respective products, using a combination of traditional attitude data and subjective judgment. The objective data provides a sound basis for assessing the lower attribute and functional consequence levels. The more personal psychosocial consequences and value levels related to the competing brands' positionings can usually be accurately assessed from their advertising communications.

Combining the segmentation and the competitive positioning analyses results in the strategic framework from which positioning options can be developed. Basically, four options emerge. The first, and least likely, is discovering a significant yet untapped orientation, one that is not currently being used in the competitive environment. Given the sophistication of today's marketer, this is becoming increasingly less likely.

Option two involves grounding a positioning by establishing ownership of a meaning, essentially creating a stronger link between what is at present a relatively weak association. For example, in the HVM in Fig. 5.4, the linkage between "dry" and "clean teeth" is seen to be weak, therefore, one positioning option would be to build a strong association here, in the context of "healthy dog." "Healthy dog" would then need to be defined in terms of another, higher order meaning, like "prolong life." The net result would be a strategic positioning that communicates to the consumer that the meaning of "dry" → "clean teeth" is a discriminating characteristic to satisfy the higher order needs they have with respect to their dog.

Option three involves developing new meanings, essentially forming a meaningful connection between two as yet unrelated concepts. Again, using the HVM in Fig. 5.4, one example would be to connect "flavor variety" to "high quality," thereby tapping into the strong (tightly connected) higher order meanings that stem from "high quality." A simple example of this would be to create "flavor varieties" (at least named as such) or descriptors that would commonly be considered or associated with a superior cut of meat by human standards (i.e., filet, choice, or tournedos). Of course, the higher level association from "healthy dog" to the most appropriate values (given the competitive environment) must also be specified in the positioning.

The fourth option involves creating a new meaning by adding a new attribute descriptor to the consumer lexicon. One example of this type of positioning development would be to define a new attribute that could readily be associated with "nutrition," given the central role it plays in the HVM. A possible alternative would be a "medically grounded supplement" such as a unique combination of needed vitamins and minerals, which could be easily linked to superior "nutrition" and ultimately reinforcing to more personal value drivers at the higher levels. An approach like this could offer significant potential if the specifics of canine nutrition could be defined with a unique contrast to human dietary requirements, essentially creating a new knowledge framework the consumer could use to ground the rational component of his or her decision-making.

As is apparent, the HVM offers more than consumer insight. It is a framework to contrast current positionings and to develop "what if" scenarios which ultimately can become strategic options. Similar to the skill required to construct a representative HVM, the development of strategy cannot be done by a black-box algorithm: It requires clear and oftentimes creative thinking.

STRATEGY TRANSLATION

The specification of positioning strategy based in a means–end framework using the Model (see Fig. 5.5) is well documented in the academic literature (Olson & Reynolds, 1983; Reynolds & Craddock, 1988; Reynolds & Gutman, 1984). However, to date, no specifics have been forthcoming on how to translate the specification into a framework that creative staff can use to develop executional ideas. The abstract nature of the content

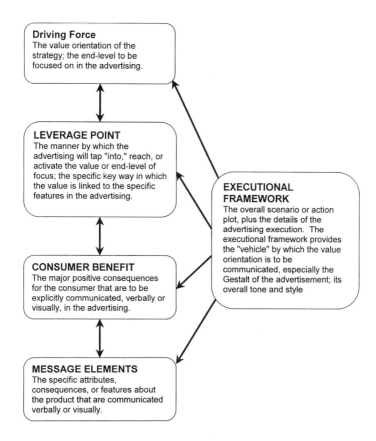

FIG. 5.5. MECCAS—Means–end conceptualization of components for advertising strategy.
Source: Reynolds, T. J., & Gutman, J. (1984). Advertising is image management. *Journal of Advertising Research, 24,* 1, 27–34.

codes and the HVM, though grounded in consumer meanings, appears more like a logical set of connections between rather simple, lifeless descriptors. The primary reason underlying this surface interpretation lies in the failure to adequately explain in detail the relevance of the concept of meaning. The first of two illustrations of this inadequacy in both explanation and understanding are made in the prior section, where meanings, defined as the connection between two concept nodes, served as the basis for the development of strategic options. Understanding the critical associative aspect of meaning offers significant potential to solve the strategy-to-creative translation problem that currently exists.

To illustrate, consider the "Super Premium" potential strategy that appears in Fig. 5.6, which creates a new linkage between "flavor variety"

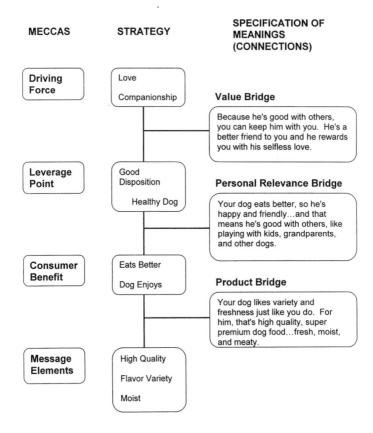

FIG. 5.6.   "Super premium."

and "high quality." Note that the specification here is repeated on the far left and the key strategic elements are presented in the center section. This form of strategy specification offered by the two left-most sections appears less than bland to the insightful creative. What is missing, again, is the concept of meaning; for it is the creative goal to create meanings that will make the product personally relevant to the consumer.

The simplicity and brevity of strategy specification in this manner, although apparently limiting, actually has the potential to serve the creative process exceptionally well. Not only is it unrestrictive, it also provides a unique structure for ideation. The focal point of this ideation is the associative aspect of meaning between any two given concepts.

To develop meanings, one must focus on the connecting lines between the concepts and explore the possibilities that maximize the probability that the desired meanings (connections) will result. This task directly feeds the creative process. What is required, then, is to develop executional ideas, scenarios, symbols, or feelings that will cause the association of the two concepts in the mind of the consumer. Generation of ideas in this way can initially be accomplished by answering the question: "What will cause the connection to be made?" Once ideas are developed for each of the three key strategic connections (see the right-most section of Fig. 5.6 for rough examples), the blending of these ideas can take place by creating specific scenes that serve to deliver the desired meanings, or an overall executional action plot that embodies all of the key meanings.

The initial form of strategy translation seen in Fig. 5.6 represents the basic underpinnings that would create the desired connection. The goal is to generate specific ideas thereby expanding the creative concept. For example, the "product bridge" linking the Message Elements to the Consumer Benefit could be enhanced by considering product names that infer the "high quality" and the "flavor variety" meaning. Using human meat labels such as choice or filet might accomplish this. In addition, combining the product name with the visual of the pet really enjoying the special, and thereby superior, meal may create both of the desired sets of connections.

The "personal relevance" bridge between the Consumer Benefit and the Leverage Point can be exemplified by demonstrating the good disposition of the pet, such as showing it playing with kids or being well disciplined. Tying this idea into the execution, either before and/or after feeding, offers another example of how the strategic concept can be brought to life. For the "value bridge," connecting the Leverage Point to the Driving Force, a visual demonstration of the affection latent in the bonding of the pet and its owner seems like an obvious executional idea.

Clearly, the sample creative ideas presented are merely examples limited by the lack of time spent and real creative insight. However, these ideas serve to demonstrate how the creative process can bring to life the strategy elements provided in a specification. The creative contribution is obviously the ultimate payoff — the tangible result of the positioning strategy and has to be worked every bit as rigorously as the development of strategic options. It is abundantly clear, however, that the creative output is intended to communicate meaning. Thinking specifically in these terms offers significant potential to focus the creative process.

Figure 5.7 demonstrates how another potential positioning, "Special Needs," can be developed from the HVM. In this example, a new attribute is created, one that gives the consumer a rational reason for grounding their decision-making (Reynolds, Cockle, & Rochon, 1990). The strategic goal, then, is to provide the consumer with a rational basis to believe the food is more nutritious, and thus superior to the competition, which is accomplished by building the appropriate meaning.

Continuing with this line of reasoning, the absence of specific dog-nutrition descriptors in the HVM offers the possibility of defining what dog

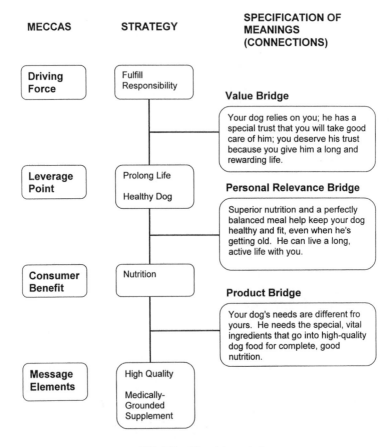

MECCAS   STRATEGY   SPECIFICATION OF MEANINGS (CONNECTIONS)

Driving Force — Fulfill Responsibility

Value Bridge

Your dog relies on you; he has a special trust that you will take good care of him; you deserve his trust because you give him a long and rewarding life.

Leverage Point — Prolong Life / Healthy Dog

Personal Relevance Bridge

Superior nutrition and a perfectly balanced meal help keep your dog healthy and fit, even when he's getting old. He can live a long, active life with you.

Consumer Benefit — Nutrition

Product Bridge

Your dog's needs are different fro yours. He needs the special, vital ingredients that go into high-quality dog food for complete, good nutrition.

Message Elements — High Quality / Medically-Grounded Supplement

FIG. 5.7. "Special needs."

nutrition is and how it differs from human nutrition. The meaning of nutrition, as defined by whatever "medically grounded supplements" can be delivered by the product, can then serve to positively differentiate the brand. Once grounded, the scenarios needed to convey the higher level connections can be developed similarly to the previous example.

As the two examples illustrate, understanding the HVM is the key to both specifying strategic options *and* to translating the options into grist for creative development. The central tenet and primary contribution of the point of view offered here can be summarized as this: the successful implementation of the means–end approach to strategy is the realization that meaning is everything. Positioning is about meaning. Analysis of consumer perceptions of the reasons that drive decision-making behavior should be framed as a study of meaning. Therefore, the development of strategic communications involves understanding how visual and verbal elements contribute to generate the desired meanings in the mind of the target consumer.

SUMMARY

Laddering is one of the most useful qualitative research techniques available to advertising researchers. It provides an opportunity for consumers to respond to choice situations in their own words and express their own feelings, yet provides enough structure to keep the conversation focused exactly on what the consumer thinks about the product category. The analysis of laddering data can be a laborious task, fraught with myriad classification decisions. The analytic tool described in this chapter provides a methodology for analyzing laddering data in a more-organized, less-error-prone, and less-opinionated fashion. This is done without suppressing the amount of information communicated to those who will eventually use the results of the analysis. The results of qualitative research should not be the biased opinion of the researcher. They should not be a selected amusing vignette or two from the best communicators in the sample interviewed. They should represent all of the perspectives of all of the individuals interviewed. Only through a careful analysis process, such as we have discussed here, can this be achieved.

Yet, even if an analysis has yielded valuable insights into consumer or industrial buyer psyche, these insights are worthless if they are not put into action. The strategic statements and positionings derived from a laddering study *must* be communicated to creative staffs developing advertising for the product. Furthermore, they must be communicated in a framework that stimulates creative ideation around the chosen positioning rather than restricting the creative staff to an overly specified message content. Such an over-restriction can be a fantastic formula for dry, unexciting advertising. For this reason, we have outlined how strategies derived from a laddering study can be successfully used as a source of ideas for creative staffs. Finding new ways to translate a product's tangible features into customers' key benefits, or to translate benefits into personally relevant feelings and values, is vital to creating advertising that is exciting and cohesive with a brand's chosen positioning. The focus of *any* communication with customers must be on the lasting product- or brand-related meanings formed in the customer's memory. This focus will not only help to build messages that contribute to a stronger brand image and positioning but will also help to preempt the creation of messages that, in isolation, may be "good ads" but in a holistic perspective dilute the positioning of the brand and confuse the brand image.

ACKNOWLEDGMENTS

We would like to express our gratitude for contributions by Steven West-berg and Jonathan Goldwater.

REFERENCES

Bass, F. M., Pessemier, E. A., & Lehmann, D. R. (1972). An experimental study of relationships between attitudes, brand preference and choice. *Behavioral Science, 17,* 6, 532–541.

Bass, F. M., & Talarzyk, W. W. (1972). An attitude model for the study of brand preference. *Journal of Marketing Research, 9,* 1, 93–96.

Gengler, C. E. (1990). An architectural perspective on advertising strategy. Unpublished doctoral dissertation, University of Texas-Dallas.

Gengler, C. E., & Reynolds, T. J. (1993). A structural model of advertising effects. In A. Mitchell (Ed.), *Advertising Exposure, Memory, and Choice* (pp. 283–302). Hillsdale, NJ: Lawrence Erlbaum Associates.

Gengler, C. E., & Reynolds, T. J. (1989, November). *Means–end structural analysis: Computer generated hierarchical value maps.* Paper presented at EIASM Workshop on Consumer Behavior: Extending the Cognitive Structure Perspective, Brussels, Belgium, November 1989.

Gutman, J. (1982). A means–end chain model based on consumer categorization processes. *Journal of Marketing, 46,* 2, 60–72.

Gutman, C., & Reynolds, T. J. (1979). An investigation of the levels of cognitive abstraction utilized by consumers in product differentiation. In J. Eighmey (Ed.), *Attitude Research Under the Sun* (pp. 128–150). Chicago: American Marketing Association.

Haley, R. I. (1968). Benefit segmentation: A decision-oriented research tool. *Journal of Marketing, 32,* 3, 30–35.

Haley, R. I. (1984). Benefit segments: Backwards and forwards. *Journal of Advertising Research, 24,* 1, 19–25.

Homer, P. M., & Kahle, L. R. (1988). A structural equation test of the value-attitude-behavior hierarchy. *Journal of Personality and Social Psychology, 54,* 4, 638–646.

Howard, J. A. (1977). *Consumer behavior: application and theory.* New York: McGraw-Hill.

Klenosky, D. B., Gengler, C. E., & Mulvey, M. S. (1993). Understanding the factors influencing ski destination choice: A means–end analytic approach. *Journal of Leisure Research, 25,* 4, 362–379.

Lehmann, D. R. (1971). Television show preference: Application of a choice model. *Journal of Marketing Research, 8,* 1, 47–55.

Little, J. D. (1979). Aggregate advertising models: The state of the art. *Operations Research, 27,* 629–667.

McAlister, L. (1982). A dynamic attribute satiation model of variety seeking behavior. *Journal of Consumer Research, 9,* 3, 141–150.

Mitchell, A. (1983). *Nine American lifestyles.* New York: Warner.

Myers, J. H. (1976). Benefit structure analysis: A new tool for product planning. *Journal of Marketing, 40,* 4, 23–32.

Olson, J. C., & Reynolds, T. J. (1983). Understanding consumers' cognitive structures: Implications for advertising strategy. In L. Percy & A. Woodside (Eds.), *Advertising and Consumer Psychology,* Vol. 1 (pp. 77–90). Lexington, MA: Lexington Books.

Peter, J. P., and Olson, J. C. (1987). *Consumer behavior: Marketing strategy perspectives.* Homewood, IL: Irwin.

Reynolds, T. J., & Craddock, A. B. (1988). The application of the model to the development and assessment of advertising strategy. *Journal of Advertising Research, 28,* 2, 43–54.

Reynolds, T. J., & Gengler, C. E. (1991). A strategic framework for assessing advertising: The animatic vs. finished issue. *Journal of Advertising Research, 31,* 5, 61–71.

Reynolds, T. J., & Gutman, J. (1984). Advertising is image management. *Journal of Advertising Research, 24,* 1, 27–36.

Reynolds, T. J., & Gutman, J. (1988). Laddering theory, method, analyses, and interpretation. *Journal of Advertising Research, 28,* 1, 11–31.

Reynolds, T. J., Cockle, B. C., & Rochon, J. P. (1990). The strategic imperatives of advertising: Implications of means–end theory and research findings. *Canadian Journal of Marketing Research, 9,* 3–13.

Reynolds, T. J., & Rochon, J. P. (1991). Means–end based advertising research: Copy testing is not strategy assessment. *Journal of Business Research, 22,* 131–142.

Rokeach, M. (1973). *The nature of human values.* New York: Free Press.

Rosenberg, M. (1956). Cognitive structure and attitudinal effect. *Journal of Abnormal and Social Psychology, 53,* 367–372.

Vallette-Florence, P., & Rapacchi, B. (1991). Improvements in means–end chain analysis: Using graph theory and correspondence analysis. *Journal of Advertising Research, 31,* 1, 30–45.

Vinson, D. E., Scott, J. E., & Lamont, L. M. (1977). The personal role of values in marketing and consumer behavior. *Journal of Marketing, 41,* 2, 44–50.

Walker, B., & Olson, J. C. (1991). Means–end chains: Connecting products with self. *Journal of Business Research, 22,* 2, 111–118.

III

DEVELOPING AND ASSESSING ADVERTISING STRATEGY

SECTION OVERVIEW

The most common application of the means–end approach has been to advertising issues and problems. Advertising strategy is a natural application because means–end chains so directly relate to communications issues (What should we say? How should we say it?). This section contains several chapters dealing with how the means–end approach can be used to develop advertising strategy and measure the effectiveness of particular ads.

• In chapter 6, Reynolds and Gutman present their vision of advertising management as seen from a means–end perspective. They see advertising as creating and maintaining meanings or images that are strategically relevant. The core idea is that advertising is about creating an appropriate means–end chain for a brand, which is one way of thinking about brand image. Therefore, the main responsibility of advertising managers is to manage the image of the brand (product or corporation). The authors show how the means–end approach is a useful framework for thinking strategically about current and desired brand images and for monitoring the changes in image created by advertising.

• In chapter 7, Reynolds and Craddock describe the MECCAS model for developing advertising strategy. MECCAS (Means–End Chain Conceptualization of Advertising Strategy) identifies five key elements of advertising strategy and shows how they relate to the elements in a means–end chain. By specifying ad strategy in means–end terms, managers can use the MECCAS framework to guide the development of ads that execute that strategy. The authors also demonstrate how MECCAS identifies the key strategic elements to measure in assessing advertising effectiveness.

• Next, Rossiter and Percy (chap. 8, this volume) contrast the means–end approach to advertising communication with their alternative framework called the a-b-e (Attribute-Benefit-Emotion) model. In a detailed critique of the means–end approach to developing positioning and advertising strategy, Rossiter and Percy make several interesting and provocative points about the means–end approach to advertising strategy. A major point of difference is that Rossiter and Percy do not emphasize the linkages between concepts (or levels) in their a-b-e model, whereas the means–end approach emphasizes the connections between the a-c-v elements. Their chapter is of interest both for their alternative a-b-e model and the critical analysis of the means–end approach.

• In chapter 9, Reynolds, Whitlark, and Wirthlin review the key elements of the means–end approach to advertising strategy. Using several actual business examples, they illustrate the entire process of creating strategic advertising communications, beginning with the means–end perspective to understand customers, to developing advertising strategy, to evaluating the effectiveness of the finished advertising communication. Their chapter is a tutorial on how to think strategically about communicating with consumers, using the means–end approach as a guide.

• In chapter 10, Reynolds and Gengler describe how researchers can use the means–end approach to guide their evaluation of the effectiveness of an advertisement. An ad strategy should be specified as a means–end chain linking specific product attributes to important consequences and to values desired by the customer. Thus, from a means–end perspective, an ad is effective to the extent it communicates the meaning elements specified in the overall strategy and connects those elements together. The authors describe the strata™ model based on the means–end approach that measures how strongly the ad communicated the key concepts and how strongly the ad linked these concepts together.

Advertising Is Image Management

Thomas J. Reynolds
Richmont Partners

Jonathan Gutman
University of New Hampshire

> *. . . translating image research to image strategies.*

As the title of this chapter suggests, the advertising function may be equated, at least in part, to the creation and management of product imagery; that is, the set of meanings and associations that serve to differentiate a product or service from its competition. Obviously, the authors are not the first ones to come upon this way of looking at advertising. One might refer back to Ogilvy's (1963) *Confessions of an Advertising Man* for a recommendation that brand image should be the basis for developing sound advertising strategies.

The *raison d'etre* for this point of view has not changed since it was first put into practice—the majority of product classes are comprised of products that do not differ from each other in any significant way. Therefore, advertising functions to enhance physical attributes and their relative importance with respect to how the consumer sees himself or herself, essentially providing psychological benefits through the image-creation process.

The purpose of this chapter is to discuss the contributions the means–end chain research model (the linking of attributes to consequences to personal values) can make to creating images for products and services. First, definitions of image and approaches for studying image are reviewed. After a review of the means–end chain model, research implementation techniques are discussed. Then an illustrative example is provided that demonstrates how the research findings can be directly translated into the specification of "image" advertising, through the detailing of a consumer-research-based strategic framework.

DEFINITIONS OF IMAGE

In order to move beyond the basic posture that brand images add value to products, one must consider defining and operationalizing image. Obviously, this is necessitated due to the fact that the way image is defined determines the manner in which research to understand image is designed, executed, and, ultimately, translated to the creative process. To illustrate, consider the various ways in which image has been translated into an operational framework:

1. General characteristics, feelings, or impressions (Jain & Etgar, 1976)
2. Perceptions of products (Lindquist, 1974; Marks, 1976)
3. Beliefs and attitudes (May, 1974; James, Durand, and Dreves, 1976; Hirschman, Greenberg, and Robertson, 1978)
4. Brand personality (Arons, 1961; Martineau, 1958)
5. Linkages between characteristics and feelings/emotions (Oxenfeldt, 1974)

Let us consider each of these in turn as the basis of defining image.

General Characteristics

Does this term simply mean descriptive phrases such as "decaffeinated coffee" or "cold water detergent?" Or, are the feelings and impressions that are derived from thinking about a product what image is all about? For example, if one mentions Johnson's baby powder, is image the warm feeling you get when you think of the loving, caring relationship between a baby and his or her mother? If so, the closely tied link between a product and these emotional feelings would appear to be a good beginning toward defining image. This also suggests that general characteristics of a product are a bit too concrete or descriptive of the physical nature of the product itself to be useful in defining the more personalized emotion-laden components of image.

Perceptions of Products

Obviously, this is a very general way of defining an image. In this context your perception of a product represents your image of that product. This conceptualization seems too broad to be of much use in defining image, although it represents the basis for multidimensional scaling's contribution to advertising strategy development (Percy, 1976; Seggev, 1982). Focus groups, although more qualitative in approach, also stem from this point of view, yielding as it were respondents' general opinions or perceptions of a product or other stimulus object.

Beliefs and Attitudes

Although this perspective is somewhat more specific than perceptions, attitude leans heavily on evaluation, whereas beliefs lead us to think about standard measurement paradigms (viz. Likert or semantic differential scales) and models (Day, 1973) that are thought to reflect image. Beliefs themselves can be defined in a number of ways (Fishbein, 1967) suggesting a considerable latitude in actually defining how image should be thought of.

The attitude-and-belief orientation of defining image has led to the use of multiattribute attitude models (Wilkie & Pessimier, 1973) that focus on attributes that are assumed to underlie preference, which in turn act as a surrogate for choice behavior. Boyd, Ray, and Strong (1972) based their advertising strategy formulation procedure on such an attitudinal framework. This approach, of course, necessitates determining which choice criteria are used to evaluate brands, thereby allowing these characteristics to be changed (added to, subtracted from, increasing or decreasing the importance of). In general, approaches such as these restrict image to consisting of product characteristics, one primary reason being the inability of paper-and-pencil procedures to effectively deal with more personal orientations.

Brand Personality

The notion of personifying the brand with characteristics we use to describe individuals certainly does suggest personal bonds of greater meaning than beliefs about product attributes. Yet, without a more general framework to know how these characteristics derive their meaning, we do not know the relation of these characteristics to those of the product or the product's degree of differentiation with respect to its competitors. Kover (1983) presented some interesting strategic applications in this area, essentially working backward by establishing the typologies of consumers by the assumed personality of a mix of brands across categories. Unfortunately, the strong emphasis on interpretation in this case, as well as making sure to look at the appropriate product classes, does not make this as methodologically rigorous an approach as one might desire.

Linkages Between Characteristics
and Feelings and Emotions

This definition seems to combine some of the best features of the prior definitions while including the notion of the connections between perceptions. Thus, when you think about a product, some feature of it typically
comes to mind. This feature itself brings something else to mind, which in
turn brings yet another thought to mind. For example, take a moment and
consider Perrier. What comes to mind? Now use your initial response as
the stimulus. What does that bring to mind? The reader following this
demonstration should be going through a sequential process of elicitation,
tracing the network of associations in memory.

As is apparent, the linking of concepts undoubtedly has descriptors in
it that in no way relate directly to Perrier. What has happened is that concepts imply other concepts, producing an implication network reflecting
memory linkages which the authors put forth as the fundamental component of image. These views are not dissimilar from two major theories of
memory, levels of processing (Craik & Lockart, 1972) and spreading activation (Collins & Loftus, 1975). The distinction that does serve to distinguish the authors' view from the traditional memory theories is the focus
on the episodic nature of the network, elements that derive their meaning
in terms of their connection to self, thus serving to modify self. This connecting of key elements that define the product to those that modify self
affords a translation of the meaning of the product to personally-relevant
descriptors that provide the basis for image.

In defining image as stored meanings that an individual has in memory,
and by relating these stored meanings to a memory network, one can suggest some research directions that go beyond those suggested by earlier
definitions. Two aspects of this definition are of importance at this point.
First, what is called up, or stored in memory — the content — provides the
meanings we attribute most basically to image (this is the perception viewpoint). Second, the organization or connections that represent the relationships, or what causes particular classifications or meanings to be called up
or linked to one another, is the structural component. As is readily apparent, if we can determine the network of personally-relevant connections associated with a particular product class, we can conduct meaningful research on image that will contribute to creating more effective advertising
strategies, and, ultimately, product positionings.

Basically, then, we need to understand types of cognitive representations consumers have with respect to products. Once the network corresponding to the product class can be isolated, what remains is to determine the relation of the component parts to the product of interest. That is,
to what differentiating characteristics it is related, and more importantly,

what linkages can be made to the personal lives of consumers to best maximize the product's perceptual position or image.

A MEANS–END CHAIN ORIENTATION
FOR DEFINING IMAGE

A means–end chain (Gutman, 1982) is defined as the connection between product attributes, consumer consequences, and personal values. Attributes are features or aspects of products or services. Consequences accrue to people from consuming products or services. They may be desirable (benefits) or undesirable. Values, or end states, are important beliefs people hold about themselves and about their feelings concerning others' beliefs about them (Rokeach, 1968). It is values that determine the relative desirability of consequences.

Embodied in the means–end chain model is the concept of levels of abstraction (Gutman & Reynolds, 1979). Put simply, *levels* refer to a way of categorizing the contents of associations about a product class that extend from physical aspects of a product to personal values. To amplify, one way to operationalize levels is to think in terms of subcategories of attributes, consequences, and values as shown in Table 6.1.

Physical characteristics are defined as being measurable in physical units, such as color or miles per gallon. The abstracted properties represent attribute designations that are more subjective in nature, like "smells nice" or "strong flavor." Functional consequences are exemplified by such outcomes as "saves money" or "don't have to wash your hair every day." Such consequences are instrumental to our achieving psychosocial consequences such as having more friends, having fun, or being more attractive to others. The instrumental-values level reflects an external orientation relating to how we are perceived by others ("makes me feel more important" or "makes me feel accepted"). The terminal or internal-values level relates to how one views oneself (self esteem or security).

TABLE 6.1
Levels of Abstraction

Abstract	Values
	Terminal–Internal
	Instrumental–External
	Consequences
	Psychosocial
	Functional
	Attributes
	Abstract Characteristics
Concrete	Physical Characteristics

Again, the key point to be made is that some system of categorization by level is required so that aspects of the product can systematically be related to important aspects of self. Conceptualizing the contents of associations in this manner aids us in probing into the nature of the hierarchical structure of the contents of consumers' associations about brands within a product class.

To recap, the levels of abstraction conceptualization represents a meaningful way of organizing the contents of memory about a particular product (i.e., its network of associations or image). What needs to be known, then, is how these components or levels are linked to one another to form an associational network representing image. In this context "attributes → consequences → values" linkages, or means–end chains, are the fundamental units of analysis in understanding image. Such structures provide useful research concepts for understanding consumer orientations with respect to image, thus providing the framework for developing image positionings.

APPROACHES FOR STUDYING IMAGE

Standard approaches in practice today for gaining insight into both the content and organization of product images, serving essentially as extensions of the theoretical formulations detailed previously, are focus groups, standard attitude and usage survey methods, and perceptual-mapping techniques. Some brief comments about these approaches have been made earlier in connection with the various definitions of image. Let us look a little more closely at them in the context of the definition of image developed in the previous discussion.

Focus groups revolve around understanding consumers' own words in a basically unstructured format, except for a directional outline, thereby permitting basic orientations and feelings to emerge. This satisfies the need to uncover contents of image. The failure of the standard content analysis to reveal, in a systematic manner, the organization or mental networking that is representative of the links between the various concepts elicited, is the major drawback of the use of this approach for studying images. That is, by simply labeling the various concepts elicited, the researcher has no real information with respect to his or her interrelationships, nor any structure to provide a basis for critical analysis. Secondarily, the group environment also has to be questioned with respect to how freely (and accurately) respondents will discuss higher value levels, which obviously represent the personal level at which image is seen to operate.

Issues relating specifically to the use of attitude models have been dealt with in detail elsewhere (Gutman, 1978, 1983). The problems with these models, with respect to studying image, center on the fact of their use of a predetermined set of items that are not guaranteed of either being important to respondents, or even of being expressed in terms meaningful to the respondents. Additionally, the classification of items generally lacks delineation as to the level of abstraction (attribute, consequence, or value) of the items (Myers & Shocker, 1981). Moreover, the linkages between items are not dealt with directly; rather they are inferred by analysis based on assumptions that are typically unrealistic, reflecting the compositional structure of the attitude model used.

An alternative methodology that addresses both the problems of predetermined items and the prespecified analytical framework, multidimensional scaling, involves the direct scaling of dissimilarity judgments obtained from an individual into a multidimensional space that denotes the relative differences between products. The underlying rationale is that these spatial distances reflect the true differentiation, reflecting the image differences of one's perceptions with respect to a particular product class. In this context, the primary problem with the scaling approach stems from the inferential process that the researcher must go through in interpreting the resulting space. Although analytic methods do help give insight to this problem, the lack of a model reflecting the relational linkages tends to make the interpretation highly subjective.

Implementing the Means–End Chain Model for Studying Image

If we are to have a better way of uncovering what goes on in people's minds, given the theoretical issues detailed previously, the following would seem to be required. First, the analytic frame of reference would be at the individual level; that is, we have to understand the individual before we can understand the group or the mass of consumers. Second, the technique should draw on the consumer's own language. Basically, it seems unreasonable to ask consumers to translate our concepts to their way of thinking; and, if they are using their own concepts it certainly behooves us to find out what they are. Third, the analysis should permit content classification by some version of the levels of abstraction notion so that the contents of image can be divided into meaningful groupings. And, fourth, linkages between levels, attributes, consequences, and values need to be directly recovered, rather than inferred, so that we can understand the defining structure of image, not merely its contents.

Translating all this into research needs results in four basic issues:

(1) How to tap into an individual's network of meanings?
(2) How to explore this structure in terms of content or levels of abstraction and determine the linkages between these levels?

(3) How to identify the common framework across respondents that can be used to summarize the data reflecting perceptual orientations across brands?

(4) How to translate these perceptual orientations into advertising strategy?

The remainder of this section presents a total methodological perspective that addresses all of the above research issues.

The Repertory Grid (Kelly, 1955; Sampson, 1972) has been used successfully to elicit distinctions consumers make among products. The Repertory Grid begins with a triadic sorting task in which the respondent is given three products and asked to think of some overall way of thinking about the three products in which two of them can be considered the same but yet different from the third. The intent here is to uncover the basic distinctions an individual uses to classify products. The respondent is asked to specify both poles of the distinction he or she is making as well as to which pole each of the three products belongs (see Reynolds & Gutman, 1983, for an interesting way of summarizing such data).

With respect to Repertory Grid applications to consumer products, it has been pointed out (Gutman & Reynolds, 1979; Reynolds & Gutman, 1983) that distinctions given by consumers to the triadic sorting task tend to be at the attribute level. To get at higher levels of abstraction and to determine the connections between the lower and higher levels, a series of directed probes is necessary. This technique, called *laddering*, entails using the preferred pole of the initial triadic distinction and then sequentially probing into why that distinction is important to the respondent. By taking the preferred pole at each level, a series of linkages connecting attributes to consequences and then to personal values is thereby uncovered.

Although these techniques are not complex, they do offer interesting analytical possibilities as well as some interesting qualitative data. The summary of this type of data has been dealt with elsewhere (Olson & Reynolds, 1983). Basically, a simple counting procedure between adjacent elements yields a hierarchical map constructed from the pairwise connections between elements above a specified criterion level. This results in a map connecting the key elements (attributes, consequences, and values). Each distinct pathway is interpreted as a possible perceptual orientation.

Thus, "tapping into" the consumer network of meanings is accomplished by the triadic sorting task, with the laddering task serving to provide the higher level interpretations of the more concrete attribute distinctions. Laddering, then, satisfies the content requirement as well as the structural by uncovering the linkages or connections between the content elements. The hierarchical analysis yielding the latent pathways or dominant orientations across respondents results from a joint analysis of the frequency of connections between common content elements. Remaining, then, is the translation of the research framework into an advertising framework.

TRANSLATING IMAGE RESEARCH TO STRATEGIC POSITIONINGS

To utilize the attribute → consequence → value connections for creating brand images with advertising, the components of advertising strategy have to be coordinated with the levels of the means–end chain. The Means–End Conceptualization of the Components of Advertising strategy, the MECCAs Model (Olson & Reynolds, 1983) accomplished this purpose. MECCAs translates (see Fig. 6.1) advertising strategy into five specific characteristics that correspond to the levels of abstraction conceptualization. The characteristics of Driving Force, Consumer Benefit, and Message Elements stem directly from values, consequences, and attributes, respectively. The Executional Framework relates to the plot, scenario, or tone for the advertising, with the specification for advertising

Level	*Definition*
Driving Force	The value orientation of the strategy; the end-level to be focused on in the advertising.
Leverage Point	The manner by which the advertising will "tap into," reach, or activate the value or end-level of focus; the specific key way in which the value is linked to the specific features in the advertising.
Executional Framework	The overall scenario or action plot, plus the details of the advertising execution. The executional framework provides the "vehicle" by which the value orientation is to be communicated; especially the Gestalt of the advertisement; its overall tone and style.
Consumer Benefit	The major positive consequences for the consumer that are to be explicitly communicated, verbally or visually, in the advertising.
Message Elements	The specific attributes, consequences, or features about the product that are communicated verbally or visually.

FIG. 6.1.   MECCAs — Means–end conceptualization of components for advertising strategy.
Source. Olson, J. and Thomas J. Reynolds. Understanding Consumers' Cognitive Structures: "Implications for Advertising Strategy." In *Advertising and Consumer Psychology*, L. Percy and A. Woodside, eds. Lexington, MA: Lexington Books, 1983.

tone coming from an overall understanding of the way of perceiving the product class as indicated by particular means–end chains.

With all these elements in mind, it is still necessary to specify just how the values-level focus for the advertising will be activated. That is how the executional components of Message Elements, Consumer Benefit, and the Executional Framework can be positioned as personally relevant to the consumer, activating or "tapping into" a personal value. This is accomplished through the concept of the Leverage Point.

The MECCAs model, then, allows for the creation of advertising that identifies important aspects of self and relates these to important consequences associated with product use, and, in turn, with key product attributes that produce these consequences. The specification of the tone and scenario for the advertising allows for the presentation of all these elements in a consistent fashion. The resulting complete strategy statements provide creative people and management with a document that provides the level of understanding necessary to focus creative energy on creating image-building advertising.

ILLUSTRATIVE EXAMPLE

Airlines are used to demonstrate the application of these research techniques for developing strategic opportunities that can be translated by the consumer into personal identifications, which represent image. Airlines were chosen because they have obvious people and equipment components that provide opportunities for image development. Further, it is easy to construct a research format using triads consisting of sets of three airlines, or one's last three flying experiences, which could yield discriminating distinctions such as: wide bodies versus regular aircraft; pleasant interiors versus unpleasant interiors; or more deals on fares versus less deals on fares.

Although these descriptors would undoubtedly be an integral part of a typical attitude and usage survey, they offer a rather limited perspective as to the higher levels of consequences and personal values that mediate these perceptions. As is apparent given the initial focus of this discussion of image, this type of input is limiting when the intent of the research is to give direction to both marketing strategists and creatives.

As mentioned previously, laddering can be initiated by ascertaining the preferred poles for each distinction and following up with a "Why?" question about why that pole is preferred. Let us say that "wide bodies," "pleasant interiors," and "more deals" are the preferred poles of these distinctions. Probing the first distinction might produce the consequence-level distinctions shown in Fig. 6.2.

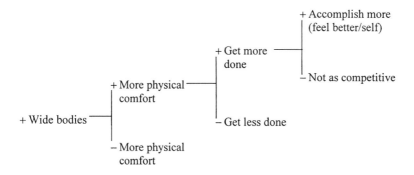

FIG. 6.2.   Consequence-level distinctions—"wide-bodies."

Stepping up the laddering summary in Fig. 6.2 illustrates the result of asking the "Why?" question to "wide bodies" that yielded "more physical comfort" that when probed further led to "get more done," and that derived its personal relevance from the need to "accomplish more." The perspective gained here is the apparent translation of the aircraft type into a perception that the additional seating provides an environment that more easily facilitates getting work done on the plane. This is meaningful due to the competitive and demanding work and travel schedule the business person is required to deal with.

It is important to note that not all of the distinctions at the various levels are represented by bipolar opposites. This is the case in particular at the higher levels, where by having the respondent detail the negative or potential negative pole, substantial insight is often gained with respect to the true meaning the respondent is trying to express. Similarly, by understanding the even more personalized meaning of accomplishment—in this case, a desire to feel better about oneself through success—although not stated explicitly, gives additional information about the orientation of the respondent.

Probing the second distinction resulted in the "pleasant interiors" to "relax" linkage that was then linked to the "in-control" distinction, which was considered important in terms of satisfying a need for "security." Thus, the diagrammatic view of laddering (see Fig. 6.3) can be analogized to a "ladder of abstraction" that follows the means–end chain, moving from attributes that are considered as part of the product/service to the personalized meaning or interpretation with respect to how the individual sees or would like to see himself or herself.

The third distinction, "more deals," when probed further, leads to the distinction, "save money." This latter distinction then leads to "feel prudent," which is important to the respondent for reasons of manifesting "security" (see Fig. 6.4). Of note here is the fact that the same term as

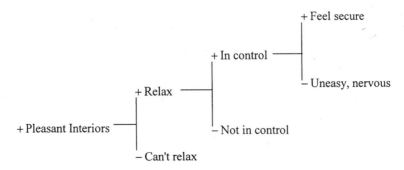

FIG. 6.3.   Consequence-level distinctions—"pleasant interiors."

above was used by the respondent, yet a different meaning was intended. The obvious fact that the specific nuances such as this must be incorporated in the analysis of the elicited distinctions is apparent.

As is readily apparent, the interpretations of even rather straightforward descriptive attributes, when moved to these higher level personalized meanings, can be quite revealing. The obvious caveat, of a highly trained interviewer, to make sure the nuances are accurately denoted as well as to insure the meaningfulness of the responses (subjectively assessed) at the various levels, and a rigidly formated content analysis, certainly need to be pointed out. Thus, the same concerns of any qualitative analysis hold true for this type of in-depth interviewing. A major advantage of this approach, however, is that the representation of elements across levels of abstraction permits a solid structural framework with which to initiate the content analysis. By simply classifying all mentioned distinctions into the appropriate breakdowns downs across and within the basic levels, the analysis is greatly expedited.

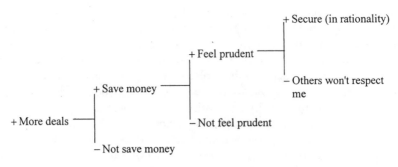

FIG. 6.4.   Consequence-level distinctions—"more deals."

Codes representing all mentioned descriptors are applied to the original data thereby permitting a nominal summarization of each level for each respondent. The issue, then, is the nature of the patterns represented in this data.

HIERARCHICAL-VALUE-STRUCTURE MAPS

A type of market-structure analysis, termed a *value-structure map*, intrinsically hierarchical in nature, can be constructed from the series of linkage ladders across respondents. Thus, the individual means–end chains referred to previously can also be used to create an aggregate map of these relations. All attribute, consequence, and value distinctions are cast as the rows and columns of a square matrix. The frequency with which each element leads to or implies each other element is represented by the cell frequencies of such a (dominance) matrix. The relationships between key elements, as summarized by the frequencies, serve as the basis for constructing the value-structure map.

A hypothetical hierarchical-value-structure map (Reynolds & Gutman, 1983) for the airline category is shown in Fig. 6.5. Note that many of the ladders are interconnected, and at the high levels, the merging of the lower level distinctions into the same value occurs. One way to examine such a map is to trace the paths from the bottom of the map to the top. As can be seen, there are a number of ways of moving from the attribute level to the consequence level and then to the values level. These paths represent common perceptual orientations, essentially perceptual segments.

"Advanced seat reservation," "aircraft type," and "first-class cabin" all lead to "more space," which in turn leads to "physical comfort." "Physical comfort" is an important node (also reached through "no distractions") leading to "status," "getting more done," and "reducing tension." These consequences are the gateways to higher order consequences and values-level considerations.

"Reduce tension" is itself also an important node in the hierarchical-value-structure map; "save time" and "dependable" lead into it. It represents a crossover point for the lower level attributes of "ground service" and "on-time performance" to reach up to the values of "accomplishment" and "self esteem." On the right side of the map, the functional benefits of "able to plan" and "prudent" lead eventually to "security." On the far right side of the map, "food quality" leads to "enjoyment," but not to any higher-order values. This demonstrates the fact that perceptions underlying preferences do not always tie into higher values.

The box in Fig. 6.5 contains the notation of "personal interaction." This interpretive addition to the map points up a nuance that might represent

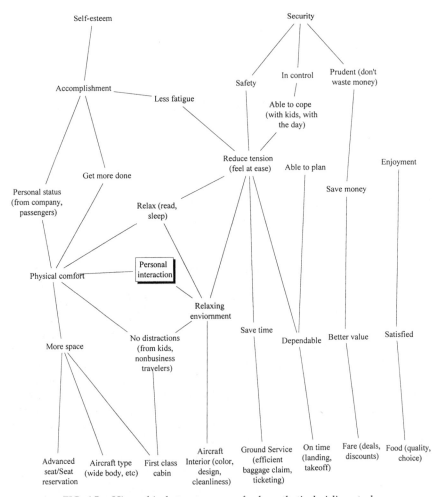

FIG. 6.5.   Hierarchical structure map for hypothetical airline study.

something respondents did not explicitly say, yet which was implicit in much of what they did say. It suggests that personal interaction is a key factor in translating "physical comfort" into "relaxing environment," leading to feelings of being "in-control," and eventually to "security." The suggestion here is that the flier gives up control when he or she makes a commitment to fly. These feelings of being locked in an artificial environment can be dealt with through the medium of personal interaction. Though certainly subjective as compared to the construction of the value-structure map, such insightful qualitative analysis as would be typical in a focus-group analysis does bring substantial richness to the interpretation of the key linkages and pathways.

Illustration of Strategic Option Development

Any or all of the perceptual orientations in the value-structure map can be the basis of an advertising strategy. Therefore, a diverse set of alternative advertising strategies can be created, each based on a way consumers have of relating to the product or service class. Figures 6.6 and 6.7 illustrate two such strategic options. The perceptual orientation on which the strategy is based is shown on the left of the figure; the strategy specification in the MECCAs framework is shown on the right.

The first strategic option, Able to Plan (see Fig. 6.6), links "on-time" as a Message Element to the Consumer Benefit of being "dependable." The Driving Force for this strategy revolves around "self-esteem." The Leverage Point, or key to linking all these elements together in the strategy is through "accomplishment"—getting more done because you can be dependable, because you can depend on your on-time airline. This suggests an Executional Framework relating to the ability to execute plans with less tension and fatigue, perhaps featuring an executive on the go with deadlines to meet in different parts of the country. Thus, however the strategy is executed, the passenger's sense of accomplishment is seen as the key to forming a meaningful connection in the consumer's mind between the other elements comprising the perceptual orientation.

Notice that this strategy specification, although it deals with the Executional Framework for the strategy, stops well short of any specification that would infringe on the purview of the creatives. It is important that management be able to supply direction to creatives, while at the same time leaving them free to create advertising within this framework. Image management consists of specifying the elements (attributes, consequences, values) that are to be linked together in the advertising and the underlying rationale for that linkage. This provides a target framework in which creatives can execute and an objective or standard against which the results can be assessed.

Level	MECCAs Model	Strategy
Self-esteem	Driving Force	Self-esteem
Accomplishment	Leverage Point	Accomplishment (get more done)
Less fatigue Reduce tension (feel at ease)	Executional Framework	Able to execute plans Reduce-tension--(less fatigue)
Dependable	Consumer Benefit	Dependable
On-time	Message Elements	On-time

FIG. 6.6. Strategic option 1—able to plan.

Level	MECCAs Model	Strategy
Security	Driving Force	Security
In-control Able to cope	Leverage Point	In-control--Able to cope (with kids, day)
Reduce tension (feel at ease)	Executional Framework	Mother/multiple kids Ground (primary) service In-flight (secondary) service-- emphasize tension reduction
Save time	Consumer Benefit	Save time
Ground service	Message Elements	Professional/personal service

FIG. 6.7.   Strategic option 2—running late.

A second strategic option (Fig. 6.7) ties "professional–personal service" as Message Elements to "save time" at the Consumer Benefit level. The Driving Force for this strategy is "security." One might think executionally in terms of a mother traveling with children. She needs personal service on the ground and in the air. The Leverage Point for this strategy is being "in-control," possibly demonstrated by being able to cope. This links the attributes and benefits to the values-level consideration of feeling secure, the rationale being that because one perceives being in control over one's situation in an environment that in reality does not offer that option, a positive feeling toward the provider of that service is created.

Thus, the two strategies differ in that one focuses on accomplishment, getting more done, whereas the other focuses on coping, being in control. Each of these foci offer opportunities for linking the coordinated efforts of the airline's personnel and equipment to important concerns of the passenger. Both strategies offer opportunities for linking direct associations with airlines to less direct, more personal associations linked to these initial distinctions. Further, by specifying the strategies in the MECCAs framework, there is the added assurance that important, personally-relevent consequences and values are portrayed as flowing from these (essentially nondifferentiatable) airline attributes. Thus, image, or the connection of product to self through relevant personalized meanings/associations with the product, is born.

RECAPITULATION

Working only with attributes is not the way to tap into or understand the components of image. The personalized translations of the attributes in terms of consequences and personal values must be identified. The more successful we are at developing a framework to distinguish across attributes, consequences, and values, the more valuable our research will be in aiding the image-creation process. The real key to understanding image lies in understanding linkages or connections between the levels that define the perceptual lens through which the consumer views the world and subsequently develops preferences for products.

Effective linkages can be established for products only when we can gain a perspective on how the product relates to the personal-value systems of consumers. By viewing means–end chains as entities, we can achieve this perspective. Admittedly, creative insight has to follow the procedures detailed above. The research process suggested here simply provides people in creative positions with the framework on which to focus their efforts, saving both time and energy.

The MECCAs framework not only makes it possible to develop effective strategies using this framework, it is also a valuable tool for identifying the thrust of competitive advertising. The MECCAs model can provide an easy-to-understand framework wherein management, creatives, and researchers can focus on an explicitly-stated agenda, whether it involves strategic options or competitive advertising.

REFERENCES

Arons, L. (1961). Does television viewing influence store image and shopping frequency? *Journal of Retailing, 37*, 1–13.

Boyd, H., Ray, M., & Strong, E. (1972). An attitudinal framework for advertising strategy. *Journal of Marketing, 36*, 2, 27–33.

Collins, A. M., & Loftus, E. F. (1975). A spreading-activation theory of semantic processing. *Psychological Review, 82*(6), 407–428.

Craik, F. I. M., & Lockhart, R. S. (1972). Levels of processing: A framework for memory research. *Journal of Verbal Learning and Verbal Behavior, 11*, 671–684.

Day, G. S. (1973). Theories of attitude structure and change. In S. Ward & T. S. Robertson (Eds.), *Consumer behavior: Theoretical sources.* Englewood Cliffs, NJ: Prentice-Hall.

Fishbein, M. (1967). A behavior theory approach to the relations between beliefs about an object and the attitude toward that object. In M. Fishbein (Ed.), *Readings in attitude theory and measurement.* New York: John Wiley.

Gutman, J. (1978). Uncovering the distinctions people make versus the use of multi-attribute models: Do a number of little truths make wisdom? *Proceedings of the 20th Annual Conference of the Advertising Research Foundation.* New York: Advertising Research Foundation.

Gutman, J. (1982). A means–end chain model based on consumer categorization processes. *Journal of Marketing, 46*(1), 60–72.

Gutman, J. (1983, May 13). Segment consumers, devise ad strategies with means–end chain analysis, "Ladders." *Marketing News*, pp. 6–7.

Gutman, J., & Reynolds, T. J. (1979). An investigation of the levels of cognitive abstraction utilized by consumers in product differentiation. In J. Eighmey (Ed.), *Attitude research under the sun* (pp. 128–150). Chicago: American Marketing Association.

Gutman, J., & Reynolds, T. J. (1983, Fall). An improved format for reporting repertory grid results. *Proceedings of American Marketing Association Educators' Conference.* (Chicago: American Marketing Association, 428–431).

Hirshman, E. C., Greenberg, B., & Robertson, D. H. (1978). The intermarket reliability of retail image research: An empirical examination. *Journal of Retailing, 54*(1), 3–12.

Jain, A. K., & Etgar, M. (1976–1977). Measuring store image through multidimensional scaling of free response data. *Journal of Retailing, 52*(4), 61–70.

James, D. L., Durand, R. M., & Dreves, R. A. (1976). The use of a multi-attribute attitude model in a store image study. *Journal of Retailing, 52*(2), 23–32.

Kelly, G. A. (1955). *The psychology of personal constructs.* New York: Norton.

Kover, A. (1988, May 13). Brand personality cluster offer vivid consumer profiles. *Marketing News,* p. 1.

Lindquist, J. D. (1974). Meaning of image: A survey of empirical and hypothetical evidence. *Journal of Retailing, 50*(4), 29–38.

Marks, R. B. (1976). Operationalizing the concept of store image. *Journal of Retailing, 52*(3), 37–46.

Martineau, P. (1958). The personality of the retail store. *Harvard Business Review, 36*(1), 47–55.

May, E. G. (1974–1975). Practical applications of recent retail image research. *Journal of Retailing, 50*(4), 15–20.

Myers, J. H., & Shocker, A. (1981). The nature of product-related attributes. In J. Sheth (Ed.), *Research in Marketing, 5.* JAI Press.

Ogilvy, D., (1963). *Confessions of an advertising man.* New York: Ballantine Books.

Olson, J. C., & Reynolds, T. J. (1983). Understanding consumers' cognitive structures: Implications for advertising strategy. In L. Percy & A. Woodside (Eds.), *Advertising and Consumer Psychology.* Lexington, MA: Lexington Books.

Oxenfeldt, A. R. (1974). Developing a favorable price-quality image. *Journal of Retailing, 50*(4), 8–14.

Percy, L. (1976). How market segmentation guides advertising strategy. *Journal of Advertising Research, 16*(5), 11–22.

Reynolds, T. J., & Gutman, J. (1983). Developing images for services through means-end chain analysis. In L. L. Berry, G. L. Shostack, & G. D. Upah (Eds.), *Emerging perspectives on service marketing* (pp. 40–44). Chicago: American Marketing Association.

Reynolds, T. J., & Gutman, J. (1984, February–March). Laddering: Extending the repertory grid methodology to construct attribute-consequence-value hierarchies. In R. E. Pitts & A. G. Woodside (Eds.), *Personal values and consumer psychology* (pp. 155–167). Lexington, MA: Lexington Books.

Rokeach, M. (1968). *Beliefs, attitudes and values.* San Francisco: Jossey Bass.

Sampson, P. (1972). Using the repertory grid test. *Journal of Marketing Research, 9*(1), 78–81.

Seggev, E. (1982). Testing persuasion by strategic positioning. *Journal of Advertising Research, 22*(1), 37–42.

Wilkie, W., & Pessemier, E. (1973). Issues in marketing's use of multi-attribute models. *Journal of Marketing Research, 10*(4), 428–441.

7

The Application of the MECCAS Model to the Development and Assessment of Advertising Strategy: A Case Study

Thomas J. Reynolds
Strategic Research, Development and Assessment

Alyce Byrd Craddock
Federal Express Corporation

The identification of viable positioning opportunities is a critical problem for marketing managers. In a mature product class, or one in which products are not uniquely differentiable with respect to product characteristics, the task is particularly difficult. To develop a unique positioning for a product in a competitive, perceptually crowded marketplace, a manager needs research tools and an interpretative framework that helps:

(1) *Identify* the perceptual orientations or segments that exist in the marketplace, including the personal motivations that provide the underlying basis for interpreting products or services.

(2) *Specify* the product's current strategic position as well as that of its competitors.

(3) *Integrate* the consumer perceptual information and the current assessment of strategic positionings into the identification, assessment, and choice of alternative strategies and communication.

The failure of most attempts to resolve this fundamental managerial problem is due to the lack of a framework that permits integration of both consumer research and advertising strategy specification. The problem is confounded by the fact that it is also extremely difficult to think divergently in the creation of new strategic positions. The ability to develop a meaningful set of advertising strategy options requires a framework that permits the strategist to generate alternatives that are grounded both in consumer perceptions and in the competitive environment of the marketplace.

The purpose of this chapter is to explain the use of one such frame-work, the MECCAS model (Reynolds & Gutman, 1984), to specify adver-tising strategy. To do so, we discuss an empirical application of the method to strategy development in the Overnight Delivery Service (ODS) market.

First, we discuss the theoretical literature and conceptual framework pertaining to the research methodologies that are used. Using examples, we detail how the understanding of the consumer gained from the re-search can be represented from a strategic perspective. Second, we pre-sent the MECCAS model and demonstrate its use to specify the compo-nents of advertising strategy. Third, we discuss how competitive advertis-ing strategies can be objectively contrasted using this conceptual framework. Lastly, we demonstrate the integration process by which the understanding of the consumer and the understanding of the competitive advertising can lead to the specification of a new advertising strategy. The example of this process using Federal Express advertising is then con-trasted on a pre–post basis.

BACKGROUND

Conceptual Perspective

From a conceptual standpoint, the advertising strategist's fundamental problem is to understand consumers at a strategic level and to use this knowledge as the basis for developing alternative positionings. A practi-cal solution to this problem has been accomplished by adopting an aggre-gate *means–end* chain approach to understanding consumers (Gutman, 1982; Young & Feigin, 1975). According to means–end theory, people have valued end-states toward which they strive and choose among alternative means of reaching those goals. Products and their attributes are valued because they are instruments — means — to valued ends. Thus the means that are in the products have salience only because they help reach the ends that are in the people.

The connections between the product and the person represent the per-sonal interpretation that serves to explain *why* a product or service is seen as being different and desirable. (And, as such, should be the primary goal of the communication process.) The linkage of the product to self can be seen to span three basic conceptual thought-process levels or levels of ab-straction. The product-specific level, attribute, represents both physical and abstract characteristics of the product/service. The person-specific level, personal values, represents the category-specific end states that are desirable. The critical link between these two levels is the consequence (of consumption or use) level, which comprises both positive and negative outcomes — see Table 7.1 for an example of a partial list of attributes, consequences, and values for the ODS category. (Note the relation of the definitions of levels of abstraction to the commonly used concept of benefit, which refers in means–end terminology to positive consequence. The

TABLE 7.1
Lexicon of Meaning for Overnight Delivery
Service Category (for Secretaries)

Attributes
  On-time
    delivery
    pickup
  Drop box

Consequences
  Reliable
    consistent, dependable
    guaranteed delivery
  Can do more
    more productive
  Save time
    less time wasted
    more efficient
  Makes me look good
    I'm credible
  Make more money
  Convenient
    no hassle
    easy to use
  Get promoted
    more responsibility
  Less worry
    makes job easier
    avoid responsibility for errors of others
  Avoid looking bad (to boss)
    not making mistakes

Values
  Peace of mind
    able to cope
  Personal satisfaction
    happiness
    a better person
  In control
    avoid taking responsibility
  Self-esteem
    self-assured
  Accomplishment
    achieve goals
    success

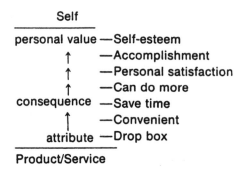

FIG. 7.1.   ODS perceptual pathway example.

avoidance of the contrasted negative consequences, then, are defined as being distinct from benefits. For example, avoiding a sun burn would not be considered a benefit in the means–end lexicon of meaning. It would instead be the avoidance of a negative consequence.) Attributes, then, can be thought of deriving their salience because of their ability to satisfy, provide, or avoid a given consequence, which in turn is deemed important because it satisfies a higher level personal value. Figure 7.1 shows a simple schematic of this relationship and corresponding examples across the levels from the ODS category.

The unique strength of the means–end paradigm is that it shows not only what key elements motivate consumers but also what the connections are between these motives and the tangible product or service attributes.

Perceptual Orientations

A perceptual orientation or perceptual segment represents a unique combination of an attribute (A) - consequence (C) - and a personal value (V). It is a unique way in which the product is interpreted with respect to self, through the translation of the A/C/V chain. The schematic in Fig. 7.1 of the translation of "drop box" through "convenience" to "accomplishment" and "self-esteem" serves as a prototypical example of this translation process to higher level meanings for one target segment of ODS, secretaries. It is important to note that these hierarchies represent *prototypical* orientations, which means that each respondent need not utilize every level in the respective hierarchy. Indeed, any given respondent is likely to effect a translation using only a subset of the total number of elements represented in the hierarchy.

The representation of these perceptual orientations in this way suggests that a summary map can be constructed that would minimize the redundancy between the orientations and thus make them easier to contrast and assess. Such a map is called a *hierarchical value map* (HVM). The HVM identifies the key content elements of memory and the associations that give meaning to the differences that consumers perceive between and among competitive products (Olson & Reynolds, 1984). The map seen in Fig. 7.2 is arranged hierarchically, with the more abstract values at the top and the concrete attributes at the bottom. It shows three different orientations, each representing a unique type of perceptual orientation toward the product category. The intermediate points within the orientation may be considered to be intermediate subcategories within the three major "levels of abstraction" content categories (see Olson & Reynolds, 1984, for a complete review of the various methods by which to classify these intermediate categories).

To illustrate, "reliable" seen in Fig. 7.2 is interpreted by secretaries in distinct ways, depending on their perception orientation. In this case, they value either the positive desire to look good or the ability to avoid looking bad (negative consequence). This apparently minor nuance, representing apparent bipolar opposites, is critical in that the more personal value orientations, which drive perceptual, are different. The motives of these segments are different and thus offer alternative positioning options. Again using the example, the instrumental level ("peace of mind"), meaning the

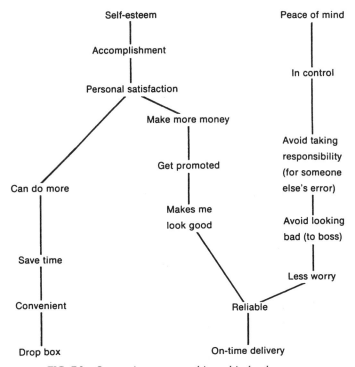

FIG. 7.2.   Secretaries summary hierarchical value map.

level just preceding the highest level personal value ("security"), supplies the meaningful interpretation or leverage into this end state. In combination, these high-level connections represent the driving forces that advertising may be oriented toward—the strategic direction.

Communication Perspective

Product positioning and the communication strategy that serves as the foundation for positioning, however, go far beyond simply identifying the driving force behind a particular product category. Successful advertising results when the communication operates simultaneously at many levels. In using the MECCAS framework, the researcher learns the elements of consumer motivation in the words consumers use (as opposed to manufacturer's jargon). The result is that the communication can be better integrated with perceptual keys that are more likely to affect the consumer—verbally (the right message with the right words) and visually (the setting for the advertising or how the characters behave or interact).

A complete strategy must also detail the message elements, which are in great part determined in the marketing environment by asking the question "Who owns what already?" A complete strategy must also spell out the specifics of the translation process across all levels of abstraction. One must also bear in mind the significant contribution the executional format can have in facilitating the translation process. Table 7.2 defines this communication-as-a-translation-process paradigm that is referred to as the Means-End Conceptualization of the Components of Advertising Strategy (MECCAS) (Reynolds & Gutman, 1984).

The strategic framework outlined by the MECCAS model addresses issue 2 by identifying the position of a product and its competitors. Moreover, it does so in a standard, strategically-based format. Although the analysis is subjective, numerous applications of the model have shown that marketing managers, marketing researchers, their agency counterparts, and agency creatives produce consistent evaluations that can usually be agreed on by all concerned. A particular benefit of this methodology is that because of its standard format for detailing strategy and because consumers supply their own words, it provides a much-needed lexicon that facilitates both client-agency interactions and agency management-creative interactions. This last point is critical. Prior to the MECCAS model no complete communication strategy paradigm existed that was predicated on positioning the product or service in terms of personal relevance to the consumer.

The identification of strategic alternatives requires a perceptual view of the marketplace within the means–end framework such as that exemplified by the secretaries' summary HVM presented in Fig. 7.2. That is, a value structure map for the target market of concern must be constructed, identi-

TABLE 7.2
MECCAS Model of Advertising Strategy

Level	Definition
Driving force	The value orientation of the strategy; the end-level to be focused on in the advertising.
Leverage point	The manner in which the advertising will "tap into," reach, or activate the value or end-level of focus; the specific key way in which the value is linked to the specific features in the advertising.
Executional framework	The overall scenario or action plot, plus the details of the advertising execution. The executional framework provides the "vehicle" by which the value orientation is to be communicated, especially the gestalt of the advertisement—its overall tone and style.
Consumer benefit	The major positive consequences for the consumer that are to be communicated, verbally or visually, in the advertising.
Message elements	The specific attributes, consequences, or features about the product that are communicated verbally or visually.

Source.   Reynolds and Gutman, 1984.

fying the key content elements and their dominant connections. Analysis of the current positions of the competition on the value structure map permits the construction of new strategy options in the same framework by locating a hierarchy yet untapped. The strategist can do this either by combining the elements in a new and meaningful way or by focusing on what is currently a unique level, or connection, within the existing hierarchy.

Clearly, the task of assessing and constructing strategies in the way is also subjective, relying on management interpretation. Yet the entire strategy process at present is virtually totally subjective with no real frame of reference for decision making. The MECCAS model provides a *framework for thinking* that permits managers to consider and contrast various strategic options, thereby significantly reducing subjectivity. Clearly, the key to developing innovative strategic alternatives lies in the understanding of the interaction of the content levels (the translation process indicated by the connections of linkages between concepts) for the consumer.

The process requires, first, that the value structure map be known as well as the complete set of meanings that underlie each content element. The problem then becomes one of identifying in consumer language the key content elements across the levels of abstraction and their respective linkages.

RESEARCH METHODOLOGY

A method that has been successful in providing the necessary content and linkage information in several varied product and service classes is a technique termed *laddering* (Gutman & Reynolds, 1979; Meyers, 1984; Peter &

Olson, 1987). The technique requires in-depth interviews in which respondents are confronted with products with which they are familiar. They are asked to make personal distinctions with respect to differences in perception or preference between or among competitive products. The researcher uses a series of directed probes to discover why these distinctions are personally relevant to them. The goal is to understand the links that connect the basic perceptual differences to the highest levels possible. The strategist seeks to understand the personal value that represents the underlying consumer motivation component.

Thus, two components of the laddering process are apparent. The first involves the elicitation of perceptual distinctions between and among products, using, for example, the triadic sort (Kelly, 1955) where the respondent is asked for some overall way within a three-product set in which two of the products or services could be considered different from the third. For example, when a secretary was asked to distinguish between Express Mail, DHL, and Federal Express, the basis of her developing a distinction is the perception that Federal Express has a drop box, and the other two do not. Once both poles of the distinction are elicited (drop box vs. no drop box), the respondent is asked which pole is preferred. It is this preferred pole that serves as the basis for the second component of laddering, which is the probing process. The process uncovers the personal connection or relevance of the attribute distinction in terms of what it means to the consumer.

This questioning process is personalized for each respondent, in an attempt to move continually higher, thereby uncovering the reasons that give each preceding level meaning and importance. The purpose of laddering can thus be seen as forcing the consumer up the "ladder of abstraction," uncovering elements across all attribute, consequence, and value levels. Typically, for each respondent several ladders can be elicited, representing the translations of the key salient attributes.

The development of an aggregate HVM across key target segments, which is usually based on 50 to 100 respondents, is accomplished by a two-step analysis that first requires a traditional content analysis of all elements elicited by the laddering procedure. Summary codes, representing the content categories output from the content analysis corresponding to the unique categories of response, are then used to summarize and codify the original ladders (see Table 7.1). The second step involves scoring and summarizing the dominant connections between key content elements (see Fig. 7.2). It is this summarization that yields the HVM map (see Reynolds & Gutman, 1988; for a complete exposition on both the laddering interviewing procedures and analysis methodology).

The value structure map or HVM once constructed then provides the ability to integrate in the same theoretically-based, consumer-driven framework the perceptual orientation information and the assessment of the current marketplace environment, from an overall strategic perspective. This permits the development and specification of advertising strategy alternatives (denoted earlier as issue 3).

Having come full circle in terms of specification and explanation of both the theory and research framework, the three highly interrelated issue areas can now be further explained by way of an example.

FEDERAL EXPRESS ADVERTISING STRATEGY RESEARCH AND IMPLEMENTATION

Although Federal Express was the initiator of the overnight delivery business and had award-winning advertising on-air, the entry of serious competition in the marketplace (DHL, UPS, Purolator, and the U.S. Postal Service's Express Mail) caused some serious questioning in the spring of 1983 about the long-term appropriateness of their advertising strategy. This questioning, focusing primarily on strategic issues, suggested the use of MECCAS as an approach to offer both assessment of the competitive environment as well as strategic direction.

The output from the consumer research phase was to be used in two ways. The first was to build a set of statements to be used to objectively assess, on a strategic level, the competitive advertising. (In addition, a substantive issue emerged on how the humor trademark that Federal Express was known by would fit into the MECCAS framework.) The second research issue concerned the specification of HVMs for each key target market, namely, secretaries, traffic managers, and executives of small and large corporations, as well as an overall value map across all groups. It is these maps that would serve as a basis of developing an understanding of the consumer orientations to the ODS market, which would then serve as the framework to specify the components of advertising strategy.

A total of 81 2-hour laddering interviews were conducted across the four target segments, the only additional screening requirement being that the individual was the primary decision maker as to what air express company was selected. Half the interviews were used for the purpose of developing a strategy assessment instrument. Following a procedure suggested by Gutman and Reynolds (1986), statements were generated that corresponded to each concept elicited by the respondents at each level of abstraction. These statements were then used in the remaining interviews to assess the commercials.

The specific research and assessment findings presented in the following sections have been limited in terms of the target group (secretaries, "facilitators" of ODS) and the advertising reviewed. This was done due to the proprietary nature of such strategic findings.

Strategy Assessment

The MECCAS summary of advertising strategy for two competitors and the then current Federal Express campaign appears in Tables 7.3, 7.4, and 7.5, respectively. The specifics of the execution are also expressly detailed so that the reader can recall or at least visualize the actual advertising. The examples of how MECCAS is utilized in the specification of the strategic

TABLE 7.3
MECCAS Representation of DHL

Primary target:	Business executives/"generators" of ODS
Driving force:	Achievement/success
Leverage point:	Trust in (service of) company re: in control
Executional framework:	A. C. Nielsen, chairman of A. C. Nielsen Company, explains that American businesses count on his Nielsen ratings. He discusses reasons why he counts on DHL for time-critical overnight deliveries.
Consumer benefit:	Reliable/can count on convenience
Message elements:	Thirty-thousand locations
	More on-time deliveries to more places around the world than anybody
Tagline:	"Next best thing to taking it there yourself"

TABLE 7.4
MECCAS Representation of Express Mail

Primary target:	Secretaries/"facilitators" of ODS
Driving force:	Accomplishment
Leverage point:	Personal satisfaction re: in control
Executional framework:	Secretary in office with her boss, sitting in the background. Boss appears rather frantic. Secretary mimics a client who demanded a package overnight from her boss. She recites a mocking dialogue she had with her boss relating to her choice of overnight delivery service. The client calls the secretary about receiving the package. With signs of relief, the boss confidently retorts back to secretary.
Consumer benefit:	Makes me look good
	Less worry
	Reliable
Message elements:	Deliver 70,000 packages on-time every day
	Two-pound package just $9.35, about half of what most others charge
Tagline:	"We make you look good for less."

TABLE 7.5
MECCAS Representation of Federal Express (1983)

Primary target:	Business executives/"generators" of ODS
Driving force:	
Leverage point:	In control (weak)
Executional framework:	Humorous execution. Executive telephoning delivery service agent about the urgency of receiving package at specific time in the morning. The package contains slides for a major business presentation. The agent repeatedly responds that the package will arrive on-time while background co-workers are ineptly working. The next day the executive calls inquiring about undelivered package. With the failure of delivery, the executive reverts to performing hand animations on the projection screen in meeting room while waiting for the package.
Consumer benefit:	Less worry Avoid looking bad
Message elements:	10:30 AM delivery
Tagline:	Next time send it Federal Express — when we say "you got it, you'll get it."

components follows, prior to a more objective assessment of the ads. The understanding gained by first becoming completely familiar with the MECCAS framework is essential in that the formal specification of a new strategic direction requires a working knowledge of the interrelation of the various components. MECCAS is thus viewed as a framework of thinking in consumer-based terminology, one that mirrors the translation process that communications are intended to facilitate.

Basically, DHL's use of a credible spokesperson, Arthur Nielsen (who is relatively well-known for his business requirements of accuracy and reliability), provides an excellent executional frame that serves to communicate both the credibility of the company and the rationally based reasons why the company is superior, namely, "key service facts" including the vast number of "delivery locations" served. The primary target of this ad would appear to be businessmen or "generators" of documents, with office workers or "facilitators" as secondary. This DHL execution appears to work well, at least subjectively assessed, at all levels of MECCAS and can be viewed as successful in translating the service attributes to personally relevant characteristics contained in the higher order value orientations.

Paradoxically, the obvious strength of the ad and the potential weakness of the strategy is in the choice of Arthur Nielsen as the spokesperson. The assessment summarized with the other two ads in Table 7.6 shows that the advertisement clearly benefits from Mr. Nielsen. A nearly identical DHL execution of the same executional format (and strategy) with Ted Turner as the spokesperson performed significantly worse (in terms of subsequent strategic communication assessment) than the Nielsen spot.

TABLE 7.6
Statements Distinguishing Selected ODS Advertising Strategies
(Percentage Statement Endorsement: 0 = 0%; 10 = 100%)

Statements	DHL	Express Mail	Federal Express
Driving force			
Self-esteem	5	1	1
Peace of mind	6	2	1
Accomplishment	[7]	1	1
Leverage point			
Trust in company	[9]	3	[4]
In control	[7]	3	2
Personal/job satisfaction	4	[5]	2
Executional framework			
Ad shows reality	[7]	4	4
Can laugh at situation	0	4	[7]
Ad too cute	0	4	1
Demonstrates personal service	[8]	2	2
Characters believable	[9]	4	2
Situation demeaning	0	[5]	2
Situation hectic	1	[6]	[9]
Consumer benefit			
Convenient to use	[8]	2	2
Makes me look good	5	[7]	3
Dependable service	[9]	1	[7]
Less worry	[8]	5	4
Inexpensive	0	[9]	0
Message elements			
Numerous delivery locations	[9]	3	3
Relevant service facts	[8]	[7]	4
Gives actual prices	0	[9]	0
On-time delivery	1	6	[8]

Clearly, in this case, the spokesperson to a great degree is the strategy. Therefore, this strategy suffers from potential lack of recognizability by primary and secondary target markets. In addition, the ability to find other spokespersons as credible as Mr. Nielsen is of issue.

The Express Mail ad from the U.S. Postal Office, apparently targeted at "facilitators," secretaries, and office help, clearly stresses price as their superior point of differentiation. "Looking good" reinforces the secretarial benefit as does the "hectic situation" portrayed. Ultimately, the personal satisfaction obtained from being "in control" of the situation as well as reinforcing the key role the secretary plays in the office-to-office communication process pays off in the feeling of "personal and job satisfaction." Overall, the ad communicates the competitive advantage on price of this overnight service quite well, with the higher level meanings being represented, albeit not very powerfully.

The classic Federal Express advertising is summarized in Table 7.5. The communication of "on-time delivery," leading to the consumer benefit, "dependable service," is humorously portrayed in the clever executional frames. It serves to provide the key communication elements of the overnight delivery category. The higher levels, representing the personal meanings, however, are not as well communicated as in the other two competitors' strategies. Clearly, the humor and identification with Federal Express, together with the fact that the name Federal Express had become virtually a synonym for overnight delivery, has resulted in great equity both in the advertising and in the name. The great strength of the initial dramatization of negative consequences through humor had been a great success in building awareness for this new service. But with the new competitive environment, the question about a long-term strategic focus is raised.

The importance of operating at all levels was considered to be important, thereby ensuring as much personal relevance as possible that can be translated to the product as well as bolstering the rational foundation, message elements, that permits positive product and service differentiation. This latter point, given the price superiority that virtually all the competition enjoyed and their ever-increasing, on-time performance statistics, put Federal Express in a potentially vulnerable position. And finally, although a stronger strategic frame (calling for a new strategic focus) at all levels was apparently desirable, it was also clear that the consumer equity of the humor in the executions should not be abandoned.

The examples of the initial, subjective MECCAS assessment detailed earlier can now be contrasted with the objective summary presented in Table 7.6. In addition, the results of simple percentage endorsements of statements corresponding to the key concepts for all three ads can now be used to contrast the communication effectiveness of the respective executions on a strategic basis. Note that these simple percentages represent only a subset of the actual statements used. In empirical application, strategic assessment of this type requires typically from 50 to 60 such statements. The key statements used in the assessment of these ads are bracketed. A brief summary of the interpretation follows.

At the message element level, the Federal Express ad does communicate on-time delivery, which can be seen as the fundamental basis for any use of ODS. The fact that the competition, as noted earlier, is reaching an equivalent level of performance on this dimension suggests that finding another basis that is not as potentially vulnerable is advisable. The DHL ad uses as an attribute basis, or reason to believe, the "numerous delivery locations" that serve to give them credibility as being a viable alternative to Federal Express. The Express Mail ad focuses on price as a leverage at the attribute level, which is apparently considered a relevant service fact.

The summary assessment of items at the consumer benefit level reveals the translations of the attributes or message elements into personally meaningful terms. The on-time delivery for Federal Express corresponds to dependable service. The DHL ad communicates even more strongly dependable service, as well as less worry and convenient to use. The effect of Mr. Nielsen as the spokesperson is seen to have a direct influence on the assessment of the service. The price message in Express Mail is translated, as expected, to "inexpensive," whereas the secretary-based execution also results in the communication of "makes me look good."

Executionally, the trademark of humor in the Federal Express advertising is evidenced by the strong joint endorsement of "situation hectic" and "can laugh at situation." The inferiority of Federal Express on "demonstrates personal service," however, as compared to DHL can be seen to be problematic. The use of a realistic situation in the DHL ad ("ad shows reality") and "believable characters" permits not only the consumer benefit of "dependable service" to be communicated but also serves to provide the basis for higher level meanings to be communicated. The Express Mail execution demonstrates an interesting problem. The endorsement of the "hectic situation" statement reflecting the executional frame probably influences the strong endorsement of "dependable service" at the consumer benefit level, but due to the fact the secretary is apparently in charge of the boss, the statement "situation is demeaning" is also endorsed. This leads one to speculate whether the ad may be serving to alienate one potential target market, the generators.

Evaluation of the higher levels, leverage point and driving force, shows the failure of Federal Express to move beyond and translate their executional humor into anything personally relevant, at least in reference to the "facilitator" target group. This is also true of the Express Mail ad. In contrast, DHL, again due primarily to Mr. Nielsen, does communicate accomplishment, through being in control and trust in company.

Overall, the DHL strategy appears as the most integrated across all levels, thus providing the best translation into personally relevant terms. The Express Mail ad focusing on price works well at the service characteristic levels. The executionally driven Federal Express ad, however, appears not to be as firmly grounded in the basic characteristics of the service and does not permit the higher levels to be reached. The question, then, is what options for the modification of strategy exist, while retaining the basic humor trademark?

Strategic Direction

The second objective of the consumer research, the determination of key linkages across content elements (Table 7.1) representing perceptual communications for different target markets, serves as the framework for evaluation of strategic alternatives. For purposes of illustration, only the secretaries' HVM presented in Fig. 7.2 is used as a basis to demonstrate how this approach, based on understanding consumer motivation, can be used to provide strategic direction. For brevity, the evaluation of the critical target market considerations central to any strategy is left out of this discussion. For purposes of exposition, the focus is limited to the secretary's perspective detailed in the example date.

Prior to the detailing of the manner in which the maps can be interpreted, a few general comments about MECCAS need to be made. The best analogy for overviewing communication as a translation process is that of the brightness of an electric light and the circuit that provides it the energy to burn. It is assumed in the MECCAS framework that the more tightly a product or service is linked to self, thereby achieving personal relevance, the more likely the product or service will be preferred. Like electric current, then, the wiring or linking of strategic elements (A/C/V) from the product to the person must be solidly connected across all intermediate points. A loose connection allowing only part of the current to be passed on results in a weaker light and, analogously, a weaker strategy. Further, this analogy suggests that if one level does not exist, the connection cannot be made.

In our example, all levels need to exist to make the best connection between the product and self. Of course, the analogy offered here is meant to be interpreted on a conceptual level. Clearly, this simplified device does not imply that managers should ignore concepts such as the product life cycle, the current market, and the communications environment. However, as a basic perspective, this analogy would appear to have merit and can serve as a fundamental way of thinking about communication strategy.

Another general rule of thumb concerning MECCAS is that a firm foundation or point of differentiation at an attribute level is a necessity. This attribute level basis, however, may be explicitly or implicitly communicated. Without a solid attribute foundation, the circuit can be envisioned to have no source and thus no chance of providing the necessary current to the light. Although the bases of preference have been shown to be driven at the higher levels of abstraction as compared to attributes (Jolly, Slocum, & Reynolds, 1988; Reynolds, Gutman, & Fiedler, 1984; Reynolds & Jamieson, 1984), the attribute-based "reason why" is required by the consumer to rationalize his or her choice behavior. To reinforce this fact, the consumer decision makers in the previous-mentioned studies consistently rated the relative importance of the attribute levels, in terms of preference, significantly higher than either consequences or personal values. This was true even though the research showed their preferences to be driven by higher level concepts.

The rational hook to justify choice, in particular in a category such as this where justification of choice may be required, should be considered a critical basis of any strategic positioning. And, more specifically, the strategic issue at hand given the major price differences that exist in the marketplace makes this perspective gain more validity.

In the following section, we attempt to review each of the components with a brief rationale as to the underlying basis of the strategic considerations. Given the logical rules of MECCAS, the first place to assess and contrast the relative strengths and inherent weaknesses of the 1983 Federal Express advertising strategy would be at the message element level.

Contrasting the two competitive ads to the Federal Express execution reveals that the communication of "relevant service facts" for the competition lends the basic support for delivering the respective consumer benefits. The rational "reason why" gives the consumer a foundation from which the service can be interpreted with respect to self. From a strategic perspective, there existed a need to investigate unique service facts that positively differentiate Federal Express from the competition and are not things that can be attacked or potentially dominated by the competition. Thus, a directed effort at finding such a fundamental basis for differentiation was undertaken.

The resulting answer to this issue was to focus on the advanced satellite communications system upon which Federal Express bases their unique service features. The viability of this approach, which led ultimately to its implementation, stems from the fact that it was generalizable due to the numerous facets or components of the network that could be portrayed. Additionally, the ability to tap into various target segments and job roles corresponding to the relevance of these network components also played a role in its ultimate acceptance.

It was decided that at the consumer benefit level "dependable service" was basic and must therefore be maintained. In addition, however, a strong desire to permit a more personal interpretation was also sought. "Less worry" became a second strategic element within the consumer benefit component that was decided upon as desirable and thus was included as a strategic goal.

Moving to the higher personal value levels, a strategic goal of "peace of mind" was thought to fit well with the ultimate translation of "advanced satellite communications" to "dependable service" and "less worry" and thus became the driving force component. The selection of the leverage point, though usually the most difficult specification, was in this case relatively easy. The success of communicating "trust in company" and being "in control" in the DHL advertising was seen to be a natural bridge to the already specified components, one that could be grounded in more specific, more relevant message elements.

Because all components of the communication strategy except for the executional framework were specified, the sole remaining task was to bring the strategy to reality. The major constraint of this process was to maintain the look of the traditional Federal Express ads, specifically the humorous style, while building key linkages from the new message support to the personal interpretation. The summary of the specification of the strategic components and its specific implementation executionally is reported in the MECCAS summary of 1986 advertising seen in Table 7.7.

The common executional frame utilized in all the ads generated from this strategy was to show a typical ODS crisis, show a hand outside the scene interrupt, and have the voice to which the hand belongs explain why the integrated, satellite-based, communication network that Federal Express has permits the resolution of the problem of interest. Thus, much of the executional humor stemming from the situation and the characters portrayed was still maintained, but the new "reasons why" Federal Express was superior to the other ODS alternatives could be communicated.

Table 7.8 shows a comparison of the key strategic components of 1983 and 1986 Federal Express advertising. One statement was added to the 1986 research, namely, "advanced communication system," this being the new message element component of the strategy. A review of the gains in degree of endorsement percentages made across the levels, with very few sacrifices, indicates more the creative expertise in developing the new ads. From a strategic perspective the new strategy delivers well at all levels, delivering an integrate communication to the consumer.

The success of the new communication strategy for Federal Express, as measured by its ability to meet *prespecified* objectives, is seen. The relevant communication of a differentiating message element and its linkage

TABLE 7.7
MECCAS Representation of Federal Express (1986)

Primary target:	Secretaries–"facilitators" of ODS
Driving force:	Peace of mind
Leverage point:	In control re: company can trust
Executional framework:	Humorous execution with a secretary working hard at finding status information of an ODS. The boss and employee are interrupted and taken by guide to view Federal Express satellite communication system used to track exact status of overnight letters and packages. Secretary realizes the benefit available in using Federal Express.
Consumer benefit:	Reliable–dependability
	Makes work easier
Message elements:	Superior tracking system
	Integrated satellite communications network
Tagline:	"Why fool around with anyone else?"

TABLE 7.8
Statements Distinguishing Federal Express Advertising Strategies
(Percentage Statement Endorsement: 0 = 0%; 10 = 100%)

Statements	1983	1986
Driving force		
Self esteem	1	1
Peace of mind	1	[5]
Accomplishment	1	2
Leverage point		
Trust in company	[4]	[7]
In control	2	[5]
Personal–job satisfaction	2	[5]
Executional framework		
Ad shows reality	4	[6]
Can laugh at situation	[7]	[6]
Ad too cute	1	1
Demonstrates personal service	2	5
Characters believable	2	4
Situation demeaning	2	4
Situation hectic	[9]	[7]
Consumer benefit		
Convenient to use	2	5
Makes me look good	3	1
Dependable service	[7]	[9]
Less worry	4	[9]
Inexpensive	0	0
Message elements		
Numerous delivery locations	3	0
Relevant service facts	4	[7]
Gives actual prices	0	0
On-time delivery	[8]	5
Advanced communications system	*	[10]

*Not asked in the initial 1983 assessment.

across the levels of abstraction that correspond to the perceptual orientation of the facilitators' target group, secretaries, is achieved.

CONCLUSION

As marketers, we believe that choices of strategic positions that result from the understanding of consumers' perceptions, preferences, and buying motives will in general be superior to those that do not. As managers, we recognize that the strategy is the important thing, and insist that programs we develop and implement support that strategy. In this article, we discuss a framework that encourages the integration of consumer research into advertising strategy specification. Although developing advertising strategy is never an entirely objective task, the use of the MECCAS framework is seen to provide an objective basis on which the strategic process can be grounded.

In marketing practice, the ability to use as much detailed consumer input as possible as an aid in the strategic process is considered crucial, and thus drives significant marketing research programs. A problem arises when the knowledge base gained from consumer research is to be translated for application to strategic planning and decision making. Traditional marketing research does not have a framework by which the understanding gained can be either directly assessed for the development of strategic options or can be specified in a consumer-based strategy format. The result of not having such a consumer-based strategy framework is undue subjectivity in the translation process of research findings underlying the development of advertising strategy.

Although the MECCAS model illustrated in this chapter derives its primary research input from the laddering component, the opportunity to perform strategy specification in consumer terminology can be seen to have broad value in terms of potential application. Having a framework that condenses the knowledge base of consumer meanings, including the particular ways in which consumers' interpret relevant product information with respect to higher level personal motivations, provides a simple structure that can be used to focus on the specific strategic issues. The framework, then, is the key to managing the development and assessment of strategic alternatives.

The MECCAS framework, grounded in consumer perceptual theory, appears to offer marketing management four key advantages. First, MECCAS permits the exact specification of how the product is to be positioned with respect to the consumer, by explicitly showing the motivations that drive product perception and preference. Second, MECCAS provides a common communications framework for the discussion of strategy issues among the client, the agency, and their respective research groups. Third, the MECCAS framework provides a common basis on which the competitions' advertising strategies can be discussed. Finally, MECCAS can be used not only to develop advertising strategy but also to assess the creative product on a strategic level.

ACKNOWLEDGMENTS

We would like to thank Jon Gutman, John Norton, and Monique Vrinds for their helpful discussions and editorial assistance.

REFERENCES

Gutman, J. (1982). A means-end chain model based on consumer categorization processes. *Journal of Marketing, 46,* 2, 60–72.

Gutman, J., & Reynolds, T. J. (1979). An investigation at the levels of cognitive abstraction utilized by the consumers in product differentiation. In J. Eighmey (Ed.), *Attitude research under the sun* (pp. 128–150). Chicago: American Marketing Association.

Gutman, J., & Reynolds, T. J. (1986). Coordinating assessment to strategy development: An advertising assessment paradigm based on the MECCAS approach. In J. Olson & K. Sentis (Eds.), *Advertising and consumer psychology* (Vol. 3, pp. 242–258). New York: Praeger.

Jolly, J. P., Slocum, J. W., & Reynolds, T. J. (1988). Application of the means-end theoretic for understanding the cognitive bases of performance appraisal. *Organizational Behavior and Human Decision Processes, 41,* 153–180.

Kelly, G. A. (1955). *The psychology of personal constructs.* New York: Norton.

Meyers, W. (1984). *The image makers.* New York: Times Books.

Olson, J., & Reynolds, T. J. (1983). Understanding consumers' cognitive structures: Implications for marketing strategy. In L. Percy & A. G. Woodside (Eds.), *Advertising and consumer psychology* (pp. 77–90). Lexington, MA: Lexington Books.

Peter, J. P., & Olson, J. (1987). *Consumer behavior: Marketing strategy perspectives.* Homewood, IL: Irwin.

Reynolds, T. J., & Gutman, J. (1984). Advertising is image management. *Journal of Advertising Research, 24,* 1, 27–37.

Reynolds, T. J., & Gutman, J. (1988). Laddering theory, method, analysis, and interpretation. *Journal of Advertising Research, 28,* 1, 11–31.

Reynolds, T. J., Gutman, J., & Fiedler, J. (1985). Understanding consumers' cognitive structures: The relationship of levels of abstraction to judgements [sic] of psychological distance and preference. In L. Alwitt & A. A. Mitchell (Eds.), *Psychological processes and advertising effects: Theory, research and practice* (pp. 261–272). Hillsdale, NJ: Lawrence Erlbaum Associates.

Reynolds, T. J., & Jamieson, L. (1985). Image representations: An analytic framework. In J. Jacoby & J. C. Olson (Eds.), *Perceived quality: How consumers view stores and merchandise* (pp. 115–138). Lexington, MA: Lexington Books.

Young, S., & Feigin, B. (1985). Using the benefit chain for improved strategy formulation. *Journal of Marketing, 39,* 70–72.

8

The a-b-e Model of Benefit Focus in Advertising

John R. Rossiter
Australian Graduate School of Management

Larry Percy
Marketing Consultant

Probably the most important purpose of advertising is to promote the benefit or benefits of the advertiser's brand. However, the term *benefit* is used rather generally in advertising to refer to several points of promotional focus (Rossiter & Percy, 1987) that include *attributes* (what the product has), *benefits* per se (what the buyer wants), and *emotions* (what the buyer feels). According to this a-b-e distinction, attributes, the first potential focal point, are relatively objective properties of the product or service. Benefits, the second potential focal point, are subjective reinforcers, often, but not necessarily, resulting from an attribute. Emotions, the third potential focal point, are the affective experience of the reinforcement itself. Often called the end-benefit, emotions may derive from a benefit or, we note, may be a free-standing emotional association with the brand. For a brand of coffee, for instance, good-quality coffee beans are an attribute, good tasting is the benefit, and gustatory enjoyment is the emotional consequence. For a bank, for instance, numerous ATM machines are an attribute, fast service is the benefit, and relief from one of life's hassles by being able to allot a predictably short time to banking transactions is the emotional consequence.

Which point or points of benefits to focus on in an ad is an unsolved and somewhat randomly approached problem in advertising. Should the ad focus on the attribute point, or on the benefit point, or on the emotional point? Relatedly, should the ad attempt to establish paths (implied causal sequences) between points, such as attribute-to-benefit or benefit-to-emotion? No model to date has comprehensively addressed these questions — not even the means–end model that is the theme of this volume. In this chapter, we propose an a-b-e (attribute-benefit-emotion) model that we believe to be an improvement on the means–end model and that is designed to answer the question of which point to focus on in ads.

The chapter proceeds as follows. First, we consider the obvious but infrequently asked question of whether benefits (of either the a, b, or e type) are necessary in ads. Second, we introduce the a-b-e model and examine what we believe to be its advantages over the well-known means–end model. In the third, fourth, and fifth sections of the chapter, we postulate the conditions for attribute focus, benefit focus and emotion focus, respectively — including relevant paths that end with one of these points as the focus. Finally, we review what remains to be done to develop the a-b-e model further.

ARE BENEFITS NECESSARY IN ADS?

Brand awareness and brand attitude, in Rossiter and Percy's (1987, 1997) theory (see also Percy & Rossiter, 1992; Rossiter, Percy, & Donovan, 1991), are regarded as the two universal communication objectives that every ad must address. Whereas brand attitude usually is triggered by the presence of benefits in ads, it can also be cued by the brand name alone. There are a number of cases in which "benefit-less" ads are employed. We should examine these carefully because they logically pose the question of whether "no benefit" should be one of the points (a null-alternative point) in our model.

Resnik-Stern Content Analyses

A number of content analyses initiated or influenced by the original Resnik and Stern (1977) study and summarized in Stern and Resnik (1991) have attempted to measure the proportion of advertisements in various media that contain *information*, defined as "cues ... to assist a typical buyer in making an intelligent choice" (Stern & Resnik, 1991, p. 36). From the studies cited by or conducted by Resnik and Stern, it appears that about 90% of business publication ads, 80% of consumer magazine ads, but only 51% of major network TV commercials contain information. The informational cues permitted by Resnik and Stern are, understandably, focused on physical attributes of the product or service. For instance, in 1986 network TV commercials, Resnik and Stern (1991) found the following incidences of types of informational cues:

components or contents — 22%;

new ideas — 15%;

price or value — 9%;

performance — 8.5%;

special offers — 7%;

nutrition — 7%;

usage demonstrations — 6%;

packaging or shape — 4%;

availability — 3.5%;

quality — 3%;

guarantees or warranties — 33%;

taste — 1%; and

safety — 0%,

although this last type was found in earlier content analyses. These types of information cues would be characteristic of what Rossiter and Percy (1987) called the informational advertising style.

Resnik and Stern explicitly excluded image ads or the transformational style of advertising in Rossiter and Percy's terminology. Although excluding them from their studies, however, they admitted that image ads may be informative for consumers seeking to satisfy psychological or social motives (Stern & Resnik, 1991). Image advertisements often contain benefits that are not directly attribute-derived and emotional cues that can guide the buyer's choice. Thus, it would not be correct to conclude from the Resnik–Stern content analyses that approximately half of TV commercials are benefit-less. Rather, most ads, including TV commercials, would include one or more benefits in the broad sense of attributes or benefits or emotions.

Brand-Awareness-Only Ads

Advertisements that contain nothing more than the brand name or visual brand logo can positively influence choice and purchase behavior — a fact that has long been established. This is because, in order for choice to occur and indeed for brand attitude to be operational, the prospective buyer must first be aware of the brand (Rossiter & Percy, 1987; Rossiter et al., 1991; see also the popular ASSESSOR new product trial model as described, for example, by Lilien, Kotler, & Moorthy, 1992). This can be expressed by the conditional equation:

$$P \text{ (Choice)} = P \text{ (Preference} \mid \text{Aware)}$$
$$= P \text{ (Brand attitude} \mid \text{Brand awareness)}$$

Thus, choice of a particular brand can increase simply by raising its awareness even with attitude held constant (Nedungadi, 1990). For instance, on a 0 to 1 scale, where 1 represents maximum favorability or maximum strength, a buyer might have equal attitudes, 0.7 and 0.7, toward Heineken and Beck's beer brands. However, if Heineken can raise its brand awareness to 0.8 while Beck's stays at, say, 0.6, then the relative choice probabilities in the conditional model are 0.56 for Heineken and 0.42 for Beck's. Thus, Heineken will be more likely to be chosen on the next purchase occasion. Moran (1990) has called this brand awareness effect *salience*. We would add that the type of awareness heightened by advertising must be correct in terms of brand recognition or brand recall according to the buyer's choice process (Holden, 1993; Rossiter & Percy, 1987; Rossiter et al., 1991).

For a new brand, it would be most unlikely that advertising would be initiated with only brand awareness content and no brand attitude (and therefore no benefit) content. Whereas it is known that repeated exposure to a name or logo alone can increase attitude via the mere exposure effect (Birnbaum, 1981; Moore & Hutchinson, 1985; Zajonc, 1968), this effect is relatively weak, and it would be inadvisable for advertisers to try it when launching a new brand.

For an established brand, however, benefit-less advertising is a different matter. In a very interesting analysis, Fraser Hite, Hite, and Minor (1991) recommended the use, when certain conditions hold, of what they somewhat pejoratively call *dissipative ads*—ads that mention the brand name only or the brand name and price in the case of retail advertising. The conditions for recommending the use of a dissipative ad are, firstly, that the brand is an established one and, secondly, that there is a reasonably large segment of consumers who wish to reduce their search and brand comparison time and are willing to pay a slight premium for doing so. It has been estimated that consumers are willing to overpay, on average, by about 12% for brand-name items that *Consumer Reports* or other objective rating sources have shown to be no different in performance quality from lesser-name brands (Anson & Silverstone, 1975 [who estimated a 14% premium], Fraser Hite et al. (1991); Hjorth-Anderson, 1984, Sproles, 1986). Comparative brand performance quality is often practically unascertainable by consumers. Because *Consumer Reports* tests brands side-by-side, differences are often found; however, consumers test products in a sequential fashion during normal usage, and their indirect comparisons are often insufficient to detect differences between brands.

However, we would emphasize that there is still a need for brand attitude content (benefit) in the brand's prior advertising, even if its later, mature-status advertising can be reduced to what is essentially a brand awareness advertisement. Only later it is likely that the brand name or logo alone is a sufficient cue for the prospective buyer to mentally supply a previously-established favorable attitude (perhaps via a cognitive response or simply by an automatically elicited affective response) without a direct brand attitude or benefit cue having to be present in the ad.

We should also mention the related case of sponsorship, whereby billboards or posters at sporting events or other public venues contain simply the brand name or logo. In Rossiter and Percy (1987), we note the example of LaCoste ads at tennis tournaments. The likelihood here is that either the target audience supplies a previously established favorable attitude or that the context in which the ad is shown, for instance a prestigious tennis event, supplies the favorable emotional cue that forms a brand attitude during exposure.

Ads for Socially Negative Established Products

There is one other circumstance in which no benefit would be recommended from the advertiser's standpoint. This is for socially negative, but established products. The reason for avoiding benefits is to prevent counter-arguing, by both social critics and the target audience, who already know the benefits of the brand. For instance, the single word *Marlboro* is now virtually sufficient for its advertising. The Marlboro cowboy is being rendered in abstract or phased out (Hwang, 1992). Whether the attitude will stay positive, over the long run and with new consumers, is doubtful, however, although we observe that the Marlboro brand attitude is well supported by interpersonal influence among younger smokers.

Overall, we see that there are rare circumstances in which truly benefit-less ads are used. Where benefits are not used, there are supplementary explanations as to why the brand attitude objective is nevertheless likely to be met. Certain types of sponsorships are the only circumstance in which benefit-less ads may have to be used. Established but socially negative products are one circumstance in which benefit-less ads should be used. Retail (re-) advertising of well-known brands is a circumstance where benefit-less ads can be used. These circumstances could justify our formulating an a-b-e model. However, we concentrate on the far more prevalent circumstances of the explicit use of benefits in ads, for which we propose the a-b-e model.

THE a-b-e MODEL OF BENEFIT FOCUS

Attributes, Benefits, and Emotions

As we commented at the outset, advertisers use the term *benefit* in a rather general way. More specifically, a benefit is any potential negative or positive reinforcer. This is in line with Rossiter and Percy's (1987) definition of

TABLE 8.1
Definitions of Attributes, Benefits, and Emotions
in the a-b-e Model. Also Defined is Motivation

Term	Colloquial Definition	Technical Definition
Attribute	What the product *has*	Physical features of product (e.g., caffeine content) or objective characteristics of service (e.g., waiting time)
Benefit	What the buyer *wants*	Negative (relief) or positive (reward) reinforcer, subjectively experienced by buyer or user
Emotion	What the buyer *feels*	Affective experience of the reinforcer itself (e.g., anxiety → peace of mind; or elation)
Motive	*Why* the buyer wants it	Fundamental drive-reinforcement energizing mechanisms, namely: problem removal, problem avoidance, incomplete satisfaction, mixed approach-avoidance, normal depletion (negatively originated or informational motives), sensory gratification, intellectual stimulation or mastery, and social approval (positively originated or transformational motives)

brand attitude as representing overall delivery (a super-belief about the brand) on a negatively originated or positively originated purchase or usage motivation. A *reinforcer* is any stimulus that tends to increase a response. It could be a positive reinforcer, as in the good-tasting coffee example, or a negative reinforcer, as in the bank's reduced waiting-time example. For benefits in ads, the reinforced response is brand attitude. Occasionally, the advertiser may wish to decrease an attitude and may include *disbenefits* or punishers, as in public service campaigns.

For the a-b-e model, however, we must distinguish more sharply between attributes, benefits, and emotions. Table 8.1 provides definitions of these terms, as we use them. An *attribute* is what the product has — physical features, for a product, or objective characteristics, for a service, such as delivery time. A *benefit* is what the buyer wants — subjective relief or subjective reward. An *emotion* is what the buyer feels — sometimes before or after a benefit and at other times, independently. In this framework, if a benefit is what the buyer wants, then a *motive* is why the buyer wants it — that is, to satisfy a currently relevant motivation.

All ads display or imply benefits in one form or another — as attributes, benefits, or emotions. At the micropositioning level, the advertiser has to decide whether to focus primarily on the attribute (a), or on the benefit (b), or on the emotion (e). Of course, combinations of these focal points are possible and are theoretically specified in our model.

The a-b-e Model of Benefit Focus

An a-b-e model of the alternative points of focus in an ad is shown in Fig. 8.1. The graphic model is adapted from the work of consultant Gayle Moberg (1988). We have extended her model, notably by including negative as well as positive emotions and supplied its functional properties. In the a-b-e framework shown in the figure, it can be seen that there are no less than 3 focal points and 3 focal paths that can be used in advertising:

1. Attribute focus (e.g., a thick potato chip): a
2. Benefit focus from an attribute (e.g., better chip taste because it's thick): a(b)
3. Benefit focus (e.g., better tasting, no reason given): b
4. Benefit focus from an emotion (e.g., dissatisfied with taste of thin chips; solution is better taste of thick chips): e^-(b)
5. Emotion focus from a benefit (e.g., fun because of better taste): b(e^+)
6. Pure emotion focus (e.g., simply "fun"): e^+ or e^-

Whereas other paths are possible, such as a to e, or a to b to e, the paths listed above are the most likely (and theoretically most important) ones. A

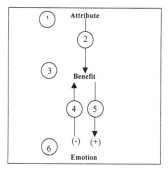

Example A: Potato Chips
1. thick chip
2. better tasting because it's thick
3. better tasting
4. better tasting (previously dissatisfied)
5. fun because it's better tasting
6. just fun

Example B: Health Choice Dinners
1. low salt, fat, cholesterol
2. heart-healthy because of low fat, etc.
3. heart-healthy
4. heart-healthy (previous health fear)
5. trendy because it's heart-healthy
6. just trendy

FIG. 8.1.   The a-b-e model of benefit focus. Focus may be on the level itself (1,3,6) or on a sequential path ending at the level (2,4,5).

second example—for Healthy Choice—is shown in the figure to illustrate the potential focal points and paths.

In presenting our a-b-e model, we concentrate on whether the primary focus should be on attributes, or on benefits, or on emotions (or on their associated paths). Before doing so, however, we point out differences between the a-b-e model and the means–end a-c-v model.

Comparison to the Means–End Model

The a-b-e model is superficially similar to the means–end model proposed by Gutman (1982) and Reynolds and Gutman (1984). In their model, Reynolds and Gutman (1984) distinguish attributes, consequences, and values a-c-v, which form ladders or benefit chains. Figure 8.2 shows the a-c-v model and the in-ad application of it, called *MECCAS*. Because the means–end model is used so widely, it deserves detailed comment.

The a-c-v and MECCAS models, in our view, have three significant problems: definitional, methodological, and overall conceptualization. We briefly point out these problems below and indicate how our model may improve on these earlier models.

Definition Problems. The first term in the a-c-v model is *attributes* (operationalized as message elements in the MECCAS model), which is the same as in our model. However, attributes are sometimes inappropri-

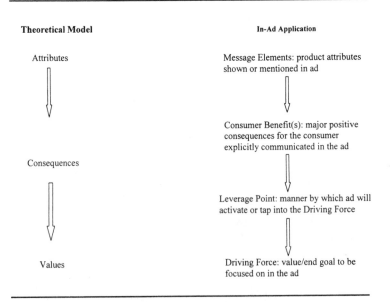

FIG. 8.2.   The a → c → v model and the MECCAS in-ad application (from Reynolds & Gengler, 1990).

ately operationalized in the MECCAS model in that consequences are included in the identification of message elements (Reynolds & Gutman, 1988; Reynolds & Rochon, 1991). For example, in Reynolds and Rochon's (1991) example of a ladder for Miller Lite, they give "less calories" and "great taste" as message elements. The former is clearly an attribute and the latter a consequence (a benefit, in our terminology). In Fig. 8.2, which depicts the a-c-v and MECCAS models, we omitted consequences from the definition of message elements.

The second term in the a-c-v model — *consequences* (or consumer benefits in MECCAS) — has two main problems. One is the very word "consequences," which implies that these are always the result of an attribute. This is an unnecessary implication, as we discuss under the conceptual criticisms following. Secondly, when translating consequences as consumer benefits in the MECCAS model, Reynolds and Craddock (1988) drew a questionable distinction between (positive) "benefits" and "avoidance of negative consequences" (p. 44) when clearly *both* are benefits to the consumer. (In our definition of benefits, the first is a positive reinforcer and the second a negative reinforcer.) Indeed, in the example Reynolds and Craddock gave for Federal Express, they listed "less worry" and "avoid looking bad" (p. 48) as consumer benefits and thus obviously deny their own definitional distinction.

The third term in the a-c-v model, *values*, and the driving force in the MECCAS model, also is problematic. Values are inferred as the latent end-goal of the advertising and are tapped into manifestly in the ad via the leverage point. The assumption that all advertising, indeed all consumer choices, must be motivated by values is far too broad. Many if not most consumer choices become purely habitual, even zero-order stochastic (Bass, Givon, Kalwani, Reibstein, & Wright, 1984; Howard, 1977). In Howard's (1977) theory, for instance, values are involved only at the first (extensive problem solving) stage of consumer learning. Similarly, questionable is the assumption that the consumer's self-concept (because all values are self-values) is inevitably engaged in consumer choice and should be addressed in advertising. To quote Reynolds and Rochon (1991): "The central principle of the means–end approach is the interpretation process between the brand and 'self' " (p. 136). Psychologists from James (1890) onward would dispute the notion that the self is always implicated, consciously or unconsciously, in behavior. People's personal values are sometimes directly or indirectly engaged, particularly when values are the source of importance weights (or emotional weights) for benefits. But importance weights can also come from purely mechanical learning, such as the negative importance of flatness in a beer, which, we would maintain, has nothing to do with values. To make values the necessary end point of the model limits its validity.

Lastly, we note the questionable worth of Rokeach's (1973) distinction between instrumental and terminal values, which is sometimes invoked in an extended version of the theoretical means–end chain (e.g., Gutman, 1982; Valette-Florence & Rapacchi, 1991). We observe that all of Rokeach's (1973) instrumental values are adjectives, such as "ambitious," "responsible"; whereas all of the terminal values are nouns (or noun-phrases), such as "wisdom," "a comfortable life." This, we contend, produces a methodological confounding in the measurements of values. We doubt that Rokeach's (1973) distinction would hold up empirically if we were to exchange the parts of speech used to measure instrumental and terminal values—for example, changing "responsible" to "a responsible life," or changing "a comfortable life" to "comfortable."

Thus, the instrumental or terminal distinction seems tenuous at best. In fact, Feather (1988) has shown that the Rokeach (1973) values can be translated directly into Osgood, Suci, and Tannenbaum's (1957) emotional dimensions of evaluation, potency, and activity. Cacioppo, Petty, and Geen (1989) go one step further and show that potency and activity can be adequately scaled in terms of the single evaluative dimension. This suggests that the functional aspect of values is an emotional response.

In our a-b-e model, we use the term "emotions" rather than values. These seem somewhat closer to the leverage point in the MECCAS application in that we, too, see emotions as manifest elements in ads that tap into something latent—namely motives rather than values (Rossiter & Percy, 1987). Motives are much more generally operative than values, and a good case can be made that they underlie *all* purchase (and usage) acts, noting that we include our normal depletion motive to explain the repetitive behavior of brand loyals.

Methodological Problems.   A first methodological problem with a-c-v laddering stems from the assumption that consumers are aware of, and can validly report, all three levels of their linkages. If all three levels — attributes, consequences, and values — are always operative, then why, in the empirical studies of laddering, do the self-reported incidences consistently decline across these levels? Not only is this observed empirically, but the a priori target levels of a, c, and v in the MECCAS applications always show declining percentages for a, c, and v in a ladder (e.g., Reynolds & Rochon, 1991).

A second methodological problem is that the a-c-v ladders typically are aggregated across consumers. For instance, consumer 1 may exhibit the ladder a_1-c_1-v_1, consumer 2 produces the ladder a_1-c_2-v_2, and consumer 3 has a ladder a_2-c_1-v_2. In aggregate, the common ladder is a_1-c_1-v_2 because each of these terms appears twice; however no individual consumer actually exhibits this ladder. Of course, it could be argued that the aggregate ladders are merely hypothetical. Recently, Gutman (1991) appeared to be making this argument (which other ladder modelers have not) when he selected prototype ladders, presented them to consumers, and had them rate the extent to which they agree "that's me." This methodology implicitly recognizes that ads do not have to reflect existing ladders but may indeed present new ones, as in positioning a new brand or deliberately repositioning an old brand.

The aggregation methodology also tends to lengthen the ladders artificially (in that few individuals exhibit long ladders). This is based on the unsupported theoretical claim that longer chains are better for advertising development (Reynolds & Craddock, 1988; see also Valette-Florence & Rapachi, 1991). The aggregation procedure is one way of ensuring that all three levels, a, c and v, are represented, which they may not be in the individuals' ladders. But this is spurious, surely. Currim and Schneider's (1991) analysis of shoppers' protocols, for instance, suggested that individual chains are typically only one or two levels. There is no evidence that consumers naturally pass through all levels either when encoding ads or when making brand choices as a result.

Related to the aggregation methodology is the necessity that many of the links between a's, c's and v's are imputed rather than natural. Reynolds and Gengler (1990) improved on imputation by asking consumers to (subsequently) rate the likelihood or strength of a connection ("little," "somewhat," "totally," which were then given the arbitrary multipliers 5%, 35%, and 75%). Reynolds and Rochon (1990), however, simply multiplied the aggregate incidences of any two levels together to infer the existence and the strength of the linkage. For example, "75% less calories × 84% less filling = 62% linkage" between this attribute and this consequence. This procedure is completely arbitrary. Better, but still imputed, is Gutman's (1991) suggestion of asking consumers to estimate the conditional probability that a linkage exists, such as "What is the probability that a beer would be less filling given that it contains less calories?" This is closer to the imputation or inference that consumers as advertising audiences have to make when confronted with a hypothetical ladder proposed in an ad. Again, however, Gutman's (1991) example shows the implausibility of values being universally engaged. He gave an example of the probability of success given one's being refreshed by Pepsi's Slice beverage. This is an unrealistic c-v linkage, which Gutman realized was stretching the theory and would not work in practice.

Finally, the a-c-v and MECCAS models omit importance weights. The aggregate percentages calculated at each level of a ladder probably represent only an aggregate belief strength measure (sum of 0, 1 mentions), or perhaps a tangled aggregate estimate of belief × importance if one assumes that the proportion of individuals mentioning this level indicates importance. It is impossible to clearly evaluate the worth or persuasive potential of one ladder versus another without knowing the importance weights. For instance, the abbreviated ladder "fruit juice" ("being refreshed") is probably more prevalent than "fruit juice" ("daily vitamin C intake,") but is it more important? In contrast, our a-b-e model includes attributes, benefits or emotions in an ad only if they are known from prior research to be important, deliverable, and unique. This is our I-D-U model of benefit emphasis (see Rossiter & Percy, 1987). We cannot see how an advertising strategy can be formulated or evaluated without knowing benefit importances.

Overall Conceptualization Problems. The means–end a-c-v and MECCAS models have a number of overall conceptual problems. First and foremost, in comparison with the a-b-e model, is the assumed linear, causal sequence of attribute-consequence-value. In Reynolds and Craddock's (1988) words, the consumer must be "forced up the ladder of abstraction" (p. 47). We have already argued that values are not the inevitable end-points of consumer choice behavior. Even if we substitute our terms, attribute-benefit-emotion, it is clear that this causal sequence is not universal. We do not have this restriction in our model. For one thing, levels may occur on their own. For instance, consider the placebo-based effectiveness of many over-the-counter drugs for many consumers. On what attribute does this benefit depend? Similarly, consider the emotional feeling that Levi's are a psychologically comfortable brand of jeans to buy — on what attribute or benefit does this depend? For another, the links may be reversed. Notably, *problem/solution advertising* basically works because a (negative) emotion occurs first (the problem) followed by a benefit (the solution): an e-b sequence rather than a b-e sequence in our model or the unidirectional c-v sequence in the a-c-v model. For instance, reminding the consumer of a value prior to the attribute may be necessary for the ad to work, such as ecological concern (look for "no hydroflourocarbons" on the label. The concept of a necessary a-c-v sequence and a one-way sequence, at that, is not justified.

Related to this is the notion (in the MECCAS model) that all levels — a, c, and v — must be represented and hierarchically linked in an ad. Even if the "all-levels" hypothesis were true, surely it is more important that the consumer makes the links (by inference or cognitive response again, or even subconsciously) rather than spell them out in the ad. Indeed, in the studies reported to date, the declining perceptions of the existence of a, c, and v in most ladders would require that the missing levels be subconsciously operating. More basically, as we show in our a-b-e model, there are situations in which the ad would deliberately *not* mention higher levels (notably, attribute-only ads aimed at experts, who know or infer their own idiosyncratic benefits). Also, some ads might use a benefit for which there is no attribute foundation (as for many image brands). The all-levels assumption in the means–end model is in many cases forced and unnecessary. Even if this assumption is relaxed to allow implicit if not explicit representation of all levels in the ad, this makes the specification of what should be in the ad very vague indeed.

In the early work based on the a-c-v model, its proponents implied that the desirable position was always on the value end of the chain. This came from the insistence that ads must force consumers "up the chain" (Reynolds & Craddock, 1988, p. 47). However, this has been modified in at least one recent study (Perkins & Reynolds, 1988) that recognized different foci may be appropriate. But their revised a-c-v model is inadequate in specifying conditions for alternative levels of focus. In the Perkins & Reynolds (1988) model, only one condition was given—light-user target audience versus heavy-user target audience. They hypothesized that light users of the brand would be more likely to be persuaded by the attributes start of the chain, whereas heavy users would be most influenced by the values end of the chain. Some support for the hypothesis was obtained at the attribute end but not at the value end. More generally, they hypothesized that novices would respond to attributes, and experts respond to values. Our a-b-e model makes the opposite prediction and specifies other conditions for either an a, b, or e focus.

The a-c-v and MECCAS models also seem unable to handle pure transformational advertising. Rather, the means–end approach assumes an informational persuasion model. As Reynolds and Craddock (1988) stated: "the attribute-based 'reason why' is required by the consumer to rationalize his or her choice behavior" (p. 55). Whereas we would agree that information is often used for this purpose in high-involvement and transformational ads, such as for luxury cars, it certainly is not required. In low-involvement and transformational ads, information rarely is even desirable (recall the Resnik-Stern, 1977, content analyses, discussed earlier, where 50% of TV commercials have no information). Coca-Cola ads, for instance, would not be feasible according to the MECCAS formula. Moreover, ads that employ subliminal cues (see the section entitled "Benefit Focus" of this chapter) would be out of the question.

In summary, our opinion is that the means–end model (consisting of the a-c-v and the in-ad-application, MECCAS models) is problematic theoretically and is overly restrictive for advertising applications. Certainly the claim that MECCAS is the complete theory of advertising strategy (cf. Reynolds & Craddock, 1988, p. 46; and Reynolds, Cockle, & Rochon, 1990, p. 11) is ill advised. We would not make such a claim for our a-b-e model, which is only one small part of advertising strategy and indeed is only one part of advertising positioning strategy (see Rossiter & Percy, 1997). The a-c-v model's limitations open the way for our a-b-e model to be proposed as a significant improvement. The discussion is now turned in detail to the new model, examining the conditions for a, b, or e focus.

ATTRIBUTE FOCUS

The standard dictum in marketing and advertising texts is to emphasize the benefit to the customer. This means the emphasis should be on the subjective reinforcement from the (actual or perceived) attribute rather than on the attribute itself. However, the a-b-e model posits that there are positioning situations in which the attribute itself should be the focus (point 1 in the a-b-e model diagram in Fig. 8.1). The main situations are expert target audience, intangible service, and as an alternative to emotion focus for homogeneous-benefit brands. Explained next is each of these situations for which attribute focus is recommended.

Expert Target Audience

Attribute focus is appropriate when positioning the brand to an expert target audience because experts know the benefits that derive from the attributes. Indeed, it can be argued that it is more effective to present only attributes to experts because their perceptions of the importance or emotional weights of these attributes, an e element in our model, probably will vary (experts often differ), and therefore experts are more likely to self-persuade based on the attributes presented alone (Shavitt & Brock, 1986).

Sujan (1985) provided a demonstration of the attribute effect with expert consumers. She presented descriptions of two cameras — one a simple instamatic camera and the other a more advanced 35mm single lens reflex (SLR) camera. Based on their prior knowledge of cameras, the consumers in this study were classified as either experts or novices. For half of the consumers Sujan switched the labels on each description, so that these consumers saw the simple camera description with the complex-camera label "35mm SLR" and the complex camera description with the simple-camera label "110 camera." The experts were not fooled; they preferred the more advanced camera regardless of whether it had a correct or misleading label. Novices, on the other hand, judged by the label, regardless of the actual attributes.

Maheswaran and Sternthal (1990) provided another good demonstration of the attributes-for-experts effect. In their study, they prepared three product descriptions for a fictitious new personal computer: attribute focus, attribute-plus-benefit focus, and benefit focus. Examples of the attribute claims and the benefit claims for the personal computer are shown in Table 8.2, along with the results. Again, consumers in the experiment were divided into experts and novices, based on a pretest of their computer knowledge. Maheswaran and Sternthal manipulated involvement (perceived risk) in the experiment, telling half the consumers that they were participants in an anonymous survey, thus making their brand choice low involvement. They told the other half of the consumers that their opinion would decide whether or not the new product would be introduced, and they could expect to be contacted later by the manufacturer for a demonstration of the product, thus making their brand choice high involvement.

We selected the high-involvement results for novices because they would probably only be looking at a personal computer ad if they were seriously planning to buy a personal computer. On the other hand, we selected the low-involvement results for experts because their product category knowledge means that they would probably look at computer ads anyway in forming their future consideration sets. The high-involvement results for experts were similar to the low-involvement results in that an attribute focus was still highly effective, although the combination of attributes plus benefits was equally good when experts are closer to the purchase decision, both being better than benefits alone. As the results show, the novices' brand-attitude ratings of the new product were highest when the benefits were pointed out to them, whereas the experts' brand attitude ratings were highest when only attributes were provided.

TABLE 8.2

Brand Attitude Ratings of a New Personal Computer by Novices and Experts as a Function of Attribute Focus, Benefit Focus, or Both, in the New Product's Description (From Maheswaran & Sternthal, 1990)

	Product Description Focus		
	Attributes	Benefits	Both
Novices	4.8	6.0	5.9
Experts	6.1	4.8	4.5

Examples of Attributes and Benefits Used in the Study:

Attribute	Benefit
Open architecture with technical tutorial for self-developed software	The technical tutorial provides extensive and simple instructions to help users do their own programming
Single disk with boot-in facility	It uses disks to store data, which increases the amount of data that can be stored

Note. Brand attitude ratings on 1 (negative) to 7 (positive) scale, with 4 as the neutral mid-point.

An example of an extreme attribute-focus was a 1992 Australian newspaper advertisement for the Audi 90 automobile. The ad showed a small illustration of the car surrounded by descriptions of no less than 80 attributes. This ad may have been too extreme in terms of information overload because, two months later, the company ran a simplified ad showing the same image of the car along with a greater benefit focus in the headline ("Now even less money buys more German luxury"). However, the revised ad still had a considerable attribute focus with a listing of some 20 attributes. Presumably, these attribute-focus ads for Audi were aimed at luxury car buyers who see themselves as experts in discriminating the available makes and models in terms of their various features. It also is possible that these ads would work with novices, by impressing them with the sheer number of attributes (via the peripheral route to persuasion, as suggested in Petty & Cacioppo, 1986).

Intangible Services

A second situation in which an attribute focus is recommended is when positioning a product that is not a product in the concrete sense but rather is an intangible service. Financial services, insurance, and auto servicing and repairs are typical examples of *intangible services*. Of course, the end result of these services is quite tangible. For instance, at a bank, you actually experience polite or rude service, or accurate or inaccurate service. If your house is robbed, you will abruptly experience precisely what home-and-contents insurance covers, and poor or good car servicing is evident in a fairly concretely way, as well. However, the point is that when you first make the decision to purchase one of these services, the benefits are not yet forthcoming and thus are intangible.

An innovative hypothesis proposed by Shostack (1977, 1981) is that the more intangible the product or service, the more it requires tangible attributes in its promotion. This is because the tangible attributes serve as surrogate indicators of the yet-to-be-experienced benefits. This hypothesis has not, to our knowledge, been put to a formal experimental test, but real-world observations suggest that it is valid. For instance, consumers are more likely to initiate and maintain a relationship with a bank whose facilities are modern and whose employees are neatly dressed and polite, although these attributes may have little to do objectively with the ultimate service that is provided. Insurance companies that are perceived as large are probably more successful than those that are not. Car service garages that are tidy and where the employees are not disheveled and grubby are more likely to get your business than places that look like backyard operations, and so forth. In sum, it seems a reasonable conclusion that companies offering intangible services have a greater need to demonstrate that their services are worth patronizing, by focusing on attributes as evidence of good service.

Alternative to Emotion Focus for Homogenous-Benefit Brands

When brands in a product category are virtually identical in terms of benefits, one well-known strategy (covered in the following) is to attempt to differentiate the brand on emotional associations. An alternative strategy is not widely recognized—if most brands in the category are advertising the same benefits, it may be effective for our brand to go back to attributes as a means of differentiation.

The theory is that a distinctive attribute can serve as a parity-breaker even if the attribute is fairly trivial in terms of delivering a benefit to the consumer. This strategy has been used for many years in advertising. Classic campaigns include Budweiser's "beechwood-aged," Shell gasoline's "X-100," Procter & Gamble's Folger's coffee, with "mountain grown" beans in its regular coffee and "flaked coffee crystals" in its instant coffee. Or, consider Ivory Soap's "99$\frac{44}{100}$% pure," a famous Claude Hopkins claim from the turn of the century that the brand still uses.

Another successful example is in the ketchup category, where most leading brands' benefits are much the same. Heinz seems to have gained an advantage by focusing on the thickness of its ketchup, an attribute that makes it "slow-pouring" (McQueen, 1990). Slowness in pouring is hardly a benefit for adults, although it may be for those who have sloppy kids! Of course, the implied benefit from the sauce's thickness is that it is "richer." Notice that the Heinz ketchup ads do not mention the benefit, contrary to the stipulation in the MECCAS model (discussed earlier) that each level is explicitly addressed in the ad. Whether mention of the benefit would make the ads more or less effective is an obvious question that Heinz probably answered in pretesting and settled on attribute focus.

Until recently, the effectiveness of the trivial-attribute-as-parity-breaker strategy had not been proven under controlled experimental conditions. Carpenter, Glazer, and Nakamoto (1994) provided an experimental demonstration of this strategy. They found consumers were much more likely to prefer a brand that, among otherwise identical brands, added a trivial attribute. The effect was shown for all three product categories studied—a brand of ski-jacket that advertised "alpine-class down fill," a pasta brand described as "authentic Milanese style," and a compact disc player that advertised a "studio-designed signal processing system." We note that deception or consumer misunderstanding is not the explanation. Half the consumers in the experiment were told that the added attribute was irrelevant or meaningless, yet most of these consumers still strongly preferred the brand that offered it. Thus, attribute focus, like emotion focus as described later, is worth considering when competitive brands are emphasizing much the same benefit or benefits.

Altogether, then, we have seen that there are at least three advertising situations in which the attribute point in the a-b-e model is the recommended focus: (1) when advertising to an expert target audience, (2) when advertising an intangible service, and (3) as an alternative to emotion focus for homogeneous brands. We now consider the next level, benefit focus.

BENEFIT FOCUS (ATTRIBUTE BENEFIT OR EMOTION BENEFIT)

Benefits, in the specific sense that we are using the term here, are subjective reinforcements that are perceived to be provided by the brand. These subjective benefits may or may not derive from the objective attributes that the brand has. Yi (1989) noted that benefits can be either physically caused by attributes (e.g., the size of an automobile, an attribute, causing the comfort benefit and also the safety benefit) or be merely correlated with them (e.g., for automobiles, European, an attribute, and prestigious, a benefit, are correlated in the minds of many U.S. car buyers). Also, an attribute that the product's designers see as important can turn out not to be a benefit to the prospective buyer.

An apparent example of a benefit that is only vaguely related to attributes is the ubiquitous claim, "natural," apparently a meaningless word. A.C. Nielsen Company (1984) conducted a content analysis of "natural" claims in food packaging. They found an incredible variety of meanings (attributes) for the claim "natural," including "no preservatives," "no added salt or sugar," "no cholesterol," "low in calories and low in sodium," "made with honey instead of sugar," "unprocessed cheese," and even "decaffeinated" (for a brand called All Natural Tea Bags).

However, the vague attribute basis of "natural" does not mean it is any less effective as a benefit. An amazing campaign in Australia substantially reversed a 40% per capita decline in sugar consumption by emphasizing that sugar is natural. Sugar does, after all, grow naturally; it occurs naturally in fruit, it is naturally present in the body via blood sugar, and so forth. (However, the chemical difference between natural and artificial foods is, of course, nonsense.) The campaign theme, "Sugar, a natural part of life," was largely responsible for restoring Australia's sugar consumption levels by disinhibiting people from adding sugar to food and beverages. A continuation of the "Sugar is natural" campaign then successfully held off the threat from artificial sweeteners that had entered the market as a diet aid. This is all the more remarkable considering that many other products claim they are natural precisely because they do not contain (or add) sugar.

Accordingly, benefit focus can be regarded as being either a sole focus on a benefit (point 3 in the a-b-e model) or as linking benefits to underlying attributes (attribute(benefit, path 2 in the model). Also, as seen later, a benefit may be linked to a prior emotion. (Technically, this requires an emotion shift; see Rossiter & Percy, 1987, 1991, for details.) Usually this is a negative emotion with the benefit providing relief (emotion-benefit, path 4). The common element is that the ad ends by stating or portraying a benefit. There are three situations in which we recommend benefit focus: brand with hard-to-imitate benefit, negatively-motivated (informational) brand, and logical attack on entrenched emotion-based attitude. The first situation, perhaps, is fairly obvious, but the second and third are not so clear. All three are discussed in the following.

Brand With Hard-to-Imitate Benefit

Clearly, if a brand has one or more differential advantages that are hard for competitors to imitate, those benefits should be the focus (point 3 in the model). This is the normal recommendation in marketing, but the hard-to-imitate aspect is crucial (Frazer, 1983). Benefits in the form of price and also price promotions, usually do not qualify, as they are easy to imitate, unless the company has a low-cost advantage and is prepared to sustain a predatory price position (as has been the case in some markets presently dominated by Japanese manufacturers).

We should emphasize that for a brand with a *superior* benefit or benefits, the advertising focus should be on the benefit (the subjective relief or reward for the buyer) and not on the attribute or the emotion. This is because differential attributes are not necessarily differential benefits from the customer's standpoint. Also, at the other extreme, differential emotions are, by and large, a less sustainable means of differentiation than if the brand has a differential benefit or benefits.

Brand Choice Based on Negative (Informational) Motives

Informational advertising (Rossiter & Percy, 1987, 1991), which is recommended when brand choice is based on a negative purchase motivation (relief), should hype the negative emotion first (the problem) and then demonstrate the benefit (the solution). In terms of the a-b-e model, the sequence (path 4) is e^--b. That is, the negative emotional state caused by the problem is relieved, sequentially, by the benefit. It is optional, not necessary, that the benefit be further accompanied by a positive emotional state after its delivery. To illustrate the effective e⁻-b sequence, consider two ads for liquid laundry detergents from the early 1990s.

One ad, an ad for Wisk, hyped the negative emotion of washing clothes by listing various ways to avoid "tsks" (life's little problems that occur when dirt or stains get on clothes) — "don't work," "don't eat," "don't drink," "don't kiss," "don't play," and so forth. The ad went on to say that one could "use Wisk liquid laundry detergent to dissolve the dirt bonds that lock 'tsks' to your clothes and get your whole wash clean." This ad showed the negative emotion (of having to avoid fun or necessary situations to remain clean) but did not visually show how the benefit provided by the brand is the solution to the problem.

We think another ad, an ad for Tide liquid detergent, would be more effective, because it was better balanced. The Tide ad, using a before-and-after format, portrayed the negative emotion by showing a shirt stained with "dad's secret recipe," a bar-b-que sauce, and then portrayed the benefit by showing the same shirt now clean after laundry with "mom's secret weapon," Tide. Moreover, the tag-line for Tide was also benefit-focused: "If it's got to be clean, it's got to be Tide."

Logical Attack on Entrenched Emotion-Based Attitude

Consumers who have an entrenched brand attitude are particularly resistant to approaches by competing brands (Rice, 1991). This is because they perceive high risk in switching from their current brand and also consider alternative brands as inferior. If their entrenchment is based on strong emotional consequences of using the brand, it could be argued that the only way to shift the entrenched attitude is to mount a logical or rational attack rather than an "emotional" one. An emotional attack would stimulate the ready supply of emotion that the buyer has for using the brand and thus could be easily rejected.

A logical attack, on the other hand, might catch the buyer less prepared to defend his or her attitude. This would be an attribute(benefit approach (path 2 in the model). Here, our position is counter to the functional theory of attitude (Katz, 1960), which would recommend a same-function attack. For instance, if the motivational base of attitude is ego defense, then Katz' theory would recommend an ego-defense attack. The opposite function attack theory for negative target audiences has been proposed most recently by Millar and Millar (1990), although their experiment provided only marginal support for the hypothesis. However, they used a mainly low-involvement product, soft drinks, and we believe that the idea is valid only for high-involvement choices. Our view is supported by Pratkanis and Aronson's (1990) review of the "latitude of rejection" research wherein a high-credibility presenter may be able to override the narrow latitude of acceptance that is held by an entrenched target audience. The effectiveness of the attack is due to blocking of counterarguments; therefore, by the same process, we would expect that the opposing function attack should be similarly successful.

Social problems such as teenage smoking, heroin use, and AIDS are examples of buyer behavior that is reinforced by strong, emotion-based attitudes. To change these behaviors, a logical (benefit-based) approach by social agencies may offer the only hope. Consider the case of AIDS, for example. The revelations by public figures, such as Rock Hudson, Anthony Perkins, Arthur Ashe, and Magic Johnson, that they had contracted the disease should be regarded as rational benefits in that they dramatically changed many people's personal estimate (subjective probability) of their chances of contracting AIDS. Most people already know the negative emotional consequences of the disease, and preventive campaigns based simply on negative emotion seem less likely to be effective.

Overall, the benefit level in the a-b-e model is the most frequent focus for advertising. A major reason for its frequent use is that it fits informationally motivated products, which are the most prevalent category in buyer behavior. However, we identified two other advertising situations where benefit focus is recommended. One is where the brand has one or more hard-to-imitate benefits (whether informational or transformational). Another is when mounting a logical attack on an entrenched emotion-based attitude. We look now at emotion.

EMOTION FOCUS (BENEFIT EMOTION OR HEAVY NEGATIVE EMOTION BENEFIT)

The final option to be considered in the a-b-e model is emotion focus. This can take two forms, as shown in Fig. 8.1: a benefit-positive emotion path (path 5) or a pure emotion focus (point 6), which would normally be e^+ but could be e^- if the ad is intended to discourage a certain behavior, as with the previously mentioned social problems. However, we also distinguish a third form, which is the same path as e^--b in benefit focus (path 4) but where the initial emotional emphasis is very heavily negative and pronounced. The situations in which emotion focus seems most appropriate are:

- Brand with easy-to-imitate benefits
- Positively-motivated (transformational) brand
- "Emotional" attack on entrenched attribute-based attitude

These three situations are discussed next.

Brand With Easy-to-Imitate Benefits

A large number of brands compete in basically homogeneous product categories where the benefits delivered by competing brands are essentially identical. One positioning option in this situation is to go back to attributes, as we saw in the example of Heinz ketchup. The other is to go forward to emotions or emotional consequences of benefits. The latter is sometimes skeptically referred to as the "If you've got nothing to say, sing it" school of advertising, but it works! For a brand whose attributes or benefits are easy to imitate and are likely to be imitated quickly by a competitor, emotional positioning provides an additional differentiation that may help preserve its uniqueness. For this purpose, the benefit-positive emotion sequence (path 5) would be used, but with focus on the emotional consequence of the benefit, which the brand should try to make unique.

A well-known example of benefit-positive emotion (with emotion focus) that has apparently been successful for many years (McQueen, 1990) is the campaign for United Airlines, "Fly the friendly skies of United." Another example that is quite touchy with Australians is the practice of auto manufacturers selling identical cars under different manufacturers' badges. Amply demonstrating that there is differential equity in a brand name alone, the same car can command a $1,000 or so price difference depending on which manufacturer's name it carries. Another excellent example of benefit-positive emotion with emotion focus is Toyota's creative device, "Oh what a feeling" (accompanied by euphoric jumping), used as a clearly emotional ending for its otherwise benefit-oriented car ads.

Although we may question the ethics of the emotional differentiation approach, it could be answered that, if buyers are subjectively happy with their emotional choices, the approach is justifiable. Several schools of moral philosophy, such as Bentham's utilitarianism, would make this argument.

Pure Emotion Focus

The interesting option of "pure emotion" focus (the single point 6 in the model) is one approach that has been perfected by the late German researcher Werner Kroeber-Riel (1986, 1988). The pure emotion-focus approach, almost always e^+, might be expected to apply only to low-priced products such as soft drinks, beer, and cosmetics. However, Kroeber-Riel (1992) applied the approach successfully to higher-priced products such as kitchenware and to services such as banks and insurance companies (personal communication). For example, an ad for a German insurance company, developed with the help of Kroeber-Riel's advertising expert system, contained the headline, "We're opening the horizon." There was no explicit benefit. Essentially the ad contained only an attention-getting and emotionally-arousing illustration of a young woman in a gauzy dress standing in front of an open door with light streaming through the opening and the wind blowing her dress and shawl. Benetton, too, has used a similar "pure emotion" focus approach, although this time daring to use e$^-$ explicitly (the social controversy theme of Benetton's ads is well known) although the inferred end result is almost certainly e$^+$. The ads have met with great success everywhere except in the United States where most of the ads were banned (*The Wall Street Journal*, 1992). In 1991, the first year of its controversial campaign, Benetton's profits grew by 24% worldwide, but fell to near break-even in the United States.

It could be argued that many cases of apparently pure-emotion focus, such as the German insurance company ad and the typical Benetton ad, are in effect benefit(emotion ads in that consumers are likely to interpret a benefit belief although none is explicitly stated. For instance, consumers exposed to the German insurance ad might have inferred that "We're opening the horizon" means that the company is promising to make your future less worrisome. Similarly, consumers may infer benefit beliefs from the Benetton ads such as the company is socially responsible, or simply the brand has avant-garde advertising (which itself may be a positively weighted benefit belief for some people). If so, then these examples could be seen, not as a pure emotion focus (point 6), but as the e$^-$-b path (path 4) in both instances. However, this argument is not strictly valid, because the a-b-e model only indicates what messages to put (explicitly) in ads; it is not a model of how consumers, or anyone else, will interpret the ad.

Worth discussing is the use of subliminal sexual imagery in ads. This is certainly a demonstration of pure emotion in advertising, because the persuasion process is evidently not based on conscious cognitive consideration of attributes or benefits or conscious consideration even of the emotion. The more sensational, unproven claims by Key (1974) of subliminal sexual imagery or death imagery in ads (corresponding to the Freudian theory of Eros or sexual drive and Thanatos or death-wish drive) have rightfully been dismissed. However, subsequent experiments by Freudian psychologist William Ruth and his colleagues (Ruth & Mosatche, 1985; Ruth, Mosatche, & Kramer, 1989) suggest that the sexual arousal effect is real, that it can occur unconsciously, and that it favorably affects brand attitude. Ruth and his colleagues conducted their experiments with ads for liquor, a product category where the benefits are similar across brands. Moreover, it could be maintained that, for liquor products, sexual arousal (usually a sensory gratification motive, but sometimes social approval) is a relevant benefit (emotion focus).

In the first experiment (Ruth & Mosatche, 1985), consumers were shown six one-page liquor ads taken from weekly news and sports magazines. Three of these ads were judged by the experimenters to contain phallic and vaginal symbols — indeed, two phallic symbols and two vaginal symbols per ad (experimental group). The other three ads contained no such symbols (control group). All of the ads depicted objects only, not people, so there was no explicit portrayal of sex in any of the ads. Consumers were told there would be a recall test after looking at the ads. However, they actually were administered a psychoanalytic Thematic Apperception Test (TAT). The TAT is an ambiguous picture projective test (like the famous Rorschach Inkblots but with people in the pictures) in which the individual is asked to write a story about what was going on in the TAT picture. The stories were then scored, blind as to experimental condition, for presence of sexual imagery, using the standard TAT coding scheme. In a postexperimental interview, none of the consumers showed awareness of the true purpose of the experiment. As predicted, consumers who saw the liquor ads containing phallic and vaginal symbols exhibited approximately twice as much sexual content in their subsequent descriptions (of the ambiguous TAT cards, not the ads) as those who saw the nonsymbolic ads. Men and women both showed the effect. This first experiment demonstrates that sexual drive can be unconsciously aroused by normal but symbolically-particular stimuli in ads.

In the second experiment (Ruth, Mosatche, & Kramer, 1989) with a new sample of consumers, the effect of sexual symbolic content was taken one step further by examining purchase intentions for advertised liquor brands. Seven paired ads were selected — again actual ads from consumer magazines. Although no people were shown in either ad, one ad in each pair contained copulatory symbolism (implying male–female intercourse), whereas the other ad had no sexual content. The ads used in the experiment were quite normal. For example, the copulatory symbolism ads used illustrations such as a bottle protruding diagonally from a Christmas stocking and the nonsexual ads used illustrations such as a winter snow scene glimpsed through a frosty window. The ingenious prior step was that the brands and liquor types in the pairs were matched beforehand for purchase intentions based on the name alone, rated by a separate but similar group of consumers. In this pretest, the brands in the pairs differed by less than 0.2 of a rating point on the 7-point purchase intention measure.

The experiment, with a new sample of consumers, followed the pretest. Table 8.3 shows the results. Purchase intentions for brands advertised in the Freudian copulatory symbolism ads were rated approximately 1 rating point higher on the 7-point purchase intention measure than the brands in the nonsymbolic ads. Moreover, demonstrating generalizability, this highly significant effect was observed for men in the experiment on five of the seven ads and for women on six of the seven ads. It is

TABLE 8.3
Freudian Copulatory Symbolism in Liquor Ads Increases Purchase
Intention* (from Ruth, Mosatche, and Kramer 1989)

	Control Ads (No Symbolism)	Freudian Ads (Copulatory Symbolism)
Men	3.6	4.5
Women	3.4	4.5

Note. Ratings on scale of 1 = low intention to 7 = high intention to purchase. Mean differences for both men and women between types of ads significant at p < .001.

unlikely that other factors such as the esthetics or likability of the ads produced these differences because the control ads were probably more attractive than the experimental (symbolic) ads. Unconscious sexual arousal (an effect of e^+ focus in the Freudian ads) is the most likely explanation. We note that the effect was obtained with only one exposure to the ads, although the laboratory-like forced exposure conditions of the experiment probably translate to about three real-world exposures. Pending replication, we accept these experiments as valid demonstrations of subliminal sexual imagery working in ads — and as an intriguingly successful demonstration of pure emotion focus.

Brand Choice Based on Positive (Transformational) Motives

The positive reward motivations in Rossiter and Percy's (1987) theory were sensory gratification, intellectual stimulation or mastery, and social approval. For brand choice based on these motives, transformational advertising is recommended. An important line of research by John Deighton (Deighton & Schindler, 1988) suggested that advertising that focuses on the emotional consequence of a benefit can actually affect the buyer's experience of that benefit when the brand is subsequently purchased and used. Thus, if the advertising has portrayed the positive benefit in an emotionally authentic way, then those exposed to the advertising are more likely to rate the brand's benefit delivery as better when they experience it later, compared to those not previously exposed to its advertising. Perhaps this is why Coca-Cola works so hard to achieve emotional authenticity in its TV commercials (the company tests only finished TV commercials, not rough versions, because roughs do not have sufficient emotional authenticity).

More generally, the transformational style of advertising (Rossiter & Percy's, 1987 definition, not the Puto & Wells, 1984 definition in which almost all advertisements that make a promise are regarded as transformational) depends vitally on a positive emotional end state. The sequence is usually b-e⁺ (path 5), or simply e⁺ (point 6). For the negative motivations, the end state can be emotionally neutral (relief or relaxation). For the positive motivations, on the other hand, the end state *must* be a positive emotion (Rossiter & Percy, 1987, 1991).

Emotional Attack on Entrenched Attribute-Based Attitude

Again, let us consider the entrenched buyer of a particular brand, in which the brand could be some form of personal or social behavior instead of a brand in the commercial product or service sense. If the buyer's brand attitude is rationally based on an attribute, and we want to change it, then an emotional attack is worth considering. In terms of the a-b-e model, this is a-b attacked by e⁻-b (path 4). Although technically this should be labeled as a benefit path because it ends in a benefit, the key is the heavy, negative emotional beginning; hence we classify it as emotion focus.

Threat or fear appeals in advertising (or in personal selling) are the best-known application of this approach. The effect of fear, a negative emotion, is to distract the person from mounting rational counterarguments (Ray & Wilkie, 1974; Rogers 1983). Well-known examples of fear appeals in advertising (LaTour & Zahra, 1989) include the TV commercials for American Express Travelers Checks in which overseas travelers are robbed ("What kind were they?") and the Prudential Insurance TV ads of the early 80's in which a father dies on the operating table or a mother drowns, thus emphasizing the need for life insurance. The overall conclusion from many years of research on fear appeals is that the higher the fear level, the more effective the attack on brand attitude will be, provided that the recommended behavior change is perceived as do-able by the individual (Pratkanis & Aronson, 1991). If the behavior change is not do-able, any level of fear will exacerbate the original behavior (Rogers, 1983). The "do-ability" proviso is important. Perhaps the best examples are not in the areas of addictive habits such as smoking and drinking, whose consequences are largely emotionally reinforcing, but rather in the example of voting behavior. Voting is easily do-able. Whereas one would think that the public's political choices in state and national elections should be based on rational appraisal of the issues (attributes), many recent elections seem to have been strongly influenced by opposing parties' emotional attacks on the personal background of the candidates. Pratkanis and Aronson (1991) provided an interesting discussion of how emotional positioning can be effective in otherwise attribute-based arenas.

Summarizing the advertising situations in which emotion is the recommended focus, we see that there are at least three: (1) when the brand has only easy-to-imitate benefits, remembering that attribute focus is also an alternative; (2) when the brand choice is positively motivated (the b-e⁺ sequence); or (3) for an emotional attack (e⁻-b, but with heavy e⁻ focus) on an entrenched attribute-based attitude. These quite diverse but conditionally specific situations go beyond the simplistic exhortation to use "emotional" advertising.

SUMMARY AND PROSPECTUS

The a-b-e model provides a useful set of conditions or contingencies for choosing an appropriate focus for benefit claims or portrayals in ads — where the term "benefit" is now expanded into its attribute-benefit-emotion components. Figure 8.1 shows the model and Table 8.4 summarizes the recommended applications of the a-b-e model.

In the a-b-e model, the generic term "benefits" is broken down into three specific components: *attributes* (what the product has); *benefits* (what the buyer wants); and *emotions* (what the buyer feels before or after the benefit, or independently). In marketing communications, usually advertisements, for the brand's positioning, the focus can be on attributes, benefits, or emotions, or on particular sequential combinations of these components.

• *Attribute* focus should be used when the brand is positioned for an expert target audience, if the brand is an intangible service, or as an alternative to emotion focus for a brand competing in a category in which other brands offer virtually identical benefits.

• *Benefit* focus should always be used if the brand has a hard-to-imitate benefit. Also, benefit focus is the normal recommendation for a negatively motivated (informational) brand — more specifically, a sequential path of negative emotion(benefit delivery is recommended. Thirdly, benefit focus is worth trying if the brand wishes to attack an entrenched emotion-based

TABLE 8.4
Summary of the Conditions in the a-b-e Model of Benefit Focus

Attribute (a) focus
 • Expert target audience
 • Intangible service
 • Alternative to emotion-focus for homogeneous-benefit brands
Benefit (b) focus
 • Brand with hard-to-imitate benefit
 • Negatively-motivated (informational) brand
 • Logical attack on entrenched emotion-based attitude
Emotion (e) focus
 • Brand with easy-to-imitate benefit
 • Positively-motivated (transformational) brand
 • Emotional attack on entrenched attribute-based attitude

attitude—specifically, an attribute(benefit path is used to attack a bene-fit(emotion path.

• *Emotion* focus typically is a recommended option for a brand that only has easy-to-imitate benefits. If most brands in the category offer the same benefits, our brand can either go "back to" attributes (adopt the attribute focus above) or "go forward" to emotions (use an emotion focus). The attribute focus or the emotion focus may provide differentiation that could not be achieved by benefits alone. Emotion focus is also the normal recommendation for a positively motivated (transformational) brand; this could be represented by a benefit(positive emotion path or simply by pure (positive) emotion focus. Emotion focus, specifically the heavy negative emotion(benefit path, also can be used by a brand that is trying to attack an entrenched, attribute-based attitude.

The a-b-e model is a reasonably straightforward contingency approach that addresses the decision of which point or aspect of benefits should be the focus in ads. This decision, which occurs in the planning of every advertising campaign, has not been addressed previously in any thorough or systematic manner.

The a-b-e model is a considerable improvement on the means–end approach (the theoretical attributes-consequences-values model and its ad application model, MECCAS). Our key terms—attributes, benefits, and emotions—are defined more precisely. The a-b-e model, by its focus on different points and paths, rejects the assumption that consumers must be led right up the ladder in all ads. Indeed, it does not assume a hierarchical approach at all (as in a-c-v). Rather, it recommends specific foci either on their own or as the respective end-points of various linkages, or two-step sequences, of attributes, benefits (negative or positive reinforcers), or emotions (negative or positive). The a-b-e model is a vast improvement over simplistic models from the advertising world such as those that state that ads should always emphasize a consumer benefit or, more recently, that emotional ads work best. Advertising cannot be so simple. Clearly a contingency theory is required, and the a-b-e model provides such a theory.

Much remains to be learned, however, and the present version of the a-b-e model cannot be regarded as a final formulation. Because the model was developed entirely on logical analysis and secondary research findings, new research is needed to fully test the conditional hypotheses that the model proposes. Also, it is likely that other conditions will be identified to fit each of the recommendations for a, b, or e focus. However, the a-b-e model begins to address a big knowledge gap in advertising theory and this initial version of the model will prove very useful to advertisers.

ACKNOWLEDGMENTS

We wish to thank the faculty and Ph.D. students at the University of Minnesota and Pennsylvania State University and the managers at Campbell Mithun-Esty advertising agency in Minneapolis for feedback on the ideas in this chapter from its presentation in seminars during the first author's sabbatical visits. In particular, we thank Jerry Olson, Rik Pieters, and Kris Moller for their helpful discussions.

REFERENCES

A. C. Nielsen Company (1984). Natural foods—the consumer's perspective. *The Nielsen Researcher, 1*, 13–20.

Anson, C., & Silverstone, R. F. (1975). Supermarket strategy summary, in *Maryland Center for Public Broadcasting's Consumer Survival Kit*, Owing Hills, MD: Maryland Center for Public Broadcasting.

Bass, F. M., Givon, M., Kalwani, M. U., Reibstein, D., & Wright, G. P. (1984). An investigation into the order of the brand choice process. *Marketing Science, 3*(4), 267–287.

Birnbaum, M. H. (1981). Letter in the *American Psychologist, 36*(1), 99–101.

Cacioppo, J. T., Petty, R. E., & Geen, T. R. (1989). From the tripartite to the homeostasis model of attitudes. In A. R. Pratkanis, S. J. Breckler, & A. G. Greenwald (Eds.), *Attitude structure and function* (pp. 275–305). Hillsdale, NJ: Lawrence Erlbaum Associates.

Carpenter, G. S., Glazer, R., & Nakamoto, K. (1994). Meaningful brands from meaningless differentiation: The dependence on irrelevant attributes. *Journal of Marketing Research, 31*(3), 339–350.

Currim, I., & Schneider, L. G. (1991). A taxonomy of consumer purchase strategies in a promotion intensive environment, *Marketing Science, 10*(2), 91–110.

Deighton, J., & Schindler, R. M. (1988). Can advertising influence experience? *Psychology & Marketing, 5*(2), 103–115.

Feather, N. T. (1988). The meaning and importance of values: Research with the Rokeach Value Survey. *Australian Journal of Psychology, 40*(4), 377–390.

Fraser Hite, C., Hite, R. E., & Minor, T. (1991). Quality uncertainty, brand reliance and dissipative advertising. *Journal of the Academy of Marketing Science, 19*(2), 115–121.

Frazer, C. F. (1983). Creative strategy: A management perspective. *Journal Of Advertising, 12*(4), 36–41.

Gutman, J. (1982). A means–end chain model based on consumer categorization processes. *Journal of Marketing, 46*(1), 60–72.

Gutman, J. (1991). Exploring the nature of linkages between consequence and values. *Journal of Business Research, 22*(2), 143–148.

Hjorth-Anderson, C. (1984). The concept of quality and the efficiency of markets for consumer products. *Journal of Consumer Research, 11*(2), 708–718.

Holden, S. J. S. (1993). Understanding brand awareness: Let me give a c(l)ue! *Advances in Consumer Research, 20*, 383–388.

Howard, J. A. (1977). *Consumer Behavior: Application of Theory*. New York: McGraw-Hill.

Hwang, S. L. (1992, September 14). New Marlboro Man is a mere shadow of his former self. *The Wall Street Journal*, B1, B5.

James, W. (1890). *Psychology*. New York: Holt.

Katz, D. (1960). The functional approach to the study of attitudes. *Public Opinion Quarterly*, 24(2), 163–204.

Key, W. B. (1974). *Subliminal seduction*. Englewood Cliffs, NJ: Prentice-Hall.

Kroeber-Riel, W. (1986). Nonverbal measurement of emotional advertising effects. In J. Olson & K. Sentis (Eds.), *Advertising and Consumer Psychology, Vol. 3* (pp. 35–52). New York: Praeger.

Kroeber-Riel, W. (1988). Advertising on saturated markets, working paper, Saarbrucken, Germany: Institute for Consumer and Behavioral Research, University of the Saarland.

LaTour, M. S., & Zahra, S. A. (1989). Fear appeals as advertising strategy: Should they be used? *Journal of Consumer Marketing*, 6(2), 61–70.

Lilien, G. L., Kotler, P., & Moorthy, K. S. (1992). *Marketing Models*. Englewood Cliffs, NJ: Prentice-Hall.

Maheswaran, D., & Sternthal, B. (1990). The effects of knowledge, motivation, and type of message on ad processing and product judgments. *Journal of Consumer Research*, 17(1), 66–73.

McQueen, J. (1990). The different ways ads work. *Journal of Advertising Research*, 30(5), RC-13–RC-16.

Millar, M. G., & Millar, K. U. (1990). Attitude change as a function of attitude type and argument type, *Journal of Personality and Social Psychology*, 59(2), 217–228.

Moberg, G. D. (1988, January 4). Strategy testing: To execute or not to execute? *Marketing News*, 30.

Moore, D. L., & Hutchinson, J. W. (1985). The influence of affective reactions to advertising: Direct and indirect mechanisms of attitude change. In L. Alwitt and A. A. Mitchell (Eds.), *Psychological processes and advertising effects: Theory, research and application* (pp. 65–87). Hillsdale, NJ: Lawrence Erlbaum Associates.

Moran, W. T. (1990). Brand presence and the perceptual frame. *Journal of Advertising Research*, 30(5), 9–16.

Nedungadi, P. (1990). Recall and consideration sets: Influencing choice without altering brand evaluations. *Journal of Consumer Research*, 17(3), 263–276.

Osgood, C. E., Suci, G., & Tannenbaum, P. H. (1957). *The measurement of meaning*. Champaign-Urbana, IL: University of Illinois Press.

Percy, L., & Rossiter, J. R. (1992). A model of brand awareness and brand attitude advertising strategies. *Psychology & Marketing*, 9(4), 263–274.

Perkins, W. S., & Reynolds, T. J. (1988). The explanatory power of values in preference judgments: Validation of the means–end perspective. *Advances in Consumer Research*, 15, 122–126.

Petty, R. E., & Cacioppo, J. T. (1986). *Communication and persuasion: Central and peripheral routes to attitude change*. New York: Springer.

Pratkanis, A., & Aronson, E. (1991). *Age of propaganda*. New York: W. H. Freeman.

Puto, C. R., & Wells, W. D. (1984). Informational and transformational advertising: The differential effects of time. *Advances in Consumer Research*, 11, 638–643.

Ray, M. L., & Wilkie, W. L. (1970). Fear: The potential of an appeal neglected by marketing. *Journal of Marketing*, 31(1), 54–62.

Resnik, A., & Stern, B. L. (1977). An analysis of information content in television advertising. *Journal of Marketing*, 41(1), 50–53.

Reynolds, T. J., Cockle, B., & Rochon, J. P. (1990). The strategic imperatives of advertising: Implications of means–end theory and research findings. *Canadian Journal of Marketing Research*, 9, 3–13.

Reynolds, T. J., & Craddock, A. (1988). The application of MECCAS model to the development and assessment of advertising strategy: A case study. *Journal of Advertising Research*, 28(2), 43–54.

Reynolds, T. J., & Gengler, C. E. (1990). A strategic framework for assessing advertising: The animatic versus finished issue. *Journal of Advertising Research, 31*(5), 61–71.

Reynolds, T. J., & Gutman, J. (1984). Advertising is image management. *Journal of Advertising Research, 24*(2), 27–37.

Reynolds, T. J., & Gutman, J. (1988). Laddering theory, method, analysis and interpretation. *Journal of Advertising Research, 28*(1), 11–21.

Reynolds, T. J., & Rochon, J. D. (1991). Means–end based advertising research: Copy testing is not strategy assessment. *Journal of Business Research, 22*(2), 131–142.

Rice, J. (1991, September 2). Ever try converting a staunch Catholic to Buddhism? *Marketing News*, 40.

Rogers, R. W. (1983). Attitude change and information integration in fear appeals. *Psychological Reports, 56*(1), 179–182.

Rokeach, M. (1973). *The nature of human values*. New York: Free Press.

Rossiter, J. R., & Percy, L. (1987). *Advertising and promotion management*. New York: McGraw-Hill.

Rossiter, J. R., & Percy, L. (1991). Emotions and motivations in advertising. *Advances in Consumer Research, 18*, 100–110.

Rossiter, J. R., & Percy, L. (1997). *Advertising communications & promotion management*, 2nd. ed., New York: McGraw-Hill.

Rossiter, J. R., Percy, L., & Donovan, R. J. (1991). A better advertising planning grid, *Journal of Advertising Research, 31*(5), 11–21.

Ruth, W. J., & Mosatche, H. S. (1985). A projective assessment of the effects of Freudian sexual symbolism in liquor advertisements. *Psychological Reports, 56*(1), 183–188.

Ruth, W. J., Mosatche, H. S., & Kramer, A. (1989). Freudian sexual symbolism: Theoretical considerations and an empirical test in advertising. *Psychological Reports, 60*(2), 1131–1139.

Shavitt, S., & Brock, T. S. (1986). Self-relevant responses in commercial persuasion: Field and experimental tests. In J. C. Olson & K. Sentis (Eds.), *Advertising and consumer psychology, vol. 3* (pp. 149–171). New York: Praeger.

Shostack, G. L. (1977). Breaking free from product marketing. *Journal of Marketing, 41*(2), 73–80.

Shostack, G. L. (1981). How to design a service. In J. H. Donnelly & W. R. George (Eds.), *Marketing of services* (pp. 221–229). Chicago: American Marketing Association.

Sproles, G. B. (1986). The concept of quality and the efficiency of markets: Issues and comments. *Journal of Consumer Research, 13*(1), 146–148.

Stern, B. L., & Resnik, A. J. (1991). Information content in television advertising. *Journal of Advertising Research, 31*(3), 36–46.

Sujan, M. (1985). Consumer knowledge: Effects on evaluation strategies mediating consumer judgments. *Journal of Consumer Research, 12*(1), 31–46.

The Wall Street Journal (1992, June 24). Shrinkage of stores and customers in U.S. causes Italy's Benetton to alter its tactics, B1, B10.

Vallette-Florence, P., & Rapachi, B. (1991). Improvements in means–end chain analysis using graph theory and correspondence analysis. *Journal of Advertising Research, 31*(1), 30–45.

Yi, Y. (1989). An investigation of the structure of expectancy-value and its implications. *International Journal of Research in Marketing, 6*(2), 71–83.

Zajonc, R. B. (1968). The attitudinal effects of mere exposure. *Journal of Personality and Social Psychology Monographs, 9*(2, part 2), 1–27.

9

Effectively Translating In-Depth Consumer Understanding Into Communications Strategy and Advertising Practice

Thomas J. Reynolds
Richmont Partners

David B. Whitlark
Brigham Young University

Richard B. Wirthlin
The Wirthlin Group

ABSTRACT

This chapter provides a brief overview of means–end theory and outlines the guiding principles of using laddering research to identify and apply customer-focused communications strategies. It provides a summary of personal observations, practical experience, and discussions with leading professionals in the field of advertising and communications regarding the effective use of a means–end approach to formulate, specify, and execute communications strategy. Said another way, it represents a set of "school-yard lessons" in applying laddering research to real communications problems. Information is organized around 12 principles or lessons for developing and applying communications strategy with examples drawn from contemporary advertising and promotional campaigns. This chapter also provides an overview of the reasons for and the concepts governing the strategic assessment of advertising.

For more than a decade, means–end theory and research techniques such as laddering (Gutman & Reynolds, 1979; Reynolds & Gutman, 1984b) have been used to develop effective advertising and promotional strategies for many leading corporations, industry organizations, public service groups, and political candidates. We believe the strategies succeed in the marketplace because they are customer focused. The strategies build public interest, involvement, and commitment because they tap into personal needs, goals, or values that provide the motivation underlying everyday living and decision-making.

Over the past several months, industry experts have shared with us the many challenges and breakthroughs they have experienced when working with clients to bring to bear the full power of means–end theory and research. These discussions, combined with our own observations and experience, have led us to set down 12 practical lessons for developing and applying communications strategy.

We separate the 12 lessons into three areas: strategy formulation, specification of strategy, and execution of strategy. The lessons provide much-needed guideposts for taking full advantage of means–end research. We have learned that making the most of means–end research is as much art as science and that there are many hazards along the way to distract, confuse, and sometimes discourage those anxious to employ a means–end approach to their communications program. However, many marketers now applying means–end thinking will attest that the rewards for uncovering and employing a truly customer-focused strategy makes the trouble well worth the effort.

In the first section of this chapter, we show the relation between being customer-focused and applying the fundamental ideas of means–end theory and suggest some reasons why a means–end approach provides marketers with a better way to compete. Next, the chapter outlines the key concepts of means–end research and makes a distinction between a means–end approach and traditional survey research. We then turn to the central purpose of this chapter and present 12 lessons for developing and applying communications strategy from means–end research. Lessons are illustrated using contemporary advertising and promotional campaigns that have drawn our attention as being particularly good examples of one or more of the underlying principles we associate with means–end communications strategy. Finally, in describing the twelfth lesson, we introduce the reasoning and fundamental concepts underpinning the strategic assessment of advertising.

MEANS–END THEORY

Customer-Focused Framework

Means–end theory (Gutman, 1982) provides one of the most powerful premises for developing a customer-focused communications strategy. In the means–end framework, product attributes and their functional conse-

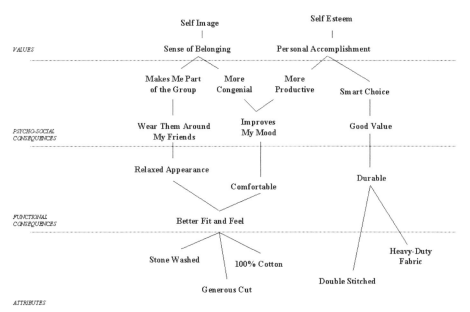

FIG. 9.1. Consumer decision-making map: Relaxed-fit jeans.

quences are just the means to an end. The *end* is a personal need, goal, or value that reflects the perceptual orientation of the consumer and shows how he or she translates a seemingly inconsequential product into an object having deep personal relevance and importance.

To be customer focused, marketers must understand the end as well as the means of consumer decision-making. In Fig. 9.1, we see that the end people seek when purchasing a product like relaxed-fit jeans is not the bundle of product attributes or even the physical experience of comfort and durability associated with consumption but actually a set of psychological and/or sociological rewards and advantages associated with satisfying one or more personal values, motives, or goals. In a means–end world, competitors contend with each other to establish and control linkages between the distinguishing attributes of their products and one or more personal values or goals that, in turn, are associated with personally relevant psychological or sociological rewards or advantages.

The fundamental objective of a means–end communications strategy is to position products, services, corporations, political candidates, and public issues by exploiting our understanding of the personal value structures through which consumers perceive the world. Means–end theory and its associated methodology are focused on uncovering the personal, often hidden reasons why consumers believe some attributes and consequences are more important than others.

A Better Way to Compete

The majority of marketplace competition centers around the "attribute versus attribute" level. In contrast, with a means–end communications strategy, the axial challenge is to determine the personal value or goal that best fits with the distinctive attributes of the product, forge a strong connection between personal value and product attribute, and fight off competitive products that want to do the same.

A stream of academic research starting as early as Cartwright (1949) has consistently reported results indicating that a product's success at tapping into personal needs, goals, or values tends to be the best predictor of consumer preference. The basic finding is consistent across many different types of products and situations. For example, Reynolds, Gutman, and Fiedler (1984) found the result among restaurant patrons: Reynolds and Jamieson (1984) among department store patrons; Perkins and Reynolds (1987) for snack chip consumers; Jolly, Reynolds, and Slocum (1988) with respect to the performance appraisal of subordinates.

Means–end theory asserts that effective advertising will link together several levels of product information, that is attributes, consequences, and values. Moreover, means–end theory asserts that advertising will be the most persuasive when the psychological and sociological benefits of consumption, that is, psychosocial consequences, are shown to develop rationally and consistently from a set of distinctive product attributes. Reynolds and Gengler (1991) reported that it is unusual for an ad to generate significant product affect unless the ad can make at least one strong connection between an adjacent pair of communications levels.

Means–End Fundamentals

The means–end model classifies and links together four levels of information that underpin consumer decision-making. At the most concrete level, attributes are the physical, tangible features or characteristics of a product. In the mind of the consumer, these tangible features translate into functional consequences. Functional consequences can be described as the physical, tangible experiences associated with product consumption. At higher levels of abstraction, product attributes and functional consequences tap into personal values or goals through satisfying key psychosocial consequences. Psychosocial consequences, themselves, spring from the emotional experiences of consumption driven by psychological and/ or sociological rewards or punishments.

The means–end chain traveled by a consumer when connecting product attributes with personal needs or goals represents their perceptual orientation with respect to the product and the buying situation. It shows why the product is self-relevant or involving. Consequently, one might argue that the perceptual orientations depicted by personalized networks of means–end chains provide the key strands of information needed to explain product-related attitudes and behavior.

The strength of connection between person and product is reflected by the level of involvement a consumer has with the product category (Walker & Olson, 1991). Consumer involvement grows when marketers bring out personally relevant psychological and sociological reasons for consuming their products, and consequently, involvement can be manipulated by marketing programs (Peter & Olson, 1994). For example, small-package delivery was a low-involvement, low-loyalty commodity business until Federal Express introduced the overnight delivery of small packages and made it self-relevant by showing the important psychosocial consequences associated with using their delivery service for business-related packages. Indeed, the primary goal of a means–end communications strategy is to build consumer involvement.

MEANS–END RESEARCH

Distinctions From Consumer-Attitude Survey Research

The key distinction between means–end research and traditional consumer-attitude research is the relative emphasis the two approaches put on determining the specific reasons why product attributes are important to consumers (Reynolds, Cockle, & Rochon, 1990). Traditional attitude research focuses on determining the relative importance of attributes and measuring perceptions about how well products perform with respect to important attributes. Means–end research focuses on determining the key choice criteria underlying a purchase decision, identifying how the choice criteria relate to product attributes and understanding the reasons why the product attributes and related choice criteria are important or personally relevant to consumers.

Marketing research that addresses attribute importance and performance becomes much more actionable when marketers also learn how the consequences of product attributes can be communicated effectively and how to link product attributes with reasons why superior performance of an attribute matters to the decision maker. Furthermore, with a consumer-relevant context that relates a product to the real needs underpinning product purchase and consumption, the marketer gains more insight into how to use marketing research to create a sustainable competitive advantage.

Means–end research can provide new ideas for product development, consumer promotions, communications strategy and advertising execution, pricing, distribution, and many other important marketing issues. Intuitively, successful marketers know that product attributes and the functional consequences of those attributes are not the motivating "end-states" leading to trial, repurchase, and positive word-of-mouth. They sense that product traits are a means to some end but are unsure about how consumer end-states change depending on the event triggering the buying situation, the target audience, and other aspects of the purchasing context relevant to the consumer.

Guidelines for Laddering Interviews

In-depth laddering interviews provide the primary machinery for conducting means–end research. Although often misused by marketing research companies, this style of interviewing amounts to much more than just unstructured note taking directed at recovering a respondent's general knowledge about a product or product category. It also markedly differs from narrowly-drawn, open-ended questions about important reasons for selecting a product. To be effective, laddering interviews must be in-depth, yet crisp and pointed. Unlike survey research that is often shallow and broad (dozens of short-answer, closed-end questions asked across a large sample of respondents), means–end research and laddering should be focused and deep (five or six interdependent, closed-ended and open-ended questions asked across a small, targeted sample).

Laddering research works best and produces the most actionable results for marketers when it is directed at achieving a specific marketing goal such as increasing sales revenue through increasing the number of people buying in the product category, attacking a leading brand, or encouraging current customers to use the brand more often. To accomplish such a goal, marketers must utilize a well thought out research design consisting of a purposive sample, context-specific interview drivers, appropriate elicitation techniques for detecting choice criteria, suitable methods for uncovering personal relevance, and unbiased ways to measure competitive strengths and weaknesses.

A purposive sample is selected to create contrast between different consumer points of view and to isolate factors that will "tip the balance" in favor of buying from a product category, selecting a particular brand, or increasing one's frequency of brand use. Furthermore, the interview itself and the method for eliciting reasons for choosing one product over another must be dimensionalized to include relevant people, places, social occasions, and purchase or consumption timing.

Distinctions between alternatives, that is, choice criteria, can be elicited in several different ways, including triadic sorting (Reynolds & Gutman, 1984b), but are usually determined by asking about reasons for choosing one alternative over another. Reynolds and Gutman (1988) provided detailed explanations of alternative elicitation methods. Finally, the full set of choice alternatives, whether they are direct competitors like Coke and Pepsi or indirect competitors like Coke and tap water, should be included in the choice exercise. Furthermore, marketers should resist the urge to myopically focus their total effort on brand competition where gains are the hardest and competitive reactions are the strongest.

Choice criteria elicited in the laddering process must be linked with tangible product attributes as well as to the intangible reasons why the criteria matter to the consumer and their value system. This often requires interviewers to ladder down before they can ladder up. In our experience, respondents only occasionally mention concrete product attributes as the reason for selecting one product over another. Respondents are more likely to mention a functional or, in some cases, a psycho-social consequence as the choice criterion. Untrained or poorly trained interviewers often take consequences as the starting point for a ladder. Consequently, they frequently do not differentiate between attributes and the functional consequences of attributes. As a result, they have difficulty uncovering the connection between product and person and seldom identify the respondent-specific cues that can clearly communicate a functional consequence.

In conjunction with the laddering interview, competitive strengths and weaknesses must be measured with respect to key choice criteria and the means–end chain of attributes, functional consequences, psychosocial consequences, and personal values to which they relate. Effective communications strategy fundamentally grows out of playing to strength. Consequently, without a pattern of competitive strengths and weaknesses to overlay on the network of means–end chains resulting from laddering interviews, there is no basis to judge whether a particular communications strategy can help build or sustain a competitive advantage. In short, marketers need more than an aggregate map of means–end chains to formulate, specify, and execute an effective communications strategy. Understanding competitive strengths and weaknesses and the barriers and opportunities they create also is critically important.

Analysis of Means–End Research

Laddering interviews uncover means–end chains associated with consumer-specific product meanings. These product meanings represent the different perceptual or buying orientations of various benefit segments within the target market. Understanding the key product elements and connections between elements together with the associated overlay of competitive strengths and weaknesses forms the basis for devising a customer-focused communications strategy.

There are four general approaches to creating competitive advantage through an analysis of means–end chains:

- *Uncovering an untapped or emerging buying orientation that represents a significant market opportunity.* As examples, consider the emerging buying orientations of the elderly living as retired people many more years than anticipated, the baby-boom generation going through mid-life crisis, or the large numbers of young people now gaining unprecedented buying power.
- *Strengthening ownership of a buying orientation that is already, or at least somewhat, associated with your product.* It is not unusual for new products to sell successfully in the marketplace without the marketing manager knowing exactly why. Similarly, many marketers cannot easily specify the higher level reasons underpinning the purchase and consumption of their brand. In these situations, understanding the importance in a consumer's decision-making process, means–end orientation that attracts consumers provides the stepping off point for reinforcing and defending one's market position.
- *Creating a new buying orientation that better fits the distinctive traits of your product.* New buying orientations may be created by either connecting yet unrelated concepts or interjecting new attributes or context-specific consequences into the network of choice criteria. This general approach to strategy can create marketing miracles along the lines of Honda who revitalized and dramatically expanded motorcycle sales in the United States by making a new connection between small motorcycles, convenient transportation, and young-at-heart, friendly riders.
- *Reframing a buying orientation initially owned by a key competitor.* Turning a strength into a weakness is one of the most powerful strategic ideas a marketer can employ. In a means–end world, this can be done most effectively by playing to the relevant set of psychosocial consequences. Consider the resounding success of Cannon personal copiers against Xerox relative to the very limited success of the larger, stronger competitors Kodak and IBM. Kodak and IBM tried to compete on the basis of superior product attributes and consequences in the context of centralized copying which Xerox owned. On the other hand, Cannon turned the distinctive competence of Xerox in centralized copying into a liability for many potential customers by stressing distributed copying that gave more personal control, a psychosocial consequence, to employees and business managers.

COMMUNICATIONS STRATEGY
AND ADVERTISING PRACTICE

Aside from the general approaches to creating competitive advantage previously outlined that can be uncovered by means–end research, which have been to some extent discussed in several papers (e.g., Olson &

Reynolds, 1983; Reynolds, Cockle, & Rochon, 1990; Strategic Assessment, Inc., 1992), few specifics or examples have been published explaining how one can translate means–end research into effective communications strategies and executional ideas. We offer the following strategic principles and contemporary examples as a help to marketers, communications consultants, advertising executives, and public-relations practitioners interested in applying the lessons of means–end marketing. The practical lessons outlined in this chapter are an outgrowth and extension of principles and research findings previously published by several authors (e.g., Olson & Reynolds, 1983; Reynolds & Gutman, 1987; Reynolds, Cockle, & Rochon, 1991; Strategic Assessment, Inc., 1992). We also draw heavily from our personal correspondence with these and other leading professionals in the field of advertising and communications.

Strategy Formulation

Lesson 1: Identify and Take Into Account What Gives Product Attributes Their Relative Importance in a Consumer's Decision-Making Process

Persuasive advertising depends directly on emphasizing the distinctiveness of product attributes and successfully tapping into the connections people make between product attributes, functional outcomes, and personal needs or goals (Cartwright, 1949). Communications that simply describe product attributes and consequences without demonstrating the role they play in satisfying the personal needs and goals of consumers fall short of an important requirement for persuasive advertising. A consumer-focused framework that shows how product attributes are linked with personal needs will help marketers understand how consumers think about the product. An actionable communications framework will provide insight into how consumers process information about the three-way combination of product, category, and context so as to give meaning to their purchases and consumption. Means–end theory provides a simple framework with which to represent the consumer thought process and points the way to defining the functional role of communications in influencing consumer choice.

Reynolds and Gutman (1988) conceptualized *meaning* as the connection consumers make between two adjacent communications levels. Each connection or meaning arises from the concepts being linked and the context of their association. For example, when we observe in the context of purchasing financial services that "saves time and effort" is connected with "smart use of money," we can say that "saves time and effort" is an aspect of financial service that means "smart use of money" for investors paying for professional help in managing their financial resources. An important goal of communications is to create or strengthen these types of connections. The connections between adjacent communications elements represent how consumers interpret product knowledge and information at each level of the means–end chain.

A communications strategy should guide the creative staff by indicating the connections or meanings that must be made or reinforced in the mind of the consumer. The creative task then becomes one of developing the appropriate visual and verbal cues and contextual setting that will cause the right connections to be made by the target audience. The campaign strategy followed by President Reagan's political advisors provided an example of this principle (Reynolds, Westberg, & Olson, 1994).

Consider the Reagan–Bush situation shown in Fig. 9.2. When formulating a campaign strategy for Ronald Reagan's candidacy for reelection, his political advisors wanted to build on Reagan's key strengths "decisive" and "gets things done" that voters translated into "strong leadership." Voters also thought that "strengthening the military" was another of Reagan's strong qualities, yet they believed that a key strength of Mondale was his pacifist world-view that offered a more direct way of decreasing the chance of war.

In order to turn Mondale's strength into a weakness, the advisors recommended undermining Mondale's "arms control leading to world

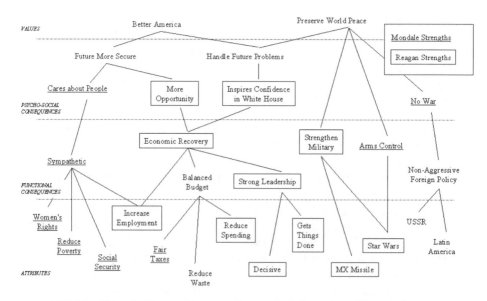

FIG. 9.2.   Voter decision-making map: Reagan-Bush '84. Adapted from Fielder and Bahner (1985).

peace" message by strengthening links between Reagan's powerful leadership qualities and his ability to build a stronger military and then by reinforcing the link between building a stronger military and peace through communicating that a stronger military is the logical way to prepare for lasting peace. In short, a stronger military was reframed to mean a decreased chance of war and arms control was reframed to mean an increased chance of war.

In an effective ad called "Bear," political advisors reframed Mondale's position on arms control. The ad simply showed a bear walking through the woods to finally confront a man face-to-face. With the sound of a beating heart in the background the announcer reads, "There is a bear in the woods. For some people the bear is easy to see. Others don't see it at all. Some people say the bear is tame. Others say it is vicious and dangerous. Since no one can really be sure who's right, isn't it smart to be as strong as the bear. If there Is a bear."

In another ad named "Kids," voters were given more evidence why Reagan's strong leadership qualities of "decisive" and "gets things done" were important. The execution shows happy and content children playing and enjoying life. At one point, children are shown on a porch next to a gently waving American flag. The scene is followed up by a sound bite and video clip of President Reagan addressing an audience. The advertising also used the tagline, "President Reagan . . . Leadership that's working."

In the voice-over, President Reagan says:

> We've faced two world wars, a war in Korea, then Vietnam. And I know this. I want our children never to have to face another. A president's most important job is to secure peace, not just now but for the lifetimes of our children. But it takes a strong America to build a peace that lasts. And I believe with all my heart that working together we have made America stronger and prouder and more secure today. And now we can work for a lasting peace for our children and children to come. Peace is the highest aspiration of the American people. Today America is prepared for peace. We will negotiate for it. Sacrifice for it. We will not surrender for it now or ever.

Lesson 2: Communications Strategy and the Means–End Research on Which it is Based Must be Framed With Specific Goals in Mind

There are many ways in which marketers can define marketing objectives. For example, marketers may want a communications strategy that outlines a campaign for increasing product sales by getting more people into the store or facilitating greater contact between people and products during the decision-making process. In addition, rather than focusing exclusively on brand competition, marketing objectives could be directed at encouraging more people to buy in the product category or for suggesting ways that your customers can increase their frequency of product use.

Just as laddering interviews should be more than unstructured note taking and accomplish more than obtaining general information regarding how consumers think about products, communication strategy should set its sights higher than communicating positive beliefs about a brand relative to its competitors. For example, if we want to expand the percentage of buyers in a product category or even increase the average frequency of product usage among current customers we must bolster the general set of positive beliefs about our product by adding in new concepts or linkages that will help more people view the product in the same way as our best customers.

Goal-directed means–end research can answer the difficult questions about what do our best customers believe about the product that others do not, and what are the barriers to achieving broader product acceptance. As an example, consider the case of Honda motorcycles documented by Pascal (1984). Although the example unfolds years before the advent of means–end research, the story demonstrates how having a specific goal in mind and using an understanding of best customers can lead to effective advertising.

Honda Motorcycle.   From 1960 to 1965, motorcycle registrations in the United States more than doubled from about one half million to over one million. Before 1960, Harley-Davidson was the market leader. After 1960, Honda became the market leader by selling a low-priced, low-powered, easy-to-handle motorcycle. The success surprised Honda management, who had felt their small 50cc motorcycle was poorly suited to the U.S. market.

In the spring of 1963, an undergraduate advertising major at University of California at Los Angeles first suggested the "You Meet the Nicest People on a Honda" campaign as part of a routine class assignment. The campaign theme was written from the perspective of a satisfied customer. The ad first reinforces widely held, positive beliefs that the bike is small, economical, and easy-to-handle. Then the ad shows what only satisfied buyers had discovered, that is, the bike gives the rider personal freedom and brings people together in a positive way. On one hand, the ad helped others understand the bike in the same special way as satisfied customers. On the other, it cleverly addressed the leather-jacketed, teenage rebel-without-a-cause stereotype that created barriers for many potential buyers. Through 1963, due to the new ad campaign, Honda motorcycle sales increased their pace considerably. By the end of the year, nearly one half of all motorcycles sold in the United States were made by Honda.

In its initial efforts to open the U.S. market, Honda unsuccessfully tried to compete head-on with Harley-Davidson, using their own comparably sized, large motorcycles. Success came quickly, however, when Honda found themselves in a situation that de-emphasized brand competition. With their small bike, they dramatically increased the percentage of people buying in the product category by tapping into a new market segment by finding an entirely different buying orientation centered around new functional, psychological, and sociological benefits of riding motorcycles.

Lesson 3: Take Into Account Competitive Advertising as Well as Your Own Competitive Strengths and Weaknesses

Understanding your own product and playing to strength in the context of a competitive marketplace is a requirement for differentiating your product in a way that target audiences will find meaningful, relevant, and persuasive. Within a competitive framework, the creative staff should ask such questions as: "How do we speak directly and uniquely to people with that buying orientation?" "What set of circumstances will cause this connection to be made in the viewer's mind?"; "What new concept does this product offer to consumers that will satisfy higher level needs?"; and "What sorts of mental connections must be made in order to show consumers that these product attributes are strengths and not weaknesses?"

Among the best examples of using means–end research to successfully play to strength in a hostile communications environment comes from the astute communications campaign sponsored by the American Plastics Council. In the summer of 1992, national attitudes toward the plastics industry were turning decidedly hostile. More Americans felt that plastic hurt society than those who thought it helped society. Public attitudes were reflected in public behavior. The deselecting of plastic packaging and components in both consumer and industrial markets caused serious concern among industry leaders, yet in about 18 months time an ad campaign and collateral industry activities were able to turn around the situation. An informal poll sponsored by the American Plastics Council among manufacturers estimated that by early 1994, the selection of plastic grocery bags in supermarkets had increased over 50% compared to the previous year. In fact, the communications campaign was so successful that the paper industry launched their own promotional campaign in response.

American Plastics Council. Since the 1980s, groups concerned about the environment have raised issues about the use and disposal of plastic packaging and products and encouraged the use of environment-friendly alternatives like paper. Plastics industry officials, on the other hand, felt if people were just informed that plastic was less harmful to the environment than paper, deselection of plastic packaging and products would decline. Consequently, the plastics industry met the negative claims of environmentalists head-on, yet made little progress on changing public attitudes or behavior.

In the initial advertising campaign, the plastics industry did not play to strength but instead attempted to confront directly and dispel perceived weaknesses. In April, 1993, however, a new approach was adopted with the ad called "Today." The opening scene showed a boy being tackled in a football game with his parents looking on. The announcer read: "Today, Dave Ryan will understand the benefits of a little extra protection." The scene shifts to a shower, and the announcer continued: "Today, Bradey Blackwell will come to appreciate a shatter resistant shampoo bottle." We were then shown a family standing in front of an orthopedic hospital, and we watched as a young girl touched her grandfather's hip while the announcer read: "Today, for the first time in years Sheila Conner's grandpa will be able to walk with less pain." The ad then returned to the football game with the crowd cheering as the announcer finished with, "Today will be a better day for a lot of people simply because of a material we call plastic."

The functional consequences of living safer and healthier lives and the associated feelings of less worry over personal and family safety and health emphasized in the ad "Today" stem from a general belief among the U.S. public that, relative to other materials, plastic is particularly good because it is shatterproof, durable, and has many important safety and medical uses. In turn, the ad makes a strong connection between these perceived strengths and the sense of being a responsible parent and having greater personal security.

Finding a way to tie the noble characteristics of plastic to personally relevant goals like family responsibility and personal security has the potential for significantly reducing feelings of guilt people experience when buying plastic products or products packaged in plastic. Playing to competitive strength is much more effective than directly addressing perceived weaknesses, particularly in a communications environment that sends out many negative messages and makes counterarguments of confrontational ads very easy.

Lesson 4: Contextual Factors Such as Different Consumption Occasions Create Differences in Consumer Preferences

Reynolds (1985) reported that different consumption occasions lead to differences in consumer preferences. Consequently, it is natural that contextual factors, such as people, places, social setting, and timing of purchases and consumption must be considered when formulating a communications strategy.

Identifying the dominant perceptual or buying orientations that span a product category provides a powerful basis for applying benefit segmentation. Within each buying segment, we can answer why the benefits sought by each audience are important and valued. Rather than only being a complex diversion, understanding the role of context in creating product meaning can become an important ally in achieving marketing goals. As an example, consider a recent advertising campaign sponsored by Federal Express that builds on the same product feature to speak to two separate target audiences.

Federal Express. Two ads, the first called "Applause" and the second called "Gotcha" both call to our attention that Federal Express tracking software is a distinctive product attribute. On the other hand, the ads show us why the attribute is important to people in two very different ways. As shown in Fig. 9.3, the two unique reasons underlying the importance of the package-tracking software attribute arise from two different buying orientations that characterize different market segments for Federal Express—administrative staff (i.e., facilitators of overnight delivery service and business executives), that is, generators of overnight delivery service. The administrative staff segment seeks self-esteem and to make a

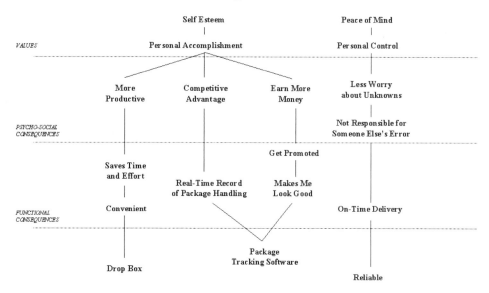

FIG. 9.3. Consumer decision-making map: Express mail delivery. Adapted from Reynolds and Craddock (1988).

positive impression on co-workers. The business executive segment wants to win and attain feelings of personal accomplishment.

The first ad, "Applause," is directed at administrative staff. The context created in the ad shows a large open room filled with many workers. In this setting, all your co-workers know about your mistakes and your successes. It is a typical workday and an irritable senior manager charges into the room and starts yelling, "Martha, that package you sent to Denver, it never got there!" To which an intimidated Martha replies, "Well . . . (Announcer: "Tracking software from Federal Express.") . . . it was picked up at 5:20 last night. It was delivered at 9:20 a.m. and signed for by Kate Donovan. Shall I call her for you sir?" "Never mind," whispers the manager as he charges back out of the room. (Announcer: "Now you can track packages right from your computer at your desk.") In the closing scene all the employees stand up and give Martha a round of enthusiastic applause, who reluctantly stands up and takes a bow. The ad effectively plays to an administrative staff member's need for self-esteem and to make a positive impression on others by showing how the tracking software can give them a measure of control over their working environment and help them look good in front of co-workers.

The second ad called "Gotcha" uses an entirely different context that is more relevant for business executives or senior staff members. The setting is a high-rise office with senior staff members surrounding the key decision-maker for a business deal. The executive decision-maker murmurs, "I know. Say we didn't get the package." (*Phone rings.*) The staff member answers, "Martha." Martha replies, "Tom, did you get our package?" "Gee, it never got here," answers Tom. To which Martha remarks, "Really . . . (Announcer: "Tracking software from Federal Express.") . . . It was delivered to your place at 9:22 a.m." Tom retorts with, "Oh, it's probably stuck in the mail room." "No," says Martha, "it was signed for by your partner Brian." (Announcer: "Now you can track packages right from your computer at your desk.") After an embarrassing pause, Tom responds, "Oh, that package . . . we can negotiate a deal if you. . . ." The ad effectively plays to a business executive's compulsive need to win. The tracking software has appeal because it can give executives the upper hand in the marketplace and consequently, satisfy their desire for personal accomplishment.

Lesson 5: The Communications Strategy Should Build on Perceived Strengths and Also Address Societal and Personal Barriers That may Prevent the Desired Behavior

Advertising consists of campaigns, not just single ads. This is a key point because, in general, agencies have found that ads telling a single story, making a single point, are more effective than ads attempting to cover all the bases. Said another way and in the context of consumer marketing, an ad campaign should consist of ads specifically targeted at either building product affect or at helping viewers overcome societal or personal barriers associated with product purchase and consumption.

Consider three ads from the national prolife campaign sponsored by the Arthur S. Demos Foundation. The campaign touches on all three aspects of persuasion by increasing support for the prolife stance helping women with unexpected pregnancies to deal with both societal and personal barriers associated with abortion alternatives. The first ad, "Decision," builds general support for the prolife position. "Moments" shows that society admires and esteems women who decide to give up their children for adoption rather than have an abortion. The third ad, "Loneliest," helps women facing an unexpected pregnancy deal with self-doubt about real-life alternatives to abortion.

National Prolife Campaign.   The ad called "Decision" builds general support for the prolife position. It shows scenes of a young boy and his family moving happily through life. The female voice-over represents the young boy's mother. She says, "When I got pregnant with Timmy 10 years ago, we almost chose not to bring him into the world. We were young and unmarried; we didn't have much money, and at the time it seemed like the right decision. But now every time I look at him I can't imagine life without him." The closing scene focuses on the close relationship the boy has with his father and the announcer says, "Life, what a beautiful choice."

In the next ad called "Moments," the announcer tells us that:

> Last year 50,000 women found families to adopt their unexpected children. They decided instead of abortion to tough it out and bring their babies into the world. They held to their belief that nothing is more precious than human life. To all these mothers, the families who adopted these children would like to say thank you. Life. What a Beautiful Choice.

The ad shows that society admires women that value human life and appreciates greatly their personal sacrifice in choosing adoption not abortion.

A third ad called "Loneliest" helps women experiencing an unexpected pregnancy deal more effectively with feelings of remorse and self-doubt. The announcer first shows empathy for the woman's situation and says, "One of the loneliest feelings in the world is being faced with an unexpected pregnancy. You've no one to turn to, no one to talk to. You know you need help, but you don't know where to find it." Next, the announcer provides an avenue for helping the woman better cope with her situation and overcome uncertainties regarding alternatives to abortion. "But the fact is, there is help, and it's as near as the yellow pages of your phone directory. Just look under abortion alternatives where you'll find caring, real-life alternatives to abortion." The announcer than reassures the woman that there are people, easily accessible to her, that will help her succeed. "So if you are faced with an unexpected pregnancy, remember there's help at the other end of the line."

Strategy Specification

Lesson 6: Formally Specify the Communications Strategy by Fully Stating the Communications Objectives for Each Level of the Means–End Model

The framework provided by the Means–End Conceptualization of the Components of Advertising Strategy (MECCAS) model (Olson & Reynolds, 1983; Reynolds & Gutman, 1984a) helps translate information from means–end chains and aggregate decision-making maps into components of a communications strategy. The MECCAS model consists of four levels corresponding to different levels within the means–end chain. *Message Elements* are the distinctive product features emphasized in the copy. *Consumer Benefits* shown in the ad represent the functional consequences of consumption linked with distinctive product attributes. The *Leverage Point* provides the bridge between product and self. It is a psychosocial consequence associated with the key emotional benefits of consumption. The *Driving Force* provides the values orientation for the ad. It serves to clarify the role of the leverage point in connecting product with self.

The simplicity of the MECCAS framework sometimes results in a misimpression that crafting an advertising campaign is no more difficult than sketching out a dot-to-dot picture. Communications objectives, however, are more often complex than uncomplicated. There are few, if any, advertising campaigns that consist of one attribute being linked to one functional consequence that is in turn associated with only one psychosocial consequence and one personal value.

Ford Motor Company.   U.S. automobile companies face a complex set of issues. On one front, they must build public support for a wide variety of segment-specific automobiles countering strong domestic and foreign competitors. On another front, they must address the loss of consumer confidence in the reliability of American-made cars and domestic dealerships. In addition, they must address consumer perceptions of unwanted sales pressure from dealers and complicated pricing policies that create sales barriers. Finally, they must deal with employees both in terms of showing their important role in manufacturing quality vehicles and showing that domestic automobile manufacturers are responsible, civic-minded employers.

From a means–end perspective, the MECCAS framework can be used to specify the details of how the various communications objectives can be accomplished. The message elements, whenever possible, should stress distinctive product features. For example, Ford may want to call attention to their customer-driven automotive design, long-standing tradition for building quality cars, responsive manufacturing technology, and a set of dedicated, talented employees. These message elements can be associated with many consumer benefits, such as comfortable and reliable vehicles, competitively-priced vehicles, and vehicles that fit the needs of the U.S. public. For leverage points, Ford can include components such as making positive, customer-driven changes, being a company that cares, making cars that people can rely on, and making cars that people can be proud to drive. Finally, the leverage points can be linked to driving forces such as personal security, self-esteem, and self-image.

Consider a Ford Motor Company advertisement from their "Quality is Job 1" corporate campaign. With customers and employees in the background trying out, talking about, and recording feelings about new cars, the announcer reads:

> We Americans have some very particular ideas of what we want in our cars and trucks. One company gets input from customers at every stage of new product development to find out exactly what they're looking for. That may be why five out of the top ten vehicles selling in America are built by the same company—Ford Motor Company.

A Ford design engineer than walks into the foreground and says "With your help, our quality gets better all the time." The announcer then continues, "Ford Motor Company where Quality is Job 1. It's working." The communications elements included in this ad together with the communications elements that Ford may need to address in a corporate campaign are shown in Fig. 9.4. Communications elements and linkages stressed in the ad are shown in bold.

Lesson 7: Specify how Components at Adjacent Communications Levels Will Fit Together to Form a Cohesive Strategy

It is not unusual for ads to show some degree of inconsistency between the communications elements presented at the beginning of the ad and the communications elements presented at the end of the ad. To be persuasive, the message elements should lead naturally to the leverage point and

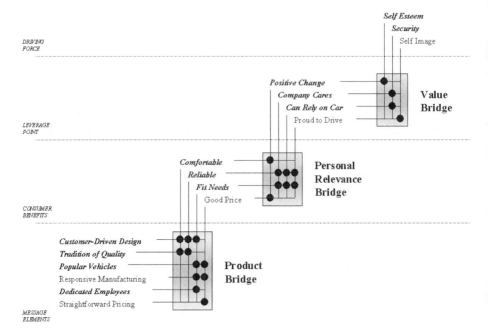

FIG. 9.4.   MECCAS summary chart: Ford Motor Company corporate campaign.

driving force. The advertising context, rational appeal, and emotional appeal should fit tightly together to form a cohesive package for the viewer.

Even with complex communications objectives, like those that Ford Motor Company must address, the many, multilevel components of a communications strategy must fit together and reinforce one another. In the MECCAS framework, the ability of the communications elements to work together is measured by considering three communications bridges illustrated in Fig. 9.4. The three bridges—product, personal relevance, and value—link together components at adjacent levels of communications. The *product bridge* measures the strength of connection between message elements and the consumer benefit. The *personal relevance bridge* measures the strength of connection between the consumer benefit and the leverage point but more broadly indicates the degree of personal involvement with the product generated by the ad. The *value bridge* indicates the ability of the leverage point to tap into the driving force. It is important to carefully consider the strength of the three communications bridges because they are key ingredients for teaching potential customers the relative advantage of your product compared to what they currently use. In total, the quality of the product bridge, personal relevance bridge, and value bridge along with ad affect are the best predictors of an ad's success in the marketplace (Reynolds & Gengler, 1993; Reynolds & Trivedi, 1989).

As an example, consider how Ford Motor Company might address their communications challenges. The product bridge should, at the very least, create strong connections between customer-driven automotive design and comfortable, reliable vehicles; long-standing tradition of quality and reliable vehicles; dedicated, talented employees and vehicles that fit customer needs; popular, top-selling cars and vehicles that fit customer needs; responsive manufacturing and competitively priced vehicles that fit customer needs. The personal relevance bridge should create strong connections between competitive pricing and making positive changes; comfortable and making positive changes; reliable vehicles and being a company that cares; reliable vehicles and making cars that people can rely on; vehicles that fit customer needs and making cars that people are proud to drive; vehicles that fit customer needs and being a company that cares. The value bridge should create strong connections between making positive changes and self-esteem, making cars that people can be proud to drive and self image, making cars people can rely on and personal security, and being a company that cares and personal security. Based on an analysis of the ad shown in Fig. 9.4, it appears as though Ford Motor Company is using an effective communications strategy.

Lesson 8: When Specifying the Content of the Communications Strategy use Consumer Language That the Target Audience Will Find Meaningful and Personally Relevant

Consumer beliefs and consumer language define marketing reality. Identifying their beliefs and language is the stepping-off point for understanding, developing, and applying communications strategy. In addition, specifying a strategy in consumer language permits a direct assessment of the degree to which the desired strategy is being communicated by the advertising.

Coca-Cola in Multicultural Communities.   Specifying a communications strategy for multicultural communities using Madison Avenue "marketing-ese" creates frustration for the creative group in trying to explain their execution and confusion for the managers trying to evaluate the execution. As an example, consider the Coca-Cola ad called "Phat Gear." The ad begins with a young man standing on the top of a tall building with other tall buildings in the background overlooking cars driving by in the city streets below. The young man "hiphop" chants more than speaks:

Yo! What goes on. I got the fly taste, right. Check my phat gear. Don't sleep. Check out the flash part, yo! Coca-Cola Classic in the new bottle. Fab right, yo! You can't even front it's goin' on. Honeys 'll be like—'ooh, he's got the flavor! ooh, he's got the flavor!' Say, yo! Be the first on your block to nab props. Because it is the flavor. Coca-Cola Classic in fresh new gig, kid. You know what I'm sayin?

A key strategic element for cola soft drinks, refreshment, is not mentioned in the ad. Yet, among inner-city audiences the ad is very successful in communicating refreshment along with real cola taste generating high levels of both ad and product affect. To the creative group, the words, images, and contextual setting provide the right vehicle to express superior refreshment and great taste in a personally relevant way to an inner-city, multicultural audience.

The MECCAS framework makes it easy for the creative group to explain and for the brand managers to understand how audience relevant phrases and cues speak to the strategic components of an advertising campaign. The framework also makes it easier for the communications strategy to be consistently applied from ad-to-ad and campaign-to-campaign. Reynolds and Gutman (1984a) demonstrated how strategic components can be matched with executional elements for a hypothetical campaign promoting airline service.

Strategy Execution

Lesson 9: Attract the Interest and Attention of the Target Audience by Making Rational and Emotional Appeals Connected With Real Needs People Have in Their Lives

First, with the ease of which people can change or mute television channels, the advertisement must make people want to watch. Second, people are reasonable. If a marketer can give them a compelling, values-based reason tied to distinctive product traits for purchasing and consuming a product, experience tells us that people will respond. In general, effective advertising will speak to the means–end orientation of a consumer or create a new orientation that plays more directly to a distinctive product attribute and functional consequence. This approach is consistent with Krugman's (1964) definition of involvement that can be described as the bond between product and self. Persuasion, then, results from successfully connecting multiple levels of thought, not merely by communicating the relative advantage of a product on a single communications level.

Marketing Carbonated Soft Drinks in Japan. Japan probably represents the most complex beverage market in the world. With so many popular beverage alternatives, selling carbonated soft drinks presents a particularly difficult challenge. As one Japanese commentator observes, a bottled cola drink looks like just one more bottle of soy sauce. Moreover, in Japan, carbonation is often linked to bad health. What rational or emotional appeal could gain attention and then convince Japanese consumers to drink a beverage that looks like soy sauce and they feel could be unhealthy?

In an ad called "Session," Japanese television viewers watch a live recording session in which a group of young people with a somewhat older and experienced director is recording a song promoting Coca-Cola. The ad is upbeat, youthful, and quick paced. The session, however, is not going well until the director has everyone drink a round of ice-cold Coca-Cola. In addition to being ice-cold, the carbonation of the drink is also shown as creating refreshment that ultimately leads to group achievement as the group energetically records the Coca-Cola jingle. "Session" gains viewer attention in a way that not only creates viewer interest in the ad and Coca-Cola but also makes strong connections between carbonation and refreshment and refreshment and group achievement.

Lesson 10: Before Developing the Execution,
Determine the Relative Degree of Emphasis
to put on Each Communications Level

It is particularly important to strike the right balance between the emotional and rational components of an advertisement. Depending on factors such as the product or issue being promoted or the stage in the product lifecycle, too much emotion will make the ad appear heavy-handed and may draw strong counterargument from viewers. On the other hand, an ad with no emotion does not have the power to motivate action.

As a rule-of-thumb, ads promoting new products must give more weight to communicating product attributes than ads promoting established products. On the other hand, ads promoting established brands in familiar product categories in which product attributes are well-known can afford to put greater weight on bringing out the psychosocial consequences of consumption. Said another way, new products must compete at an in-kind level (product attribute) or functional level (product benefit or functional consequence), whereas established products can compete at an ego-emotive level (emotional benefit or psychosocial consequence). Incidentally, products competing at the ego-emotive level are more involving and consequently are likely to generate more brand loyalty than products competing at the in-kind or functional level.

Paine Webber. Advertisements in the retail financial-services market can easily play too directly to emotions with taglines or copy. Obviously, people care deeply about the security of their money and are concerned with financial uncertainty. For example, consider the strong counterargument potentially raised by ads that flash "peace of mind" across the screen, have actors say they choose a particular financial-service provider because it offers greater "peace of mind," or have an announcer emphasize the substantial financial risk we all face and that our only option is to sign up with the biggest, most powerful financial-service provider. These types of appeals are likely to make people feel like they are being manipulated.

In a set of excellent ads for Paine Webber financial services, good friends or family members talk about how they are successfully meeting the financial challenges in their lives because of the foresight of a Paine Webber broker. The source of the broker's financial foresight? The ad simply says "he asked." In an unobtrusive way, the ad makes a connection between "good relationship with broker," "competent broker," and "a broker that cares and has my best interest at heart" with "being prepared to handle the financial uncertainties we all face in life" that in turn leads to feelings of "less stress over finances," "personal security," and "peace of mind." The financial challenges facing people in the target audience are made explicit, but by not speaking directly to values and only saying a simple phrase "he asked," the ad strikes the right balance between the rational and emotional appeal needed to reach the target audience.

Lesson 11: Make the Product a Catalyst for Generating the Behavior That Satisfies Key Psychosocial Needs

Product-as-catalyst sets a higher standard for ads than the time-honored advertising agency maxim of product-as-hero. We have seen many ads for which one could argue that the product is the hero, but yet the product is not the catalyst driving the action shown in the ad. For established brands or product categories, more than any other aspect of advertising, this one factor is critical for making the product personally relevant and attractive to the target audience. By viewing ads with this one principle in mind, one can gain considerable insight into the ultimate success or failure of an ad. If product usage or consumption leads directly to satisfying important psychosocial consequences, the ad has a good chance for success. If the product is only a sidebar to the core activity shown in the ad, that is, if the product does not create the action, the ad has a poor chance for success.

Coca-Cola and the Teen Market.   As an example of this principle consider two ads produced for Australia by Coca-Cola. Both ads rely heavily on images and music to make their respective points, but the way the product is introduced into the two ads is quite different. In a very successful ad, "Skysurfer," the teenage skysurfer is riding in a small plane and wants a drink of Coca-Cola, but the ice chest is empty. Below he sees a building with Coca-Cola painted on its roof. To the amazement of his friends, he jumps out of the plane, skysurfs, then parachutes down to the store where he is joined and admired by several attractive young women and his skysurfing friends. The message: The superior cola taste and refreshment of Coca-Cola gets you to do great things, it gives you what you need to be your best and brings young people together in a positive way. In this ad, Coca-Cola is the catalyst. It is the key for satisfying important and personally relevant goals.

In contrast, consider the ad "Special Delivery." In this ad a young, female, Australian rock star calls for a pizza. The young man receiving the order decides to take along a couple of Cokes when making the special delivery to the hotel where the singer is staying. The teenage boy cleverly avoids security and other barriers to successfully deliver the pizza. He then is able to live out a personal fantasy and share a Coca-Cola with the young star. The action in this ad is created by the young man's desire to meet and be accepted by the rock star. The young woman creates the action. She is the catalyst for satisfying the young man's key psychosocial needs, not the drink. In a sense, Coca-Cola is the "hero" by being a part of the young man's fantasy, but Coca-Cola definitely does not create the action. As a result, although it generates substantial ad affect, "Special Delivery," is particularly weak in generating product affect and motivating purchase.

Lesson 12: Assess Strategically the Advertising While it is Undergoing Development and Then Again After the Finished Ads are Produced

Strategic ad assessment is a vital step in creating effective advertising campaigns. Of the principles of copy testing generally accepted within the advertising industry reported by Yuspeh (1982), the first and governing principle is that "a good copy testing system provides measurements which are relevant to the objectives of advertising" (p. 2). Consequently, because the ultimate objective of advertising is positioning (Seggev, 1982), good copy testing should include an assessment of how well an ad communicates the desired positioning (Reynolds & Gengler, 1991). Said another way, copy testing must include measures of how well the goals of the communications strategy are being implemented. That is, marketers must measure how clearly the ad's executional framework communicates and links together strategic elements.

The creative process should aim to provide an executional vehicle that gains positive attention, generates significant product affect, and motivates purchase by showing how distinctive product traits satisfy important personal goals. In the means–end approach this is done by communicating strategic elements clearly and making the tightest possible connection between adjacent strategic elements in a contextual setting that the target audience finds interesting and personally relevant. A strategic assessment of advertising will measure all of these factors.

A 10-year-study conducted by Information Resources, Inc. in cooperation with several leading advertising agencies indicated that traditional copy testing is ineffective (Lubetkin, 1991). Based on matching split-cable advertising tests with associated copy tests, the research established that ad recall and simplistic measures of persuasion, such as remembering key copy points or overall viewer affect, do not predict how well an ad will perform in the marketplace. Strategic ad assessments, on the other hand, are quite different from traditional copy testing, and their capacity as a leading indicator of marketplace success has been validated through television direct-response advertising campaigns.

Testing is good, but assessment is better. It has been said that one test is worth a thousand expert opinions. We believe copy testing runs into trouble because of what is tested and how it is tested. Reynolds and Rochon (1991) pointed out that copy testing rarely addresses levels of product meaning higher than product attributes and their functional consequences and never measures the strength of connection between adjacent levels of product meaning. Moreover, copy testing does not assess the fit between an advertising execution and a communications strategy or relate the fit between execution and strategy to the desired marketing outcome.

When an ad works with consumers in the marketplace, marketers have difficulty answering whether the ad delivers a great execution of a mediocre concept, a mediocre execution of a great concept, or a great execution of a great concept. Is it any wonder then that we often observe companies following up successful ad campaigns with less successful campaigns? Copy testing does not provide a framework to explain the mechanism underlying the failure or success of an ad and therefore does not make successful advertising campaigns more predictable and reproducible or unsuccessful campaigns more avoidable. Consequently, once a campaign runs its course, marketers and ad agencies often must start developing a new executional envelope without a thorough, strategically-based understanding of why consumers responded the way they did to the previous campaign.

The positive impact of doing ad assessments can be multiplied by researching the ad before it is produced. At the point of a copy test the ad usually has been produced and the decision is one of how much media weight to put behind each execution. Under this system, because the "sunk costs" of production are rarely treated as sunk by managers, even poor ads receive some media weight. So testing ads only once they are finished results in media money being wasted on unproductive ads and affords no opportunity or in fact any real guidance to make improvements to advertisements that have been tested.

We recommend that strategic assessments of advertising be conducted before finished ads are produced. Reynolds and Gengler (1991) reported that strategic assessments of ads at the animatic stage and at the finished stage yield up very consistent results. In fact, they observe that differences between animatic and finished ad assessments only occur when the finished ad contains unique properties the animatic cannot capture such as the screen-presence of a celebrity endorser. Strategic ad assessments can make production and media dollars more productive by turning off bad executions before they are produced and improving good executions before they are produced and aired. They provide building blocks for gaining an ever-improving, long-term understanding of target audiences and how to communicate to them effectively.

Guidelines for the Strategic Assessment of Advertising

To assess the fit between communications strategy and advertising execution, the content of the desired communications elements, relative weight among elements, and desired executional effect must be prespecified. There are several published examples of how to apply the MECCAS model to the assessment of communications strategy (Gutman & Reynolds, 1987; Reynolds & Craddock, 1988; Reynolds & Gengler, 1991; Reynolds & Rochon, 1991). Beyond the mechanics outlined in the previous chapters there are several simple and practical rules-of-thumb to keep in mind when devising a system to strategically assess advertising.

First, the biggest hazard of formally specifying and assessing a communications strategy is allowing the ads to rely too heavily on using words to make their points. When it comes to communications and the spoken word, more is often less. It is estimated that less than 20% of what gets communicated in our society is verbal (Marketing Science Institute, 1993). Perhaps people simply do not have the patience to listen to a lot of advertising copy because, in general, advertising is not considered by consumers to be a very credible information source because of the marketer's vested interest in selling the product (Assael, 1987).

Advertiser's can not depend on copy alone to persuade consumers. In fact, too much copy can get in the way of an effective ad. In today's society, it appears as though the more an ad relies on images and music to convey its message, the more persuasive the ad will be. This may put ad agencies in a difficult position when working with the MECCAS model. On the one hand, the creative group wants to put together what they think will be a persuasive ad, on the other, they may want to include copy speaking directly to the MECCAS framework to show their work is "on-strategy." However, such problems can be avoided if one remembers the goal of the advertising is to effectively communicate and link the key strategic concepts and not necessarily to use the exact words specifying the communications strategy or, for that matter, use any words at all.

Another serious and frustrating problem is the tendency of respondents to become advertising experts. One way to address this issue is to show several ads together, one after another, then ask about the impact, content, and communications characteristics of the ads. Having respondents compare several ads, two at a time, also may be effective. Moreover, a laboratory setting for conducting ad assessments may help because one viewing of an ad often is not enough to gather all the pertinent information.

An ad assessment should also provide a foundation for learning how to make better advertising executions in the future. Consequently, the success of the executional framework in showing key points and creating the right mood must be measured. In addition, one may want to measure shifts in viewer attitudes toward the product, behavioral intentions, and how well viewers like the ad so that these factors can be related back to specific communications and executional elements.

Strategic Assessment of Competitive Advertising

Working on your own advertising is often so personally involving that it is easy to overlook the opportunity to learn more about competitors and how to position your product in the competitive environment by conducting a strategic assessment of competitive advertising. Assessments of competitive advertising bring out the strengths and weaknesses of competitors in the marketplace. Moreover, these assessments can clarify the nature of the target audiences being addressed by competitors and the buying orientations into which they are trying to tap.

In our experience, taking the time to look critically at and understand competitive advertising and positioning strategies has been among the most effective ways to leverage means–end research into an effective communications strategy that builds on strength, stresses defensible points of distinction, and reframes the consumer decision-making process in a way that creates competitive advantage.

The first step in assessing competitive advertising is expressing the content and executional elements of competitive ads in the MECCAS framework. An assessment can then be conducted with respondents evaluating a set of competitive ads along with the your own ads. In addition, similar to drawing a sample for a means–end laddering study, the sample for a competitive ad assessment should be targeted to include people with differing buying orientations, product preferences, and usage patterns.

SUMMARY

It is difficult to summarize in a few words the combined knowledge and experience of many industry experts in applying a means–end communications strategy to making advertising more persuasive by making it more customer focused. Clearly, means–end research, in and of itself, is a worthwhile enterprise. However, the research alone often will not make the choice of the best communications strategy immediately obvious. It is also clear from the examples cited in this chapter, many of which did not spring directly from applying means–end theory, that good advertising can and does happen without the added benefit of using means–end research.

We believe, however, the best and most reproducible advertising will emerge from a communications strategy that builds on means–end research to gain a greater understanding of potential customers and current competitors. Likewise, applying a broadened understanding of the target audience within the guiding principles outlined in this chapter should be a significant help in developing stronger and stronger advertising campaigns. Figure 9.5 presents a summary of the strategic lessons and the associated advertising campaigns.

Means–end theory, its accompanying methodology, and general framework for thinking about motivating people are effective tools for

STRATEGY FORMULATION

1. Find out why product attributes are important.

2. Keep specific marketing goals in mind.

3. Take into account competitive advertising and positioning.

4. A different contextual setting may create a different preference.

5. Play to strength, but also address societal and personal barriers.

Reagan-Bush 1984
Honda Motorcycles
American Plastics Council
Federal Express
Arthur S. DeMoss Foundation

STRATEGY SPECIFICATION

6. Specify the content of strategic elements at each communications level.

7. Specify how strategic elements at adjacent levels fit together.

8. Specify the strategy using consumer language.

Ford Motor Company
Ford Motor Company
Coca-Cola US

STRATEGY EXECUTION

9. Gain attention and interest by connecting with real needs.

10. Strike the right balance between rational and emotional appeal.

11. Product-as-catalyst transcends product-as-hero.

Coca-Cola Japan
Paine Webber
Coca-Cola Australia

12. Strategically assess advertising during development and after production.

FIG. 9.5.   Summary of lessons and example advertising campaigns.

formulating, specifying, and executing effective communications strategies. Laddering interviews, individualized means–end chains, aggregate decision-making maps, the MECCAS model, and the strategic assessment of advertising are tools that every marketer should understand and use.

REFERENCES

Assael, H. (1987). *Consumer behavior and marketing action* (4th ed.). Boston: Kent Publishing.

Cartwright, D. (1949). Some principles of mass persuasion: Selected findings of research on the sale of United States war bonds. *Human Relations, 2*(3), 253–267.

Gutman, J. (1982). A means–end chain model based on consumer categorization processes. *Journal of Marketing, 46*(2), 60–72.

Gutman, J., & Reynolds, T. J. (1979). An investigation of the levels of cognitive abstraction utilized by consumers in product differentiation. In J. Eighmey (Ed.), *Attitude research under the sun* (pp. 128–150). Chicago: American Marketing Association.

Howard, J. A. (1977). *Consumer behavior: Application of theory*. New York: McGraw-Hill.

Jolly, J. P., Reynolds, T. J., & Slocum, J. (1988). Application of the means–end theoretic for understanding the bases of performance appraisal. *Organizational Behavior and Human Decision Processes, 41*, 153–179.

Krugman, H. (1964). The impact of television advertising: Learning about involvement. *Public Opinion Quarterly, 29*, 351–364.

Lubetkin, B. (1991). Additional findings from "How Advertising Works" study. Advertising Research Foundation.

Marketing Science Institute (1993, September). Seeing the voice of the customer: The Zaltman Metaphor Elicitation Technique (Report No. 93-114). Cambridge, MA: Zaltman & Higie.

Olson, J. C., & Reynolds, T. J. (1983). Understanding consumers' cognitive structures: Implications for advertising strategy. In L. Percy & A. Woodside (Eds.), *Advertising and Consumer Psychology* (pp. 77–90). Lexington, MA: Lexington Books.

Pascale, R. T. (1984). Perspectives on strategy: The real story behind Honda's success. *California Management Review, 26*(3), 47–72.

Perkins, W. S., & Reynolds, T. J. (1987). The explanatory power of values in preference judgments: Validation of the means–end perspective. *Proceedings of the Association of Consumer Research*, Boston.

Peter, P., & Olson, J. (1994). *Understanding consumer behavior*. Burr Ridge, IL: Irwin.

Reynolds, T. J. (1985). Implications for values research: A macro versus micro perspective. *Psychology and Marketing, 2*(4), 297–305.

Reynolds, T. J., Cockle, B., & Rochon, J. (1990). The strategic imperatives of advertising: Implications of means–end theory and research findings. *Canadian Journal of Marketing Research, 9*, 3–13.

Reynolds, T. J., & Craddock, A. B. (1988). The application of the MECCAS model to the development and assessment of advertising strategy: A case study. *Journal of Advertising Research, 28*(2), 43–54.

Reynolds, T. J., & Gengler, C. (1991). A strategic framework for assessing advertising: The animatic versus finished issue. *Journal of Advertising Research, 31*(5), 61–71.

Reynolds, T. J., & Gengler, C. (1993). A structural model of advertising effects. In A. Mitchell (Ed.), *Advertising Exposure, Memory, and Choice*. Mahwah, NJ: Lawrence Erlbaum Associates.

Reynolds, T. J., & Gengler, C. E. (1995). Consumer understanding and advertising strategy: Analysis and translation of laddering data, with T. J. Reynolds, *Journal of Advertising Research, 35*(4), 19–33.

Reynolds, T. J., & Gutman, J. (1984a). Advertising is image management. *Journal of Advertising Research, 24*(1), 27–36.

Reynolds, T. J., & Gutman, J. (1984b). Laddering: Extending the repertory grid methodology to construct attribute consequence–value hierarchies. In R. Pitts & A. Woodside (Eds.), *Personal values and consumer psychology* (pp. 155–167). Lexington, MA: Lexington Books.

Reynolds, T. J., & Gutman, J. (1987). Advertising strategy development and assessment: A MECCAS model. In J. Olson & K. Sentis (Eds.), *Advertising and consumer psychology.* Praeger.

Reynolds, T. J., & Gutman, J. (1988). Laddering theory, method, analysis, and interpretation. *Journal of Advertising Research, 28*(1), 11–31.

Reynolds, T. J., Gutman, G., & Fiedler, J. (1984). Understanding consumer's cognitive structures: The relationship of levels of abstraction to judgments of psychological distance and preference. In A. Mitchell & L. Alwitt (Eds.), *Psychological processes of advertising effects: Theory, research, application.* Hillsdale, NJ: Lawrence Erlbaum Associates.

Reynolds, T. J., & Jamieson, L. (1984). Image representations: An analytical framework. In J. Jacoby & J. Olson (Eds.), *Perceived qualify: How consumers view stores and merchandise* (pp. 115–138). Lexington Books.

Reynolds, T. J., Olson, J. C., & Rochon, J. P. (1994). A means–end approach to evaluating advertising strategy. *Proceedings of Advertising and Consumer Behavior Conference, University of Minnesota*, Minneapolis, MN.

Reynolds, T. J., & Rochon, J. (1991). Strategy-based advertising research: Copy testing is not strategy assessment. *Journal of Business Research, 22*, 131–142.

Reynolds, T. J., & Trivedi, M. (1989). An investigation of the relationship between the MECCAS model and advertising affect. In A. Tybout & P. Cafferata (Eds.), *Advertising and consumer psychology.* Lexington, MA: Lexington Books.

Reynolds, T. J., Westberg, S. J., & Olson, J. C. (1994). A strategic framework for developing and assessing political, social issue and corporate image advertising. In L. Kahle (Ed.), *Advertising and consumer psychology.* Mahwah, NJ: Lawrence Erlbaum Associates.

Rokeach, M. (1973). *The nature of human values.* New York: Free Press.

Rosenberg, M. (1956). Cognitive structure and attitudinal effect. *Journal of Abnormal and Social Psychology, 53*(3), 367–372.

Seggev, E. (1982). Testing persuasion by strategic positioning. *Journal of Advertising Research, 22*(1), 37–42.

Vinson, D. E., Scott, J. E., & Lamont, L. M. (1977). The role of personal values in marketing and consumer behavior. *Journal of Marketing, 41*(2), 44–50.

Walker, B. A., & Olson, J. C. (1991). Means–end chains: Connecting product with self. *Journal of Business Research*, 111–118.

Yuspeh, S. (1982). PACT. Positioning Advertising Copy Testing, A consensus credo representing the views of leading American advertising agencies. *Journal of Adverting, 11*(4), 1–29.

10

A Strategic Framework for Assessing Advertising: The Animatic Versus Finished Issue

Thomas J. Reynolds
Richmont Partners

Charles Gengler
Baruch College

Advertising expenditures for individual firms, particularly consumer goods firms, continue to increase, representing a significant portion of revenues. For example, in 1988 Philip Morris became the first single company to crack the 2 billion dollar mark for annual advertising expenditures (Endicott, 1989). The immensity of these annual commitments to advertising expenditures reflect the importance that industry places on the role of advertising in the marketing process. The management of this critical marketing function demands that the maximal efficiency, or strategic quality, be sought.

Current trends indicate that one area in which firms are aggressively seeking to better manage their television advertising expenditures is by evaluation of ads at earlier stages of the production process through the use of rough prototypes of the finished advertisements, termed animatics, photomatics, or steal-a-matics (Bunish, 1987). Because the average production cost of a television commercial usually ranges from $250,000 to $500,000 (compared to less than $10,000 for the animatic production), the reduction of expenditures on ineffective advertisements represents a goal, early on in the creative process, by which the goal of maximal efficiency can be formally investigated. Of primary interest, then, is how the complex concept of advertising efficiency, or strategic quality, can be assessed early in the creative process, at the animatic stage of copy development.

BACKGROUND

Many methods of assessing the effectiveness (or quality) of advertising have been advocated and implemented. Yuspeh (PACT, 1982) presented the views of a group of the leading advertising agencies on the topic of advertising copy testing. Of the nine principles that were the consensus of these views, the preeminent, first principle cited is that "A good copy testing system provides measurements which are relevant to the objectives of the advertising" (PACT, 1982). Along this vein, Seggev (1982) suggested that ". . . the primary goal of advertising is to effect positioning." Thus, if positioning is the primary goal of advertising, then a major component of the evaluation of copy should therefore be the assessment of the strategic positioning message communicated, reflecting its strategic quality.

At present, a majority of copy is assessed after the final stage of production. Obviously, several aspects of the communication process are all at question simultaneously at this point. The advertisement must gain an audience's attention and must communicate the desired message to the consumers that they will remember. Measures of whether or not a particular aspect of the message was delivered or whether the ad was remembered typify traditional copy-testing research methodologies. However, these types of research methods often ignore the specific, strategically based positioning content of the message. The fact that no a priori framework of strategic positioning is utilized for the assessment forestalls any direct assessment of the relative effectiveness of the execution or any systematic contrasting of the quality of alternative executions. Clearly, advertisements should be assessed to monitor the degree to which they communicate the desired positioning, or in other words, to assess how well these messages deliver the intended strategy. Following this argument, Reynolds and Rochon (1991, p. 131) stated:

> Standard copy testing methods adequately measure intrusiveness, be it known as recall, recognition or simple memorability of key copy points. Standard copy testing fails to measure, however, the degree to which the desired strategy was communicated. (p. 31)

It is proposed that the most consistent, and most important, aspect of an advertisement across all stages of production is the particular strategy-related positioning message it contains. Obviously, standard intrusiveness measures, although important in their own right, are inapplicable for animatics, as is any related form of recall or recognition research. The strategic evaluation of animatics is primarily a judgment of quality of the *content* of the communication, reflecting the extent to which a desired positioning was obtained. Dual research issues emerge: (1) specify a theoretically sound framework for the assessment of advertising strategy; and (2) assess the correspondence of the analysis of the strategic message represented in animatics with respect to analysis of the message communicated in the final production.

DEFINING ADVERTISING STRATEGY

Reynolds and Gutman (1984, p. 28) described advertising communication as "the set of meanings and associations that serve to differentiate a product or service from its competition." With this in mind, advertising strategy is simply defined as "the specification of the manner by which the brand will be meaningfully differentiated by the target consumer" (Reynolds & Rochon, 1991). A specific strategy, then, is the particular set of meanings and associations linked to the brand, or cognitive structure, which is being communicated.

Several structural viewpoints of communications, with respect to how meaning or cognitive structure is derived, have been proposed. Cartwright (1949) proposed a goal orientation in understanding motivational structure communicated in advertising. Young and Feigin (1975) presented the Grey Benefit Chain, which links physical traits of products to more personal "emotional payoffs," which represent, similarly, the motives of the consumer. Consistent with the motivational approach, Levy (1981) presented a structural perspective of product meaning based on social structure in which products are linked to individuals' perceptions of the type of people they feel use those products. Another related model of meaning was presented by Cohen (1979), who linked product attributes to valued outcomes. Similarly, Chattopadhyay and Alba (1988) studied levels of abstraction in cognitions generated from advertising, ranging from "Factual Details" through "Single-Fact Interpretations," "Abstractions," to "Global Evaluations." Seeking a more comprehensive research paradigm, means–end theory (Gutman, 1982) proposed a structural viewpoint of meaning based on consumer cognitive categorization processes, which are the essence of product differentiation.

Means–end theory is based upon a personal values orientation (Howard, 1977; Rosenberg, 1956; Vinson, Scott, & Lamont, 1977), where personal values are the motivating "end-states of existence" that individuals strive for in their lives (Rokeach, 1973). The core of an individual's self-concept can be viewed as a bundle of values (Homer & Kahle, 1988), which govern perception, memory, and ultimately behavior. Products are viewed as a schema of physical attributes (see Peter & Olson, 1987, for a comprehensive review of this concept). Means–end theory simply suggests that the way in which these physical attributes of products are linked to personal values of individuals is the manner by which products gain personal relevance, essentially, the manner in which meaning is established. Thus, a physical attribute of a product is important only to the extent to which this attribute delivers a benefit or consequence to the consumer through the perception of product usage. The perceived consequence of product usage, then, is important only to the extent that this consequence is linked to another higher level, psychosocial consequence and, ultimately, to an individual's personal value orientation. A technique known as laddering (Reynolds & Gutman, 1988) has been demonstrated as a methodology for eliciting from individuals what their individual meaning structures are for a product category defined by attributes, consequences, and personal values. Essentially, laddering provides the basis from which an individual's cognitive structure can be obtained, including both content and structural components. The aggregation of ladders across a sample of consumers, then, yields a representative cognitive structure for an entire product category.

Following this theoretical perspective, a model to define the cognitive components of meaning for advertising strategy has been presented, termed the MECCAS model (Olson & Reynolds, 1983; Reynolds & Craddock, 1988; Reynolds & Gutman, 1984). This model (see Table 10.1), predicated on means–end theory, presents four conceptual elements of an advertising message that should be considered in strategy development and specification. In the model, Message Elements refer to the differentiating physical attributes of the product that are communicated. Consumer Benefits are the direct consequences consumers could gain through product usage. Leverage Points are the ways in which the message taps into, or activates, the individual's personal value system. This level is oftentimes considered to reflect brand personality traits of the product that serves to provide the link from the physical descriptors of the product to the higher level definers of "self." Driving Forces, then, are the high-level value orientations, that define self, communicated or activated by the ad. The final component of MECCAS, the Executional Framework (EF), is the specification of the delivery vehicle for the four fundamental strategic components and, as such, is not considered part of strategy specification. It is important to note that *not* all ads are required to communicate at each of the strategic levels; rather, MECCAS represents a framework which is broad enough to deal with all types of advertising strategic specification and assessment.

To illustrate how strategy can be specified with MECCAS, a summary derived from an assessment of telecommunications ads (Gengler & Reynolds, 1993) is presented in Table 10.1. Note that the key strategic elements corresponding to the MECCAS definitions are specified in the appropriate boxes. The blank box for EF represents the unique contribution

TABLE 10.1
MECCAS Specification and Example

Specification	Example
Driving Force (DF)	
The value orientation of the strategy; the end-level to be focused on in the advertising.	• Peace of Mind • Personal Security
Leverage Point (LP)	
The manner by which the advertising will "tap into," reach, or activate the value or end-level of focus; the specific key way in which the value is linked to the specific features of the product.	• Care • Commitment to Positive Change • Trust
Consumer Benefit (CB)	
The major positive consequences for the consumer that are explicitly communicated, verbally or visually, in the advertising.	• Can Count on to Work • Make My Life Easier • Save Time
Message Element (ME)	
The specific attributes, consequences, or features about the product that are communicated verbally or visually.	• Uses New Technology • Good Longstanding Reputation • Wide Selection of Products/Services

of the advertising agency, namely, the optimal executional story or device to communicate and link together in an impactful way the four strategic elements. A strategic specification in this form, then, indicates what the key meanings that are to be communicated by the ads, which essentially defines how the telecommunications product or company is going to be made personally relevant to the viewer. In a real-world environment, the specification would also include the relative strength desired at each respective level, thereby providing the marketing strategist the ability to communicate to the agency the particular area of focus desired for the desired positioning. Interestingly, the responsibility of the advertiser can be defined as one of developing and specifying a positioning strategy, whereas the dual responsibility of the advertising agency is to simultaneously provide the meanings desired as well as maximizing the connections or associations between these meanings.

The MECCAS model has been used to assess strategic components of specific advertisements (Reynolds & Craddock, 1988). Reynolds and Trivedi (1989) studied the relation between components of the MECCAS model communicated and the overall affect generated by the ad in the snack-food product category. In their research, significant correlations were found between components of the model and overall affect. Two key omissions were made, however, in design of the initial Reynolds and Trivedi (1989) study. First, an aggregate affect measure was used that combined both ad affect and brand affect, although these have been demonstrated to be separate constructs (Gresham & Shimp, 1985; MacKenzie, Lutz, & Belch, 1986; Mitchell & Olson, 1981). Second, and of equal importance, the Reynolds and Trivedi (1989) study concentrated entirely on communication of meanings at the levels of MECCAS and ignored measures of association between conceptual meanings communicated in the ad. It is this latter point that offers unique potential in the assessment of advertising quality from a strategic perspective, both for finished as well as animatic ads (Reynolds & Rochon, 1991).

Recently, Gengler and Reynolds (1993) addressed both of these issues in a new approach to assessing the meaning on which product positioning and advertising strategy is predicated. A separate construct was designed for brand affect generated by the ad and for affect for the ad, and subject perceptions of the associations communicated between the strategic components of the advertisement were gathered. Their findings indicate that both the MECCAS components and the associations between components were found to offer independent contributions to the prediction of brand affect for ads in the telecommunications category. The critical finding showed that the associations communicated between strategic elements, thought to be the basis of meaning, were indeed related to affect for the brand. Furthermore, a pattern was observed in the results that indicates that for the ads in which stronger contribution from associations was found, the affect generated for the brand by these ads was systematically higher.

This basic finding with respect to the importance of the levels of abstraction in communication, as represented by the MECCAS model, and the connections or linkages between the strategic elements at the respective levels presents a unique opportunity to develop a new data presentation format that summarizes both the relative strength of a given set of strategic elements as well as the myriad of potential connections between adjacent levels. The opportunity presented here is to develop a data presentation framework that, in essence, provides a complete summary of the cognitive elements and associations activated by a given execution. From the Gengler and Reynolds data, a diagrammatic model representation of the strength of the communication of both the strategic elements corresponding to levels of the MECCAS and the strength of the associations between each pair of elements is developed. Figure 10.1 illustrates this new approach to summarize the sum of meanings communicated by an execution.

In Fig. 10.1, the key statements reflecting the strategic elements of each level of MECCAS are presented along with the relative strength of the communication of that concept for each ad (on a 0 to 100 scale). Note that the stepswise presentation format necessary requires that the communication strength of each element for the Consumer Benefit (CB) and the

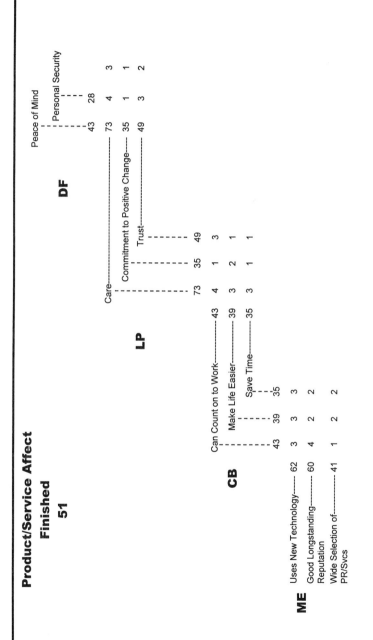

FIG. 10.1. A diagrammatic representation of key strategic elements and their relevant association strengths for finished assessment: Ad A.

Leverage Point (LP) levels be presented twice for ease of interpretation. For example, the strategic CB concept of "dependability," summarized by "Can Count on to Work," scores a 43, which is reported both in reference to the lower level Message Elements and the higher level Leverage Points. The statements summarized in Fig. 10.1 represent the strongest strategic elements communicated in the specific ads assessed.

The three matrices of scores between the adjacent levels of MECCAS represent the degree of association (on a 0 to 9 scale) between each pair of key strategic elements. To illustrate, for the ad represented in Fig. 10.1, the Message Element "Uses New Technology" can be seen to have a mean communication rating of 62, and the Consumer Benefit "Save Time" has a mean communication rating of 35. The association communicated between these meanings has a rating strength of 3. Thus, although somewhat complex, this data presentation format can be seen to provide a complete and convenient summary across all the strategic elements and associations that comprise the meanings or relevant associations communicated by a given ad.

To date, virtually all research concerning advertising strategy has been performed upon finished copy. Significant savings can be made, however, by performing this type of critical analysis earlier in the advertising production process. Animatics represent an opportunity for such an instance of earlier analysis and have received a steady pattern of increased attention and usage over the last decade (Halliday, 1982; Laufer, 1986; Bunish, 1987). The primary research question, then, is: To what degree do the meanings generated by an animatic correspond to those generated by the finished ad? More specifically, the new summary format described above offers a framework for directly contrasting the animatic analysis of meaning, which serves as the basis for strategy specification, with the finished counterpart. A second, more fundamental, question is: To what degree can this type of strategic analysis be used to make decisions, with respect to which executional frameworks hold the most promise for communicating more effectively a given strategy?

METHODOLOGY

To address the basic research issues, animatics were obtained for two of the finished telecommunications ads analyzed by Gengler and Reynolds (in press), hereafter referred to as Ad A and Ad B. The finished ads were very consistent with the animatics in terms of the similarity of scenes presented and accompanying voiceover. A sample of 49 subjects recruited under the same sample specifications as the sample from the finished ads—from a geographic region where the finished ads had not been aired — was utilized, thereby ensuring no previous exposure to the finished ads.

Subjects were administered a questionnaire in exactly the same fashion as was performed in the original assessment of the finished ads, a personal computer-based procedure, termed strata™ (which is an acronym for strategic assessment). This system integrates a personal computer and a video cassette recorder such that the ads being assessed and the questions directed to the subjects can be shown alternately on the same color monitor. Responses are given verbally by subjects to a trained interviewer, who then enters them into the computer. The average amount of time required to complete the task, assessing both ads, was 53 minutes.

Strata is designed to assess the strategic communication effects of advertising through implementation of the MECCAS model discussed earlier. Prior to the initiation of a research study, the key elements for the entire product/service category, usually jointly obtained from the laddering process and a strategic review of competitive advertising, are translated into statements corresponding to the levels of abstraction prescribed in the MECCAS format. An outline of the presentation format of the different types of questions is detailed in Appendix A. Randomization of questions within the question categories is performed.

The scale utilized in strata for assessing the strength of a specific strategic element has three response options: (0) "does not apply," (60) "clearly applies," and (100) "perfectly applies." Pretesting was performed and the resulting scale point weights were assigned. Of note is prior research conducted by Reynolds and Trivedi (1989) that showed little difference between a two-point and a five-point scale in a similar study. The scale utilized for the strength of association between key elements, defined as those that are endorsed as either "clearly" or "perfectly" applicable to describing the specific ad, also has three points: (1) "little," (2) "somewhat," and (3) "totally" connected. These questions are presented in the form of a graphical scale using color-coded Venn diagrams with differing degree of overlap between each relevant pair of strategic elements (approximately 5%, 35%, and 75%, respectively). The resulting associations score is derived from a multiplicative form of the three scores (element i, element j, and their direct association measure ij), which is rescaled using a probabilistic function to a 0 to 9 scale. More specifically, the scores for a given pair of statements (i,j) representing adjacent levels of MECCAS are multiplied by the score reflecting the strength of connection (1, 2, or 3). This multiplicand is then scaled on a 0 to 9 scale with each increment corresponding to probabilistically equal steps.

The primary quantitative output of the strata methodology, the strength of communication of the key strategic elements, and their pairwise strength of associations between adjacent levels can then be summarized in the new stepwise data format developed above.

RESULTS

Following the previous Gengler and Reynolds (1993) research, this study was concerned only with potential differences in the measures of brand affect. The same two statements, namely, "This ad makes me feel even better about using the product/service" and "This ad makes me really want to get the product/service," were used. The scores of these two statements across both ads yielded a Cronbach alpha reliability in the previous study with finished ads of .70 as compared to .73 in this study with animatics, indicating no significant difference. (Of note is that what are termed as brand-affect questions in this research paradigm closely resemble what many refer to as persuasion scores, possibly broadening the interpretation of these findings to persuasion-like scores.)

For each of the two ads (A and B), stepwise summary representations were constructed (see Figs. 10.2 & 10.3). These representations differ in content from Fig. 10.1 in that they are comparative, containing scores in the same format for both the animatic and finished executions. This combined format permits straightforward contrasting of the two independent research findings. Differences in obtained scores between animatic and finished for the same ad are indicated by circles or ellipses around those significantly different (t-test, $p < .05$).

Level of Meaning

For both ads assessed, the overall pattern of scores between animatics and finished were quite similar, except for consistently stronger scores at the Message Element level. This difference, noted for five of the six lower level elements across both ads, was likely due to the difference in executional format. That is, the reason animatics are scoring higher at the Message Element level is apparently due to increased attention being paid to the more concrete product-related aspects, stemming from the lack of distraction from becoming involved in the story line of the finished execution. Said another way, the viewer involvement with the story flow in the finished execution causes the viewer to attend to more of the dynamic flow of information and images as opposed to the more static "picture" approach executed in animatics. As such, the assessment of animatics will probably result in more perceptual emphasis on the concrete aspects of product information of the communication.

At the higher levels, two significant differences of the 16 possible for both ads can be observed. For Ad A, "Commitment to Positive Change" at the LP level scores significantly higher for the animatic (58) than for the finished (35). The stronger ME communication may well account for this net result. Similarly, the LP element of "Care" for Ad B is again more

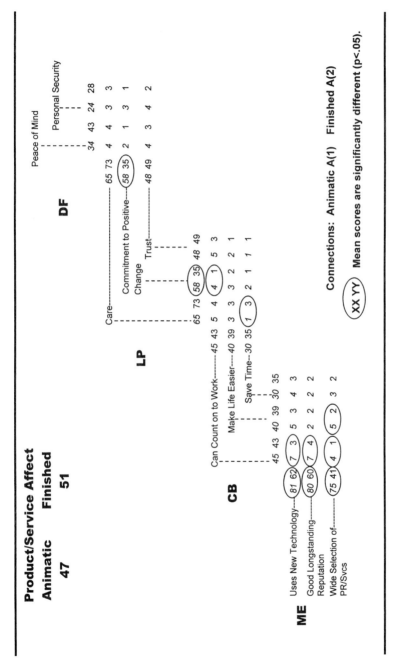

FIG. 10.2. A diagrammatic representation of key strategic elements and their relevant association strengths for animatic versus finished assessment: Ad A.

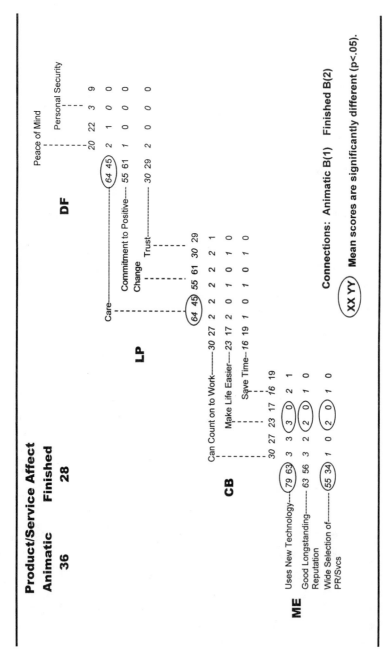

FIG. 10.3.   A diagrammatic representation of key strategic elements and their relevant association strengths for animatic versus finished assessment: Ad B.

strongly communicated by the animatic, 64 and 45, respectively. In total, the scores for the strategic elements on the higher levels do appear to correspond closely between the animatic and finished executions.

Analysis of the differences in the strength of associations is generally consistent with the above findings: Differences emerge at the lower levels. The explanation is obvious. Given that the absolute magnitude of the ME is significantly more strongly communicated, the likelihood of making a connection to higher level elements is also significantly increased. For Ad A, two significant differences appear, which, interesting for one of them ("Save Time" to "Care"), is not a result of a significant difference for either of the strategic elements. This difference cannot be readily explained. However, the other difference for Ad A, "Can Count on to Work" to "Commitment to Positive Change," appears consistent with the prior explanation, namely, the strength of the lower level communication produces potentially higher connection scores to the higher levels. With this specific example, however, the observed strength of communication for the statement "Can Count on to Work" is not significantly different between animatic and finished, suggesting that the network of cognitive meanings may not be perfectly linear and stepwise in nature as proposed by the specification format of MECCAS. Different networks of connections may well produce different types, connections, or routes of meaning in producing persuasive communications. For Ad B, no significant differences in associations at the higher levels between animatic and finished were found.

Brand Affect

No statistically significant differences ($p < .05$) were found between the animatics and the finished ads. The scale used to assess brand affect was the same three-point ordinal scale as was utilized in the measurement of the strength of strategic elements. The brand-affect summary scores for Ad A were virtually identical, 47 and 51, respectively. For Ad B, the animatic scored 36 as opposed to a slightly lower score of 28 for the finished execution, again indicating little difference in the overall affect measures.

Decision-Making Value

To address the second research issue, namely, contrasting of alternative execution vehicles for the same strategy at the animatic stage with the purpose of deciding which offers the most potential to deliver the desired strategy, Fig. 10.4 was constructed.

Contrasting of the summary affect score, although not statistically significant, does give the animatic for Ad A a slight advantage (47 vs. 36).

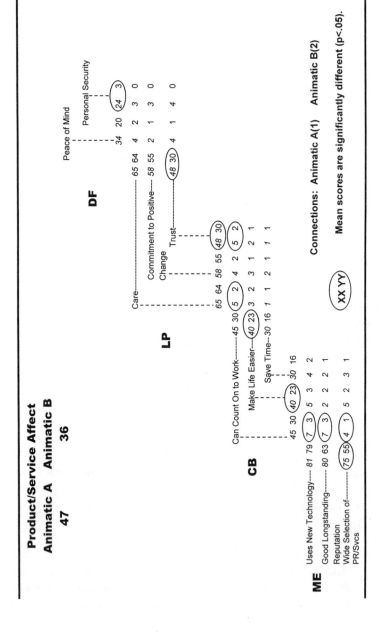

FIG. 10.4. A diagrammatic representation of key strategic elements and their relevant association strengths for a comparison of animatics: Ad A versus Ad B.

More importantly, the scores for Ad A do significantly outscore Ad B on one element at each of the four strategic levels: "Wide Selection of Product/Services" (ME), "Make My Life Easier" (CB), "Trust" (LP), and "Personal Security" (DF). Depending, of course, on the desired positioning strategy, the stronger communication of these key strategic elements in combination with the stronger set of associations between levels, does appear to suggest that the animatic for Ad A offers significantly more strategic quality potential.

The research question of assessing strategy or positioning in this way strongly suggests that an a priori specification of strategy be made. The primary application of strategy assessment is to determine to what degree a given animatic delivers against the desired strategy. Desired strategy, in this case, means predetermining the key strategy elements and their relative strengths. Secondarily, however, the ability to assess the strength of the connections "of meanings" between and across key strategic elements presents a diagnostic that can serve the creative process, either in terms of indicating a potential weakness prior to final production, or, to serve as reassurance that a particular executional device does in fact deliver the desired linkage or connection.

Experience with the strata methodology with animatics across a broad range of executional types yields two basic findings. One, rarely do ads that do not have at least one strong connection between at least two MECCAS levels generate significant affect for the brand (for both animatic and finished execution). And two, the only real differences that exist between animatic and finished occur only where the execution cannot or has not been captured in the animatic. For example, an execution that relies totally on borrowed interest from a unique aspect of a celebrity endorser is difficult to represent in animatic form and, as such, typically scores more strongly in the finished form.

SUMMARY

This study developed a summary assessment format, grounded in the cognitive aspects of means–end theory and the MECCAS model of advertising strategy specification, applicable to both animatic and finished advertising. This assessment format combines scores indicative of both the strength of the communication elements across the levels of meaning and the strength of association or connection between adjacent levels of meaning in the same data presentation. This format permits a comprehensive summarization of the network of meanings communicated by a given piece of copy, either in animatic or finished form.

The results of this study have demonstrated that strategy assessment is feasible at the animatic stage of copy development. Both the strength of communication of the strategic elements and the associations between those meanings that subjects interpret from animatics correspond, in general, closely to those for the finished executions. This implies that a positioning strategy can be assessed early on in the advertising process, thereby providing management with a tool to assist in the development of effective, strategically sound executions.

The very nature of animatics, however, does create a positive bias in terms of the assessment of concrete, product-attribute-related strategic elements. The static nature of an animatic, as compared to its more dynamic finished counterpart, permits the viewer to attend more fully to the basic product characteristics, thereby inflating the communication scores on those elements, and on their respective strength of associations to the higher level meanings.

APPENDIX A

Summary of Components (20) of Strata Interviewing Methodology

Part	Strata interviewing methodology
1.	View Ad A.
2.	Qualitative Questions (e.g., "main point," etc.)
3.	View Ad B.
4.	Qualitative Questions (e.g., "main point," etc.)
5.	View Both Ads A and B.
6.	Affect Statements (both Brand and Ad).*
7.	Message Element Statements.*
8.	Consumer Benefit Statements.*
9.	View Both Ads A and B.
10.	Executional Framework Statements.*
11.	Leverage Point Statements*
12.	Driving Force Statements*
13.	View Ad A.
14.	Ad A Connections for ME to CB.**
15.	Ad A Connections for CS to LP.**
16.	Ad A Connections for LP to DR.**
17.	View Ad B.
18.	Ad B Connections for ME to CB.**
19.	Ad B Connections for CS to LP.**
20.	Ad B Connections for LP to DF.**

*Administration of two-step rating process. Step 1 involves answering a question to which ad(s) the statement applies, if any. Step 2 involves, for each ad that the statement was applicable, judging to what degree.

**Administration of all adjacent level pairs which were judged as applicable to the three-point Venn diagram scale reflective of degree of connectedness.

REFERENCES

Bunish, C. (1987, September 11). A lot more sophisticated: Commitment to animatics growing. *Back Stage, 25.*

Cartwright, D. (1949). Some principles of mass persuasion. *Human Relations, 2, 3,* 253–267.

Chattopadhyay, A., & Alba, J. (1988). The situational importance of recall and inference in consumer decision making. *Journal of Consumer Research, 15,* 1, 1–12.

Cohen, J. B. (1979). The structure of product attributes: Defining attribute dimensions for planning and evaluation. In A. D. Shocker (Ed.), *Analytic approaches to product and marketing planning* (pp. 239–256). Cambridge, MA: Marketing Science Institute.

Endicott, R. (1989, September 27). Philip Morris ad spending muscles past $2 billion. *Advertising Age, 60,* 1–2.

Gengler, C. E., & Reynolds, T. J. (1993). A structural model of advertising effects. In A. Mitchell (Ed.), *Advertising exposure, memory, and choice.* Hillsdale, NJ: Lawrence Erlbaum Associates.

Gresham, L. G., & Shimp, T. A. (1985). Attitude toward the advertisement and brand attitudes: A classical conditioning perspective. *Journal of Advertising, 14,* 10–17.

Gutman, J. (1982). A means–end chain model based on consumer categorization process. *Journal of Marketing, 46*(2), 60–72.

Halliday, D. G. (1982, September 10). Testing thrives; So do animation houses in NY. *Back Stage, 20.*

Homer, P. M., & Kahle, L. R. (1988). A structural equation test of the value–attitude–behavior hierarchy. *Journal of Personality and Social Psychology, 54*(4), 638–646.

Howard, J. A. (1977). *Consumer behavior: Application of theory.* New York: McGraw-Hill Book Company.

Laufer, A. (1986, March 28). Clients press to test: Many factors lead to rise. *Back Stage, 24.*

Levy, S. J. (1981). Interpreting consumer mythology: A structural approach to consumer behavior. *Journal of Marketing, 45*(3), 49–61.

MacKenzie, S. B., Lutz, R. J., & Belch, G. E. (1986). The role of attitude toward the ad as a mediator of advertising effectiveness: A test of competing explanations. *Journal of Marketing Research, 23*(2), 130–143.

Mitchell, A. A., & Olson, J. C. (1981). Are product attribute beliefs the only mediator of advertising effects on brand attitude? *Journal of Marketing Research, 17*(3), 318–332.

Olson, J. C., & Reynolds, T. J. (1983). Understanding consumers cognitive structures: Implications for advertising strategy. In L. Percy & A. G. Woodside (Eds.), *Advertising and consumer psychology* (pp. 77–90). Lexington, MA: Lexington Books.

Peter, J. P., & Olson, J. C. (1987). *Consumer behavior: Marketing strategy perspectives.* Homewood, IL: Irwin.

Reynolds, T. J., & Craddock, A. (1988). The application of the MECCAS model to the development and assessment of advertising strategy: A case study. *Journal of Advertising Research, 28*(2), 43–54.

Reynolds, T. J., & Gutman, J. (1984). Advertising is image management. *Journal of Advertising Research, 24*(1), 27–37.

Reynolds, T. J., & Gutman, J. (1988). Laddering theory, method, analysis, and interpretation. *Journal of Advertising Research, 28*(1), 11–31.

Reynolds, T. J., & Rochon, J. (1991). Means–end based advertising research: Copy testing is not strategy assessment. *Journal of Business Research, 22,* 131–142.

Reynolds, T. J., & Trivedi, M. (1989). An investigation of the relationship between the MECCAS model and advertising affect. In P. Cafferata & A. Tybout (Eds.), *Cognitive and affective responses to advertising* (pp. 373–390). Lexington, MA: Lexington Books.

Rokeach, M. (1973). *The nature of human values.* New York: Free Press.

Rosenberg, M. (1956). Cognitive structure and attitudinal effect. *Journal of Abnormal and Social Psychology, 53*(3), 367–372.

Seggev, E. (1982). Testing persuasion by strategic positioning. *Journal of Advertising Research, 22*(1), 37–42.

Vinson, D. E., Scott, J. E., & Lamont, L. M. (1977). The role of personal values in marketing and consumer behavior. *Journal of Marketing, 41*(2), 44–50.

Young, S., & Feigin, B. (1975). Using the benefit chain for improved strategy formulation. *Journal of Marketing, 39*(3), 72–74.

Yuspeh, S. (1982). 'PACT'. Positioning advertising copy testing, a consensus credo representing the views of leading American advertising agencies. *Journal of Advertising, 11*(4), 1–29.

THE MEANS–END APPOACH TO DEVELOPING MARKETING STRATEGY

SECTION OVERVIEW

The means–end approach can help marketing managers understand how and why consumers make purchase decisions and then use this understanding of customer motivations to guide their thinking about marketing strategy.

A marketing strategy should specify how a particular group of consumers should perceive the personal relevance of a product or brand. It is useful to specify a marketing strategy as a means–end chain that identifies the salient product attributes, consequences (benefits), and values to be emphasized, and also identifies how these elements are linked together. Each means–end chain defines a particular form of customer–product relationship or a particular sense of personal relevance for the target consumer. Selecting an appropriate means–end basis for the consumer–brand relationship is the essence of a marketing strategy.

The means–end approach to developing marketing strategy usually begins by understanding how current customers see the personal relevance of a product category. This would usually entail conducting laddering interviews that would produce a set of means–end chains obtained from a group of customers. Then the researcher would combine the various means–end chains and portray the resulting structure as a *map*. Once called a Hierarchical Value Map (HVM), today researchers are more likely to use the term Consumer Decision Map (CDM). The CDM portrays the most common means–end chains elicited from a group of consumers. Because the CDM is an aggregate structure of the perceptions of a group of customers; it is bigger than the means–end structure for any single consumer.

The chapters in this section focus on three basic issues regarding using the means–end approach to developing marketing strategies. First, they show how to aggregate the means–end chains produced by laddering to form a CDM. Second, they show how the CDM can provide deep understanding of consumers' relationships with products and brands, including the reasons for and against product purchase and use. These pro and con feelings about products (or brands or companies) are called *equities* and *disequities* because they are contribute to positive and negative evaluations from the company's point of view. Third, each chapter uses actual business examples to illustrate how managers can translate customer understanding represented by the CDM into possible marketing strategies. In sum, these chapters show how to use the CDM like a strategic playing field on which managers and researchers can use their creativity and imaginations to develop alternative strategies and try out different strategic ideas.

• In chapter 11, Reynolds, Rochon, and Westberg show how the means–end approach was used to understand the motivations of a particular group of customers and how that understanding was used to develop a highly successful strategy. In this case, the key customers were Mary Kay salespeople, not the end purchaser or ultimate consumer of Mary Kay cosmetics. The authors used the means–end approach to understand the motivations of sales consultants in making three types of decisions: joining Mary Kay, staying with Mary Kay, and quitting their association with Mary Kay. Based on their understanding of these customers, the authors created a marketing strategy designed to recruit and retain sales consultants. The strategy was specified in terms of the means–end chains that linked positive features of working with Mary Kay with the benefits and values sought by the sales consultants. Mary Kay managers have used this video tape successfully to communicate the value of working with Mary Kay as a key element of their recruiting strategy for attracting new sales consultants.

• Next, Reynolds and Rochon (chap. 12, this volume) describe how managers can use the means–end approach to segment a market, in this case for ChemLawn's lawn-care services. The goal is to identify groups of customers that are similar in their perceptual or value orientations toward lawn-care services. Based on a means–end data, the authors identified six distinctive motivations for using lawn-care services. Each orientation was defined as a distinctive means–end relation between the certain attributes of lawn-care services and certain important (self-relevant) benefits and values sought by customers. Customers who possess the various means–end orientations should respond differentially to market offerings; therefore, they can be treated as a separate market segment. The authors show how knowing those motivational orientations can help a company create strategic plans, even to the tactical level that should appeal to each type of customer.

• In chapter 13, Reynolds and Novell discuss the interesting application of using the means–end approach to understand philanthropic behavior, such as contributing to fund-raising efforts. Their chapter illustrates the general applicability of the means–end approach to understanding the motivations underlying behaviors other than purchase of consumer goods.

• Then, Reynolds and Norton (chap. 14, this volume) describe yet another application of the means–end approach. The authors discuss how the means–end approach can be used to address a number of important issues in business-to-business marketing contexts. Similar to chapter 13, this volume, their analyses demonstrate the generality of the means–end approach.

• In chapter 15, Reynolds and Westberg discuss the important notion of equity or value. The authors provide a useful taxonomy of equity, in essence different sources, or bases for value. From a means–end perspective, equity is neither in the company nor the brand. Rather, equity exists in the minds (and behaviors) of customers. Equity is a function of the type of relationship that customers have with the product, brand, or company. Reynolds and Westberg argue that managers must go beyond the basic financial approach to measuring equity to understand the basis for customers' perceptions of value. Means–end chains are useful for modeling these value perceptions, which are the foundation of true equity. The authors present several ideas about how to manage equity and leverage it strategically.

11

A Means–End Chain Approach
to Motivating the Sales Force:
The Mary Kay Strategy

Thomas J. Reynolds
Strategic Research, Development and Assessment

John P. Rochon
Richmont Partners

with

Steven I. Westberg
Southern California Edison

INTRODUCTION

Marketing solutions that work have one thing in common: a customer orientation. Success, however, depends not only on orientation, it depends also on understanding and action. Despite the rapid evolution of marketing methods toward a more accurate and detailed understanding of the marketplace, managers have difficulty translating the results of the research process into effective marketing solutions. Success and failure often hinge on the manager's skill at implementation. Marketers have not provided clear answers to the manager's fundamental question: How do I really know what to do? Managers need a problem-solving framework that allows them to break away from old habits and tap into the power of customer-oriented marketing practices.

This chapter examines how one company, Mary Kay Cosmetics, made use of means–end marketing to solve a major strategic problem that threatened the continued viability and growth of the company. In presenting this case, we detail a problem-solving process that can help almost any company identify and adopt an effective customer orientation. To be successful, a customer orientation must embrace all of the relevant details surrounding the customer during the critical moments when that customer makes a choice, and then focus on the customer's decision-making process to find out why the choice was made.

The managerial problem-solving process involves answering six critical questions. The first four help managers frame the marketing problem from the customer's perspective. The last two then motivate in-depth customer research. The information is used to construct a template or map of the perceptual marketplace, including the reasons that customers both choose and reject alternatives. Based on the template, management can specify positioning strategy in customer language, which allows direct translation into communications and other marketing activities. An important characteristic of the process is that these communications address the personal motivations and beliefs that drive customers' behavior.

BACKGROUND

In early 1986, Mary Kay Cosmetics, Incorporated (MKCI) was in trouble. A recent management buy-out left them heavily in debt, with interest and principle repayments scheduled to begin at the end of the year. A 22% decline in sales over the previous 2 years, from $325 million to $249 million, required that management take immediate and substantial action to meet debt payments and remain solvent.

At the time MKCI was the eighth largest cosmetics and toiletries company in the United States. The highly fragmented and mature cosmetics industry had grown at an inflation-adjusted annual rate of less than 2% since the mid-1970s. MKCI products were sold through a network of independent sales consultants, not in retail stores. Thus, MKCI competed not only other direct-sales cosmetics companies such as Avon and Amway for salespeople but with cosmetics companies such as Estee Lauder who distributed through retailers.

Mary Kay's sales consultants were organized into a hierarchy consisting of four levels: beauty consultants, sales directors, senior sales directors, and national sales directors. All sales people started as beauty consultants and could be promoted contingent on meeting sales and recruiting goals. Sales consultants purchased products from MKCI at a wholesale price and then resold them to customers at the suggested retail price. Periodic promotional events gave consultants additional opportunities to earn bonuses and prizes.

MKCI also provided substantial incentives to the sales force to recruit and train new beauty consultants. Although the beauty consultants purchased products directly from MKCI, the recruiter was paid a percentage bonus based on products purchased by people she recruited. Sales directors also received bonuses based on the number of beauty consultants recruited into her unit as well as products purchased by all consultants in the unit.

Recruiting is critical to any direct sales organization, including MKCI. In the past, both revenues and operating profits were determined primarily by the number of consultants and directors in its sales force. During the recent revenue decline, sales revenue earned per consultant at MKCI had actually increased slightly, but the size of the sales force had gone down. Also, recruiting tended to be countercyclical. When the economy was doing well, fewer people wanted to work as sales consultants. When the economy faltered, recruiting for direct-sales organizations tended to increase.

But the problem was more complex than just recruiting. Indeed, a primary motivation behind the MKCI buyout was to reduce the effects of reported performance and stock price on recruitment, retention, and productivity. To become a beauty consultant, the new recruit had to invest $600 in product inventory at the outset. When Mary Kay's stock price was down, potential recruits became skeptical about investing in the company. Existing sales consultants also lost motivation, which contributed to further declines in performance and profitability. Although the buyout reduced future negative effects of stock price on performance it did not halt the decline in sales.

At a meeting of top managers, both immediate and long-term solutions to increase cash flow were proposed. Operating, efficiency, a more diversified product line, and new product development were discussed, but all practicable near-term solutions focused on marketing related issues. The principle options considered included the following: (a) raising both retail and wholesale prices; (b) increasing sales force recruitment, sales productivity, or the length of time that a consultant stayed with the firm; (c) increasing product availability through retail channels; and (d) developing advertising and other consumer communications to boost the image of the company and its product line. Options were discussed in detail and many issues were raised. For example, management knew that product imagery was old fashioned, dominated by pink Cadillac's, although technical product quality was as high as that of premium retail brands. It was further noted that MKCI was spending literally nothing on advertising.

Management had to take some form of action but realized they needed more information. To this end, they decided to commission a market research study to more fully explore the potential consequences of the options they were considering. Learning from the research, they decided, would help them come to a decision about how to solve the problem of declining sales. Before the research could begin however, MKCI management had to answer some tough questions about the market environment in which they were operating.

FRAMING THE MARKETING PROBLEM

Solving marketing problems by adopting a customer orientation must begin with framing the problem from the customer's perspective. First, MKCI management had to identify who was their key, customer. To identify their key customer, management had to consider a fundamental marketing concept — the two primary methods of selling a product. In the *pull* method, the manufacturer directs its marketing efforts at the end-user, who then actively seeks out the product and "pulls" it through the distribution system. In the *push* method, the manufacturer motivates the distribution system with incentives and promotions, relying on the distribution system to get the product into the end-user's hands.

Mary Kay management had to decide where they should focus their marketing efforts to have the most influence. If pull could become the primary driver of sales, then the end-user would represent the most important customer. On the other hand, if push could provide the highest returns, then the salesperson would be key. From the beginning for MKCI, revenues correlated almost perfectly with the number of sales consultants. Management also knew that productivity had increased slightly over the past few years, but recruitment and retention were what had really suffered. Management correctly reasoned that consumer acceptance was not the problem, rather motivating the sales force was. Hence, MKCI's key customer was the sales consultant, not the end-user. Management, then, had to develop a marketing strategy that focused on the needs of the sales force.

Next, management had to determine what were the relevant behaviors of the sales force that subsequent marketing activities would have to address. *Marketing* can be described simply as a process of either changing or reinforcing people's behaviors. Therefore, relevant behaviors can include what management wants key customers to do and what customers actually do. Behaviors are not always physical actions. They can be decisions that later on become actions. For example, eating at a destination restaurant usually requires a decision about where to go before the actual behavior of going there. Also, behaviors and the decision about behaviors can be singular or take multiple steps. Drinking a cold beer might simply involve opening the refrigerator and pulling one out. In contrast, buying a car might first include deciding what decision criteria are most important, and then what car magazines to read, what people to talk to, what dealerships to visit, and what models to test drive before dickering over the price. These behaviors must be understood so that subsequent marketing activities target the most critical behaviors.

The relevant behaviors for MKCI were not complicated. Management needed to know about three primary outcomes or events that corresponded to being a sales consultant. The first two were desired behaviors that had to be reinforced in order to duplicate the company's past success. These were becoming a sales consultant and continuing as a sales consultant. The third behavior, quitting as a sales consultant, represented the other side of the coin, the undesired behavior. Understanding this dark side was just as important as understanding the positives because much decision behavior is motivated by avoiding undesirable outcomes. Each of these behaviors further defined that the key customer becoming a consultant was a relevant behavior for new consultants, continuing as a consultant was a relevant behavior for those who were experienced and successful, and quitting was a relevant behavior for former consultants.

Identifying behaviors provided guidance for developing hypotheses for further investigation. MKCI management realized that they must understand why people joined Mary Kay and then what factors contributed to their success. Also, because many consultants quit after just a short time with the company, management realized that there were inconsistencies between what these people expected and what they actually experienced.

In this case, management deliberately avoided getting involved in how the sales force actually sold their products. All consultants received training and sales support from the sales directors and the company, but to sustain the entrepreneurial spirit that MKCI represented to women, consultants were encouraged to use their own ingenuity and ambition to develop a client base.

Once MKCI management identified their key customers and relevant behaviors, the third question that management had to answer was: What were the relevant contexts of the key behaviors? Behavior does not occur in the abstract. All behavior is contingent on situational factors that, in part, determine the behavior. Thus, the relevant context can refer to the situation or physical occasion in which the behavior occurs. Context can involve consumption of products or services, purchase of products or services, or information gathering. In this case, it was the need for a job.

Defining variables of an occasion context can include the physical time of day, location, activity, and participants. For example, an occasion for restaurant choice could be described as, "during breakfast, weekday, near the office, with a client, setting up a new account." Such an occasion would likely result in a very different choice of restaurants compared to, "during breakfast, with the kids, weekend, near home, suffering from a hangover." Situational variables might be psychological, physiological, demographic, or cut across multiple occasions. An example of a psychological situation could be, "approaching midlife crisis and questioning your self-worth," whereas a physiological situation might be, "over 40 and getting wrinkles."

Preliminary research identified the relevant contexts for women deciding about becoming a Mary Kay beauty consultant. One such context was an "earn money" orientation, described by "I've got kids and my husband earns enough to support us, but I want to contribute." Another was a career orientation, illustrated by "I've worked a lot of dead-end, low-paying jobs, but now I want a career." A third was a personal growth orientation—for example, "I want to be self-sufficient, but I don't have the necessary skills." Each of these orientations represented a lifestyle or life situation context. Several personal factors including age, family status, and educational background helped determine these lifestyle situations. Understanding context was important because it influenced the beauty consultant's decision about joining staying with and quitting Mary Kay Cosmetics. Context was part of the cognitive process that resulted in these three key outcomes.

Because making decisions is predicated with having options, the fourth framing question that Mary Kay management had to answer was: "What were the options that required the decision?" Behavior is almost always a choice between competitive alternatives. Alternatives can be similar, for example, "should I drink Coke or Pepsi." Or, they can be dissimilar, "should I drink Coke or coffee?" Alternatives can even be completely unrelated, "should I drink Coke or go to the gym?" Competitive alternatives relate to the behavior of interest and they frequently differ by context and by key customer group. Because Mary Kay beauty consultants could either choose or reject Mary Kay as an employment opportunity, their competitive choice alternatives included other jobs that were available to them. For many of these women, the most realistic job alternatives included (a) working for another direct-sales organization such as Amway or Avon, (b) working a secretarial 9-to-5 job, and (c) working shifts in retail sales. Understanding what alternatives the potential beauty consultants were considering allowed management to focus on the critical reasons for choice, which for many consultants differed from the reasons that they liked different alternatives. For example, a consultant liked both Mary Kay and Avon because direct sales provided flexible working hours, but this same person chose Mary Kay over Avon because Mary Kay offered more opportunity for personal growth.

To review, MKCI management had to answer four problem-framing questions: Who were the key customers? What were the relevant behaviors? What were the relevant contexts? And what were the competitive choice alternatives? Although the process has been demonstrated by answering the questions in sequence, an iterative approach was followed in practice, with management confirming answers to previous questions when answering the later ones.

At this point, management could have written a formal problem statement in terms of their answers to the framing questions. For example, a useful statement might have read: Develop a marketing strategy that (a) provides both immediate and long-term sales growth (b) by focusing on the relevant life experiences that Mary Kay can provide (c) versus alternative job or career options (d) that will motivate new salespeople to join Mary Kay and that will give them the orientation that will influence their chances of finding long-term success in the company.

UNDERSTANDING CONSUMER DECISION MAKING

Having framed the problem, the next step for management was to understand the decision-making process of their key customer, the beauty consultant. Understanding decision making included two parts: The first was to determine what choice criteria consultants used to distinguish among their job alternatives, and the second was to understand why the choice criteria were personally relevant to the consultants.

A research study was designed to get at these critical issues. During interviews, consultants were asked three questions to elicit underlying factors driving key choices made with respect to MKCI. The three questions were:

1. Why did you join Mary Kay?—asked of all consultants in the sample;
2. Why do you stay with Mary Kay?—asked only of successful consultants who stayed with the company; and
3. Why did you quit Mary Kay?—asked only of those who had quit.

During actual interviews, these questions were customized for each respondent, depending on the respondent's predetermined behavior classification, context, and competitive alternatives. For example, an interviewer might have said, "Why did you join Mary Kay instead of staying with your secretarial job with IBM?" Reasons for joining and staying with Mary Kay represented the positive aspects of being a Mary Kay beauty consultant, whereas reasons for quitting Mary Kay represented negative aspects of the job and the company.

Most of the responses given by consultants were grouped into three broad categories: financial, social, and job characteristics. Financial reasons included having one's own money and having additional money for the family. Social aspects were being able to teach others about skin and beauty care, and the people orientation of the job, embodied in characteristics such as meeting new people and working closely with other people. Finally, the job characteristics focused on being one's own boss, which provided considerable job flexibility.

Once these initial choice distinctions were identified in the interview, the interviewer had to understand *why* the distinctions were important to the respondent. Identifying choice criteria is only an academic exercise, unless we also determine why the criteria are important. Knowing the reasons why makes the research more actionable and provide the means for making stronger ties between the characteristics of the job and the psyche of the sales consultant. For example, a successful consultant indicated that she stayed with Mary Kay because "I am able to help my customers." Being able to help customers was important to this person because it makes me feel like I've got a special role with them. Having this special role was important because it meant, "I'm learning more myself," which in turn was important because it provided a "feeling of accomplishment." Accomplishment was the motivating internal drive or personal value behind the choice criteria.

Another consultant who had quit Mary Kay did so because "I didn't earn much money." Not earning money was important because it meant that "I wasn't contributing anything to our household income," which then led to dissatisfaction because "I wanted to prove that I could do it . . . that we could afford to buy a few luxuries." Not being able to afford luxuries caused her to "still feel dependent on others," which is exactly the opposite of the independence value that she wanted to achieve.

These chains of connected ideas, from choice criteria to personal values, are called ladders (Olson & Reynolds, 1983; Reynolds & Gutman, 1988) because the interview process involves moving up the ladder of abstraction from concrete choice criteria to abstract personal values. The closer one gets to personal values, the more internal and feeling-oriented the remarks become. Eliciting these ladders is usually done by asking some form of the question is that important to you beginning with the initial choice criteria.

Beauty consultants from the three key groups — new joiners, successful consultants, and quitters — were interviewed in this manner to uncover the personally relevant reasons associated with their choice criteria. Once the full range of these connected associations and ideas were uncovered, they were summarized in a Customer Decision Map (CDM; or Hierarchical Value Map, Reynolds & Gutman, 1988), a graphical presentation of the ladders (Fig. 11.1).

Each phrase or idea on the map was found in a substantial number of the ladders. The words on the map were simply coded responses that represented the actual verbatim remarks made by the respondents in the interview. Each line on the map indicated that a substantial number of ladders contained both of the connected elements. Each pathway that could be traced, from the choice criteria at the bottom to the personal values at the top, represented a perceptual orientation of the market, in this case the beauty consultants' reasons for accepting or rejecting Mary Kay.

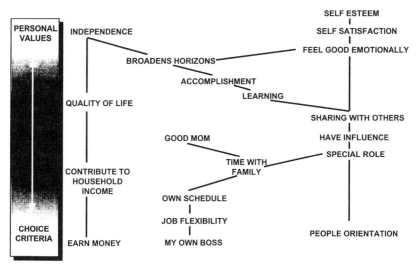

FIG. 11.1. MKC customer decision map.

This map had five primary orientations—more than management had previously believed existed. One was financial: On the far left side of Fig. 11.1, the CDM, Earn Money appears at the bottom, connected through Contribute to Household Income and Quality of Life to Independence at the value level. A second orientation, in the center of the map, was grounded in My Own Boss, which then led to Job Flexibility, Own Schedule, Time With Family, and finally Good Mom. A third branched from Time With Family to Special Role, Have Influence, Sharing With Others, Feel Good Emotionally, Self-Satisfaction, and finally, Self-Esteem.

A fourth orientation began at People Orientation and led through Special Role, Have Influence, Sharing With Others, Leaning, Accomplishment, Broadens Horizons and Independence. The fifth orientation followed the same path as the fourth through Broadens Horizons but then went to Feel Good Emotionally, Self-Satisfaction, and finally Self-Esteem.

Although informative, the map was incomplete without additional information about which orientations were associated with the three primary consultant groups in the sample and the positive and negative associations between MKCI and the choice criteria and other elements. Stepping back from the map, management had to understand the two sides of choice—selection and rejection.

Understanding the relevant ladders of consultants who had chosen and stayed with Mary Kay as well as the ladders of those who had rejected Mary Kay allowed management to identify the elements on the map that were perceptual strengths and weaknesses of the company compared with other job alternatives. Once this was accomplished, it became evident to management why they had to first segment their respondents based on the consultants' relevant behaviors. To alter behavior, management had to understand the differences in beliefs between those consultants with the desired behavior and those without—that is, those that were successful sales people and those that were not and quit.

The perceptual strengths that represented the primary reasons that all consultants joined Mary Kay were labeled as common equities of Mary Kay. On the map, three key pathways existed here: The Earn Money to Independence orientation, the Be My Own Boss to Good Mom orientation, and the Be My Own Boss to Self-Esteem orientation.

The primary reasons that consultants left Mary Kay were called *disequities*. On the map, the elements that were reasons for consultants to quit were also among some of the same reasons that they joined. Specifically, MKCI's disequities were associated with the Earn Money orientation. This suggested that those consultants who quit did so because of unfulfilled financial expectations. Recruiting had, indeed, focused primarily on the ability to earn money as a Mary Kay beauty consultant by pointing out those relatively few consultants who had done very well. The majority of sales consultants, however, never earn as much as these top performers. Many consultants quickly realized this and quit.

Leverageable equities were those elements that were the primary reasons successful consultants stayed with Mary Kay. These elements were unique to the successful consultants. Those who quit and those who had recently joined did not mention them. Somehow, successful consultants learned about this orientation, from People Orientation to Independence, during the time that they had been consultants. For this group, achieving Independence through Learning and Broadens Horizons supplanted the financial pathway to Independence. Armed with this understanding of the perceptual marketplace in which the company was operating, management next had to specify a positioning strategy that would become the basis for subsequent recruiting and sales force communications.

IDENTIFYING POSITIONING STRATEGY

Positioning strategy was defined as the specification of how Mary Kay would be meaningfully differentiated to their sales consultants. Specification required identifying the key components of the strategy in terms of the elements on the map. The CDM then became the game board to think about positioning strategy. Meaningfully differentiating Mary Kay required identifying how the company would appear special and superior to alternatives.

In general, effective strategies operate across all levels of the decision-making process. Differentiation, then, could occur at any or all levels. Also, effective strategies supplant disequities and leverage equities. Supplanting disequities could be accomplished by either convincing beauty consultants that the negatives they associated with Mary Kay were actually positives or by providing alternatives to the negative elements. This second method in effect would reduce or eliminate the importance of the disequity. Leveraging equities could be accomplished by strengthening the current positive beliefs about Mary Kay and by introducing these ideas to consultants who might not have or associate these positive concepts with MKCI.

Following these guidelines, management specified a positioning strategy. The strategy had to focus on recruiting new sales consultants and then keeping them once they joined. Therefore, the elements that were selected for the core strategy included all of the leverageable elements identified on the map: People Orientation, Special Role, Have Influence, Sharing With Others, Learning, Accomplishment, Broadens Horizons, and finally, Independence (Fig. 11.2). This core strategy was chosen because it supplanted the existing financial and job characteristic reasons for joining Mary Kay with the reasons that the successful consultants stayed. This reduced unfulfilled financial expectations and at the same time provided management with the opportunity to differentiate Mary Kay from other direct sales organizations that also offered Earn Money and Be My

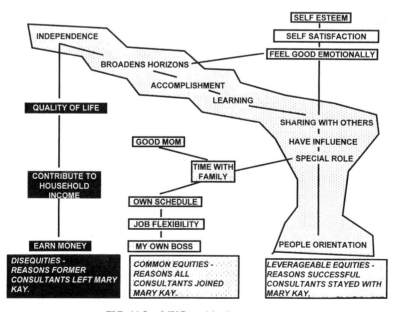

FIG. 11.2.   MKC positioning strategy.

Own Boss. Incidentally, both the Earn Money and the Be One's Own Boss orientations were still included in the strategy but the emphasis on these two pathways was greatly reduced.

Another advantage of the core strategy was that it tended to attract people who already had this orientation for success, for example, those people who placed higher value on the reasons that successful consultants stayed with the company and less on the financial ones. This helped reduce the high-turnover rate among beauty consultants.

COMMUNICATING POSITIONING STRATEGY

The final phase in the process was to translate the strategy into effective communications. MKCI management chose to produce a recruiting videotape called "Focus on Independence" that informed potential recruits about the key ideas and their connections from the positioning strategy. A video was selected because it could be quickly produced and distributed for nearly immediate results, and it demonstrated MKCI's commitment to current consultants by providing them with a tool that could help them succeed. The video included a montage of interviews with successful consultants and exposition about MKCI's commitment to helping them achieve their independence. The video was made available to current consultants, and about 15% of them bought it during the year.

To assess the video's effectiveness, MCKI managers compared the results achieved by 1,200 matched pairs of sales consultants. One consultant from each pair had used the new video while the other had continued using an old video that talked only about the financial potential of the job and the benefits of being one's own boss. Recruitment increased by 42% in one year for the consultants using the new tape over the old. Based on these impressive results, the company implemented company-wide distribution of the new tape. Additional internal communications including a monthly newsletter and sales promotional material were produced and distributed that also focused on the key elements in the strategy. Both recruitment and sales almost immediately returned to their prior 16% to 20% annual growth rate. They have continued at this pace ever since and continued to do so at the time of this publication (Fig. 11.3).

CONCLUSIONS

In summary, MKCI's management was able to solve their marketing problem by taking a customer perspective that involved four steps: (1) framing the marketing problem in terms of their key customer, (2) under-

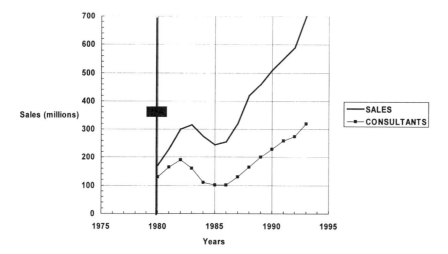

FIG. 11.3.   Results of sales consultant strategy.

standing customer decision making in terms of reasons for choice and rejection, (3) developing a positioning strategy based on understanding
their customer, and (4) creating a communication tool to implement the
strategy. Management framed the marketing problem by asking four important questions about their customers, Who is the key customer? What
are the relevant behaviors? What are the relevant contexts? What are the
competitive choice alternatives? Then, management commissioned interviews that probed into their customer consultants' minds to understand
their reasons for choice: What choice criteria do customers use, and why
are these choice criteria personally relevant and important to the customer? Finally, management developed positioning strategy based on understanding the perceptual equities and disequities of Mary Kay in terms
of the elements of the CDM. This understanding readily transferred into a
video communication that helped increase recruitment and retention,
thus providing MKCI with the opportunity to increase sales and profit-
ability.

The problem-solving skills discussed here are not limited to a direct-sales cosmetics company. In fact, the framework outlined here can
help managers solve almost any marketing problem in any category for
any business. What this framework provides is the rigorous structure
needed to both develop and then implement a positioning strategy that is
compelling, motivating, and captivating to customers and potential customers.

A manager's job requires innovative action. This discussion began by
noting that managers have trouble implementing new ideas although new
information gives them better understanding of the marketplace. This

phenomenon is called *paradigm paralysis*. Symptoms include managers who continually have difficulty answering these questions: Who should I target? What message should I get across? How do I really know what to do next? Using the framework described here, management can not only avoid paradigm paralysis, but can achieve marketplace success.

REFERENCES

Olson, J. C., & Reynolds, T. J. (1983). Understanding consumers' cognitive structures — Implications for advertising strategy. In L. Percy & A. Woodside (Eds.), *Advertising and consumer psychology (Vol. 1)* (pp. 77–90). Lexington, MA: Lexington Books.

Reynolds, T. J., & Gutman, J. (1988). Laddering theory, method, analyses, and interpretation. *Journal of Advertising Research, 28*(1), 11–31.

Rochon, J. P., & Reynolds, T. J. (1989). Applying qualitative techniques to real world problems: The Mary Kay case study. Presentation at the Third BI-Annual ARF Qualitative Research Workshop, New York.

12

Consumer Segmentation Based on Cognitive Orientations: The ChemLawn Case

Thomas J. Reynolds
Strategic Research, Development and Assessment

John P. Rochon
Richmont Partners

INTRODUCTION

Segmentation divides a heterogeneous marketplace into smaller and more manageable homogenous components. These smaller market segments can be targeted with more personally relevant positioning strategies that have greater appeal to individuals within the group. In theory, marketers can tailor a unique marketing mix to each segment that can be optimally effective in persuading consumers in the segment to choose their brand or increase brand usage. Thus, the potential benefits of efficient segmentation are substantial, particularly given the fragmented media market that exists today. Evidence of this is given by the emergence of micromarketing practices that target individuals with customized selling propositions through direct mail, direct solicitation, or cable programming.

To provide efficient segments, differing segmentation classifications have been developed, including demographic characteristics of the consumer, benefits sought by the consumer, and behavioral measures of the consumer (Wilkie, 1989). Segmentation by demographics (Company A targets only males, whereas Company B targets only people living in the Northwest) is very popular and quite easy to do. But broad demographic segments and most other unidimensional segmentation schemes provide only a piece of the segmentation puzzle. In most cases, the unidimensional classification schemes have to be combined with other segmentation variables in order to market to what appears to be a more homogenous target.

Lifestyles and psychographics can provide these additional variables and are segmentation forms that more closely reflect the way people live and why they buy. Lifestyle segmentation, for example, would group together those people who are suburbanites or those who are "generation X," whereas psychographic segmentation is based on consumer psychological profiles that presumably define their consumption behavior.

Many segmentation approaches, however, are limited in their ability to provide actionable guidance to managers, because segments are ill defined or they exist more in the data than the reality of the marketplace. In extreme cases, segmentation becomes an end unto itself rather than a marketing tool. Segmentation efforts further suffer from a lack of causal relations between the defining characteristics of a segment and the behaviors of interest (Winter, 1984). Also, it can be difficult to accurately classify a consumer into a segment without knowing details about the individual, including demographic, psychographic or behavioral characteristics. These are some of the fundamental reasons why attempts at broad-scale segmentation often fail to provide managers with useful information that leads to better, let alone optimal marketing solutions.

Indeed, inappropriate customer classification can mislead managers into unnecessarily limiting their target market. A segment defined by both behavioral and demographic variables will exclude potential customers who might qualify on behavioral variables alone. Likewise, some segmentation schemes might include low-probability prospects in the same group as high-probability prospects. For example, segmentation based only on psychographic variables or personal characteristics might include both users and nonusers of a category. Further study of such segments, without identifying more refined subgroups, would tend to hide potentially critical differences, such as the barriers that keep people out of the category or the brand franchise.

But are these potential results serious problems for marketing management? One can think about segmentation error the same way one thinks about statistical effort. Type I segmentation errors result in people being excluded from the market segment in which they should have been included. Type II segmentation errors result when people are included in the segment who should have been excluded.

What are the downsides of Type I or Type II segmentation errors? How large do these errors have to be before they matter, and which error is more serious? The answers depend on the costs of communication to groups of prospects and the probability of making a sale to these prospects. In most marketplace situations, both types of error are inefficient and waste limited marketing resources. Clearly, the ability to target consumer groups with the most appropriate strategic message offers both a significant challenge and an opportunity to marketing management.

This chapter introduces a methodology of segmentation based on understanding the consumer's choice process. This approach has the potential to reduce these two sources of segmentation error. The methodology is based on our belief that effective segmentation is a result of differentiating a heterogeneous population based on the decision-making criteria used to select a product, as well as by the dimensions of consumer behavior of greatest interest to the marketing manager. Therefore, we believe that segmentation schemes should include both attitude and behavior variables to allow management to efficiently target customers with appropriate communications. A second challenge facing the marketer is delivering the most appropriate message to the target group, which we discuss as well.

BACKGROUND

Segmentation is

> disaggregative in its effect in that it tends to bring about recognition of several demand schedules where only one was recognized before. . . . Market segmentation . . . consists of viewing a heterogeneous market (one characterized by divergent demand) as a number of smaller homogenous markets in response to differing product preferences among important market segments. Segmentation reflects the desires of consumers for more precise satisfaction of their varying wants.

Said another way, disaggregation shows that the relation between price and quantity, the demand schedule, will be quite different based on individual needs and wants. This is good news for marketers because disaggregation may identify high-value–high-profit needs and wants that are unobservable in pooled data. Smith has since been acknowledged as the forefather of segmentation (Wind, 1978, Winter, 1984). However, demand may not always be the most appropriate basis for segmentation, particularly if the underlying reasons for demand are not consistent across members of the segment. Further dividing segments based on these underlying reasons for purchase may provide additional insight and guidance concerning the types of marketing activities or communication appeals that might work best for each segment.

Winter (1984) provided a definition of cost-benefit segmentation that is perhaps more useful for selecting marketing activities and developing communications. He wrote:

> Market segmentation is the recognition that groups or subsegments differ with respect to properties which suggest that different marketing mixes might be used to appeal to the different groups. These subsegments may

then be aggregated if the reduction in cost exceeds the reduction in benefits (revenues). This aggregation is based on the fact that both subsegments respond most to the same marketing mix.

Winter (1984) further pointed out the problems with most segmentation analysis: weak relations between demographic characteristics of a segment and behavior, no causal base, and a lack of actionability. For example, what does one do with a segment identified as "Our primary target market for frozen pie crusts consists of females 35–60 with a high school education living in the Midwest and Southeast, making $20,000–$35,000 per year and with 3.2 children who no longer live at home but who visit two times per month?" (Wansink, 1993). Winter offered a procedure of segmentation trees that is based on understanding specific consumer needs to overcome some of these problems. The segmentation tree approach accounts for two key factors. First, the situation may dictate the segment into which the consumer falls. Second, segments based on needs rather than behavior help select the marketing mix strategy that will be most effective. Thus, marketing activities aimed at subsegments identified by a tree approach are likely to be less wasteful of marketing resources. The problem remains, however, to identify the "optimum" tree.

At this point, managerial goals must enter the process. What will management do with the segments? There are two primary applications of segmentation. One is to identify markets for new or potential products. This might be useful in the product development and design stages, as well as for new product introductions into the market. More often, the goal of segmentation is to identify or refine markets for existing products and then sell to them. Segmentation for this purpose would assist the development of the marketing mix. Distribution, pricing, and communication strategy might all be of issue. Our focus is communication strategy because of the fundamental difficulties in developing and implementing targeted communications such as direct mail, television or print advertising, and sales promotions. Segments for communication strategy must then reflect homogeneity of the characteristics, ideas, or concepts concerning the product or service that are included in the marketing communications.

THE THEORETICAL BASIS FOR A COGNITIVE SEGMENTATION APPROACH

Marketing communications, in general, are meant to alter or reinforce beliefs and attitudes, which in turn alter or reinforce behavior (i.e., communications are meant to be persuasive). Petty and Cacioppo (1986) provided a model that recognizes persuasion as a process of multiple determinants. In their Elaboration Likelihood Model, there are two routes to persuasion.

The central route requires cognitive effort and results in relatively stable and enduring attitudes that tend to predict behavior. The peripheral route involves little or no cognitive effort and results in unstable attitudes that are less predictive of behavior. A persuasive result or attitude or belief change, then, is a result of one or both of these routes. Logically, segmentation for communication strategy should be based on the key elements that lead to persuasion. Often, central-route persuasion is desirable because this route leads to more enduring attitudes and associated behavior.

Means–end theory describes consumer decision-making as a cognitive process involving different levels of associations (Gutman, 1982; Gutman & Reynolds, 1979). These levels combine in memory to provide the consumer with the personal motivation to choose and use a product or service. Thus, means–end theory describes a cognitive process that corresponds to central-route persuasion. In means–end theory, the product is defined by tangible attributes at the most concrete level. In contrast, very abstract, personal goals or values that motivate behavior define the consumer. The consequences of product attributes that help consumers satisfy or achieve their goals represent the cognitive link between the external product or service and the internal personal value orientation of the person. These consequences can be physical in nature, such as "quenches my thirst" or psychological, such as "I feel refreshed."

People have multiple values or goal orientations, and they place differing emphases on the respective orientations that exist for them. Values, then, might serve as an initial basis for segmentation because they represent the motivations for behavior. Unlike the popular Values and Life Styles (VALS) approach, however, means–end theory recognizes that a person strives to satisfy different values across different consumption occasions that further differ across product classes. Said another way, means–end theory recognizes that people interpret their world in different ways depending on the product and context of consumption (Reynolds & Gutman, 1984). For example, a professional photographer might consider a deer standing in a meadow for a graphic project in order to fulfill a value termed *financial security*, whereas a zoologist might study the deer's behavior as a way to achieve success. The converse may also be true — namely, the photographer could be driven by success, whereas the zoologist is driven by security. Therefore, using values as the only criterion for segmentation is not enough.

People learn to associate certain chains of ideas that connect a product or service with self. Summaries of these means–end chains, called *Hierarchical Value Maps* (HVMs) (Olson & Reynolds, 1983, Reynolds & Gutman, 1988), provide graphical representations of the perceptual marketplace. Each pathway on the map represents a dominant perceptual orientation among consumers. Importantly, each pathway includes both the value orientation of the consumer, as well as the personal interpretations of how the product or service fits with the consumer's self-goal and values. The pathways are based on experiential or media learning or on cognitive reasoning. In either case, the pathways are always context specific for the respondent. Reasoning occurs within situations from the real world or with equal validity, in "minds-eye" frames. Segmentation based on these perceptual orientations yields segments that will differ in response to marketing messages because the consumers' decision hierarchy served as the basis for identifying the segments.

The following case example demonstrates this segmentation process, from problem identification to segmentation based on consumer decision-making to the process of developing communicative tactics for each segment.

THE CHEMLAWN CASE

ChemLawn Services Corporation of Columbus, Ohio was the first company to offer lawn-care services on a national basis. This new service was met with widespread acceptance, while ChemLawn's only competition included the "do-it-yourself" market and local "mom and pop" operations. From 1975 until 1986, consumer acceptance remained high while disposable incomes grew. During this period, several national companies entered the market, and additional local companies were formed to compete directly with ChemLawn. By the late 1980s, ChemLawn's period of rapid growth and expansion had ended due to the combined forces of increased competition, ChemLawn's high level of penetration in many markets, decreasing levels of disposable income, and increased consumer concerns about environmental safety. Nevertheless, ChemLawn remained the U.S. leader in lawn-care services, with an approximate 30% share of all revenues in the industry, compared with less than 10% for its nearest competitor.

Growth throughout the lawn-care services market also came to an end in the late 1980s. The number of lawn-care service customers peaked in 1986 then began to decline with the onset of hard economic times. Customer turnover in the industry rose to 32% per year. Competition, already intense due to the number of players in the industry, became fierce. Most major competitors adopted price as their competitive platforms with a focus on recruiting new customers to deal with the increasing turnover problem. At the same time, widespread publicity over industry practices and materials led to increased consumer concerns about health and the environment. Do-it-yourself product manufacturers, taking advantage of these concerns and the economic downturn, greatly improved their marketing efforts.

In an attempt to counter these negative trends, ChemLawn increased its service offerings and expanded into new markets, but neither of these strategies proved effective in slowing ChemLawn's customer-base erosion. In fact, ChemLawn's annual customer turnover rate approached 42%, considerably more than the industry average. Also during this time, all national lawn-care service companies, save one, continued to lose market share to small regional and local companies.

There were two possible explanations for this. One, the smaller companies had lower cost and overhead structures and thus could charge a lower price. This belief, though, assumed that the industry had become mature, with no real difference among service providers or the quality of their service. In such a scenario, the only solution would be to cut costs. An alternative view was that the national providers had not been effective at differentiating their services from the regional and local companies and were out of touch with how these differences might appeal to particular market segments. This suggested an urgent need to understand segments of the market.

If changes in their positioning were then made based on an adequate market segmentation, ChemLawn could adapt effectively to market circumstances it could not control, thereby exercising command of its own fate.

Laddering Interviews and Analysis

The first step in developing a positioning for ChemLawn consisted of 80 in-depth consumer interviews across a representative sample of Chem-Lawn service users, competitive service users, and do-it-yourselfers. The interviews, using the laddering technique (Reynolds & Gutman, 1988), identified five motivational value orientation groups. Laddering is a one-on-one interview process that uncovers the personally motivating reasons and feelings associated with the functional and physical aspects of the product or service that serve as stated initial reasons for choice. Laddering also uncovers the barriers to choice when it focuses on the reasons for rejecting an alternative. Examples of both benefit and barrier ladders for lawn-care services are shown in Fig. 12.1. Although each customer respondent typically has multiple ladders or perceptual pathways associated with the different physical features (attributes) of the product or service, individuals' dominant reason for choice can be represented by primary pathways. These dominant reasons also are called the individual's *perceptual orientation*.

The laddering data was used to develop an "HVM of the lawn-care services industry, which included multiple segments based on how the customer related the tangible service aspects to their personal motivating

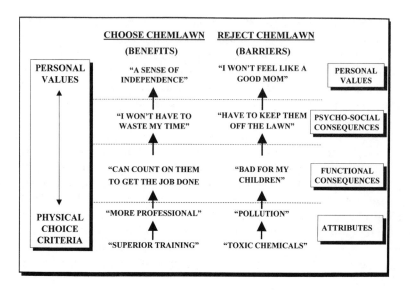

FIG. 12.1.

value or goal orientation. Analysis of the laddering interview data in the HVM revealed six distinct customer segments shown in Fig. 12.2a and 12.2b representing six primary decision-making orientations: (1) Environmentalist, (2) Parent, (3) Justifier, (4) Busy Guy, (5) Perfection Seeker, and (6) Green Thumb. Individual consumers typically had characteristics and beliefs from more than one of these categories, but their primary motivations were associated with one of these dominant pathway. Thus, they could be classified into one of these groups.

An example of how to translate the laddering data into a descriptive segment is shown for the Justifier segment. Based on the primary decision-making ladder associated with this group and additional quantitative analysis, we developed an understanding of the group's buying behavior. The Justifier was not satisfied with a quality product; he or she had to justify its purchase through the judgment that it was a good value. Thus, the Justifier was price sensitive but also recognized the worth of value-added attributes. Justifiers were unique in the market because of their emphasis on cost-benefit relationships for the purchase decision. This made them a hard sell but potentially a good target group. They did not make snap-buying decisions, but once convinced of the value of the product or service, they did not change their minds unless they perceived a change in value.

In addition to grouping consumers based on attitudinal and motivational factors, segmentation must be able to contrast beliefs between people with and without desired purchase or consumption behaviors. From a

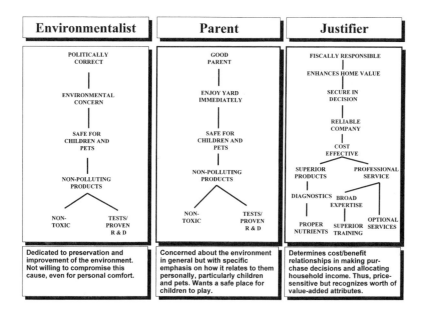

FIG. 12.2a.

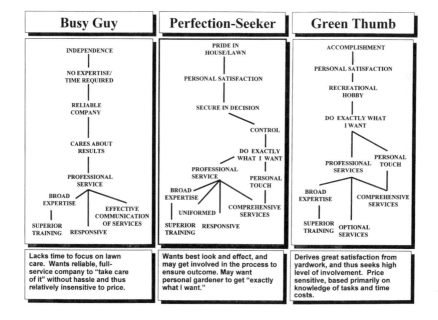

FIG. 12.2b.

Key Customers
(Percent)

	ChemLawn *(1,100,000)	Other Services *(4,000,000)	Do-It-Yourself *(25,900,00)	Total Homes ('000s)
Busy Guy	33	30	1	1,822
Justifier	24	22	12	4,252
Perfection-Seeker	19	18	2	1,447
Parent	12	15	24	6,948
Green Thumb	8	5	35	9,353
Environmentalist	4	10	26	7,178
Total	100	100	100	31,000

* Number of households

FIG. 12.3.

managerial perspective, marketing activities must affect behavior—in particular, purchase and consumption behaviors. One of the best ways to deal with this issue is to contrast the perceptual orientations of groups with the relevant purchase or consumption behavior. In the case of ChemLawn, the critical behavior of interest was based on the consumer's relationship to ChemLawn. For example, the behavior of interest among ChemLawn's current customers was to "continue to employ ChemLawn." The desired behavior among customers of other national providers of lawn-care service was to "switch to ChemLawn." The key behaviors for do-it-yourselfers were first "consider employing a service" and then "begin using ChemLawn." Finally, the relevant behaviors for nonusers of lawn-care products were to "start using fertilizers or lawn chemicals," and then "employ a service" and "begin using ChemLawn."

Clearly, the primary emphasis in this analysis was to understand the consumer types in ChemLawn's current customer base to better meet their needs and reduce turnover. The secondary focus was on the do-it-yourselfers because the do-it-yourselfers represented substantial industry growth and seemed easier to recruit than customers of other services and non-users.

Market Survey

To provide estimates of the relative sizes of the segments and additional qualitative and quantitative information focusing on the perceptual differences between the segments, we conducted a survey of 539 lawn-care service users including both customers of professional service providers and do-it-yourselfers (see Fig. 12.3). In the survey, each respondent was given brief descriptions of all six customer segment profiles described previously. Respondents were to order the profiles with respect to how well each one described them. The top two profiles were used as a basis of questioning to determine which consumer group was most representative. Each respondent was then classified into one of the six groups, and estimated segment sizes were determined. In addition, each respondent evaluated each of the service providers and the do-it-yourself option, on the elements identified by the laddering research. Respondents rated both the importances of the elements and associations between elements and lawn-care alternatives. These evaluations would be used later to help identify the key elements to include in communications to each segment.

The survey confirmed that ChemLawn dominated its competitors in the current customer market for lawn care; however, they had been less than effective in addressing their customers' personal needs. Even more apparent was the combined size of the do-it-yourself market, which at five times the size of the current base of lawn-care customers, represented considerable growth potential. Based on this analysis, ChemLawn had an opportunity to target critical customer segments to maintain their current base — Busyguys, Justifiers, and Perfection Seekers. ChemLawn also could target other segments to grow both their share and the category — Parents, Green Thumbs, and Environmentalists. Of course, some share growth could come from attracting customers of other lawn-care services, but category growth would come primarily from attracting new customers from the do-it-yourself segments.

DEVELOPING STRATEGIC COMMUNICATIONS

The segmentation approach described previously identified the key perceptual pathways and motivational orientations that could form the basis of a positioning strategy for each of the target segments. Before communications could be developed, however, we must identify the leverageable elements in these pathways. *Leverageable elements* are those concepts in the HVM rated as important by both current customers and do-it-yourselfers, and seen by current customers as substantially positive for ChemLawn but not so by do-it-yourselfers. This suggests that if do-it-yourselfers could be taught the positive characteristics that customers already knew about ChemLawn, their likelihood of choosing ChemLawn should be increased. By comparing the strategic elements within each the three perceptual segments that comprised the majority of do-it-yourselfers with the key elements for the three segments that were the majority of Chem-

Lawn's current customer base, we identified the leverageable elements that would become the focus of communications.

The next question to be answered was how to design the appeal to reach each segment. The first step was to translate the leverageable functional and psychosocial consequences into simplified, benefit-oriented concepts that could then be used in marketing ChemLawn's products. With the Justifier segment, for example, the primary marketing concepts that would reinforce or stimulate purchase were Reliable and Value. Although these represented the most salient motivators, other elements identified in the perceptual orientation diagram for this group may well have played secondary roles in the decision process. The Benefit Concepts also had to be supported by ChemLawn's tangible service features or attributes in order for a Justifier to switch to or continue with ChemLawn.

Barrier elements were identified in the research as well. For example, safety concerns prevented the parent do-it-yourselfers from selecting a professional provider. Therefore, in the final development of marketing messages, both benefit concepts and barrier concepts had to be determined. Message development is a powerful use of the decision-making ladder. Successful messages are both personally relevant and believable to the target segment because they are directed at the most important needs of the prospective customer as supported by (linked to) product and service attributes.

An example of a message that would communicate "Reliable" to the Justifier segment follows. Although the words used here do not represent the actual phrases of final copy, they were the keystone messages or ideas on which actual copy would be based.

> ChemLawn provides proven, professional service through its highly trained and experienced team of Landscape Specialists.
>
> ChemLawn's experienced team of Landscape Specialists are trained to recognize and diagnose the needs and problems of your landscape and to offer reasonable and immediate solution options.
>
> A healthier, more beautiful landscape is easier to achieve with ChemLawn's team of highly trained Landscape Specialists. With years of experience, these specialists use only the best landscape care products, proven effective through extensive research and development in ChemLawn's own research facility.

The next step was to identify delivery strategies for the key messages for each segment. For example, the Justifier consumers use cost-benefit relationships in their purchase decisions. They are price sensitive but recognize the worth of value-added attributes. They do not make snap decisions, and therefore are not a candidate for short-term trial. Justifiers use information to analytically support or refute their decisions and need a lot of critical information before making a purchase.

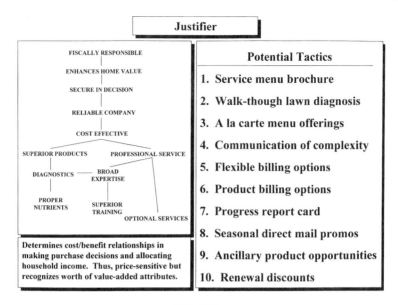

FIG. 12.4.

Television, radio, and newspapers are unlikely to be effective because of the information requirements of the Justifier. Direct-mail pieces showing a lush, beautiful lawn would likewise miss the mark because the Justifier needs to hear that his or her investment will be returned in value. Two steps may convince the Justifier of ChemLawn services.[1] The first was a lengthy, direct mail piece laden with information that strongly portrayed the critical Reliable and Value messages. The second was a face-to-face visit from a ChemLawn representative when the sale would actually be made. Other tactics, as outlined in Fig. 12.4, could also be used to reach and persuade the Justifier.

The delivery strategies, or tactics, created for the Justifier segment were also valid for other segments. For example, the direct-mail piece was also appropriate for the Partner segment, and a modification was appropriate for the Perfection-Seeker, Busyguy, and Yardwork-Hater segments. A communication matrix based on an understanding of the delivery tactics that would work best for each segment was developed as a managerial tool for allocating resources and conducting cost–benefit analyses for each segment (Fig. 12.5).

Identifying these people in the real world was the final challenge that remained. Here, demographic characteristics or a self-selecting question-

---

[1]The research outlined here was conducted during negotiations for the acquisition of ChemLawn. The acquisition was not successful; thus the communication strategies were not implemented.

Strategic Tactics	Current Base			New Prospects		
	Busy Guy	Justifier	Perf. Seeker	Green Thumb	Parent	Environ.
Walk through lawn diagnosis	X	X	X	X	—	—
Service menu brochure	X	X	X	X	—	—
Ancillary product opportunities	X	X	X	X	—	—
Follow-up phone calls	X	X	X	X	—	—
Progress report cards	X	X	X	X	—	—
800 number information/order line	X	X	X	X	X	X
Customer preference card	X	—	X	X	X	X
Newsletter	—	—	—	X	—	—
Strengthen brand awareness	X	—	—	—	—	—
Safety Information	—	—	—	—	X	X

FIG. 12.5.

naire could have been used. Several sophisticated demographic and psychographic tools (e.g., Claritas and Cluster-Plus) could identify the most effective ways of reaching these specific market segments as well.

This case review is but a single example of the utility of information derived from means–end based consumer research. Other strategic marketing and communication issues also can be addressed using the resulting deep understanding of market segments.

CONCLUSIONS: THE MANAGERIAL PROCESS

Virtually all successful marketing communication strategies emerge from carefully structured development processes, perhaps similar to the one outlined here. The really good strategies — those that accomplish their objectives to the fullest possible extent for the maximum possible time — seem to result from processes with five common elements.

1. Develop a comprehensive understanding of both how and why the consumer reaches a decision about whether or not to purchase a specific product or service. Means–end research with laddering interviews can provide these insights.
2. Thoroughly analyze the various segments of the market into which consumers fall and weight each by the measurable potential it holds for the company.

3. Identify specific strategies and tactics based on the information developed in the first two steps, as we did with the previous Justifier segment.
4. Assess and refine the identified tactics and concepts through market research. Further cost–benefit measures of the strategic tactics needed for each segment can provide additional guidance to management.
5. Test the tactics by launching them in pilot markets and measuring customer response.

These five steps recognize that marketing activities are part of a behavioral process that focuses on the consumer. Therefore, consumer responses and reactions must be included explicitly at both the initial, customer-understanding stage of the process and at the final, communication assessment stage. Also, this process recognizes that the best test of marketing activity effectiveness is in the marketplace. The main premise of segmentation is that unless different marketing mixes are to be offered to different segments, segmentation provides no additional benefit to management.

ACKNOWLEDGMENTS

We would like to thank Dwight Smith and Steven J. Westberg for many helpful contributions in preparation of this manuscript.

REFERENCES

Gutman, J. (1982). A means–end chain model based on consumer categorization processes. *Journal of Marketing, 46*(2), 60–72.
Gutman, J., & Reynolds, T. J. (1979). An investigation of the levels of cognitive abstraction utilized by consumers in product differentiation. In J. Eighmey (Ed.), *Attitude research under the sun* (pp. 128–151). Chicago: American Marketing Association.
Olson, J. C., & Reynolds, T. J. (1983). Understanding consumers' cognitive structures: Implications for advertising strategy. In L. Percy and A. Woodside (Eds.), *Advertising and consumer psychology* (Vol. 1, pp. 77–90). Lexington, MA: Lexington Books.
Petty, R. E., & Cacioppo, J. T. (1986). *Communication and persuasion: Central and peripheral routes to attitude change.* New York: Springer-Verlag.
Reynolds, T. J., & Gutman, J. (1984). Advertising is image management. *Journal of Advertising Research, 24*(1), 27–36.
Reynolds, T. J., & Gutman, J. (1988). Laddering theory, method, analysis, and interpretation. *Journal of Advertising Research, 28*(1), 11–31.

Wansink, B. (1997). Visualizing customer profiles for accurate targeting: The technique and the validation. In L. Kahle & L. Chiagouris (Eds.), *Values, lifestyles, and psychographics.* Mahwah, NJ: Lawrence Erlbaum Associates.

Wilkie, W. L. (1989). *Consumer behavior, 2nd Edition.* New York: John Wiley & Sons.

Wind, Y. (1978). Issues and advances in segmentation research. *Journal of Marketing Research, 15*(3), 317–337.

Winter, F. W. (1984, January/ February). Market segmentation: A tactical approach. *Business Horizons, 27*(1), 57–64.

13

Fund-Raising Strategy: Tapping Into Philanthropic Value Orientations

Thomas J. Reynolds
Strategic Research, Development and Assessment

James Norvell
Private Consultant

Using a sample of 200 millionaires, a recently published book identifies personal motives underlying philanthropy among wealthy donors. Although there seem to be many different reasons for giving, what these millionaires want from charities apparently can be boiled down to different shades and mixtures of only two factors — degree of personal control and the need for public recognition. By combining these two factors together with the types of charities supported, we can identify seven giving-types that range from *altruists* (people who provide unrestricted funds to support social causes and wish to remain anonymous) to so-called *communitarians* (people who want a big say in how their contributions are used to support local cultural, religious, or educational concerns and expect generous amounts of public acknowledgment and personal attention). The basic insight of the research on wealthy donors is that both the characteristics of a charity and the personal motives of donors are important in understanding philanthropy. Our own experience in fund-raising tells us that personal involvement greatly increases when donors can see and feel a tight connection between the characteristics of a cause or a nonprofit organization and their own personal goals or values. Experience also teaches us that gaining the personal involvement of prospective donors is the key to successful fund-raising.

The purpose of this chapter is to show how to build personal involvement among current and prospective donors so as to solidify and expand a nonprofit organization's base of support. We suggest new ideas for how to make a tight connection between the characteristics of a nonprofit organization and the personal values of prospective donors. To formalize these ideas, we propose a definition of philanthropic strategy based on understanding the prospective donor's decision-making process, and then we explain and demonstrate the methods used to develop an effective strategy.

PRESENT AND FUTURE CHALLENGES
FOR NONPROFITS

It is the rare nonprofit organization that has not suffered significant setbacks during the worldwide economic slowdown of the early 1990s. As the economy began to make a modest recovery, the roll out of delayed fund-raising campaigns threatened to overwhelm prospective donors especially in combination with the increase in the number of organizations looking for funding in the wake of governmental budget cuts.

Based on the experience of corporate America since the 1980s, more customer choice often means more customer power. Donors of all types now have more choices of where to put their time and money than ever before. In the short term, many nonprofits that laid low during the recession without investing in a more complete understanding of their donor constituency may face further reductions in financial support and losses of key personnel. In the long term, it will become critically important for all nonprofits to adjust what they do within their organizations and what they communicate both inside and outside their organizations in order to better satisfy the growing demands of current and prospective donors.

SEEING THE OPPORTUNITY

In a marketplace crowded with many alternatives, organizations must establish meaningful distinctions over their competitors. Meaningful distinctions are associated with delivering real value to their customers. Today's winning companies have been among the first to accentuate their distinctiveness by adopting customer-based marketing and positioning strategies. Such strategies help managers deal with their growing uncertainty regarding how to position a product and develop an action plan that will retain and cultivate established customers, and in some cases, attract whole new market segments. This approach to strategy is successful because it outlines the means whereby a close connection can be made between product qualities and the personal motives of customers. Tightly connecting product qualities with personal motives provides customers both the rational reason and the emotion-based motivation to purchase and repurchase the product. Such a basis for product positioning raises competitive barriers, reduces price sensitivity, and often increases frequency of use.

As a first step in translating the concepts of "customer orientation" to nonprofit organizations, it is useful to start by defining and outlining the principles of a customer-based philanthropic strategy. *Philanthropic strategy* is the specification of a customer-based template for guiding the operations, communications, and public relations activities of a nonprofit organization so as to differentiate the organization's case for support from other social or personal investments in positive and personally relevant terms among key donors and donor prospects, members of the community, and other important stakeholder groups. Adhering to the basic principles of strategy that arise from the preceding definition allows organizations to leverage a customer orientation into marketplace success.

Principles of a Customer-Based Philanthropic Strategy

Principle 1. Philanthropic strategy guides a coordinated set of actions through the use of a strategic template. Strategy brings together and coordinates resources to accomplish highly focused objectives. A core strategic concept is to pick targets of opportunity that enable one to match many resources against a competitor's few. Also, successful organizations follow a strategic pattern or template, even if it is not written down, that enables them to gain efficiency by focusing all of their resources on the same target or goal. A *strategic template* is different than a formal strategic plan. A template succinctly captures the strategic intent of the organization in an outline form that facilitates the assessment of an organization's behavior, communications, or appeals against a strategic standard of measurement.

Principle 2. Philanthropic strategy differentiates the organization's case for support from other social or personal investments. People contribute charitable donations and service for a wide variety of reasons, attenuated by their preferred area of support, preferred type of support, desired level of recognition, and the amount of personal control. Identifying the right mix of powerful, motivating reasons is critical. To attract substantial investment, an institution's case for support must be sharply drawn, distinct from other social and personal investments, and be centered in activities and practices that donors value. Institutions differentiate themselves by communicating to constituents or donors that through contributing to or becoming an important part of the organization, the donor will receive psychological or social rewards that satisfy their important driving goals or values.

Principle 3.   Philanthropic strategy uses positive terms. Many organizations dwell on how they have corrected past mistakes rather than moving on to stress their unique benefits. Problems must be fixed, but publicizing their repair will not guarantee success. Sharing a positive vision based on the delivery of unique benefits strengthens continuing support and attracts new investment. Unique benefits are defined in the context of competitive weaknesses. A good strategist will turn a competitors strength into a weakness and consequently find a competitive edge.

Principle 4.   Philanthropic strategy uses personally relevant terms. Strategists make it a point to gain a better understanding of the "landscape" than their competitors, and clever use of the landscape creates competitive advantage. With a philanthropic strategy, one is competing on a mindscape. We can gain competitive advantage by using personally relevant words and experiences that tap into the ideas and associations forming the donor's mindscape. In this terrain, an experienced guide can uncover a case for support that prospective donors will find convincing and motivating. Of course, for a philanthropic strategy, one of the most important facets of personal relevance revolves around the peer group. Donors want to be sought out, but not by just anyone. A case for support will not be personally relevant unless donors believe they are being sought out by a befitting peer group or organization.

Principle 5.   Philanthropic strategy focuses on key donors and donor prospects, members of the community, and other important stakeholder groups. Good strategists define the battlefield on their own terms, not someone else's. In philanthropy, the field of competition is the marketplace of donors and public opinion. A key to effective strategy is not simply identifying who these people are, but defining who we want them to be in terms of *external* factors (demographics and socioeconomic status) and *internal* characteristics (attitudes, beliefs, and values).

The need for fund-raising is often the impetus for taking a closer look at how a nonprofit is operating and communicating. To be truly customer-based, nonprofits need to have a master plan to bring all of their activities in tune with the physical and emotional needs of their constituencies. A philanthropic strategy is a master plan. Its development and use will bring a sense of uniqueness, consistency, and relevancy to the organization and its fund-raising activities.

Developing strategy requires three broad steps: (1) framing the fund-raising issues; (2) identifying the compelling reasons and associated physical and emotional benefits that underlie donor contributions, given the specific frame; and (3) developing appropriate communications that link these compelling reasons with the organization, activity or fund-raising campaign.

FRAMING THE FUND-RAISING ISSUES

To uncover which physical and emotional needs matter most to donors and therefore serve as reasons for choice and to determine how they can be used to link the characteristics of the organization or activity to the individual's personally relevant goals or values, we must answer four questions.

1. What constituencies should be considered?
2. What are the relevant behaviors of the constituents?
3. What situational contexts are relevant?
4. What are the constituents' choice alternatives?

Answers to these four questions help frame subsequent donor research that will yield actionable and successful marketing and positioning strategies. Consider the example of Mardan School, a case in which school officials ran a real risk of not keeping pace with the growing needs of the learning-disabled children within their community. The Mardan School is a day school for learning disabled children, offering many types of education ranging from special needs' tutoring to full-time instruction. In 1984, it had an enrollment of approximately 50 children and was marking its tenth anniversary in the former City Hall in the downtown area of Costa Mesa, California.

Enrollment growth led the school to purchase two mobile classrooms that were placed in the parking lot. The board of trustees commissioned an architect to prepare a plan for the building's renovation and expansion. However, although the community held very positive beliefs about the quality of the school and clearly felt that the service provided was very important, the level of fund-raising support for the expansion was judged as being poor to fair. What had the board of trustees overlooked in arriving at their decision to renovate the building?

Before the board could move forward, they realized they had to take a few steps back to assess the issue more thoroughly. Clearly, the problem was to understand the reasons for this apparent lack of interest and formulate a solution that enabled the school to fulfill its purpose. Following a customer-based approach, the first step was to answer the four framing questions.

First, the key constituencies needed to be identified. The constituencies included all potential donors, of whom 10% would be expected to provide 90% of the dollars for the fund-raising campaign. Thus, the key constituency was the smaller group of anticipated large donors. Most of these donors were known to the board, so further identification research was not necessary.

Once the key constituencies were identified, Mardan's trustees needed to know what relevant behavior had to be addressed. The obvious answer was to give generously, but in order to support this key behavior, Mardan's board had to establish positive attitudes toward substantial giving to the Mardan school among key donors. Also, some of these donors in turn would be asked to solicit donations from their peers or associates. Thus, Mardan had to provide them with persuasive arguments to support the School.

The relevant context was the next issue to be addressed. Donors generally want to be recognized as worthwhile members of a worthwhile group. Consequently, the organizational mission, reputation for excellence, and quality of staff, physical facility, and business decisions made by Mardan School were matters of personal pride for key donors. In addition, a study of county records indicated that in the years ahead, school-aged children would be predominantly located in growing residential areas several miles south of Costa Mesa. To continue to serve its traditional constituency effectively, Mardan would have to move south with young families. Thus, the social context within which Mardan School's donors would be expected to contribute involved receiving civic recognition and seeing that the gift was used efficiently.

The fourth framing question involved identifying the choice alternatives available to the key donors. External to the school were numerous worthy causes, some offering similar services to Mardan. Within the school, there were several opportunities other than the original expansion plan. For example, potential donors knew that many schools in the community surrounding Mardan were vacant. To them, this meant that there were opportunities for Mardan to relocate to a nearby vacant school under a favorable long-term lease.

Once the framing issues were laid out, it became apparent that the next step was to better understand the personal values of key donors that made the renovation project unacceptable. Interviews with the potential donors revealed that many donors believed the renovation of an existing building was not at all warranted. Moreover, they were disturbed that board members had asked for renovation plans before they had obtained a better grasp of the situation.

From the potential donor's perspective, the renovation planned for Mardan School would result in a high-priced, clumsy-looking, ill-suited building in a location far removed from the growth area of the county. To them it felt like bad business, and they believed that once completed, it would become a source of public embarrassment, not public pride. What was needed was a one-time, long-term solution for the school that would reflect favorably on the judgment and leadership of the donors.

Once the perspective of potential donors was identified together with key situational factors and the choice alternatives, the campaign progressed rapidly. With the help of a local developer, school officials located an affordable three-acre site across from a park in a growing residential area. Because the existing location was ideal for low-income housing for elderly, the city of Costa Mesa repurchased the City Hall building from Mardan at a price that paid for most of the new site. A beautiful, modern new school was built that far exceeded any facilities envisioned or possible at the previous location.

What made the Mardan campaign a success? We believe the research effort to uncover the personal reasons for donor participation in the project made a big contribution. Clearly framing the problem situation, then uncovering the key donor-decision criteria, and then understanding why they were important helped Mardan's directors create a vision of what the project could mean to the major donors and the community. When Mardan's directors were able to communicate the vision to donors, they created a heightened personal involvement and enthusiasm for the project, which ensured a successful fund-raising campaign. Although the donor-based plan required more money than the original renovation plan, the donor plan received substantial support because it tapped into the personal goals of the donors.

LOOKING BEYOND THE DONOR CONSTITUENCY

Large corporations conduct business in an ocean of public opinion. Among other advantages, a favorable public image can help companies maintain sales during tough situations. For example, although stores to either side were burnt to the ground, McDonald's restaurants were left relatively untouched during rioting in Los Angeles, so McDonald's was open for business whereas competitors were still cleaning up debris. The benefit of favorable public opinion and public trust is also evident in the ability of Johnson & Johnson to get past the Tylenol poisonings, as well as the speed with which major airlines rebound after devastating airplane disasters.

On the other hand, certain industries and companies have not invested in accumulating a deep well of favorable public opinion. For example, Exxon has lost competitive ground since the Exxon Valdez Alaskan oil spill because at least some consumers find it socially unacceptable to buy gasoline from a company that reinforces their perceptions that oil companies do not act responsibly toward the environment.

Public opinion is also one of the most vital elements for a nonprofit organization to consider when planning and implementing a fund-raising campaign. Few development officers would admit that public opinion has a serious impact on fund-raising activities because the majority of charitable support comes from so few people. Yet, public opinion should not be overlooked. As already mentioned, what a key donor's peers think about the organization he or she supports or the group with which he or she affiliates is an important factor in explaining his or her philanthropic behavior. What one's peers think about an organization or its governing board can be strongly influenced by public opinion. Consequently, when public opinion of a nonprofit turns sour, as was the recent case with the United Way, the organization can often face serious challenges for many years.

In some instances, the management of public perceptions can be the determining factor between failure and success for a nonprofit venture. As an example, consider the challenges addressed by a home for dependent children located in Orange County, California.

In the early 1980s, Orange County's facility for receiving and holding minors that were placed under protective care by the county's juvenile court system was by all accounts glaringly inadequate. The facility was originally built during the 1950s as a juvenile detention center and had been converted for housing juvenile victims who because of circumstances beyond their control were temporarily or permanently left without parental care.

The Albert Sitton Home was a series of institutional barracks with an authorized capacity of 45. The facility was housing over 80 children and the census was steadily climbing. To onlookers, it appeared as though children who had already suffered so much personal pain and loss were being placed in a unwholesome situation that would cause more suffering rather than alleviate it.

Contributing to the rising number of children placed in the home was the growth of the county's population and the increasing awareness of child abuse with a concurrent willingness and legal obligation to report it. In addition to abuse victims, the Sitton Home hosted lost and abandoned children, children of parents seriously or fatally injured in accidents, and children of parents who were jailed.

The Sitton Home was designed to provide temporary housing for children ranging in age from 1 month to 18 years old. Children stayed at the home for a period that could last from a few hours to several months. Often relatives were located and other times the children were sent to foster homes. Sitton Home had to have the capability of clothing, feeding, and educating a very broad range of children. In addition, security and a barbed-wire perimeter fence was maintained because some of the children were in danger from abusive parents, and others had a tendency to try to leave the grounds. As a result of the responsibility to provide protection, the facility looked a lot like the juvenile detention center located adjacent to the home.

The county was under a court order to provide facilities adequate to the demand and appropriate to the nature of those served or face a contempt order and escalating daily fines. In answer to the need, the county, being short of capital funds, convened a 100-member blue ribbon committee of county residents to study the problem. The chief judge of the juvenile court prevailed on a personal friend to serve as the chairman of the committee. The Blue Ribbon Committee chairman was, at that time, California's most prominent home builder, former Secretary of the Air Force, co-owner of Air California (later purchased by American Airlines) and a man of the highest visibility and stature in Orange County. He was obviously a wealthy man but had no experience in local government or philanthropic fund-raising.

The committee quickly confirmed that there were no county funds to use for expanding Sitton Home facilities or hiring new staff members without seriously undermining other infrastructure needs. The members felt that the option of seeking money through fund-raising should be explored.

First, the potential donors who were expected to contribute were identified as the key constituency. The relevant behaviors and contexts were essentially the same as for Mardan School; key donors had to feel positively about giving and some of them had to be motivated to canvas their friends to give as well. Choice alternatives external to the house included other possible philanthropic or investment opportunities. Internal alternatives for the home, however, were determined by the committee to be limited to building a new facility.

As one might expect, the ensuing research study uncovered a significant reservoir of sympathy for the children. Potential donors agreed that the children should not only have adequate housing but the best housing and care that could be provided. The obstacle uncovered by the research, however, was their reluctance to provide support for any facility that was administered by the county government. Prospective donors personally distrusted the county government as it was constantly under the public eye for one reason or another. Public opinion, as well as personal experience, had made them quite skeptical about the willingness of county officials to use their money with sufficient care to build a new facility that would meet the needs of the children.

The Sitton Home had extremely high public visibility. It was clearly portrayed and widely understood to be a government facility. To make matters even more difficult, a county probation officer who was given a leadership role on the Blue Ribbon Committee was gaining prominence as a spokesperson for the home. Her position as a probation officer served to blur the public's perception of the types of children served by the home and the circumstances that brought them under the county's supervision. The public began to raise some questions why a new juvenile care facility for "troubled" children was needed. By raising its voices, the public became part of the constituency that had to be addressed.

In order to conduct a successful fund-raising campaign, it became necessary to manage public perceptions by putting as much distance as possible between the Sitton Home and the county government. Effective management would require taking the right steps to support the desired strategy of separating the home from government. An operating foundation, established to solicit and receive anticipated private support, was activated to become the driving force behind the project. The foundation was chaired by the Blue Ribbon Committee chairman and the fund-raising campaign itself chaired by another of California's leading home builders. The contact between the operating foundation and the county government was limited to the head of the Child Welfare Department who served on the foundation board along with the wife of one of the county supervisors. Some twenty other board members were prominent private citizens.

Management for the building project was not provided by the county government, but put under the control of a board member who was the president of the Mission Viejo Company, developers of a large-planned (20,000 inhabitants) community. In addition, a complex arrangement was made wherein the county temporarily deeded over the property on which the new facility was being built to the operating foundation while the buildings were constructed. Then, as buildings were completed, they were deeded back to the county with the stipulation that they would be operated for the purpose intended for a period of at least 30 years. These steps alleviated the reluctance of potential donors who believed county officials were not competent to be in charge of facility design and construction and felt that the county would use the buildings for some other purpose once they were constructed.

To focus greater public attention on the special nature of the children being served by the home, build on the feeling of community support for the campaign, and ensure the project would not be tainted by a sour public opinion of county government, a considerable amount of effort went into informing public about the composition of the foundation board and the control it would exercise over the project. The plan was successful. The campaign was overfunded. First-rate facilities were constructed and an endowment was established to provide ongoing supplemental support for the home.

Following strategic guidelines helped both the Mardan School and the Albert Sitton Home succeed in their fund-raising activities. In summary, they were able to frame the fund-raising problems that they faced, understand the motivations and beliefs of their key constituencies, and then effectively manage these beliefs to accomplish their fund-raising objectives.

Identifying the key motivations and beliefs held by constituents is critical to developing a customer-based orientation. To accomplish this, organizations must delve into the thoughts and feelings of their constituents to uncover the key reasons associated with the decisions they make concerning their behavior.

UNDERSTANDING THE PHILANTHROPIC DECISION: THE MEANS–END APPROACH

There are many models of customer decision making. Among the most powerful in predicting and understanding choice is the means–end model (Gutman, 1982; Gutman & Reynolds, 1979; Howard, 1977). In the means–end framework, physical features or characteristics and their immediate, functional benefits are just the means to an end. The end people seek is always a powerful psychological or social need, which in turn often is associated with basic, personal values that people hold. Identifying and understanding the role of these psycho-social needs and personal values in decision making leads to predictions of choice that are much more accurate than predictions based only on physical features and functional benefits. Such a perspective removes much of the risk in trying to understand how decisions are made and how people can be taught and persuaded.

A Means–End Model of Philanthropic Donations

Based on the means–end framework, we created a model that describes the decision process of the philanthropic donor (see Fig. 13.1). In this model, the organization and its activity are described by philanthropic attributes, which include all perceived tangible qualities of the organization such as the type of service that it provides, its volunteers and paid staff, the level of personal involvement it affords to donors, its organizational structure, and the organization's leadership and management. These tangible characteristics provide functional consequences to donors, which are the measurable consequences of giving. Functional consequences include benefits such as effectively using the money, fulfilling a sense of obligation for the donor, and helping others in need.

Functional consequences lead to *psychosocial consequences*, which are the emotional states attainable through philanthropic giving. Psychosocial consequences include personal feelings and emotions, such as feeling less stress and worry, feeling accepted by peers, sensing personal growth, and experiencing the thrill of seeing improvement in others. In turn, these emotion-laden needs are associated with stable, enduring personal values or goals that are central to our lives, such as peace of mind, personal security, self-image, accomplishment, and personal happiness. Psychosocial needs

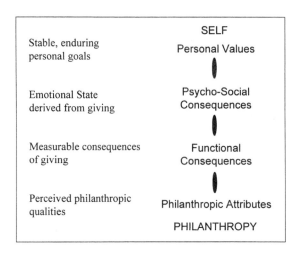

FIG. 13.1.   Philanthropic decision making: prospect model.

pull at the heart strings. When tightly linked to the objective features or characteristics of an organization, a person, a place, or a thing, they become key motivational elements for influencing thought and action.

To understand the rational (attribute and functional consequence) and emotional (psychosocial consequence and value) factors that influence constituent's decision making, one must do two things: (a) Elicit the distinctions that underpin the choice of one alternative over another in the context of the appropriate situation or frame of reference; and (b) determine the reasons why these particular distinctions or choice criteria are important and personally relevant.

Eliciting Distinctions

Eliciting distinctions can be accomplished using one of several techniques, including triadic sorting, differences by occasions, and preference or behavior comparisons (Reynolds & Gutman, 1988). In triadic sorting, three alternatives are presented to the prospective donor-respondent, who is then asked to group two of the alternatives together and describe how the two are similar to each other and different from the third. Several triads can be constructed and used in this way.

Differences by occasions is another way to elicit distinctions. Focusing on the situational context of donor behavior provides a meaningful basis from which the donor can respond. Behavior does not occur in the abstract; rather, behavior is always constrained by external factors such as time, location, and people or by externally influenced factors such as societal norms. It is important that both the respondent and the interviewer keep in mind the contextual basis when discussing differences among alternatives.

Eliciting the Basis for Preference

Using preference and behavior comparisons is a third way to frame the choice situation. To begin, you present prospective donors with a list of many different choice alternatives, then ask for them to specify any alternatives to which they last considered or would consider making a significant financial contribution. Next you ask them to rank alternatives hierarchically to reflect the relative level of support they would be willing to provide for each option. An exercise based on likelihood of support provided the charity preferences shown in Fig. 13.2. The responses were elicited from a 75-year-old male who is a CEO and founder of a national chain of restaurants. He was very active in providing both time and money for local and national charities.

Assuming the organization was Yale University, you would want to ask two general questions. Why would you give more support to St. John's Hospital than Yale University? Why would you give less support to the United Way than to Yale University? The answers to these questions represent the initial choice criteria or distinctions.

If one focuses on identifying and understanding choice criteria as the primary research goal, it is easy to write questions that will get the nonprofit organization where they need to be with respect to understanding the key perspectives of donor prospects. The difficulty is in determining the right people to interview, the appropriate situational context to use as

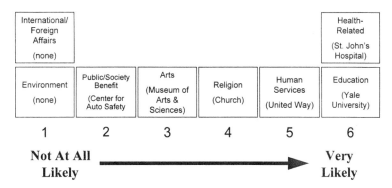

FIG. 13.2. Philanthropic decision making.

a frame of reference, and the choice alternatives that are related to the behaviors the nonprofit wants to influence.

Why Is a Choice Criterion Personally Relevant?

Once choice criteria have been identified using one of the techniques mentioned or some other method, it is necessary to understand why these particular distinctions are personally relevant or important to people. This can
be done by determining how the choice distinctions are linked to important
personal motives of the donor prospect using a laddering interview.

In its simplest form, laddering aims to uncover why attributes and associated consequences matter or are important to the respondent's physical and emotional well being. The details of this type of interview have
been described in the marketing literature (Olson & Reynolds, 1983;
Reynolds & Gutman, 1988). Laddering involves asking various forms of
the question, "Why is that important to you?" Laddering is a structured
yet conversational technique adaptable to nearly any type of interview environment, including interpersonal contacts or social gatherings among
key fund-raising representatives and potential contributors. Figures 13.3
and 13.4 show examples of decision-making means–end chains that repre-

Question	Answer
"How does that make you feel when you know others respect you?"	"It makes me feel good about myself." ↑
"Is it important for you to set an example for others?"	"Yes, because I earn respect from both the business and community." ↑
"Why is that important to you to help other students get a good education?"	"It makes me feel good...that I am leading the way for others to give...so they can help too." ↑
"Why do you want to give something in return?"	"I am able to help other students get the same great education I received." ↑
"Why is it important to you to donate to Yale just because you went there?"	"Because they gave something to me, so I want to give something in return." ↑
"Why are you less likely to make a significant donation to the United Way than to Yale University?"	"I would donate to United Way because someone asked, but I went to Yale, so I feel a loyalty to it."

EDUCATION YALE UNIVERSITY	vs.	HUMAN SERVICE UNITED WAY

FIG. 13.3.   Philanthropic decision making: negative ladder example.

Question	Answer
"Why is it important to you to have less stress?"	"It gives me peace of mind."
	↑
"Is it important to you to have good judgement?"	"Yes, it takes a lot of pressure of me. I'll have less stress."
	↑
"How does it make you feel when to know that your money is going to be used wisely?"	"I feel proud of my judgement."
	↑
"Why is it important to you to donate to an organization because you respect their leadership?"	"I know that my money will be put to good use."
	↑
"Why are you more likely to make a significant financial contribution to St. John's Hospital than to Yale University?"	"I respect the individuals in the organization."

HEALTH-RELATED ST. JOHN'S HOSPITAL	vs.	EDUCATION YALE UNIVERSITY

FIG. 13.4.   Philanthropic decision making: positive ladder example.

sent the giving orientation of the same 75-year-old CEO donor, as uncovered by a laddering interview. The laddering questions asked are shown on the left and the donor's answers are on the right.

The Decision-Making Map

Figure 13.5 depicts a decision-making map. Decision-making maps are an aggregation of information collected in laddering interviews of multiple individuals. A map includes the most frequently mentioned ideas or elements, as well as the most common associations or connections between those elements. Each element on the map is a code word that represents a set of similar ideas mentioned by respondents. Figures 13.3 and 13.4 also show examples of verbatim remarks associated with the code-word pathways on the map.

Decision-making maps reveal the different types and levels of information that people use to make choices between competing alternatives. The ladders (chains of associated ideas) frequently are based on contextual factors such as the donor's life stage, peer group, ethnic background, reasons for involvement, and past experiences with nonprofit organizations

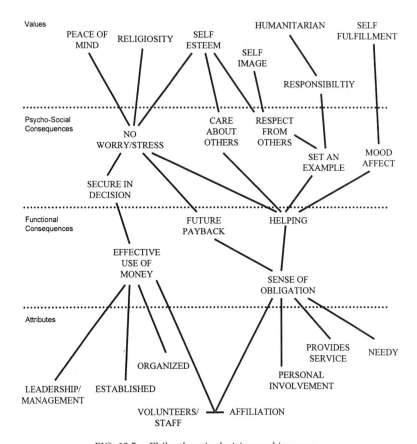

FIG. 13.5. Philanthropic decision making map.

may significantly influence. Therefore, decision-making maps also reflect the influence of these contextual factors on a person's reasons for choosing to contribute.

Quantifying the Map.   When a substantial number of ladders are collected from numerous donor-respondents, the aggregate decision-making map can be *quantified* to reveal the frequency of mentions for individual elements at each level on the map. For instance, the relative importance of the element can be indicated by expressing the number of times that element was mentioned in the ladders as a percent of the total number of mentions for a given level (e.g., psychosocial consequences or attributes). As another example, because ladders are elicited relative to specific organizations, the number of positive mentions for each organization can be contrasted with the number of negative mentions to provide a measure of competitive strengths and weaknesses.

Equities and Disequities. Ladders and decision-making maps can include both positive elements (reasons for supporting St. John's Hospital) and negative elements (reasons for supporting an organization other than St. John's). Elements with substantial positive balances (seen as much more positive than negative) are considered to be *equities* (valuable assets), whereas elements with large negative balances are *disequities*. Although this type of equity–disequity analysis may not be feasible with fund-raising problems that involve relatively few donors, it might be very useful when many potential contributors, such as the United Way or the American Heart Association. For situations with only a few key donors, one might field a fund-raising feasibility study in which potential donors first describe the giving orientation that fits them best. Then potential donors could discuss the strengths and weaknesses of each donation alternative relative to their giving orientation.

THINKING STRATEGICALLY ABOUT PHILANTHROPIC DECISION MAKING

A consumer-decision map is like a road map that can guide every strategic decision of the nonprofit organization from how fund-raising campaigns are planned and implemented to what the organization does with its funds to how people working for the organization are recruited and retained. For instance, the philanthropy decision-making map in Fig. 13.5 shows several ways for managers to create meaningful differentiation between alternatives for charitable giving. For example, one organization might stress the established leadership of their respected board and advisors that allows them to make effective use of money that, in turn, reduces the donors' level of worry and stress. Other organizations might reinforce the sense of obligation people feel based on the nature of an organization's provided service. This feeling of obligation then allows potential donors to give back and help others who face similar circumstances to their own.

Understanding the Equities and Disequities

Understanding the reasons for and against various choice alternatives (the equities and disequities) provides valuable guidance for selecting the most compelling elements to include in a strategy and for identifying the ones to exclude. For example, in the Sitton Home case, "association with local government," an attribute, was identified as a major barrier to donation behavior. Their successful strategy hinged on severing the association between government and the Home.

Identifying a Strategic Template

The decision-making map in Fig. 13.5 shows that people may use many different types and levels of information to make their donation choices. To position itself effectively, a nonprofit organization must identify the key concepts that are most salient to their target audience and convincingly demonstrate how these elements are connected to personally relevant values and goals of the target donors. This specification of the means–end linkages that connect the differentiating characteristics of an organization with donors' personal motives functions as a basic outline or *strategic template* for managers. The strategic template is a simplified description of strategic intent—what the organization wants to become. Figure 13.6 shows a possible strategic template expressed as an ameoba shape that encompasses the key attributes, functional and psycho-social consequences, and values to be emphasized in the philanthropic strategy. This template represents the strategy of an organization wishing to stress

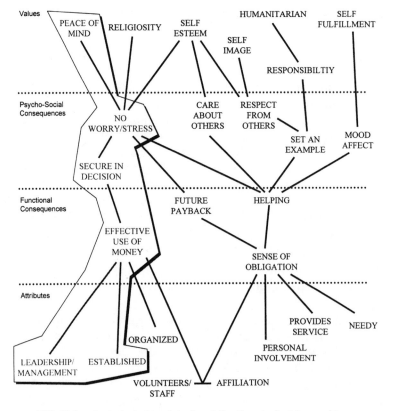

FIG. 13.6.   A strategic template for philanthropic decision making.

its first-rate leadership and management as instrumental for achieving a hierarchy of benefits (effective use of money) and emotions (secure in decision and no worries) that eventually are associated with a personal value (peace of mind).

The ability of an organization to identify a suitable strategic template and then match its internal and external behavior to that template will determine the persuasiveness of its case for donor support and its ability to meet program needs. However useful for planning purposes, the strategic template is rather lifeless until managers determine how each strategic element will be implemented, particularly in communications with the target audience.

Implementing the Strategic Template

Implementing a strategic template can create an enduring competitive advantage. However, a great deal of work must go into implementing a philanthropic strategy beyond identifying a strategic template. A major part of the implementation involves how the strategy is to be communicated to donors in a persuasive manner. The communication goal is to form a double bond of rational reasons and emotional rewards across the levels of decision making specified in the strategic template. Managers or directors should constantly ask themselves what they can do to communicate a stronger connection between the concepts that underpin the success of their organization's fund-raising efforts.

Assessing the Strategic Implementation

A fully specified strategic template can also function as an assessment tool. Using the strategic template as the target, managers can determine how well each activity within the organization fits with and contributes to the organization's strategic intent. For example, by identifying activities and tactics that are off strategy, managers can be proactive in shaping the organization and not merely be reactive to events. Identifying actions that are off strategy can be done either through direct managerial analysis of the specific activities and messages that the organization is communicating to its constituencies. Alternatively, a more rigorous method involves obtaining donor feedback on specific activities or communications. For example, a letter to be sent to potential donors might first be evaluated by a representative group of donors to determine its effectiveness in communicating the key elements of the specified strategy.

Strategic assessment based on the means–end approach may be the single most effective tool for implementing a customer-based approach to doing business. Within the area of consumer marketing, the assessment of a company's behavior relative to its strategic intent has enhanced product and corporate advertising (Reynolds & Gutman, 1984; Reynolds & Rochon, 1991), consumer promotions, corporate sponsorship activities, new product concept development, retail store operations, training and management of customer service representatives, and recruitment and retention of salespeople. In the context of fund-raising and philanthropy, a donor-based strategic assessment of an organization and its fund-raising activities should have similar success.

REFERENCES

Gutman, J. (1982, Spring). A means–end chain model based on consumer categorization processes. *Journal of Marketing, 46*(2), 60–72.

Gutman, J., & Reynolds, T. J. (1979). An investigation of the levels of cognitive abstraction utilized by consumers in product differentiation. In J. Eighmey (Ed.), *Attitude research under the sun* (pp. 128–151). Chicago: American Marketing Association.

Howard, J. A. (1977). *Consumer behavior application and theory.* New York: McGraw-Hill.

Olson, J. C., & Reynolds, T. J. (1983). Understanding consumers cognitive structures: Implications for marketing strategy. In L. Percy & A Woodside (Eds.), *Advertising and consumer psychology, Vol. 1* (pp. 77–98). Lexington, MA: Lexington Books.

Prince, R. A., & File, K. M. (1994). *The seven faces of philanthropy: A new aprroach to cultivating major donors.* San Francisco: Jossey-Bass.

Reynolds, T. J., & Gutman, J. (1988, February–March). Laddering theory, method, analysis, and interpretation. *Journal of Advertising Research, 28*(1), 11–31.

Reynolds, T. J., & Gutman, J. (1984, February–March). Advertising is image management. *Journal of Advertising Research, 24*(1), 27–37.

Reynolds, T. J., & Rochon, J. P. (1991). "Means–end based advertising research: Copy testing is not strategy assessment. *Journal of Business Research, 22*, 131–142.

14

The Application of Means–End Theory in Industrial Marketing

John A. Norton
Wirthlin Worldwide

Thomas J. Reynolds
Strategic Research, Development and Assessment

This book concerns means–end theory — how it is developed and how it is applied. This chapter illustrates the applications of means–end theory and laddering and equity analysis, in particular, to a number of business-to-business applications. Our goal is to show how business marketers operating in a wide variety of industries have used these tools and to encourage others to use them to enhance their understanding of buyer behavior. Such understanding is required to achieve leverageable and sustainable competitive advantage.

INDUSTRIAL AND CONSUMER MARKETS

Many of the examples found in this volume illustrate applications to positioning, advertising, and promotion of frequently purchased branded goods. It is a fact that consumer-goods marketing managers use relatively large market research budgets in support of advertising and promotional efforts to devise and carry out their plans, and they have been methodological pioneers. Business marketers have been later adopters of a number of well-accepted customer marketing tools, including means–end theory.

Why have we industrial-marketing types been slow to catch on? It may be that we have let our own writing on industrial marketing fool us somewhat. We like to point out the differences between the marketing processes used to take frequently purchased branded goods to end-users (marketing

Campbell's Soup or Coca Cola) and those used to bring to business or government the things it might require (engineering services bought by a city building a power plant, telecommunications services used by an insurance firm, or diesel fuel used by a fleet of long-haul trucks).

For good reasons, there are some observable differences in these processes. Because consumer-goods marketers do not often meet face-to-face with their customers, formal market research and the use of advertising as a communications vehicle are more prevalent in those markets. Because of the relative complexity of the typical product or product line in business markets, industrial "brand managers" (the title may be different) tend to be older and more experienced than their packaged-goods counterparts. Finally, because the number of accounts or customers is relatively small and geographically concentrated, and the purchase amount per account or transaction is large, direct selling is more often feasible in business markets.

One key difference in consumer and industrial markets is the concept of derived demand. Products such as synthetic fibers are components of such products as carpet, fabric, and tire cord, and the level of demand for those products is partly a function of new car sales. Although certain products such as programmable logic controllers are sold to the literal users of those products, the demand for such devices is in part a function of long-range forecasts of new car sales by those same auto makers, which in turn motivates the firms to invest in plant and equipment.

Although we have ample evidence of the effective use of means–end theory in consumer-goods markets, we have fewer examples of application-to-business markets. In consumer goods, we see the frequent use of the means–end approach in developing (and assessing) impersonal communications such as television advertising, promotional campaigns, and brand-positioning strategies. Although applications to industrial markets are not unknown, they are more rare. We think that is a mistake.

Many differences between consumer and business marketing are largely a matter of degree. For instance, in certain product classes, families engage in committee buying and family members specify products or attributes of products to be bought by another member of the family. Whereas consumer-packaged goods marketers study phenomena such as brand loyalty and switching, business marketers study their analogs: relationships and transactions.

Despite the well-documented importance of the industrial and governmental sectors of the economy and despite some occasional calls for industrial-goods marketers to learn from their opposite numbers in the consumer-goods fields, industrial-goods marketers still lag. That is a shame because understanding the decision-making process of customers in industrial markets is no more or less important than it is in consumer markets.

WE ARE SLOW TO LEARN FROM CONSUMER-GOODS MARKETERS— WE NEED TO CATCH UP

Here is why: Buying is a special case of choice, and choice is a special case of human decision making. Selling is a special case of persuasion, and persuasion is a special case of communication. In industrial marketing we live at the intersection of those special cases of decision making and communication. It makes sense that we should know as much about them as our friends at Coca-Cola do. Even in the case of strictly derived demand, although the choice of the product form may be a closed issue (the automobile requires fibers of a certain type for its carpets and tires), whose fibers to use is not closed. Vendor choice is a decision variable under the control of buyers, and we can influence that choice if we understand those buyers completely.

We argue that industrial marketers need the insights that means–end techniques can provide. In the paragraphs that follow, we describe a number of applications that helped firms do things a little (or a lot) better and illustrate the laddering probing techniques that enabled researchers to learn what they needed to know.

Salesforce Recruiting—Recruiting for Success

Means–end techniques help you avoid traps. Is your firm engaged in direct selling? If so, among the tasks your managers must master are recruiting and retaining salespeople. We know that all the hundreds of studies of who makes the best salesperson (loud or quiet, introvert or extrovert, flashy or conservative dresser) tell us—well, not much because all sorts of people can and do succeed by some measure in sales; but we also know that a good way to frustrate someone is to establish a set of unrealistic expectations for them, and a good way to get salespeople to quit is to leave them without a base of support when the inevitable setbacks occur. Here is how one company changed its recruiting pitch based on what it learned about its successful and unsuccessful sellers, which helped link selling the company's products to the self in a meaningful way.

In the mid-1980s, Mary Kay Cosmetics experienced a decline in sales and recruiting that put the firm in jeopardy. To investigate the reasons that people became beauty consultants (salespeople), the research team divided their sample universe into sets. One set comprised beauty consultants who were successful and stayed with the company; another included people who were relatively unsuccessful; a third group consisted of people who had left the company. During a laddering interview, interviewers probed for reasons why all of the beauty consultants joined and for reasons they stayed or left. To understand why they joined, researchers asked respondents to recall the decision context. In doing so, they realized that becoming a beauty consultant was not always a choice between obvious competitors such as rival direct selling organizations or cosmetics firms but sometimes a choice between working 9-to-5 in a retail store or as a secretary in a bank. By asking for the most positive aspects of being a beauty consultant for Mary Kay, as opposed to exercising another career option, managers discovered that there were a number of common themes within each of the subgroups.

Although the linkages between the company and the values people held were many, not all had the same valence for all groups. That is, some were positive only for successful consultants, and some were negative primarily for consultants who left in frustration. An example of the former was a set of linkages dealing with learning (about skin care and cosmetics and about other things such as communication skills and business discipline). Another was "teaching those skills to others." Both were linked with a feeling of self-worth. By contrast, for consultants who resigned, the linkage between monetary rewards and a feeling of contrabution to family was strong—and negative.

When successful beauty consultants spoke about their experience with Mary Kay and how it was different from prior work experiences, they acknowledged financial motives. However, they also indicated that they viewed financial results as less important than the ability to learn, to grow, and to help other people, and the way those outcomes made them feel. They were motivated by a sense of independence and self-esteem, and even on days when sales were not what they had wanted, they were sustained by other psychosocial gains. In contrast, beauty consultants whose experiences were less positive overall usually had only a financial motive for becoming a sales consultant. Examples of individual ladders in Fig. 14.1 illustrate the results of typical interviews.

The Mary Kay company used these means–end results to revise its recruiting message to prospective beauty consultants. Besides de-emphasizing money as an end result, the recruiting message also recast financial gain as one of several valued outcomes of the process of learning, growing, and helping other people that could lead to a heightened sense of independence and self-worth. The result? In 1,200 matched pairs of consultants, the changed recruiting materials produced a 42% increase in recruiting success versus the control group.

Commodity Sales: You Can Differentiate Anything

Sometimes, the traps you can avoid are those you lay for yourself. Does your firm sell products that you and your customers call commodities? Our experience shows that you can differentiate those products. The key

Why consultants stayed	Why consultants quit
I have a feeling of accomplishment	I still felt dependent on others
I'm learning more myself	I wasn't able to improve my lifestyle
I've got a special role with them	I wasn't able to contribute
I'm able to help my customers	I didn't earn much money

FIG. 14.1.   Examples of individual positive and negative ladders.

is to understand that, if attributes of the product or the extended product are nearly identical across firms, the differentiation needs to take place at the psychosocial level (in means–end theory). Usually, your customers see differences you do not, so ask them.

Consider the case of a major petroleum company selling mid-level distillates (diesel fuel, kerosene, and jet fuel). As the manager expressed it, "This is a points business, not a dollars and cents business. The 'four P' are price, price, price, and price." All of the managers believed it, their salespeople practiced it, and their margins showed it. Yet, when interviewed by members of the research team, their customers' assessment of what was important and why varied greatly. In fact, the interviews uncovered over 25 differentiators of diesel fuel by brand. For fleet buyers and for buyers of jet fuel, price was a dominant attribute. However, for other customers, a broader set of attributes was important. Among them was price, and it was an important attribute — about 10th on the list, but for most people, price was not a differentiator if it was not completely out of line with the marketplace. Why was price not more important? Because other attributes of the brand — assurance of supply, assurance of consistnecy, speed or response to requests, even courtesy and friendliness — led to more central psychosocial outcomes, and those connections were more highly leverageable than a price that was a little lower than average.

In this case, the attributes that served as differentiators were discovered by starting with a usage amount probe. Researchers asked respondents how frequently they bought each brand of fuel in the past month. For the sake of illustration, suppose a respondent reported stopping for fuel at a Shell station three times, at a Mobil station six times, and at a Texaco station seven times. The differences in those frequencies were used to initiate the laddering probes. The contrasts between purchase frequencies revealed both positive and negative differentiators for each brand. The questions used as probes for this respondent might have included the following:

- Why did you use Mobil more than Shell? (Shell negative, Mobil positive)
- Why didn't you use Texaco always? (Texaco negative)
- When you bought Shell, why did you choose it over the other brands? (Shell positive)
- What do these three brands have that others lack? (Category positive)

By conducting equity analyses of the category and the brands, team members could in fact find leverageable nonprice equity in their brand. Figure 14.2 illustrates ladders resulting from usage probes.

DEFENSIVE STRATEGY: YOU DON'T HAVE TO DEFEND AGAINST PRICE ATTACKS BY DROPPING PRICE

Understanding the nonprice dimensions of competitive advantage is another important application of the means–end approach. A company that supplied protective services (in the form of guards, uniformed or plain clothed, armed or unarmed) to embassies, shopping centers, and businesses found it needed to protect itself from price-cutting competition. Some managers believed that price had become the only dimension of im-

Texaco Shell	Shell Mobil
People can rely on me	I'm a better driver
I deliver loads on time, every time	I'm in a better frame of mind
No delays	I'm important to them
No gelling in cold weather	The lady behind the register calls me by name

FIG. 14.2.   Ladders resulting from usage probes.

portance. If that proved to be the case, then they were at a serious disadvantage. Their costs were relatively high because of rigorous recruiting standards and a training process about 100 times longer than the average for such firms. They knew that firms valued other things than price, such as the training, the appearance of the guards, their degree of formality or approachability, and the nature and closeness of supervision, but they did not know how those attributes of their firm were linked to the personal lives of the people who made the decision to retain them. Understanding the linkages to valued outcomes lets them educate their sales staff to keep them from playing the game by rules that would have put them at a disadvantage.

In this case, respondents were generally aware of a small number of competing firms. Therefore, the interviewers began their laddering probes by asking respondents to register their overall satisfaction with their current supplier of protective services: "On a scale from 0 to 100, where 0 means 'awful, couldn't be worse' and 100 means 'perfect, couldn't be better,' how satisfied are you overall with XYZ company?" The two ends of the scale (perfect, couldn't be worse) were deliberately scaled so that even the most satisfied or dissatisfied respondents would not use them. As a result, interviewers could probe for both positive and negative attributes in each case.

- You rated your satisfaction with XYZ a 90. What kept you from rating them higher? (This probe elicits an XYZ negative).
- What made you rate them so high? (This probe elicits an XYZ positive.)

When respondents mentioned price, interviewers let them vent. Then, they could ask follow-on questions such as the following:

- Suppose they did lower price, and you rated them three points higher. What is the one most important thing XYZ could do to get you to rate them higher still?
- Suppose all firms' prices were identical. Would you still prefer to use XYZ? Why?

Each of those probes revealed nonprice differentiators of interest to respondents, illustrated in Fig. 14.3.

POSITIONING: LET YOUR NAME MAKE A PROMISE

"There ain't no loyalty that two-cents-off won't overcome," or so it is said. As if to prove the statement, a telecommunications company's commercial customers described their choice of providers as coldly rational. "We

Why did you rate them so high?	Why didn't you rate them higher?
I'm a better parent	My job could be in jeopardy
I spend more time with my family	Makes me look bad
I don't have to stay late	Hurts the mall's image
Always on time	A guard's appearance was inappropriate

FIG. 14.3.   Ladder-revealing nonprice differentiators.

write down a needs statement, solicit three bids, assess the capabilities of the firms on relevant dimensions. . . ." That is hardly an environment in which "relationship" as a marketing goal seems achievable. Yet, consider the complex decision-making environment and the limited resources the business user has to direct toward making a choice. How does one choose among alternative offers of considerable complexity? What is the marginal gain to be made by taking the time and effort to process information about each offer? One way to deal with such cost and complexity is to let the promise of the brand take the place of much complex decision making. That was something this firm's customers were willing to do because the brand had earned their trust. In this case, researchers gained an understanding the components of trust, the signals that indicated that the firm could be trusted. Researchers also found the degree to which different firms were thought to possess those signaling qualities. Probes of decision makers, influencers, and deciders revealed the emotional outcomes of those signal attributes and the ways in which linkages were formed between attribute business consequence personal (emotional) consequence. Those linkages formed the basis of both *brand strength* (the ability of the brand to compete in its market) and *brand leverage* (the ability of the brand to grow beyond its current boundaries). By specifying in the positioning statement the linkages to be reinforced, managers, sales staff, and technical staff could see the elements of the marketing mix — advertising, personal selling efforts, and new-product development efforts — as part of an integrated, purposive strategy.

   In this, as in many industrial markets, when customers were asked why they preferred provider A to provider B, they responded with summary-level judgments on characteristics such as quality, reliability, and dependability. Such generic answers are not particularly helpful to a marketer trying to understand how to communicate those virtues. Interviewers in this case had to chute downward from such responses, then ladder upward, as the following example illustrates.

Interviewer: Why did you rate ABC Company so high?

Respondent: Dependability. They are very dependable.

Interviewer: How do you know?

Respondent: Because every time they say they will be there, they show up on time.

If the interviewer had asked why dependability was important, a generalized positive might have resulted: "I try to be dependable, others should be, too; I like to deal with dependable companies." By asking for the underlying attribute, a different and more personally meaningful ladder results.

Interviewer: Is it important to you that they show up on time?

Respondent: Sure. I can schedule my appointments and know thatI can meet my customers when I promise to. That way, I don't disappoint my customers and look bad.

Often, after probing downward to get the factors or cues that lead to or support a construct such as dependability or quality, the respondent does not return to the original construct but instead goes beyond to a personally relevant consequence. The factors or cues themselves are useful in defining for a service manager the signals by which buyers recognize quality or dependability in a service provider, as illustrated in Fig. 14.4.

INDUSTRIAL STRATEGY FORMULATION AND IMPLEMENTATION: POWER MEANS PREFERENCE, BUT LEVERAGE MEANS GROWTH

Some names have power. That is, within a defined category, they have been able to build purchase preference. Building power is largely a matter of understanding the equities the brand has in the minds of customers and using those equities to reinforce linkages with the self. An example of a consumer brand name with a lot of power might be Coca-Cola.

Other brands have leverage. They have permission, within the minds of customers in their current product class, to reach beyond their current sphere of business. Brand names with leverage can magnify value in other markets. An example of a brand name with leverage might be Arm & Hammer.

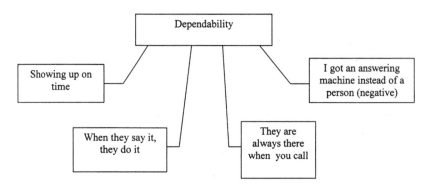

FIG. 14.4.   Cues that reveal provider dependability for one respondent.

There are ample cases in consumer packaged goods markets of firms believing that because they had achieved strong brand preference in beverages (or automobiles or typewriters), they could then brand other products such as foods (or sportswear or computers). Their success depended in part on whether they in fact had a brand name that was leverageable and therefore extensible or a name that was merely powerful. We have found analogs among business marketers as well. In some cases, identifying the bases of equity and the reasons for its personal relevance has helped a company understand the level of commitment it had to make to establish leverageability.

One firm selling project management services in a given range of project sizes aspired to capture some of the market for bigger, more complex projects. Through a laddering study, the firm was able to understand how the attributes of the firm and those of its competitors led to personally meaningful outcomes for buyers including the mitigation of psychological risk, the potential for social reward, and achieving certain levels of psychological comfort. Thus, the firm was able to understand that its primary equities gave it a great deal of power but relatively little leverage. Managers also learned what equities the company had to develop in order to make the firm's name and reputation leverageable or transferable to larger projects. Figure 14.5 illustrates how the attributes of the firm were personally relevant to contracting personnel at potential client firms.

DISTRIBUTION STRATEGY: JUST KNOWING
IT CAN BE DONE CAN MAKE IT POSSIBLE

Good theories are often quite practical. Sometimes, just knowing the phenomenon exists and conjecturing about how it might manifest itself is a help. In one case, a manager was confronted with the following situation, in a European market for industrial power monitoring and control:

We are at a distinct disadvantage. Our technical service staff is about one-tenth the size of our largest competitors. As a company, they have been in this market for 100 years. They have a very large installed base in motors and controls although that is not necessarily the key driver for decisions. We desperately need improved distributor representation. Distributors think our products are great. But those distributors, faced with a decision to carry "us or them," choose them. I need some way to get these distributors to cast their lot with us. I will tell you, however, that I have sought help from dozens of people, and the answer is unanimous: They are all glad it is my problem and not theirs, because they don' see a feasible solution other than giving away the product.

In this case, the manager and his staff knew the distributors reasonably well, and some had worked for distributors in the past. Therefore, they were able to draw on their own experiences with both firms for insight. All they needed was a framework to articulate the problem as a decision-making problem, and a brief introduction to means–end theory provided that framework. We cast them in the role of respondent distributors and had them role-play, articulating the ways in which they could tell the companies and their products apart in particular sales and service situations. The actors, playing the part of distributors, tried to put themselves in the distributors' shoes and explain why those differentiators were personally relevant to them. They were able to identify, in this case, plausible positive and negative associations with the two firms, some of which were inherent in the operating methods of the companies. In this case, too, the manager spent some time learning how to ask questions in a way that let him not only uncover needs but link those needs with personally relevant outcomes. For example, rather than asking about problems with the current supplier, they asked, "What is hard about what you do? "The respondent could then identify a felt need, and the salesperson could ask what benefit would result if that need were met, how the distributor would

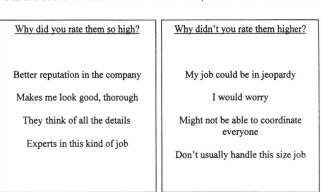

Why did you rate them so high?	Why didn't you rate them higher?
Better reputation in the company	My job could be in jeopardy
Makes me look good, thorough	I would worry
They think of all the details	Might not be able to coordinate everyone
Experts in this kind of job	Don't usually handle this size job

FIG. 14.5.   Personal relevance of the attributes of the contracting firm.

know the need had been met, and so on, engaging in a kind of laddering process.

With some instruction in the rudiments of constructing a consumer decision-making map, the manager returned to Europe cautiously optimistic. On arriving, he taught his sales staff about means–end theory and gave them materials on laddering methodology. He also told them about the mock interviews he had conducted and gave them his maps, linking performance features of the firms to personally relevant characteristics, such as the one exemplified in Fig. 14.6.

Members of his staff, already trained in asking questions and in problem-solving sales techniques, quickly understood the process and adapted their calling techniques to accommodate the new approach. About a month later, he wrote to tell us of his success at winning over an account worth tens of millions of dollars operating in three countries.

THE SELLING PROCESS

Let us return briefly to the notion of the intersection between communication and decision-making, for it is here in business marketing, as it is in consumer marketing, that the application of means–end theory can have relatively immediate impact.

It is true that advertising budgets in packaged-goods firms are large, and because expenditures that are large draw a lot of scrutiny within companies, it makes sense that consumer-goods marketers would actively

Personal values	Self-worth	Achievement
Corporate outcomes	I cannot deal with special circumstances (-)	I can do things the way I want to (+)
Supplier policies	Do things their way (-)	Willing to do anything (+)
Capabilities	Many service reps (-)	Few service reps (+)
Size of company	Very large (+)	Small in this region (-)

FIG. 14.6.   Levels of concepts associated with companies.

search for and embrace techniques to help them pull products through the distribution channels. But direct-selling budgets also are large in almost all business-marketing companies, and much effort is directed at achieving and evaluating selling effectiveness. We see significant opportunities for sales professionals in industrial or business-to-business markets to benefit from a clearer understanding of means–end theory and its application in their work.

Most sales-training programs propose a process or system that codifies the authors' experience in sales. The experience base of Miller and Heiman, explained in such books as *Conceptual Selling* (Miller & Heiman, 1987), and the experimental and empirical base that Rackham explained in *Spin Selling* (Rackham, 1988), make contributions that are proven in the field. Their books explain *what* works, or at least, some of what works. Athough we find great insight in their accounts, these books do not explain *why* what works does in fact work. That is, we do not see in these treatments evidence of a general theory of how industrial buyers make decisions. Without such a general theory and understanding, in the end they can only acknowledge that selling, and especially account planning, should be strategic. In contrast, means–end theory provides techniques that help firms establish positioning strategy by specifying the manner in which the characteristics of the brand, service, or firm are to be linked to personally relevant outcomes for a targeted set of buyers.

Using the Sales Force for Strategy Development and Implementation

In the industrial salesforce, the single most powerful change agent in an organization is capable of serving as an information source for strategy development and as an instrument for carrying out policy. The salesforce can be brought to bear as a weapon of competitive advantage in a few short steps. Salespeople already are talking to the decision makers, and they already know the value of asking questions. What they may not know is how to use directed laddering-type probes — open-ended questions aimed at taking conversations to a higher level of psychological abstraction to gain insight into personal relevance. In addition, salespeople can be taught how to construct a map — a graphical representation of their findings from their interview notes. Familiarizing the sales personnel with means–end theory and technique would go a long way toward giving them that knowledge.

Let us give an example of how such a process might work. Rackham's (1988) *SPIN Selling* differentiates among features (what we call attributes), advantages (functional consequences), and benefits (again, usually functional benefits but ones the customer has asked for specifically, expressed as a need statement). His or her process could connect to higher level psychosocial implications, but usually it does not. However there is no reason that an interview could not push to higher, more personal consequences:

Seller:	And we also have triple-duplex wiring. (A feature in Rackham's taxonomy, an attribute in means–end language.)
Customer:	What's that do?
Seller:	Keeps you from getting your muffler-bearings crossed.
Customer:	I don't have that problem. But I do need to keep the G-4 from impinging on the bearings.
Seller:	Why is that? (At this point, the customer has expressed a need; Rackham might suggest making a benefit statement in response. But we are still at the level of the functional consequence, and would like to probe a bit deeper.)
Customer:	It's critical; our customers hate when that happens.
Seller:	When that happens to one of your customers' machines, what happens in your office?
Customer:	Two things. First, they call me, and I don't blame them. And I feel like an idiot because I promised them they didn't have to worry about that.

At this point, the probes have reached a low-level psychosocial consequence associated with the attribute mentioned earlier. If it were comfortable to do so, we could continue.

Seller:	Why is that important to you?
Customer:	Because I am responsible, and because my customers should be able to rely on what I tell them.
Seller:	Is that important to you?
Customer:	Sure.
Seller:	Why?
Customer:	Are you crazy?
Seller:	(Silence.)
Customer:	Okay, I'll tell you. I only have one thing to sell, when it gets down to it: My word. If I don't have that, I don't have anything. Customers have to trust me. And they can. I'm proud of that.

In this case, we have taken this imaginary customer to the values level with repeated application of the basic laddering probes. In many business sales, that is not possible. However, we can usually take people to the psychosocial level and understand something of the emotional drivers underlying their behavior. Factors such as "gaining recognition," "I'm important," "I'm in control," "I did a good job," "makes my life easier," "get more done," "get in to other things," "not get hassled" can be important leverage points for communications. As a cautionary note, these laddering probes are inappropriate for meetings larger than one-on-one. The material is a bit sensitive for that.

USING INTERVIEW NOTES FOR INSTITUTIONAL LEARNING

Interview or sales-call notes can be kept in a kind of coding shorthand that represents individual ladders:

	Level
• Duplex wiring	(A)
• (Not) cross muffler bearings	(A)
• (Not) impinging on bearings	(FC)
• (Not) make customers mad, call in	(FC)
• (Not) make me feel like an idiot	(PC)
• Customers can rely on me	(PC)
• Proud of my reputation	(V)

Those notes can then be coded and collapsed into a consumer decision-making map. An example of a sketch that might result from such an interview follows as Fig. 14.7.

The results can be analyzed over time for both individual and corporate learning, so that moving sales people from one territory to another does not result in lost history. It also gives your sales staff and management, along with others in the firm, a common language or lexicon with which to discuss your business. That lexicon is not your own internal "company-speak" but the voice of your customers, the most valid language you can use.

SUMMARY

Although marketers of consumer goods have historically used means–end theoretic frameworks more broadly than have business marketers, there is nothing about the markets themselves that militates in favor of

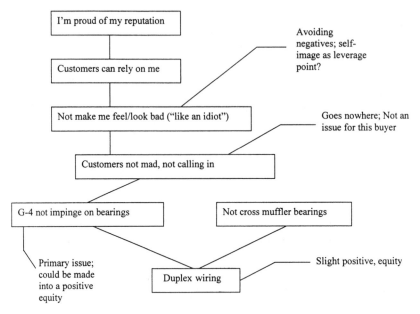

FIG. 14.7.   Toward creating a decision-making map using sales-call information.

such a condition. We have shown that the means–end framework can be (and has been) applied in strategy formulation, positioning, salesforce recruiting, strategic account planning, assessment of growth opportunities, relationship building, defending against price-based attacks, channel development and control, sales and sales training, research and development (R&D), and product support. We have provided a few specific questioning techniques that can help, although clearly there are many more. Finally, we have argued that means–end theory forms a foundation for institutional and individual learning, and that such a foundation can help the functional parts of the firm—R&D, production, finance, support, communication, sales, and even marketing—stay grounded in a deep understanding of consumer perceptions, preferences, and motives. Understanding the nexus of decision making and communication yields customer-relevant marketing strategy, the operational definition of a marketing orientation.

REFERENCES

Miller, R., & Heiman, S., with Tuleja, T. (1987). *Conceptual Selling*. New York: Warner Books.
Rackham, N. (1988). *SPIN Selling*. New York: McGraw-Hill.

Beyond Financial Engineering:
A Taxonomy of Strategic Equity

Thomas J. Reynolds
Strategic Research, Development and Assessment

Steven J. Westberg
Southern California Edison

INTRODUCTION

The misuse of leveraged buy outs (LBOs) in the 1980s is probably best illustrated by Robert Campeau who borrowed nearly 10 billion—that's 10 with nine zeros—from professional, experienced financiers, with no apparent strategically-based business plan to enable repayment. The blatant abuse of the financial system underlying this transaction is evidenced by the roughly $1 billion that went to lawyers, accountants, and investment bankers for the "invaluable services" in closing this megadeal—services that convinced future creditors that Campeau's $10 billion loan was indeed credible.

The explicit trademark of deal making in the 1980s was not really the "art of the deal." Rather, it could be described more aptly as "do the deal, and generate personal fortunes for supplying invaluable services." That such a landmark-size deal could easily land Campeau Corporation in Chapter XI, as it did in early 1990, stems from the rather straight-forward assessments of the "invaluable services" provided by Wall Street's finest—incompetent, unethical, or both. The summary assignment of some combination of incompetence or ethical misconduct, however, is not the focus of this treatise. Rather, the goal here is to detail a fatal, theoretical flaw in the financial decision-making system and seek to resolve it so such situations can be avoided in the future.

Certainly Campeau was hardly alone in being forced to seek refuge in the bankruptcy code. More than half of the mergers and acquisitions that began in the 1980s are in, or appear headed for, the courts. Their flagship brands and subsidiaries have been dragged off to the salvage yards. Assessing each of these deals involves understanding the simple fact that virtually every one of these deals resulted from sophisticated financial engineering — the respected Wall Street science of number generation, classification and thaumaturgical assessment. The moneylenders who lost billions, as well as many of those still employed on Wall Street, probably would agree that rigid analysis of financial statements, cash flows, and projected stock prices is a necessary but not sufficient technique on which to base mergers and acquisitions.

Perhaps the somewhat magical numbers and projections generated from financial engineering made sense to someone. Perhaps it seemed logical and prudent to assume such a staggering debt load or to participate in funding it. However, such actions must rest on the assumption that the assets being acquired are sufficient to support the debt, including the acquisition costs. In this case, those assumptions were based on the analysis of strategic equities (regardless of what terminology might have been used) of the numerous brands being acquired. Those equities in the Campeau example were under both the Federated and Allied banners. Therein lay the problem — there has never been a well-defined, formal definition of equity, much less any accepted method of evaluating it.

The death of financial engineering does not mean that mergers and acquisitions will no longer take place. Rather, it suggests that more realistic methods of analysis should be developed and applied to insure the financial transaction is based on realistic business and market driven assumptions, not mere number crunching. It is clear that total reliance on financial engineering was the fatal flaw. Although probably a bit melodramatic, it could be said that many of those who lived (quite well, we should note) by these strictly financially based methods also died by these same methods. What is needed are business- and market-based evaluation methods focusing on the strategies that serve as the foundation of the core business. In fact, these market driven methods must underpin all financial analyses. In brief, a paradigm is needed to identify, at a very minimum, the strategic equity of the firms, and in the best of all worlds, to translate and quantify that equity in terms of acceptable financial evaluation methods.

This chapter lays a foundation to address these key issues by providing the details of such a paradigm, beginning with a taxonomy of the concept of strategic equity. Beyond defining equity, we also describe the fundamental consumer-based component in special types of equity. In addition, we give examples of how managers can build equity in a corporate or brand franchise, thereby maximizing long-term profits and shareholder value.

WHAT IS STRATEGIC EQUITY?

Successful acquisitions of the 1980s shared a single, common factor: the combined created real value more than offset the high costs of acquisition. For example, Quaker Oats bought Stokely-Van Camp in 1984 in a deal that included Gatorade, a languishing competitor in the underdeveloped sports-drink market. Quaker Oats increased advertising, expanded the line of flavors, and refurbished packaging to transform the relatively ho-hum Gatorade on supermarket shelves nationwide. With sales up from $170 million in 1984 to $625 million in 1989, Gatorade demonstrates how the right combination of brands and brand management adds up to dramatic increases in sales, profit, and ultimately, shareholder value.

In this case, an unpretentious cereal company knew what the flamboyant Robert Campeau and all of his "invaluable" advisors did not: A key ingredient is missing from the financial engineering approach. That ingredient is *brand equity*, the value added to a product due to its affiliation with a brand name or trademark. Brand equity gives products such as Morton Salt and Crayola Crayons a virtual monopoly in a market of otherwise undifferentiated commodities. It gives the Courtyard hotel chain higher occupancy because of its association with the Marriott name. It gives Honda lawnmowers a premium price because of Honda's quality reputation for building reliable gasoline engines. The problem, then, is measuring how much of this success is attributable to what, so far, has loosely been termed brand equity—in short, why is brand equity valuable?

WHY IS BRAND EQUITY VALUABLE?

Strong brand names imply a high level of consumer loyalty. Brand loyalty is a behavior, but it is based on the perceptions of the brand that consumers carry in their minds that, in turn, drive consumer decision making. Positive memories and meaningful associations held in consumers' knowledge structures have staying power and this makes the company that owns well-known, high-quality brands stronger in at least three ways (Farquhar, 1989):

1. A dominant brand can fend off attacks by serving as a barrier to entry. For example, there is virtually no room for competitors of Arm and Hammer baking soda, Jell-O gelatin, and Vaseline petroleum jelly. This is known as *brand dominance*.
2. A good brand image can keep a brand viable through bad times and changes in consumer tastes. GI Joe was profitably resurrected after the anti-war sentiment of the seventies had passed. Budweiser re-

turned as the "King of Beers" when prohibition was repealed in 1933. Tylenol survived a major product-tampering crisis in 1982. Such examples of survivability are known as *brand resilience*.

3. Strong brands can serve as platforms from which to launch new products and services. This is the *leveragability advantage* of brand names. For example, licensed products carrying the Disney label number in the hundreds. Bally's best selling Lifecycle machines led to their successful Liferowers. Proctor and Gamble launched Ultra Tide to maintain Tide's position as a superior cleaning agent.

Before evaluating any type of equity attributable to a brand or a company, managers (as well as market analysts) must have a complete understanding of the types of equity that exist in the business environment. The following taxonomy briefly outlines the types of equity that have been identified and provides examples to illustrate these definitions (see Fig. 15.1 for the entire framework). This formal taxonomy will then provide the basis for assessing brand equity and will serve as the foundation for consumer input to the equity review and measurement process.

A TAXONOMY OF EQUITY

Strategic Equity

Strategic equity is the value of a company based on its ownership of one or more of the primary equities: brand, distribution, or resource control.

Brand Equity

Brand equity is (a) the value, current or potential, that exists because a product or service is in some way affiliated with a brand name, trademark, or other distinguishing brand identity; (b) the value of a company that exists because of its ownership of brand names and; (c) *Cognitive equity*: the value of consumers' memories, either real or imagined, about brands. (There are six specific subtypes of cognitive equity: *bridge, scarcity, borrowed, prestige, promotional*, and *latent*). For example, Waterford crystal is an example of a brand with a high level of cognitive equity. In Waterford's case, the characteristics that consumers associate with the brand are high quality and strong heritage. McDonald's (and kids), Crest (and tooth decay prevention), Coca-Cola (and superior refreshment), Levi Strauss (and ruggedness), and Porsche (and stylish speed) are other examples of brands with high levels of cognitive equity.

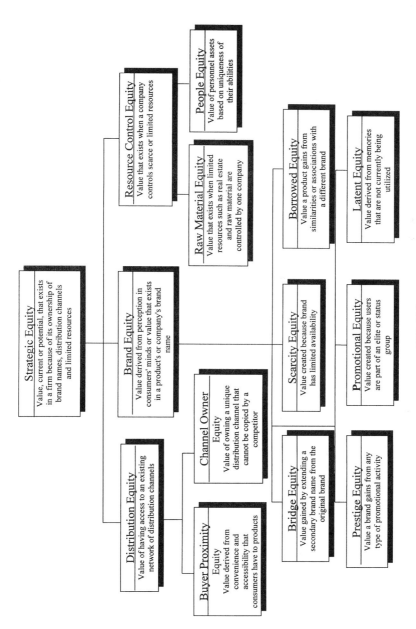

FIG. 15.1.

339

Secondary Equities in Brand Equity

Bridge Equity. Bridge equity is the value that is created by brand names attached to a new product or group of products; the original brand name can increase in value through bridging. For example, Jell-O Pudding Pops have successfully bridged the association between Jell-O gelatin and the new frozen dessert snack.

Scarcity Equity. This is the value created because a brand has limited availability. For instance, at one time, Coors beer had scarcity equity because of its limited distribution prior to the mid-1970s. Coors' equity grew by word-of-mouth, creating demand that led to its immediate success when it penetrated new markets in the south and east. More recently, Madonna's 1990 music video had scarcity equity because it had been banned by MTV and other music broadcasting stations. The video restrictions generated dramatic interest due to the unavailability of the product.

Borrowed Equity. This is the value a product gains from similarities it shares with a different brand. Usually the host brand possesses significant brand equity, and the borrowing brand purposely mimics the brand's attributes. The borrowing brand must offer some significant advantage over the host, typically price. For example, Sears profited from borrowed equity because of similarities between its Fox brand and LaCoste's popular Izod shirts. VP Planner software closely resembled the software capabilities of Lotus 123, thereby taking advantage of pre-existing equity created by Lotus in the marketplace.

Promotional Equity. This is the value a brand gains from any type of promotional activity for the brand including coupons, advertisements, publicity, and word-of-mouth, or, any positioning activity that creates or builds cognitive equity. Consider that products such as Gillette, Budweiser, Coke, and Pepsi take full advantage of promotional equity through a variety of media, including sponsorships of social and entertainment activities (concert tours and videos) and sporting events.

Latent Equity. This is the value of consumer perceptions having the potential to be linked to a brand. These perceptions are not necessarily a result of product promotion. Or, the value of reactivating consumer memories that do not now exist in a top-of-mind fashion. For instance, Converse shoes can be linked to older male consumers' fond memories of their childhood days due to the brand's virtual dominance of the sport shoe market until the 1970s.

Distribution Equity

Distribution equity is the value of having access to distribution channels that is not a result of cognitive equity or channel power. For instance, Coca-Cola's global distribution channels represent perhaps the most valuable distribution equity in existence today. As a result of this distribution power, Coca-Cola is the best known brand name in the world and dominates international soft-drink markets. Secondary types of distribution equity include: Buyer Proximity and Channel Owner.

Buyer Proximity Equity.   This is the value derived from having consumers in proximity to products that are not primarily sought. For example, products or brands in close physical proximity to check-out stands in grocery stores — like the *National Enquirer*, chocolate candy, and chewing gum — have equity due to their proximal location to the potential buyer. Similarly, bean dip gains sales when it is located adjacent to snack chips in the grocery store.

Channel Owner Equity.   This is the value derived from virtual control or ownership of a distribution channel. For instance, Avon has over one million sales people worldwide selling to well over 100 million households directly. There is significant latent value in this sales franchise, which could sell other types of goods ranging from insurance to travel.

Resource Control Equity

Resource control equity is the value that exists because a company owns or controls scarce or limited resources, including intellectual property and patents. Secondary equities include raw material and people. For example, Texas Instruments stock rose sharply in 1989 when competitors were required to pay royalty fees for using TI patents, reflecting TI's control of its intellectual resources.

Raw Material Equity.   This is the value of controlling limited resources such as real estate and physical raw material. Consider that DeBeers possesses almost 100% raw material equity of the diamond market.

People Equity.   This is the value of personnel assets based on the uniqueness of their individual or aggregate abilities; or the value of an individual's ability to bring new and creative ideas to the company. People equity is often found in technologically based companies such as Apple or IBM that hire individuals with unique talents from prestigious companies and schools. The 3M Company, for example, realizes the potential value of its employees and nurtures its people equity by rewarding those who bring new products to market. People equity, then, is also reflected in valuations based on a company's potential to develop new products.

COMBINING TYPES OF EQUITY

The specific equities defined previously represent the basic building blocks of strategic equity. Importantly, these concepts obviously are not totally independent, either in the three major types (brand, distribution, and raw material), or across the various types. For example, the following combinations are commonly seen across the major equity classifications.

Monopolistic Equity

Monopolistic equity is the value that exists because competitors cannot easily enter or effectively compete in a market without significant additional cost and the value that arises from possession of one or more primary equities that prevent significant competition. For example, Nintendo of America once dominated the home-video market by such a high penetration of households with its computer hardware that its competitors were locked out in the foreseeable future.

Cross-Cultural Equity

Cross-cultural equity is the value that exists because a brand can cross cultural boundaries. Consider that the McDonald's eating experience can be enjoyed by people from vastly different cultural backgrounds, in particular, consumers who desire to emulate the U.S. lifestyle or behavior. Levi operates in an identical manner with respect to cross-cultural equity, which the company is able to leverage in overseas markets.

The preceding definitions suggest that the concept of strategic equity is nearly universal, encompassing all aspects of strategically grounded value in a corporate environment. Likewise, brand equity encompasses much more than brand-name recognition and buying behavior. Measuring a brand's value based on perceptions in consumer's minds or the premium customers are willing to pay for the name is a necessary basis and critical to the evaluation process, but it is not completely sufficient.

Applied to acquisition strategy, brand equity can be used to create value in at least two ways: (a) leveraging latent brand equity into new opportunities, and (b) combining brand equity with one or more other components of strategic equity to create additional value. Quaker Oats' acquisition of Stokely-Van Camp, noted earlier, used both methods. First,

Quaker Oats leveraged the Gatorade brand itself. Leveraging a brand requires that the new owner extend the brand into new products or services in such a way that increases the value of the brand franchise. Second, Quaker Oats combined its distribution system with the Gatorade name to move the sports drink into new markets. This example illustrates how different forms of brand equity can be combined synergistically to create a whole that is greater than the sum of its parts.

More recently, Coca-Cola and Nestle announced an international joint venture to market canned coffee and tea drinks. Nestle hoped to combine its well known trademarks with Coke's massive global distribution system in order to bring coffee and tea products to worldwide markets much faster than either company could do alone. In other words, Nestle's brand equity and Coca-Cola's distribution equity were combined to produce additional value (representing both monopolistic and cross-cultural equity) for each firm. It is important to understand that creating value by combining equities is dependent on owning strong brand names. Interestingly, the resulting equity that could be gained from the joint venture between Coca-Cola and Nestle may well generate additional strategic equities, including equities based on distribution and (new) product. This partnership represents a prototypical example in which the total incremental value to be achieved from leveraging existing strategic equities is significantly greater than the sum of its parts.

BRAND EQUITY ASSESSMENT

Brand equity can be a powerful asset, and those who manage it need insight, not clairvoyance. Financial engineering ignores this elusive asset, so it is not surprising that crystal-ball methods prevail when Wall Street analysts attempt to predict the success of a merger or acquisition. However, with a reliable method for analyzing brand equity, both analysts and managers could correctly plan for and evaluate the merger and acquisition activities that will occur during the 1990s and beyond. Most importantly, effective brand-equity management would provide a means of adding value to firms that, in turn, would strengthen the overall economy, something Wall Street has been unable to accomplish in recent times.

Currently in the United States, accounting procedures ignore brand equity as an asset unless the firm is acquired for more than book value. The resulting intangible asset of "goodwill" is simply a default category that in no way recognizes the true worth of the brands. Since the 1970s, in lieu of a more valid strategic equity measurement, financial engineering was Wall Street's only method of valuing a firm. Successful acquisitions occurred because gut feelings about marketing issues were correct, not necessarily because the numbers added up.

In an attempt to improve on the evaluation system, several alternatives have been suggested. Wentz (1989) suggested (a) comparing the price of a branded product with the price of an unbranded product in the same category, (b) comparing profits of unbranded products to profits of branded ones, (c) determining how much the product would be worth without the brand name, and (d) conducting detailed investigations of factors such as market share, market trends, and advertising in order to arrive at a composite brand worth. Attempts have also been made to show the extent that accumulated advertising, product attributes, product quality, order of entry into the market, and the future potential of the product affect the equity of the brand. However, brand equity is more comprehensive and greater in scope than is indicated by these previous attempts to measure equity. Most importantly, a definitive measurement of the inescapable connection between the consumer and the value of the brand is missing from all previous efforts.

CONSUMER DECISION-MAKING THEORY

Brand equity dominantly lies in the perceptions of the consumer. In fact, marketing reality with respect to brand loyalty is in the minds of consumers. Consumers translate their perceptions into actions that ultimately dictate which products or services succeed and which fail. As a result, before any valuation of brand equity can be developed, it is important to understand how consumers think about products and services, and what aspects of their decision-making processes relate to their personal involvement with the product or service.

The issue, then, is to understand how consumers store information in memory with respect to brand perceptions and the decision-making process. More specifically, how do cognitive associations held in the collective memories of the marketplace motivate brand choice on an individual basis? This difficult research question can be addressed using the means-end perspective offered by the laddering methodology (Reynolds & Gutman, 1988).

Laddering assumes that the consumer perceptual and decision-making process operates on both a rational and an emotive level and includes a range of considerations from product and service attributes (rational) to personal values (emotive). Put simply, the laddering methodology attempts to uncover the associative structure between a product or service and "self," which then defines the individual decision-making process. The consumer is seen to maximize desirable outcomes or consequences of consumption with respect to higher level, more personal needs. That is, one's personal values determine the relative utilities for outcomes or consequences of consumption that, in turn, determine the relative utilities or importance weights for product attributes. The relative importance of the attributes, then, serves as the practical basis for product differentiation and ultimately rational choice. For example, the real, top-down, decision-making process for the selection of McDonald's to take the kids for lunch could be translated as:

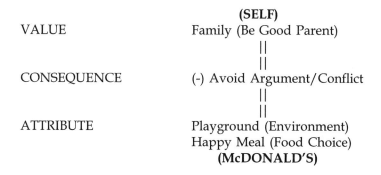

This theoretical perspective implies that consumers purchase products, not so much for their features or attributes, but for the physical and psychological consequences that stem from the attributes during consumption. In the previous example, a desire to minimize stress by avoiding conflict during the meal experience with the kids is guiding and defining the importance of key attributes that then define the selection process of the fast-food restaurant. The total set of connections between the product attribute and the consumers' value is the personal interpretation that explains why the consumer sees the brand (a fast-food restaurant) to be unique and distinct and, therefore, the brand of choice. The cognitive associations between attributes, consequences, and values (a-c-v) are envisioned as the decision-making memory traces for each consumer.

An integral part of the laddering process involves developing summary perspectives for an entire marketplace (a consumer segment), usually with specific brand loyalties as the basis for determining the relevant segments. Figure 15.2 provides an example of what is termed a *Hierarchical Value Map* (HVM) — or more simply, a consumer decision-making map (CDM) — for the fast food category, which represents the dominant perceptual orientations or decision-making ladders for a group of consumers.

A HVM that is constructed using specific user groups, like McDonald's users, provides the framework for developing an analysis of brand equity. That is, once the key decision-making criteria (the salient attributes, consequences, and values) are identified for an entire product class or a set of

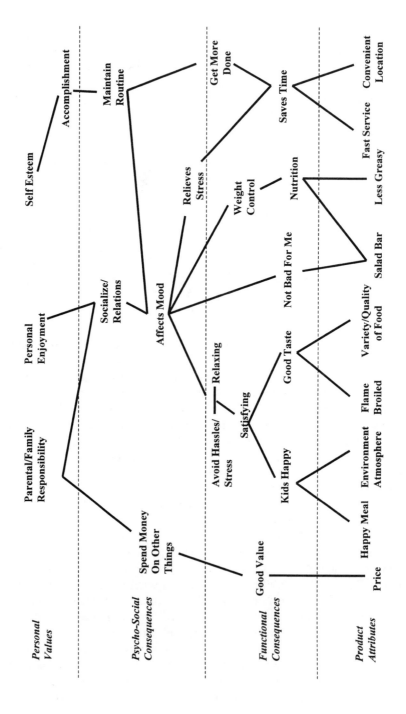

FIG. 15.2. Hierarchical value map for fast food restaurants.

competitive brands, traditional market research procedures can be used to assign relative importances and belief ratings for the respective options across user groups. What results is a differential equity index for each decision criteria (across attributes, consequences, and values) for each user group. These scores can then be contrasted to determine the relative equities and disequities of the brand with respect to the competition. This type of cognitive equity analysis explains, for example, why brand-loyal users prefer their product and why the brand-loyal users of competitive brands do not choose other brands (these reasons are the equity of the competition). Clearly, this type of information is invaluable for marketing managers in developing and specifying positioning and communication strategy.

Further, classification of consumers' perceptions of a brand into three types—product, image and personality can provide additional insight into the equity of the brand. Perceptions, as seen in the McDonald's example, are best described by physical attributes or consequences that stem from the functional form of the product or service. For example, McDonald's product perceptions might be "tasty french fries", "fast service", and "clean restrooms". Image perceptions are strongly tied to the abstract, nonfunctional attributes and consequences of a laddering summary or an HVM. For example, McDonalds' image perceptions might include "fun for kids," "American tradition," and "helping the community." Personality perceptions are those that are most strongly associated with human characteristics or traits. In these cases, a character or a person often personifies the brand. For example, McDonalds is personified by Ronald McDonald who embodies the virtues of "fun and entertainment", as well as "caring"—the latter concept derived from sponsoring hospices for seriously ill children and their families. Further examples of product, image, and personality perceptions are listed in Fig. 15.3.

Understanding how consumers perceive brands with respect this perception classification scheme can provide deeper insight into brand strengths and weaknesses. In general, strong brands will be grounded in product perceptions (giving consumers clear, rational reasons for buying the product or service). But, brands will also possess personally relevant image characteristics that both distinguish the brand from competitors and enhance consumers' usage experiences. In essence then, image perceptions can be the value-added result of marketing activities such as advertising and nonprice promotions. Personality perceptions generally serve to strengthen positive emotions consumers may have for the brand and to reinforce image and product perceptions.

A second set of initial research questions to initiate the laddering process can also be used in the study of brand equity. This type of research approach involves simply asking consumers "What comes to mind?" when a specific brand or service is mentioned. In the case of fast-food restaurants,

BRAND PERCEPTIONS

BRAND	PRODUCT	IMAGE	PERSONALITY
Tide	Superior cleaning power	Orange/yellow package	Mom
Miller Lite	Less filling, low calorie	Number one, funny ads	Ex-jocks
Ivory	White, floats, 99-44/100's pure	Good value	Grandmother
Disney	Movies, cartoons, amusement parks	Family entertainment	Mickey Mouse and friends
Sugar Frosted Flakes	Pre-sweetened corn flakes	"They're Great"	Tony the Tiger
Coca-Cola	Real cola taste, superior refreshment	"Americana", traditional	Popular, ubiquitous
Converse	Official NBA shoe	Revives pleasant memories	Larry Bird

FIG. 15.3.

suppose the restaurant asked about was Burger King. On the HVM derived from the laddering process, we see that "flame broiled," is a key product attribute that has significant equity with respect to Burger King's "most often" users and "occasional" users. However, in the "top-of-mind" association questioning, the concept of flame broiled did not come up very often. Given that the concept is an important discriminator with respect to consumer choice, and that it is not top-of-mind, strongly suggests "latent equity" that should be leveraged.

Research methods such as these provide insights for all types of brand equity, with primary contributions to directly specifying prestige, promotional and latent equity and, equally as important, brand disequities. Secondary inferences from this type of consumer research also yield strategic alternatives or options with respect to bridge and borrowed equity. The development of strategic alternatives or options then permits direct assessment of equities using traditional marketing research techniques.

The impact of these research approaches are primarily in developing marketing and business strategies, which require consumer understanding of the perceptual equities and disequities that exist with respect to the competitive marketing environment. Importantly, the development of new strategic directions that may have been overlooked or underrated gives the analyst specifics to assess in developing a sound strategically based evaluation. At the very least, the specification of the disequities in this manner yields a strong disaster check to make sure the current business strategies are both on track and devoid of potential weaknesses that may not appear in any other financially based analytic frame.

APPLICATION OF BRAND EQUITY

Consider the example of Converse in the competitive athletic shoe market. In the early 1990s, the market share belonging to Converse lagged well behind that of their primary competitors, including Reebok, Nike, and LA Gear, although at one time, Converse was the market leader in athletic footwear. Using the laddering methodology, an HVM was developed for the athletic shoe market as shown in Fig. 15.4. Note that it is possible, and often desirable, to describe the HVM with both positive and negative characteristics. For example, the attribute of "been around a long time" is strongly positive for some consumers, wheras for others this attribute is a negative (presumably because it connotes old fashioned or out-of-date).

Following development of the HVM, consumers evaluations of each brand—rated on each of the relevant attributes, consequences, and values—were quantified and compared. The brands rated higher by consumers for specific attributes, consequences, or values dominated the other

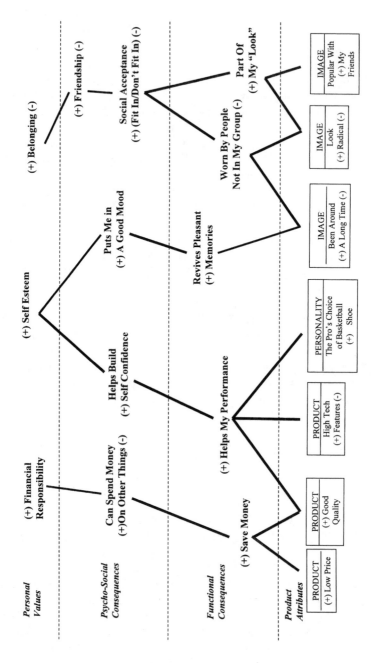

FIG. 15.4. Hierarchical value map for athletic shoes.

brands on these decision criteria. One can describe overwhelming dominance as ownership of the decision criteria. The magnitude of this dominance is a function of both the difference between consumer ratings and the relative importance of the specific attribute, consequence, or value. Top-of-mind frequency can help provide a measure of the relative importance of these characteristics. Comparing brand dominance across all dimensions gives a relative measure of the brand's overall equity against other brands. It is possible, and indeed most likely, that even weak brands may have dominance in certain relevant areas. Such was the case for Converse as shown in Fig. 15.5. In terms of strategy, then, Converse might consider three options.

1. The first strategic option is to attack from their position of relative strength by emphasizing the positive benefits of their attribute, "been around a long time." Because this attribute currently rates low in relative importance, the strategy would focus on increasing the salience of this dimension. Positive benefits currently exist in some consumers' minds (primarily among older males), so the communication should serve either to remind or persuade customers.

2. The second strategic option calls for Converse to create a new benefit of which consumers are not aware, in order to build a strong link between "been around a long time" and a value that Converse could dominate. For example, Converse could create a new functional consequence "my dad used to wear them" to link "been around a long time" with the psychosocial consequence "helps build self-confidence." In this case, the communication execution would teach consumers something new about the product, and at the same time leverage the familial bond.

3. The third strategic option involves a mixed strategy of both emphasizing their current strength of "been around a long time" and building additional strengths where competitors are vulnerable. In this case, Converse can strengthen consumers' perception of "good quality" and "the pro's choice of shoes" in order to strengthen perceptions of Converse's ability to "help my performance."

HOW SHOULD BRANDS BE MANAGED?

The real financial scorecard for brand management (other than the critical free cash flow) is the net equity gained or lost in a given time period. The value of a firm reflecting shareholder value, is a multiple of the sum of the equities described in this chapter. Following this redefinition of strategic criteria, the equity paradigm has rather strong implications for marketing strategy development and assessment and for evaluating a corporate fran-

Perceptual Brand Equities

Attribute	Importance Rating	Dominant Brand	Second	Third
Low Price	3	Converse	LA Gear	Nike
Good Quality	7	Nike	Converse	Reebok
High Tech	8	Nike	Reebok	LA Gear
Official Pro Basketball Shoe	2	Converse	Nike	N/A
Been Around A Long Time	4	Converse	Nike	Reebok
Look Radical	4	LA Gear	Reebok	Nike
Popular With My Friends	6	Nike	Reebok	Converse

Functional Consequence	Importance Rating	Dominant Brand	Second	Third
Part Of My "Look"	6	Reebok	Nike	LA Gear
Save Money	4	Converse	LA Gear	Nike
Helps My Performance	8	Nike	Reebok	Converse
Worn By People Not in My Group	3	Converse	LA Gear	Reebok
Revives Pleasant Memories	4	Converse	Nike	Reebok

FIG. 15.5.

chise. Thus, equity management should be the primary criteria for management decision making about brands.

First, management decisions can and, indeed, should be evaluated by their anticipated impact on each of the components of strategic equity. The merit of a decision will then rest on its ability to improve long-term brand performance and shareholder value. Such an approach will also insure cross communication between functional areas as managers strive to better understand the overall impact of a decision on the firm. The scorecard for decision making can be a checklist of equities, which can be reviewed for each decision.

Second, management, particularly brand managers, should be evaluated and rewarded based on their overall performance for developing and leveraging of the strategic equity of the firm. The formalized decision-making process proposed here could adopt the following sequence:

1. The brand manager presents a decision proposal;
2. The brand manager and others review and formally assess the potential impact of the decision on a scorecard;
3. Higher management or a board of directors assesses the proposal based on the results of the equity review; and
4. If the decision is executed, the actual impact of the decision is tracked and subsequently evaluated on the same scorecard.

Figure 15.6 outlines a hypothetical "Equity Scorecard" that shows the initial equity assessment of the firm, the anticipated impact of a proposed decision, and finally, the results of that decision on the various equities.

SUMMARY

The premise of this chapter is simple: understanding the strategic equities of brand franchises and the corporations that own them will provide the basis to avoid the monumental errors and abuses that took place in the merger and acquisition arena in the 1980s. The concept of strategic equity provides a way to understand the often intangible value that resides within the firm through its ownership of one or more of three primary equities: brand, distribution, and resource control. In terms of acquisition strategy, the intangible value can yield tangible profits when these equities are first understood, and then these equities can be leveraged or combined to create additional value. Because brand equity is potentially the most valuable of the three primary equities, skillful brand management is key to providing strategic direction for the brand, thereby maximizing the overall value to the firm.

Converse				
	As of 1/1191	Estimate - Decision A	Estimate - Decision B	As of 1/1/92
Brand Equity				
Bridge equity	0	0	0	0
Scarcity equity	+	0	+	+
Borrowed equity	0	0	0	0
Prestige equity	+	++	0	++
Promotional equity	+	0	0	+
Latent equity	+++	0	0	+++
Distribution Equity				
Buyer proximity equity	0	0	0	0
Channel power equity	+	0	-	+
Resource Control Equity				
Raw material equity	0	0	0	0
People equity	+	0	-	+

FIG. 15.6.   Equity scoreboard.

The laddering methodology provides managers with a way to evaluate the specific strengths and weaknesses of a brand in a competitive consumer-based context that, in turn, can lead to the specification of optimal offensive- and defensive-brand strategies. Indeed, one of the strengths of laddering is that it can uncover not only the positive equities of the brand, but also the potential negative factors, or disequities, may be associated with the brand. The result of a laddering study is an HVM that graphically depicts the playing field of the consumer decision-making process as a graphical playing field for managers to exercise their creative imaginations in creating marketing and communication strategies. The respective equities and disequities for a product category and specifically, for individual brands, are major elements of the HVM that have important strategic implications.

An overall benefit of measuring strategic equities is in the application to evaluation and assessment decisions. Armed with an equity scorecard, managers might better understand, and at least be more aware of, the intangible values that reside in the firm and might then take better care of these values through a more comprehensive decision-making process.

Although as yet unanswered, is the application of equity measurement in a financial mode. Although the methodology proposed here can provide relative evaluations of equity with respect to past levels, the ability to quantify equities in monetary terms would not only strengthen their usefulness for internal decision making but also in their application to financial accounting. The current debate surrounding accounting for brands is, to a large part, fueled by the lack of objective and consistent monetary measures. This has not stopped some firms from placing brands on their balance sheets (and thus in the hands of analysts, investors, and competitors), but it has left the users of financial statements somewhat ill informed. Further research in bridging the financial translations and implications of strategic and brand equity should be the immediate focus of any advisors and participants in merger and acquisition activity, in particular those interested in the numerous turn around opportunities that continue to emerge from the massive failures of the 1980s.

REFERENCES

Farquhar, P. (1989, September). Managing brand equity. *Journal of Advertising Research, 30*(4), 7–12.
Reynolds, T. J., & Gutman, J. (1988). Laddering theory, method, analyses, and interpretation. *Journal of Advertising Research, 28*(1), 11–31.
Wentz, L. (1989, June). How experts value brands. *Advertising Age, 60*(3), 24.

V

THEORETICAL PERSPECTIVES FOR MEANS–END RESEARCH

SECTION OVERVIEW

To a large extent, the means–end approach has evolved in an informal, somewhat haphazard manner. Many of the conceptual developments and methodological improvements were based on researcher intuition about solving a particular problem posed by a business application. With few exceptions, the theoretical underpinnings of the means–end approach remain implicit and only partially understood by its advocates.

As a result, the means–end approach lacks a clearly specified theoretical foundation. As yet, no one has developed a coherent and concise statement of the theory underlying the means–end approach. This lack of a conceptual foundation has disturbed many academic scholars and probably has limited its appeal. To many academic scholars, the means–end approach is a method used in business practice, with little theoretical interest or scholarly value. In fact, several chapters in this book reflect concerns about the "looseness" of the theoretical foundations of the means–end approach, and other chapters point out needed areas for theoretical development. Despite the general neglect of the theoretical basis for the means–end approach, we believe it is possible to position the means–end approach within a rich theoretical framework. The means–end approach has ties to several influential theories in psychology, including the work on personal construct theory (Kelley, 1957), human values (Rokeach, 1973), attribution theory, cognitive structure (Scott, 1969), among others.

Future work could and should develop these theoretical threads into an articulate conceptualization of means–end chains.

The final section of this book contains original chapters that deal with important conceptual issues regarding the means–end approach. These chapters point out directions for future research and theorizing. Although these chapters take steps toward a fully explicated theory of the means–end approach, none of them accomplish that task. Apparently, more thinking must be done. We hope future researchers will be inspired to further develop the theoretical foundations of the means–end approach.

- Claeys and Vanden Abeele (chap. 16, this volume) address the important concept of product involvement from a means–end perspective. The core of involvement is the personal relevance a consumer feels for a product (or brand, or company, or activity). Means–end chains can be used to model how a product is seen to be personally relevant and, therefore, is involving to a consumer. The authors present a study of involvement for so-called think and feel products. Consumers supposedly use cognitive or rational choice criteria to make decisions about think products; whereas affective or emotional choice criteria are used to decide about feel products.

- Cohen and Warlop (chap. 17, this volume) address the motivational orientation of the means–end approach from a somewhat critical perspective. They review some of the apparent assumptions of the means–end, and they point out where current formulations of means–end approach go wrong. Their chapter offers many ideas for further theoretical development of the means–end approach.

- Pieters, Allen, and Baumgartner (chap. 18, this volume) continue the motivational focus by showing how means–end chains relate to the important idea of goal hierarchy. They show how the means–end approach can help researchers understand the sets of interrelated goals consumers are pursuing through their decisions and actions. The entire question of goals is a rich conceptual area of great relevance for means–end theory. This chapter lays out many of the issues and offers suggestions for further research and thinking.

REFERENCES

Kelley, G. A. (1955). *The psychology of personal constructs*. New York: Norton.

Rokeach, M. (1973). *The nature of human values*. New York: Free Press.

Scott, W. A. (1969). Structure of natural cognitions. *Journal of Personality and Social Psychology*, 12, 261–278.

Means–End Chain Theory and Involvement: Potential Research Directions

Christel Claeys
Catholic University of Leuven, Belgium

Piet Vanden Abeele
Catholic Univerity of Leuven, Belgium

ABSTRACT

This chapter focuses on the utility of the means–end chain theory for the analysis of involvement. At the conceptual level, a number of ideas on how the paradigm can provide academics with a new alternative to operationalize involvement are developed. We suggest that it is necessary to extend the conceptualization of involvement from the means–end chain perspective beyond value attainment. Several characteristics of the hierarchical value map (HVM) are introduced as potential indices of involvement. We discuss their nature, their interdependencies, and their contribution to the assessment of involvement.

INTRODUCTION

Since the 1970s, involvement has been introduced as an explanatory or moderating variable in a wide variety of consumer-related research. The construct has shown to mediate such consumer behavior topics as attitudes, decision making, information processing, advertising effectiveness, cognitive structures, and brand loyalty, to name but a few. The influence of involvement on major aspects of consumer behavior justifies its central status in contemporary consumer research. Therefore, it is a reasonable research strategy to study the interactions between involvement and concepts newly introduced to the field.

In this chapter, attention is paid to the relation of involvement with the concept of means–end chains and with the laddering methodology, an area that increasingly is attracting the interest of academic researchers. In this way, this chapter contributes to an increased understanding of both involvement and of means–end chains and laddering. In addition, we hope that this approach revives consumer researchers' interest in involvement.

Despite the fact that the concept has profoundly altered the state of the art in our understanding of consumer behavior, research on involvement apparently has lost some of its attractiveness, at least in academic circles. One reason for this may be that the plurality of proposed definitions, typologies, and operationalizations have made the concept rather elusive, thereby discouraging academics from undertaking further research. Another, perhaps even more influential reason, may simply be that involvement is no longer a fashionable publishing topic. Whatever the reasons for the current lack of interest in involvement, important research topics should not be determined by fashion, nor should a body of knowledge acquired through 20 years of research accumulate dust in a dark academic corner. Such neglect is counterproductive for the consumer research discipline.

The goals of this chapter are threefold. First, we seek to establish a relation between involvement and means–end chains, primarily through the intervening construct of cognitive structures. Second, we use this relation as a starting point for a series of critical comments and thoughts on the causal implications of involvement on the content and structure of means–end chains. Third, we hope this discussion stimulates hypothesis formulation and research on the concepts of involvement, cognitive structures, means–end chains, and on the interrelations between them.

MEANS–END CHAIN THEORY

Means–End Chain (MEC) theory proposes a conceptual model for the cognitive organization, structure, and content of product knowledge in memory. The MEC model is consistent with the associative network type of memory structures but some characteristics are specific to means–end chains.

The MEC model distinguishes between three basic components: attributes, consequences, and values. A finer-grained version of the model is obtained by dichotomizing each of the basic levels into two sublevels. Product knowledge can thus be represented at six different levels of abstraction, ranging from the very concrete to the very abstract—concrete and abstract attributes, functional and psychosocial consequences, instrumental and terminal or end values. The different levels are related by causal asymmetric linkages. Thus, attributes may be perceived as producing desired consequences that in turn lead to the achievement of values. Attributes or product characteristics are the means by which the consumers search to materialize desired goals, values, or ends.

A *means–end chain* is a directed, hierarchically organized structure of interconnected levels of product knowledge of varying abstraction. A product category or brand can be typified by several means–end chains. These chains are not necessarily interrelated, although this often is the case. The entire product schema, in the means–end terminology, referred to as *HVM*, can be thought of as embedded within a larger associative network of product knowledge, including evaluations, affect or emotions, decision rules, product-usage situations, and so forth. Information in such an associative network is retrieved via the mechanism of spreading activation (Collins & Loftus, 1975).

Thus, spreading activation drives the generation of means–end chains. This mechanism implies that activation of a value automatically evokes associated constructs, such as consequences and attributes. The stronger the association between two constructs, the higher the probability of activation of one by the other. Values become salient in memory through the activation of contextual cues such as goals, product use, or decision situations. For instance, different usage or decision situations activate different goal structures and values (Walker & Olson, 1991), which in turn imply different consequences and attributes. In this way, situationally defined means–end chains can be generated within a product class. MEC theory constitutes a powerful approach to study the influence of situational context on cognitions and behavior by explicating the link between situation and activated knowledge.

The scope of MEC theory exceeds the domain of knowledge representation and organization. MEC theory offers an integrative framework for current perspectives and paradigms in consumer research in two respects. First, the means–end approach integrates insights on a facet of consumers' cognitive structures; namely, the organization of products in coherent groups on the basis of perceived equivalence or categorization. Categorization is considered a fundamental cognitive activity, and contemporary categorization theory is dominated by two seemingly opposing views on the organizing principles of classification. The oldest school of thought (represented by Rosch and Mervis, 1975) posits that resemblance in terms of features or attributes determines the category structure. This approach is commonly referred to as a *taxonomic categorization*. More recently, another stream of research (represented by Barsalou, 1983) challenges the first approach for its remoteness from human needs, goals, and values. Adherents of this school claim that classifying objects that serve a common goal constitutes a more natural way of categorizing objects in the environment. Both schools of thought have been advocated for application in consumer behavior literature.

Interestingly, the taxonomic means–end chain model—describing product knowledge at the attribute, consequence, and value level—appears compatible with both principles for categorization suggested in the cognitive psychology literature. If a consumer groups products together because they possess a set of similar attributes, hence using the information at the most concrete level in the chain, a taxonomical category structure as advanced by Rosch and Mervis (1975) is expected to emerge. Alternatively, the consumer may wish to structure his or her environment according to the perceived instrumentality of products to achieve particular consequences or values. To the extent that the means–end knowledge for products is established in the consumer's mind, this information can readily be retrieved from memory. The resulting category structure will have more of the "goal-derived" nature as advanced by Barsalou (1983). The central tenet of the MEC theory—that consumers are interested in acquiring products because of their perceived ability to achieve important ends or values—is more consistent with the concept of goal-derived categorization.

Recently, however, it was observed that category representations are rarely invariant but, rather, are contingent on situational constraints, task demands, and contextual cues. Some empirical evidence supports this issue, demonstrating that consumers are adaptive and that flexible category constructors can readily restructure a taxonomic knowledge basis in terms of goal-derived categories defined by appropriate decision criteria (Claeys, 1991; Ratneshwar & Shocker, 1990). The model of product-knowledge organization advocated by MEC theory is compatible with such a view on flexible product categorization.

The second point is that MEC theory integrates the two major approaches used to understand and predict consumer behavior—the cognitively oriented and the motivational approach.

The basic assumption of MEC theory—that products are acquired as a means to achieve certain ends—is not new to the discipline of consumer behavior. This idea is exemplified in Rosenberg's (1956) and Fishbein's (1963) theories of attitude formation that constitute the fundamental underpinnings of the multiattribute attitude modeling approach in consumer research. In the Rosenberg (1956) model attitudes toward an object are determined by the perceived instrumentality of that object to attain core values times the importance of those values to the individual. In Fishbein's (1963) approach, the *beliefs* (perceived consequences produced by the objects) about an object and their evaluation constitute the building blocks of attitude. Hence, both models imply that favorable attitudes will be developed toward products that offer us the means to attain desirable ends. Although based on similar means–end notions, Fishbein's (1963) and Rosenberg's (1956) models disagree on the ends consumers seek to achieve and that determine their ultimate attitude toward the product—consequences and values, respectively. MEC theory contributes to the field of multiattribute attitude modeling by acknowledging that attributes and consequences or values are not independent precursors of attitude or behavior; rather they are associated in a hierarchical arrangement. In this way, MEC theory formally integrates these two models of attitude formation.

In general, the MEC theory offers a more complete framework for studying and explaining consumer behavior, which reconciles the seemingly conflicting approaches available. The more cognitively oriented perspectives, supported by a wide range of quantitative techniques, have traditionally focused on the product knowledge part of the chain (attributes and functional consequences). In this view, consumers are thought to perceive products as bundles of attributes from which they derive value. In this paradigm, attitudes and preferences are explained as a function of product characteristics. The research techniques employed in the cognitive perspective differ in the abstractness of information that is used. Conjoint analysis and perceptual mapping, for example, focus heavily on product knowledge at the concrete attribute level. On the other hand, the "attributes" in multiattribute attitude models seem to encompass information of a higher level of inclusiveness because these models concentrate on perceived consequences or benefits of the product (cars are judged on reliability, goodness for city driving, or durability; toothpaste is judged on its capability to prevent tooth decay or freshen breath).

The other major paradigm, the motivational approach, focuses on personalities, lifestyles, and motivations to study consumer behavior. These different types of research are related by their common reliance on values and value systems as the driving force behind consumption behavior. Motivations, personalities, interests, and lifestyles can be thought of as different facets or outcomes of the same underlying construct—the core self-structure representing the fundamental goals and values held by the individual. Therefore, this approach posits that the self-schema constitutes the frame of reference for the individuals' consumption behavior.

The cognitive and the motivational perspective share a common restriction. They model consumer behavior on the basis of a small part of consumers' cognitive structures. The emphasis is on the product knowledge in the cognitive approach, whereas the motivational approach attaches all weight to the self-component of the knowledge structure.

It has been the merit of the MEC theory to point out that the product is inextricably linked to the self and to take into account both the characteristics of the product and the higher order benefits and values it produces as related and interdependent explanatory variables of consumer behavior. Hereby, MEC theory formally reconciles existing perspectives on consumer behavior.

INVOLVEMENT

The number of definitions, operationalizations, domains of application, and correlates of the concept of involvement is abundant. It is beyond the scope of this chapter to provide an exhaustive literature review on the topic. Instead, a definition of involvement in terms of personal or self-relevance can integrate divergent views on involvement. The conceptualization of involvement as the centrality of the product to the self-concept (often called ego-structure) originated in social psychology (Sherif & Cantril, 1947; Sherif & Hovland, 1961; Sherif & Sherif, 1967) and found support from many scholars in consumer research (Day, 1970; Houston & Rothschild, 1978; Krugman, 1966; Lastovicka & Gardner, 1979; Peter & Olson, 1987; Petty & Cacioppo, 1981; Tyebjee, 1979; Zaichowsky, 1985). A definition characteristic of this perspective on involvement is offered by Peter and Olson (1996):

> Involvement refers to consumers' perceptions of importance or personal relevance for an object, event, or activity. Consumers who perceive that a product has personally relevant consequences are said to be involved with the product and to have a personal relationship with it. (p. 101)

This definition turns out to be compatible with various treatments of and perspectives on involvement advanced in the literature. Briefly discussed is the suitability of the personal relevance conceptualization of involvement to account for the involvement typology, the distinction between situational and enduring involvement, and the causal schema distinguishing between antecedent states and consequences of involvement. Finally, we note that this perspective holds the promise of reconciling the views on involvement as a multifaceted versus a unidimensional construct.

First, conceptualizing involvement in terms of value-instrumentality can handle the various types of involvement outlined in the literature: product (product category or brand) involvement (Bloch, 1981; Day, 1970; Zaichowsky, 1985), situation involvement (Houston & Rothschild, 1978), and involvement with a (advertising) message or a communication (Andrews, 1988, Batra & Ray; 1983; Krugman, 1966; Petty & Cacioppo, 1981).

Each of these types of involvement can originate from perceived personal relevance based on the observed relation of the object, situation or communication with needs, values and interests of the individual.

The typology of involvement is intertwined with the distinction of involvement on the dimension of time. Involvement with a product is commonly assumed to be relatively permanent and enduring, whereas involvement with a situation or message only lasts for a specific time, making it situational specific and transitory. The time dimension of involvement is incorporated in the definition as well. Enduring involvement is the result of a long-term perceived personal relevance that exists across situations and on an ongoing basis. When personal, relevant knowledge, such as goals and values, is only temporarily activated due to the peculiarities of a situation, the term *situational involvement* is applicable.

Third, the personal relevance conceptualization specifies the components of the implicit causal scheme of involvement (Cohen, 1983; Mitchell, 1979). The goals and value systems of consumers constitute the antecedents of involvement. The myriad of sources of involvement indicated in the literature, such as product importance, the amount of interest evoked by the product, motivation, or commitment, are all ultimately linked to thevalues held by the individual. The internal state of arousal (felt involvement) is determined by the combination of enduring and situational perceived linkages between the product and personal interests, goals, and values (Celsi & Olson, 1988). Personal relevance can also account for the process implications advocated by some involvement theorists (Greenwald & Leavitt, 1984; Houston & Rothschild, 1978), such as extensive information searches and complex decision-making.

Fourth, the personal relevance perspective allows reconciling the treatment of involvement as a multifaceted versus a unidimensional construct. Proponents of the multidimensional view (Laurent & Kapferer, 1985) posit that typifying involvement as a variety of intensity of arousal levels, as is typical for the unitary view (Zaichowsky, 1985), ignores valuable information on the origins of involvement. Laurent and Kapferer (1985) argued that involvement is a profile shaped by the performance of the product on underlying dimensions or value orientations, such as sign value and perceived risk. Hence, the overall sense of involvement is distributed across the presumed constituent components and is not considered a valuable measure in its own right, which is in sharp contrast to the unitary approach.

The conceptualization of involvement as personal relevance in the Ostrom and Brock (1968) fashion, implied that involvement is somehow proportional to the number of values reached. Hence, the overall experience of involvement, which is the measure of concern, is based on the relatedness of products to a series of different values. The personal relevance conceptualization integrates the benefits of both approaches by attempting to offer an overall measure of involvement intensity and providing the opportunity to examine the profile of value that underlie this overall experience.

Central to the personal relevance definition is the acknowledgement that involvement is not a characteristic of the product in itself but is contingent on the personal meaning the consumer assigns to the characteristics of the product. Involvement originates from the interaction between the product schema and the self-schema. The commonly applied dichotomy between high- and low-involvement products merely denotes that some products are perceived by a large variety of consumers as having high- (low-) personal significance to them.

More recently, consensus grows that involvement is, to a large extent, determined by the situational setting (Antil, 1984; Celsi & Olson, 1988). The ultimate level of involvement reached results from the perceived personal relevance of a product to a person in a particular situation. Situational involvement, as opposed to enduring involvement, is a short-term state of arousal, established by a temporary activation of relevant self-knowledge, situation-specific and transitory. In literature, situational involvement is restricted to apply only to the purchase situation and may be interpreted as brand-choice involvement (Rothschild, 1984). In this chapter, we adopt a broader view on *situational involvement* and define it as experienced personal relevance due to both usage and purchase situations.

The concept of situational involvement further vitiates the simplicity of the *high-* versus *low-involvement* dichotomy. Products typically referred to as low involving (e. g. batteries, light bulbs, or paper clips) have the potential of acquiring personal relevance in those situations where expected benefits are not realized (Antil, 1984). For example, as long as the light bulb in one's favorite reading corner performs well, the product is probably not part of daily concern. However, when it fails, one may become very concerned about getting it replaced as its absence explicates its relatedness to the value system. Not being able to read may be perceived as spoiling the evening, which reduces the satisfaction and pleasure in life. Therefore, a good criterion to distinguish between high and low involvement may be its endurance over time. High involvement can be interpreted as involving on an enduring, ongoing basis. Low involvement often refers to the absence of enduring involvement, which is not identical to stating that there is a lack of connections with the value system.

The definition advanced by Peter and Olson (1987) does not explicate the situational facet of involvement, however it does not exclude its occurrence. A more important deficiency is the observed ambiguity at the level of the causes of involvement. Involvement or personal relevance is said to arise out of the ability of the product to help achieve consequences or values of importance to the individual. A number of questions can be raised on this issue (e.g., do both consequences and values produce a similar amount of involvement; what is the nature of the consequences and values involved; how should the importance of values and consequences to the consumer be measured?). These questions demonstrate that the definition in its current form is not suitable for a straightforward operationalization of involvement in terms of personal relevance.

Zaichowsky's (1985) Personal Involvement Inventory, generally considered a milestone in involvement research, recognized the self-relevance conceptualization of involvement as well. However, the unidimensional scale she proposed to measure (enduring) involvement does not constitute a satisfactory operationalization of the personal relevance perspective on the construct. The scale items seem to reside at the level of psychosocial consequences (e.g., boring vs. interesting, appealing vs. unappealing, beneficial vs. not beneficial) without explicitly establishing the link with the value structure as an origin of involvement.

In conclusion, in spite of the popularity of the value-instrumentality perspective of involvement, a sound operationalization of the concept is lacking in the literature. In addition, most currently available tools heavily focus on the measurement of enduring involvement.

Although involvement is a variable considered to affect major cognitive activities, such as information search and processing and decision making, its influence on cognitive structures is not extensively researched. The general intuitive assumption is that the complexity of the cognitive structure increases at increasing levels of involvement. Lastovicka and Gardner (1979) empirically supported this hypothesis by demonstrating significant differences in dimensionality and integration (level of abstraction) between the cognitive structures of high- and low-involved individuals. They found that the cognitive structures of low-involved individuals can adequately be represented by using fewer dimensions and are less integrative than is the case for highly involved people. It is also acknowledged that the knowledge organization under high involvement is characterized by strong links between salient components (Greenwald & Leavitt, 1984; Mitchell, 1983).

In addition, some interesting insights on the influence of involvement on cognitive organization can be derived from the expertise and familiarity literature due to the observed correlation between these constructs (Barnes, 1980; Jacoby & Hoyer, 1980). High involvement with a product class normally implies that the individual is motivated to devote attention and time to information search and comparison between alternatives. From this, it logically follows that high-involvement consumers demonstrate expertise in the product class they are interested in. Nevertheless, the correlation will not be perfect as the acquisition of expertise and the level of involvement are time-dependent. Deviations will occur for high-involved consumers just entering the product class and for consumers with high expertise who lost their interest or involvement in the product class. Except for these cases, it seems plausible to assume that high-involvement and low-involvement cognitive structures can be described by characteristics generally assigned to cognitive structures of experts and novices, respectively. The major findings of this literature can be summarized by stating that experts possess a refined, differentiated, complete, and veridical cognitive structure (see Alba & Hutchinson, 1987) of a large dimensionality, articulation and a high level of abstraction (Marks & Olson, 1981). Abstraction is the consequence of intensive processing and interpreting and is oftentimes referred as chunking or unitization of information (Hayes-Roth, 1977).

THE RELATION BETWEEN THE CONCEPTS
OF INVOLVEMENT AND MEANS–END CHAINS

A simple comparison between the concepts of means–end chains and involvement reveals a number of interesting similarities. First, both involvement and means–end chains are assumed to originate from the interaction between the product and the self. Second, both constructs have implications for the cognitive organization of product knowledge in memory. Third, involvement and means–end chains are similar in that they are both to a large extent determined by situational characteristics. Fourth, both constructs are defined primarily at the level of product categories rather than brands.

These similarities point to the plausibility of a relation between means–end chains and involvement. If these constructs are related, then expectations can be formed on the structural and content-related properties of means–end chains for high- or low-involved consumers. Thus, the MEC theory provides a new means to operationalize and measure involvement. Indeed, in their textbook Peter and Olson (1996) suggested that the MEC paradigm is instrumental to the analysis of involvement. These authors paraphrased their involvement definition from the MEC perspective as: "Means–end chains can help marketers understand consumers' product involment because they show how knowledge about product attributes is related to their knowledge about self" (p. 103). Hence, using means–end chains to operationalize the personal relevance perspective of involvement has promises. This endeavor fills a current gap in the involvement and MEC literature.

This chapter aims at developing (preliminary) ideas on this issue and investigates several ways in which involvement affects the structure and content of means–end chains. The theoretical insights obtained for involvement and means–end chains allow to posit and critically comment on a series of statements on the nature of the relation between both constructs.

The discussion is divided into two major parts, reflecting the distinction between enduring and situational involvement that is thought to be a central concern when implications for content and structure of means–end chains are considered.

The first part comments on the combination of means–end chains and high-enduring involvement. In the second part attention is devoted to the means–end chains characteristics for products that are, in general, only situationally involving. An additional point of concern here is the possibility of differentiating between enduring and situational involvement from the means–end chain perspective.

Enduring Involvement and Means–End Chains

As stated earlier, the observed similarities between means–end chains and involvement justify our endeavors to establish a relation between both constructs. We attempt to elaborate on the nature of this relation at the conceptual level. More specifically, we advance a number of thoughts concerning the effect of the level of involvement on the means–end chains or more generally, on the hierarchical value map (HVM),[1] the consumer holds for a product. Initially, we ignore issues and problems pertaining to operationalization of the measures proposed.

A central assumption in our discussion is that consumers do organize their product knowledge in memory as HVMs. We describe this HVM as consisting of units of information at different levels of abstraction and of linkages between these units. The linkages differ in strength. Some concepts are only weakly related, others are very strongly associated. In addition, we assume that the consumer stores information on the importance or centrality of each of the knowledge components in his or her life. Figure 16.1 illustrates such a hypothetical HVM held by a consumer for the product category "computers." In this exemplary HVM the linkages are characterized by numbers denoting the strength of association. Important values, consequences, and attributes are represented by large and bold characters (cf. happiness, efficiency, storage capacity).

The configuration of these HVMs differs across consumers for the same product. If the MEC theory is to constitute a framework to study involvement then the characteristics of the individual HVM should be indicative of the degree of involvement experienced by the consumer. We propose to

---

[1]The term *hierarchical value map* is used here to refer to the constellation of means–end chains the individual consumer possesses for a particular product.

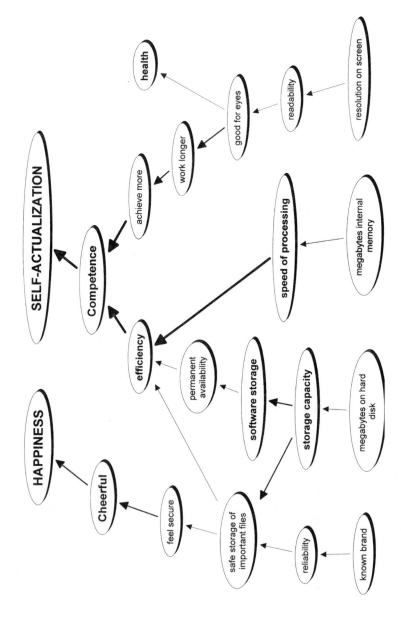

FIG. 16.1. (Hypothetical) hierarchical value map of involved computer user.

use them for the computation of an overall involvement score, that is, a measure of the intensity of involvement that is comparable across consumers and across products. Given this goal, we have to identify useful characteristics.

From the examination of the overall appearance of the HVM two potential indices of involvement emerge:the number of means–end chains elicited and the highest level of abstraction reached. In the exemplary HVM in Fig. 16.1, the number of different chains mentioned amounts to seven. The highest level of abstraction reached is the level of terminal values, represented by the values "happiness" and "self-actualization".

These general characteristics may be helpful in quickly dichotomizing between high and low involvement. However, to capture more refined distinctions on the involvement continuum, more detailed information is required. Such information can be derived from the HVM as well. Typically, means–end chains are described at the levels of values, consequences, and attributes. We may develop indices of involvement at each of these levels independently.

Characteristics available at the value level that can be useful to assess involvement are the number of values mentioned, their centrality or importance to the consumer, and their nature (instrumental vs. terminal). We illustrate these characteristics with the help of the HVM in Fig. 16.1. For this (hypothetical) consumer, computers are linked to four values, two of which are instrumental ("cheerful" and "competence") and two of which are terminal ("happiness" and "self-actualization"). Happiness is a value of major importance to this consumer, self-actualization is perceived as being a moderately important value, and cheerfulness and competence are considered of lesser importance, as is indicated in Fig. 16.1 by the character size of these values (the larger the size the more important the value is perceived to be). These three indices may be examined for their contribution to the involvement score at the level of attributes and consequences as well.

It has been emphasized previously that the merit of MEC theory primarily lies in its acknowledgement of the existence of linkages between the different components of product and self-knowledge. A good strategy to learn about involvement may therefore be to devote attention to the structure and organization of the means–end chains included in the HVM and to the interrelations between the different levels of abstraction. In this respect, possible indices for involvement are the strength of association between adjacent levels of abstraction and the degree of elaboration, this is the number of intervening steps between the starting and the ending level of the chain. In the exemplary HVM of Fig. 16.1 the attribute "speed of processing" and the consequence "efficiency" are strongly associated, whereas "safe storage of important files" is only weakly related to "feeling secure". The degree of elaboration of the means–end chains varies within the range of four (e.g., the chain connecting "resolution" to "health") to seven (e.g., the chain "resolution" to "self-actualization").

In sum, the HVM provides us with a whole range of information that may prove useful for the computation of an involvement score. We discuss each of these potential indices and the interdependencies between them in the following.

Implications at the Value Level. From the definition proposed by Peter and Olson (1987) it can be inferred that involvement is related to the attainment of consequences and values. The conclusion derived from the observation that values represent a more abstract type of information (information at the value level subsumes consequences) and that high-involved individuals tend to concentrate information at more abstract levels, is that the attainment of values versus the attainment of consequences reflects higher involvement. The same logic justifies the claim that the abstraction of the highest level reached is proportional with involvement intensity (Celsi, Olson, & Walker, 1990).

By definition then, high-enduring involvement is reflected in the attainment of important values. It is therefore convenient and attractive to start the discussion on the indices of involvement in the means–end chains at the level of values. It is also at this level that the main attention in contemporary literature on the issue is focused.

The formalization of involvement proposed by Ostrom and Brock (1968) provided initial guidelines to develop hypotheses on how involvement is reflected at the value level of means–end chains. They define involvement as the product of value centrality and value relatedness, summed over all relevant values associated with a product. This can be expressed symbolically as:

$$\text{Involvement with a product} = \sum_{i=1}^{n} VC_i \times VR_i,$$

where n = number of values considered relevant by the individual, VR_i = value relatedness, or the perceived relatedness of the product to value i of the value structure of the consumer.

VC_i = value centrality, the perceived importance or centrality of value i in the consumers core self.

The Ostrom and Brock (1968) model offered three interesting propositions. First, it implied that involvement will be related proportionally to the number of values attained. Second, the higher the perceived relatedness of the product to the value structure the higher the involvement with the product will be. This component of the model is comparable with the notion of perceived instrumentality advance in the Rosenberg (1956) multiattribute attitude model. Third, involvement will increase with increasing importance to the consumer of the values attained.

Suggestions similar to those implied by the Ostrom and Brock (1968) conceptualization of involvement have already been introduced in the means–end chain literature. Celsi, Olson, and Walker (1990) argued that the centrality or the importance of the values attained has to be taken into account ifone wants to measure involvement using means–end chains. In addition, these authors claimed that the number of means–end chain associations established between product and the values is a potential indicator of involvement as well. The assumption is that personal relevance increases if the product provides multiple benefits that are linked to several goals or values. In essence, the latter argument is conform to the claim that the more values are reached the higher the personal relevance or involvement level should be.

In sum, high involvement seems to be correlated with (a) the number of values reached, (b) the importance of those values, and (c) the perceived instrumentality of the product in attaining desired values.

The index for the number of values considers involvement as a cumulative variable. The more values that can be attained by consuming a product, the more closely it is connected to the self and the higher its personal relevance. Nevertheless the argument that multiple relations between a product and values is not a necessary prerequisite for high involvement and that one linkage with a central value in life suffices is sensible as well. Therefore it is desirable, conform to the Ostrom and Brock (1968) approach, to consider the index of quantity in conjunction with the more qualitative dimension of importance or centrality of values attained. The number of values and their importance are compensatory rather than independent building blocks of involvement. Hence, the involvement score in terms of value-attainment assigned to the HVM of Fig. 16.1 does not simply equal 4 but has to be modified by the differential weights or importances associated with the values achieved.

The index of perceived importance is currently a theoretical construct only. It is clear that MEC theory would be more complete and benefit from the measurement of the centrality of values.

The information to be extracted at the value level concerns the nature of the values as well. Drawing on the assumption that the degree of abstraction is proportionally related to involvement, it is tempting to posit that the attainment of terminal values deserves a heavier weight in the involvement computation in comparison with instrumental values. However, we cannot refute the possibility that this higher rank in weights of terminal versus instrumental values is reflected in the importance attached to the values by the individual. Following Rokeach (1973), terminal values constitute the core self of the individual and hence are considered more central or important than instrumental values, which rather refer to preferred modes of conduct to obtain the desired end states.

The analysis of the value level in itself prevails in contemporary research on involvement from the means–end chain perspective (Celsi, Olson, & Walker, 1990; Peter & Olson, 1987). Another pertinent question not dealt with in the literature yet is concerned with *how* the value level is attained. Indeed, it is an important contribution of MEC theory to explicate how product characteristics are linked to the value structure of the consumer. Therefore, it seems logical to complete the discussion on involvement by integrating the organization and structure of the entire means–end chain. The configuration of the chain as it climbs up to the value level is instrumental for the operationalization of the concept of "perceived instrumentality" advocated to affect involvement in the Ostrom and Brock (1968) conceptualization.

The perceived instrumentality of the product in attaining instrumental and terminal values can be determined by two factors. The intensity of the association between the product and the core self, reflected by the strength of association between the adjacent levels connecting the product attributes to the values, can be taken into account. In addition, the directness of the relation can be important. Directness can be defined in terms of the number of intervening constructs. The lesser intervening steps required to establish a relation with values, the more direct the association is. The latter aspect of means–end chains has been referred to as the degree of elaboration earlier in this chapter. Both aspects of means–end chains, in terms of involvement, will be discussed extensively in the following.

Implications at the Consequences Level. Information on the intensity of involvement of a consumer toward a product can be communicated at the level of consequences. Analogous features as those discussed at the value level apply here. We may try to assess involvement in terms of the number, the nature, and the importance of the consequences mentioned.

Highly involved consumers have usually acquired much product experience over time. Hence, these consumers are well placed to indicate perceived consequences and benefits associated with product purchase and use. Less involved consumers may simply be aware of a few immediate consequences (e.g., cars offer the benefit of getting you anywhere). These consequences are expected to reside predominantly at the functional consequence level if the hypothesis of low-personal relevance is to be correct.[2] High-enduring involvement seems to imply a more refined discrimination at both the level of functional and psychosocial consequences. The ar-

---

[2]Note that for clarity of exposition, we initially exclude the possibility that linkages with the self-concept are induced by the situation rather than by the product in itself.

gument on the compensatory power of the importance of a unit of information versus the quantity is equally applicable here. A more accurate measurement of involvement may be obtained by weighting the consequences for their importance to the consumer. Again, the information to be extracted from the nature of the consequences (functional vs. psychosocial) may be intertwined with the importance scores.

Implications at the Attribute Level.   Characteristics at the level of attributes can be integrated to refine the assessment of involvement even more. It has been observed in consumer research that high-involvement knowledge structures are characterized by high dimensionality and articulation (Lastovicka & Gardner, 1979). Individuals highly involved with a product class will tend to compare and differentiate between product alternatives on a high number of features or dimensions. Due to such extensive processing of information, knowledge will be acquired that enables fine discriminations within each dimension or between the levels of the features. In means–end chain terminology this implies that highly involved consumers are capable of identifying a large number of concrete attributes. However, cognitive structures of highly involved individuals are also shown to be of a high level of abstraction. Following the unitization theory of Hayes-Roth (1977) increased knowledge implies interpretation and processing of concrete information to form more abstract concepts. Information is recoded into chunks or unitary concepts that represent several associated more concrete components. Hence, knowledge elicitation within the attribute level may start at the level of abstract attributes. Low-involvement consumers, processing information to a lesser extent, are expected to literally store knowledge at the concrete attribute level and retrieve that when probed for characteristics of the product. Hence, a tentative conclusion may be that a more intense discrimination at the level of abstract attributes is observed under high involvement. On the other hand, more knowledgeable persons do not loose the ability to decompose abstract information into constituent parts if the task demands for it (Hayes-Roth, 1977). If data gathering for HVM construction is based on the laddering methodology, the subject may be stimulated to produce relatively concrete knowledge. Our involved computer user example (see Fig. 16.1) mentions "speed of processing" and "readability of the screen" as important attributes in his or her computer choice. However, when probed for it, this consumer is able to go down the ladder of abstraction and to associate abstract features to concrete properties, namely megabytes internal memory and high-screen resolution.

In summary, HVMs for high- versus low-involved consumers are characterized by a high level of discrimination at the abstract and at the concrete attribute level if they are asked for it.

Insights on involvement are thus obtained from the characteristics of the HVM at the three different levels of abstraction. It might be worthwhile to compare and weigh the value of the information at each of these levels in the final computation of the involvement score. The desirability of this approach can be easily illustrated at the attribute level. The sheer number of attributes elicited can be merely indicative of the knowledge inventory stored in memory and, to the extent that the product studied is noted very complex, a moderate degree of motivation may suffice to acquire full information on the product.

One might argue that the number of means–end chains, advanced as a rudimentary index of involvement in the introduction of our discussion, should be strongly related to the number of units of information mentioned at individual levels of abstraction. The more refined discriminations at the attribute and consequence level are expected to be reflected in the elicitation of larger number of means–end chains for high-involved consumers. Therefore, using the summary index of number of means–end chains is attractive for its apparent property of being a more convenient and manageable criterion to assess involvement while taking into account the information at the different levels of abstraction. Nevertheless, we deem it worthwhile to conduct analyses at the levels of attributes, consequences, and values separately. First, the number of means–end chains criterion is involved with the quantity of information only and ignores qualitative dimensions, such as importance, as discussed earlier. Second, this index has the potential of hiding valuable information, for example, a subset of the means–end chains extracted may show only minor differences (e.g., they start at a different attribute). By not taking this into account the final involvement score will probably be overestimated. On the other hand, if multiple chains converge to the same value, it can be inferred that the product is strongly connected to that value. In this case, the number of chains associated with a product communicates more than the knowledgeability of the consumer and seems to function as a proxy of strength of association, which is assumed indicative of involvement. Hence, ignoring this information will probably result in an underassessment of the intensity of involvement experienced by the subject. In Fig. 16.1, for example, the majority of chains elicited end at the value of self-actualization. This value assumes a central role in the establishment of a link between computers and the self and is perhaps the main cause for involvement.

Implications in Terms of Interrelations.   We point out at several previous occasions that a discussion of involvement from the means–end chain perspective is incomplete if the interrelations between the different knowledge components are not taken into account. In terms of the connections between the levels we devote attention to two characteristics, namely the strength of the connections and the number of connections made.

Previous research on the nature of cognitive structures under conditions of high involvement suggest that strength of association is a valuable index. Indeed, under high involvement, the cognitive structure is demonstrated to be well organized, which is reflected in strong links between salient components (Greenwald & Leavitt, 1984; Mitchell, 1983). Under low involvement, product knowledge is rarely experienced consciously in daily situations and is only latently present in memory. The links between the different components will be very weak or even not existent.

With respect to the criterion of strength of associations, two important issues emerge. The first is whether the strength of association between all pairs of adjacent levels of abstraction is of equal importance in determining the involvement level. It is obvious that, for instance, the link between concrete and abstract attributes is of minor value for this purpose. We conjecture that a strategy worthwhile to pursue is to assign a higher weight to the link established between the highest level reached in the part of product knowledge and the lowest level mentioned of the self-knowledge. Otherwise stated, the strength of association between product knowledge and self-knowledge is assumed to be of major importance. Based on empirical data in previous research (Claeys, Swinnen, & Vanden Abeele, 1991), we have observed that the self constitutes a relatively permanent knowledge basis where constituents components are to a high extent linked to each other invariantly. In essence, we have shown for a series of products that once the level of psychosocial consequences is reached subsequent levels of abstraction have the same probability of being activated. The self-knowledge structure constitutes perhaps for most individuals one information chunk of which relevant parts become activated as a whole. To the extent that this is true, it seems advantageous to focus on the strength of association of product knowledge with self-knowledge. A strong link at this level implies that the product in itself is connected tightly to the self and that its contribution to value attainment is not mainly determined by its (maybe small) probability to evoke psychological consequences closely anchored to the value system.

The relevance of this consideration can be demonstrated in the exemplary HVM of Fig. 16.1. We observe that the link between the functional consequence "safe storage of important files" and the psychosocial consequence "feel secure", which establishes the connection between the product (computers) and the self, is rather weak. On the other hand, the value of happiness ultimately attained in this chain is perceived to be of central importance to the consumer. This communicates high involvement if we apply the criterion discussed before that involvement is determined by values attained weighted for their importance. However, the influence of this characteristic in the final involvement determination is attenuated if one takes into account that the value is mainly evoked within the information chunk activated by the psychosocial consequence "feeling secure," which is only weakly associated to product knowledge. Conversely, the strong link between "speed of processing" and "efficiency" relating the product to the value "self-actualization" may reflect that the latter value, rated to be of lesser importance than happiness, is the trued underlying cause for involvement. This conjecture is supported by the fact that multiple means–end chains connect computers to this value.

A second issue with respect to the integration of the strength of association into the measurement of involvement is the operationalization of the construct. The MEC theory is currently in need of satisfactory (i.e., valid and reliable) way to measure strength of association.

The degree of elaboration of the means–end chain, or the number of connections established between the starting and ending level of the chain, is thought to be another correlate of involvement.

High-involvement cognitive structures are characterized by a clear organization that is reflected by the presence of closely associated salient components. Preliminary evidence for this proposition in terms of means–end chain structures comes from our empirical work on the think–feel product typology (Claeys, Swinnen, & Vanden Abeele, 1991). In this study we demonstrated that under high-involvement conditions, the differences between both types of products was accentuated. "Think" products were mainly described by concrete attributes, functional consequences and values, whereas "feel" products were identified at the level of abstract attributes, psychosocial consequences, and values. The description obtained fit perfectly with prior expectations on the salient constituent components of the knowledge structure derived from theory. Apparently, high involvement resulted in the disregard of less important or central knowledge items. Means–end chains under high involvement proved to be shorter.

An alternative perspective that is congruent with the proposition of less elaboration under high involvement is the theory of unitization or chunking (Hayes-Roth, 1977). More involved consumers are in general more knowledgeable and tend to combine concrete information into abstract concepts, hence reducing the total quantity of knowledge components. In the illustrative HVM of Fig. 16.1 the link between the components "speed of processing" and "efficiency" subsumes the knowledge that a high-processing speed results in short waiting times implying that more work can be done in the same amount of time leading to the perception of increased efficiency.

Low-involvement consumers, on the other hand, have less organized cognitive structures. They cannot discriminate very accurately between salient and less salient aspects of knowledge. In addition, the structure implied by the means–end chain formalization is oftentimes not, or only latently present. This requires low-involvement consumers to construct and to carefully climb up the ladder taking all consecutive steps. Hence, we can expect more elaborated means–end chains for low-involvement consumers relative to the number of levels mentioned. The possibility remains that in terms of total number of steps means–end chains for high-involved individuals are more elaborated than those of low-involved consumers due to their propensity of climbing higher up the levels of the self-knowledge part.

However, it must be noted that the final outcome may be contingent on task requirements. Conover (1983) showed that subjects do not necessarily reveal their ability to generalize from more concrete elements of knowledge. If stimulated by the task, they will provide detailed and concrete information. For means–end chains this implies that highly involved individuals may elicit very detailed knowledge structures containing information at each level of abstraction. This may create confusion with the constructed means–end chains of the low involved.

Means–End Chains and Situational Involvement

For clarity of exposition we have deliberately excluded the situational facet of involvement in the previous discussion. If we do, however, introduce situational involvement in the analysis, the implications of involvement for the structure of means–end chains outlined previously may become less relevant and certainly more complex. This is due to the fact that situational involvement in contrast with enduring involvement, is not necessarily related to familiarity and expertise. Hence, the premises advanced on the basis of the observed relation between (enduring) involvement and the organization of product knowledge in memory are valid to a lesser extent only. Statements with respect to, for example, strength of associations between links and discrimination at the consequences and attribute levels will have to be formulated with more prudence.

It can be argued however that the distinction between situational and enduring involvement is relevant and interesting at the theoretical level only. For managerial purposes and marketing-strategy development it suffices to know how and when the product is involving to the consumer. Analogously, in terms of behavior the consumer is expected to engage in information search, processing and in complex decision making when there is involvement, whether situation or enduring.

Notwithstanding this observation, we consider it worthwhile to elaborate on the distinction enduring versus situational involvement because of its relevance to the validity of means–end chains. A criticism often ad-

vanced is that the elicitation of chains attaining the value level is an artifact of the methodology applied (most commonly laddering). Such criticisms may derive from equating involvement with enduring involvement
and not acknowledging the propensity of means–end chains to reveal situational involvement. Indeed, the nature of the knowledge extraction
process of the means–end chain approach encourages the elicitation of
situation-dependent information. The techniques discussed by Gutman
and Reynolds (1988) to help the individual up the ladder of abstraction explicitly refer to the situational context. Hence, means–end chains of products scoring very low on the traditional involvement scales (Laurent &
Kapferer, 1985; Zaichowsky, 1985) measuring enduring involvement may
attain the value level, which is commonly interpreted as indicating (at
least partially) involvement. If the MEC theory is to benefit from its position of providing researchers with a unique framework to study situational involve, it is useful to point out how situational involvement is reflected in the characteristics of means–end chains. We identify some areas
that deserve further research to establish differences between enduring an
situational involvement.

Situational involvement implies a temporal activation of personally relevant knowledge. The link between product knowledge and the core self
becomes salient in particular situational settings only and is therefore assumed to be transient in memory. If the knowledge required to connect
products to the value structure is not or only latently present in memory, a
high degree of construction will take place. The subject will have to climb
carefully up the ladder of abstraction in order to produce the information
required. Therefore, a tentative hypothesis is that means–end chains reflecting situational involvement will be very elaborated.

A second structural difference with the means–end chains of endur-
ingly involved subjects is expected to occur at the levels of product knowledge. In general, consumers will store little knowledge on products such
as light bulbs, paper clips, or freezers that are mainly situationally involving. This lack of detailed information and familiarity should be reflected
by less discrimination at the levels of attributes and consequences. Once
the level of psychosocial consequences is attained, few differences are expected to emerge between means–end chains of situationally and endur-
ingly involved consumers. It has been argued before that the self-knowledge constitutes a fairly permanent chunk of information in memory.
Hence, whether activated by the situational aspects or by the product
characteristics themselves, the composition of the elicited self-structure
will be fairly similar.

In addition, distinctions between enduring and situational involvement in terms of the content of the means–end chains may be searched for.
We have scrutinized a wide range of chains for both types of involvement

and have the impression that two opposite principles drive the relation between product and self. If a product is involving on an enduring basis the usage, possession or presence of the product contributes actively to the achievement of a value. This will be reflected in the chain by relations of the form "if, then". On the other hand, if involvement with the product originates from situational aspects, then it seems more appropriate to state that the absence or deficiencies in the product are perceived as reducing the extent in which a value is achieved. The link between product and self is established via an "if not, then" logic or reasoning. An illustrative example may clarify this.

When probed for the product category "hi-fi's", in general more of the high-enduring involvement nature, the subject may construct the following chain:

Attribute: a good stereo sound. →
Consequence: more pleasant to listen to records of classical music. →
Value: higher enjoyment in life.

Hence, a characteristic of the product is perceived as being linked directly and actively to the value system. If the hi-fi has a good stereo sound, then the value "enjoyment in life" is achieved to a higher extent.

If, on the other hand, probed for such categories as "light bulbs" typically the means–end chains is formulated by stressing potential negative consequences.[3]

Attribute: (in)sufficient intensity of light. →
Consequence: (not) able to read. →
Consequence: (not) satisfied. →
Value: (no) enjoyment of life.

The chain reflects that a badly performing light bulb ultimately reduces one's enjoyment in life.

The previous statement may overgeneralize: They nevertheless provide useful guidelines for further research on the issue. For example, we expect that high-situational versus high-enduring involvement is reflected by a different focus on benefits sought expressed at the level of consequences in means–end chains, namely the avoidance of negative consequences and the achievement of positive consequences, respectively.

---

[3]It deserves mention that this "if not fulfilled, then what happens" pattern of thought, which is prevalent for a large number of means–end chains of low-involving products, is recommended as a technique to force the subject up the ladder of abstraction (Gutman & Reynolds, 1988). Negative motives such as problem avoidance, problem removal or incomplete satisfaction are also mentioned as the main reason for purchase of "think" products in the Vaughn (1980) and Rossiter and Percy (1987) product typology.

In all, the discussion on situational involvement explicates once more the need to broaden the conceptualization of involvement from the means–end chain perspective beyond value attainment.

In the preceding sections an extended perspective to study involvement is proposed. It was argued that one benefits from examining the pattern of characteristics of the HVM as an integrated whole. The features discussed are oftentimes compensatory rather than independent indicators of involvement. For example, a HVM described by high-involvement characteristics, such as the attainment of three important values and a strong discrimination at the consequence and attribute level, may still point to moderately or low-felt involvement if the links established between the product knowledge and the self-knowledge are weak.

Besides structural principles, content-related aspects of the HVM may be incorporated in the analysis of involvement. This may be of particular interest if the goal is to distinguish between (high) enduring and (high) situational involvement. At present, the exact implications for the HVM of involvement that is primarily situationally induced are less clear.

FUTURE RESEARCH DIRECTIONS

The previous discussion outlines several subjects and directions for future research on the relation between involvement and means–end chains and for the operationalization and measurement of involvement from this perspective.

A first avenue to pursue is to examine the scope of the potential indices of involvement identified. Do these characteristics of the HVM independently point to involvement? The major topics of discussion can be formulated a research questions to be investigated empirically:

1. Is involvement positively related to the degree of abstraction of the highest level reached in the means–end chains?
2. Can we establish a positive relation between involvement and the number of values elicited? Is a significant increase in the accuracy of the assessment of involvement obtained when the importance of values is incorporated as a weighting coefficient?
3. Does discrimination at the level of consequences reflect high involvement? Is it desirable to assign more weight to variance observed at the psychosocial consequence level in the final involvement computation?
4. Is involvement reflected by the elicitation of large number of attributes and, if so, do abstract or concrete attributes constitute the main level of concern to determine the intensity of involvement?

5. How can the strength of association between adjacent levels be integrated in the involvement computation? Is it meaningful to pursue the strategy of devoting major attention to the link between product and self-knowledge?

6. Does the degree of elaboration of the means–end chains communicate how involved one is and, if so, is involvement to be inferred from extensive elaboration or rather from chunking of information? To what extent is this contingent on exogenous and contextual factors?

7. To what extent does content analysis contribute to a better assessment of the level of involvement? Should requirements for involvement be met at the consequence level, as suggested in this chapter, or at the value and attribute level as well?

In addition to researching each of these issues in itself, there is a need to examine how these indicators can be integrated into a single overall involvement score. Efforts may be devoted to determining the contribution of each index to the involvement score and to identifying an indicator or combination of indicators that constitutes the best proxy for the full-picture assessment of involvement. Questions pertaining to the manageability and the desirability of such a detailed account of involvement for practical applications may be dealt with. If the computation of the involvement score turns out to be complex and time consuming or if a large proportion of its variance is explained by a few characteristics of the HVM, it is interesting to identify circumstances that justify the effort required to obtain such an accurate assessment of involvement.

These research questions can apply both to enduring and situational involvement. A comparative analysis of findings in the two domains will shed light on the distinction between situational and enduring involvement in terms of the hierarchical value map configuration. Further, the possibility of integrating the knowledge that situational rather than enduring involvement is concerned into the overall measure, possibly computed by assigning different weights to both types, can be examined.

Although our concern is primarily oriented toward presenting ideas for using the means–end chains perspective to study involvement at the conceptual level, we conclude this section by pointing to a number of measurement issues.

At the measurement level, attention can be directed toward examining whether laddering, the most commonly advocated instrument to measure means–end chains, is indeed a satisfactory technique to gather data for the purpose of involvement analysis. In this respect, it is worth noting that probing the consumer to actively think about the reasons why a particular product is purchased or used probably increase the level of felt involvement. Moreover, it is inherent to the nature of laddering to induce situational involvement. Therefore, laddering is perhaps a less suitable technique to identify low-enduring involvement; but then again, it was argued earlier that this is not where the true strength of the means–end chain paradigm for involvement determination lies.

Research efforts can also be devoted to issues of operationalization of constructs advances as indices of involvement in the prior discussion. The measurement of the perceived importance of value sand consequences to the consumer and of the strength of association of linkages deserves particular attention.

Useful input on the measurement of the centrality of values and consequences can be derived from the literature. The methods suggested imply reliance on direct and subjective assessment. A possible avenue to proceed could be to let the individual rank order or rate the values attained. This approach is commonly employed in value research at the aggregate level (Kamakura & Mazzon, 1992). Alternatively, the subject may be demanded to rate the entire Rokeach (1973) value inventory in terms of perceived importance in his or her own life. The latter method may be slightly superior in terms of reliability as the subject is offered the opportunity to weigh against one another central values in life. If a consumer associates "happiness" and "true friendship" with a product category, he or she may find it hard to differentiate between the importance of both values. However, in the context of the entire range of values, he or she may perceive that "happiness" and "friendship" are less important than "taking care of the family" and more central than "social recognition" or "a comfortable life". These observations may help to establish a more reliable importance judgement of the values of interest. The reliability and validity assessment of measures proposed for importance should be a prime concern given the (presumed) influential role of the construct in involvement determination. Secondly, there is a need for an adequate and reliable measure of association strength. We outline three possible avenues to pursue. The first is to rely on the memory implications of high- versus low-involvement cognitive structures and to utilize latency times in responses as a proxy for association strength (Fazio, Powell, & Williams, 1989). This measurement approach has the drawback of being very obtrusive and may be detrimental to the sense of comfort of the subject and the spontaneity of the interview. An alternative procedure is to count the frequency with which a particular link is mentioned (Gutman, 1991). The more often the link is referred to during the interview, the higher the strength of association is perceived to be. A potential criticism on this approach is that frequency of mention may originate from halo-effects. To the extent that the subject has learned that links must be established between consecutive levels of abstraction, he or she may for convenience relate a lower level to the same more abstract level. This is particularly likely to occur between functional consequences and more abstract levels. Note however that frequency of occurrence of a link between two elements is a main variable in the construction of the HVM at the aggregate level and denotes strength of association there.

A third alternative is to demand for subjective estimates of the strength of association between a sequence of components mentioned by the individual. Such direct assessment is best obtained immediately after the elicitation of the means–end chains (Gutman, 1991). There is a real danger that this procedure seriously interrupts the progress of the knowledge extraction.

In essence, creativity will have to be directed toward an operationalization of strength of association that does not impede the elicitation of means–end chains while being valid and reliable.

CONCLUSION

The means–end chain paradigm offers a valuable framework to think about involvement and its implications on knowledge organization, acquisition and processing. In addition, the theory provides academics with a new alternative to operationalize and measure this important construct. From the preceding discussion, it emerges that such an operationalization need not be a simple and straightforward task, an observation that is not too surprising given the complexity and elusiveness of the involvement concept. The research challenge is to further develop and test the ideas elaborated on.

REFERENCES

Alba, J. W., & Hutchinson, J. W. (1987, March). Dimensions of consumer expertise. *Journal of Consumer Research, 13*, 411–454.

Antil, J. H. (1984). Conceptualization and operationalization of involvement. In T. Kinnear (Ed.), *Advances in consumer research*, Vol. 11, 3e (pp. 203–209). Provo, UT: Association for Consumer Research.

Andrews, J. C. (1988). Motivation, ability and opportunity to process information: Conceptual and experimental manipulation issues. In M. Houston (Ed.), *Advances in consumer research*, Vol. 15 (pp. 219–225). Provo, UT: Association for Consumer Research.

Barnes, J. H. (1980). A discussion on survey research. In K. Monroe (Ed.), *Advances in consumer research*, Vol. 8 (pp. 304–305). Ann Arbor, MI: Association for Consumer Research.

Barsalou, L. (1983, August). Ad hoc categories. *Memory and Cognition, 11*, 211–227.

Batra, R., & Ray, M. L. (1983). Operationalizing involvement as depth and quality of cognitive response. In R. Bagozzi & A. Tybout (Eds.), *Advances in consumer research*, Vol. 10 (pp. 309–313). Ann Arbor, MI: Association for Consumer Research.

Bloch, P. (1981). An exploration into the scaling of consumers' involvement with a product class. In K. Monroe (Ed.), *Advances in consumer research*, Vol. 8 (pp. 61–65). Ann Arbor, MI: Association for Consumer Research.

Celsi, R., & Olson, J. (1988, September). The role of involvement in attention and comprehension processes. *Journal of Consumer Research, 15*, 210–224.

Celsi, R., Olson, J., & Walker, B. (1990). The relationship between means–end chains and product involvement. In H. Mühlbacher & C. Jochum (Eds.), *Proceedings of the 19th Annual Conference of the European Marketing Academy*, 233–235.

Claeys, C., Swinnen, A., & Vanden Abeele, P. (1990). Consumers' means–end chains for think and feel products. *Onderzocksrapport nr. 9018, Katholieke Universiteit Leuven.*

Claeys, C. (1991). *On the comparability of natural object taxonomies and product hierarchies.* Extract from Unpublished doctoral dissertation, Katholieke Universiteit Leuven.

Cohen, J. (1983). Involvement and you: 1000 great ideas. In R. Bagozzi & A. Tybout (Eds.), *Advances in consumer research*, Vol. 10 (pp. 325–328). Ann Arbor, MI: Association for Consumer Research.

Collins, A. M., & Loftus, E. F. (1975). A spread activation theory of semantic memory. *Psychological Review, 82*, 407–428.

Conover, J. (1983). Familiarity and the structure of product knowledge. In A. Mitchell (Ed.), *Advances in consumer research*, Vol. 9 (pp. 494–498). Ann Arbor, MI: Association of Consumer Research.

Day, G. S. (1970). *Buyer attitudes and brand choice behavior.* New York: Free Press.

Fazio, R. H., Powell M. C., & Williams, C. J. (1989, December). The role of attitude accessibility in the attitude-to-behavior process. *Journal of Consumer Research*, 280–288.

Greenwald, A. G., & Leavitt, C. (1984, June). Audience involvement in advertising: Four levels. *Journal of Consumer Research, 11*, 581–592.

Gutman, J., & Reynolds, T. (1988, February). Laddering theory, method, analysis and interpretation. *Journal of Advertising Research*, 11–31.

Gutman, J. (1991). Exploring the nature of linkages between consequences and values. *Journal of Business Research, 22*, 143–148.

Hayes-Roth, B. (1977). Evolution of cognitive structures and processes. *Psychological Review, 84*, 260–278.

Houston, M. J., & Rothschild, M. L. (1978). Conceptual and methodological perspectives on involvement. In S. C. Jain (Ed.), *Research frontiers in marketing: Dialogues and Directors* (pp. 184–187). Chicago: American Marketing Association.

Jacoby, J., & Hoyer, W. D. (1980). What if opinion leaders didn't know more? A question of nomological validity. In K. Monroe (Ed.), *Advances in Consumer Research, Vol. 8* (pp. 299–303). Ann Arbor, MI: Association for Consumer Research.

Kamakura, W., & Mazzon, J. A. (1991, September). Value segmentation: A model for the measurement of values and value systems. *Journal of Consumer Research, 18*, 208–218.

Krugman, H. (1966). The measurement of advertising involvement. *Public Opinion Quarterly, 30*, 583–596.

Lastovicka, J., & Gardner, D. (1979). Low involvement versus high involvement cognitive structures. In K. Hunt (Ed.), *Advances in Consumer Research, Vol. 5* (pp. 87–92). Ann Arbor, MI: Association for Consumer Research.

Laurent, G., & Kapferer, J.-M. (1985). Measuring consumer involvement profiles. *Journal of Marketing Research, 22*, 41–53.

Marks, L., & Olson, J. (1981). Toward a cognitive structure conceptualization of product familiarity. In K. Monroe (Ed.), *Advances in consumer research, Vol. 8.* (pp. 191–196). Ann Arbor, MI: Association for Consumer Research.

Mitchell, A. (1979). Involvement: A potentially important mediator of consumer behavior. In N. L. Wilkie (Ed.), *Advances in consumer research*, Vol. 6, (pp. 191–196). Ann Arbor, MI: Association for Consumer Research.

Mitchell, A. (1983). Cognitive processes initiated by exposure to advertising. In R. Harris (Ed.), *Information processing research in advertising* (pp. 13–42). Hillsdale, NJ: Lawrence Erlbaum Associates.

Ostrom, T., & Brock, T. (1968). A cognitive model of attitudinal involvement. In R. Abelson (Eds.), *Theories of cognitive consistency* (pp.). Chicago: Rand McNally.

Peter, P., & Olson, J. (1987). *Consumer behavior: Marketing strategy perspectives.* Richard Irwin, Inc.

Petty, R., & Cacioppo, J. (1981). Issue involvement as a moderator of the effects on attitude of advertising content and context. In K. Monroe (Ed.), *Advances in consumer research,* Vol. 8 (pp. 20–24). Ann Arbor, MI: Association for Consumer Research.

Ratneshwar, S., & Shocker, A. (1990). *Substitution-in-Use and the role of the usage context in product category structures.* Working Paper, University of Florida.

Rosch, E., & Mervis, C. (1975). Family resemblances: Studies on the internal structure of categories. *Cognitive Psychology, 7,* 573–605.

Rossiter, J., & Percy, L. (1987). *Advertising and promotion management.* McGraw-Hill.

Rothschild, M. (1984). Perspectives on involvement: Current problems and future directions. In T. Kinnear (Ed.), *Advances in consumer research,* Vol. 11 (pp. 196–198). Provo, UT: Association for Consumer Research.

Sherif, M., & Cantril, H. (1947). *The psychology of ego involvement.* New York: John Wiley.

Sherif, C., & Hovland, C. (1961). *Social judgment: Assimilation and contrast effects in communication and attitude change.* New Haven, CT: Yale University Press.

Sherif, M., & Sherif, C. (1967). *Attitude, ego involvement and change.* New York: John Wiley.

Tyebjee, T. (1979). Response time, conflict and involvement in brand choice. *Journal of Consumer Research, 6,* 295–304.

Vaughn, R. (1980, October). How advertising works: A planning model. *Journal of Advertising Research, 20*(5), 27–33.

Walker, B., & Olson, J. (1991). Means–end chains: Connecting products with self. *Journal of Business Research, 22,* 111–118.

Zaichowsky, J. (1985, December). Measuring the involvement construct. *Journal of Consumer Research, 12,* 341–350.

17

A Motivational Perspective
on Means–End Chains

Joel B. Cohen
University of Florida

Luk Warlop
Catholic University of Leuven, Belgium

ABSTRACT

The objective of this chapter is to assess the value of the means–end chains approach as a way of thinking about the behavior of consumers. What are we buying into when we adopt this approach, and what does it buy us?

It is unreasonable to expect any one approach or model to be the unqualified or ultimate solution to understanding why consumers do what they do and how they think about purchase alternatives. Model proponents who stress the all-encompassing nature of their approach, or model adopters in search of a magic wand, seriously understate the complexity of the substantive issues and minimize the significance of the inevitable tradeoffs that are reflected in any model. Behavior—consumer or otherwise—and the thinking, decision making, and circumstances that shape it require a diversity of approaches to produce valuable and useful insights.

This is a prelude to the judgment that means–end chains have been a bit over-sold. Its proponents have not lacked for enthusiasm in describing how the approach helps us to understand the motivational antecedents of customers' behavior as well as their organization of product knowledge and brand meanings. Still, even if some of the claims and hopes do not survive careful scrutiny, failing to recognize that we can profitably settle for something less than a panacea would be equally unwise.

We begin by examining the implications of the means–end chain approach for the study of consumer motivation and by providing some perspectives on its premises and guiding orientations. Later, we examine the usefulness of some of the frequently advanced memory representation assumptions and claims, including the tendency to present means–end chains as associative network structures. Finally, we discuss how means–end chain research, within the limitations that we have identified, can contribute to our understanding of consumer behavior. First and foremost, means–end chains address motivational issues, so we begin our assessment at that point.

UNCOVERING PURCHASE MOTIVATIONS

Marketing has long recognized the importance of understanding why consumers purchase the products and brands they do. Such information permits marketers to design products that are more likely to be adopted and to promote their products more effectively. It would, for example, lead to better recognition of potential positioning options and evaluation of products' ability to appeal to the needs of multiple segments.

From time to time, marketing has had an infatuation with prepackaged motivational explanations drawn from other domains in the hope that particular motives or traits would prove to be of practical significance. Traditionally, such dimensions were assigned either drive-like or value-like motivational significance. Alternatively, they may be thought of as more salient personal constructs (e.g., McGuire & Padawer-Singer, 1976; Wyer & Srull, 1986). It is generally agreed that this approach is more appropriate for predicting patterns of behavior or tendencies that distinguish people who are chronically higher along dimensions believed to be of central importance within a given theory (Kassarjian & Sheffett, 1991; Wiggins & Pincus, 1992). A *problem focus* (i.e., starting from the behavior one wishes to explain) has proven to be superior to an *independent variables approach* (i.e., starting from an interest in a particular motive, such as achievement, or a personality trait, such as dominance) in accounting for variance in specified purchase behavior. A problem focus is more eclectic and ideally recognizes that there likely will be a number of different reasons for engaging in a given behavior.

Despite the widespread adoption of such a problem focus in marketing (e.g., models designed to predict attitudes and behavioral intentions), there has been an ongoing attempt to find causal explanations of behavior by looking for explanatory constructs at a higher or deeper level in an assumed motivational hierarchy. There is ample documentation that, with sufficient creativity, even the most functional product or service can be linked to more universal themes and values. Such accounts make fascinating stories, and one is able to choose among preferred interpretivist accounts arising from a variety of psychological traditions as well as from more ad hoc social-symbolic explanations.

Reviewing the rich history and evolution of psychology's search for substantively integrative motivational explanations in detail would go too far afield (because this has been a recurrent theme in motivational theories as diverse as psychoanalytic theory,[1] modern day holistic psychology,[2] and various "self" theories).[3] For consumer researchers, the overriding lesson of this endeavor has been that there are multiple reasons for most purchases, and these range from the mundane (e.g., it looks durable, has a better warranty) to the occasional satisfaction of more personally significant goals and desires. Considerable experience has taught us to avoid searching for a single overriding and psychologically compelling motive for most purchases. Our fascination with both deeper needs and higher values should not blind us to the fact that consumers are looking for toasters that toast properly, foods that taste good, and carpets that resist wear and tear. These salient reasons for purchase may, possibly, be derived from more basic or important goals and desires, and we look at the contribution of the means–end approach in providing guidance about this motivational process (e.g., when this happens, how this happens, and how to identify these goals and desires).

For marketers, a legacy of the 1950s-inspired motivation research era has been a general distrust of deeper needs accounts of consumers' behavior, unless these could be accompanied by, at least, the appearance of methodological rigor or seemed to have face validity. The latter typically meant that the conventional wisdom among key marketing and advertising executives supported the research conclusions (a factor not usually lost on research suppliers). It is not that more cautious marketers ceased believing that there were deeper and more symbolic reasons behind many purchases. However, defending highly subjective, almost clinical methods of investigation (e.g., projective tests, depth interviews) became progressively more difficult as management began to adopt more rigorous

---

[1]Displacement of instinctual energy and the formation of substitute object-cathexes, in Freud's (see Hall & Linzey, 1957) view, produces the complex network of interests, preferences, and choices that characterize adult human behavior. Even Leonardo da Vinci's interest in painting madonnas was interpreted as a sublimated expression of a longing for intimacy with his mother (from whom he was separated at an early age).

[2]In general, there is a focus on self-actualization (which posits a sovereign, unifying theme from which other wants are derived). In Maslow's (1970) version, a hierarchy of needs—including safety, belongingness, and self-esteem—give rise to specific behaviors.

[3]A number of self-theories stress the linkage between several possible conceptions of self- (e.g., actual, ideal, potential) or compartmentalized self-concepts (e.g., self as parent, social self), and a person's attitudes and choices. These focus on self-maintenance and consistency in translating global motives to specific actions (see Cantor et al., 1986; Greenwald, 1982; Markus & Nurius, 1986; Sirgy, 1982; for relevant reviews).

and analytical standards for decision-making. Verification of investigators' interpretations proved to be elusive, and concerns increasingly were raised (Fennel, 1975; Rothwell, 1955) as to how actionable these deeper insights were (e.g., in developing segmentation strategies or planning advertising executions).

Lifestyle and psychographic research (that, after all, used hard data and multivariate methods) and more down-to-earth focus group studies attempted to fill the gap, and these were soon joined by benefit segmentation, multiattribute attitude models, and multidimensional preference scaling as ways of identifying reasons for purchase and ways of categorizing consumers. Still, the symbolic role of products in meeting more fundamental needs, attaining more important personal goals and values, and supporting or enhancing one's self-concept seems too grand a notion to be brought to ground by mere methodological refinements that took initial responses at face value. Accordingly, one could anticipate considerable interest being displayed toward a new and integrative approach to answering motivational questions, especially if it avoided the earlier pitfalls, displayed analytical rigor and theoretical sophistication (yet was surprisingly straightforward), and particularly if it provided actionable implications and was easy to implement. For many then, means–end chains represent a breakthrough of considerable importance. Let us now consider how means–end chains address the issue of where value resides.

EXPECTANCY-VALUE THEORY AS A GUIDING ORIENTATION

Means–end chains follow a time-honored approach for thinking about motivational issues. The central premise — that objects have value only because they produce desirable consequences or enable one to avoid negative consequences — is at the heart of most modern conceptualizations of motivation (Atkinson, 1964; Lewin, 1951; Tolman, 1959). More specifically, the means–end chain approach closely parallels expectancy-value theories of motivation (Atkinson, 1964; Feather, 1982; Peak, 1955) in stressing a product's role in achieving one or several desired states, rather than conceiving of the product itself as the repository of value (Cohen, 1979; Hansen, 1969).

Conceptually a means–end analysis takes no a priori position as to what the key sources of value are for any object or decision. It treats this as a largely behavior- (and situationally) specific empirical question. This is in contrast to more doctrinaire approaches that are committed to particular content areas as driving forces. The latter take a stronger position on what it is people are seeking or avoiding or which types of people are more prone to behave in characteristic ways (i.e., theories emphasizing various personality traits). The means–end premise that underlies expectancy-value approaches alerts us to the fact that we should not *assume* that value resides in product attributes (Cohen, 1979).

Sometimes, of course, the distinction between a product attribute and a desired feature is largely a matter of semantics. Often what gives a brand added value are the performance characteristics or ingredients that are built into it (e.g., easily prepared foods, vitamin-enriched cereals, a remote control for a TV, or perhaps even a mute switch). It may be useful, therefore, to distinguish between attributes that are strictly descriptive (e.g., visually salient features, some of which may be important in categorizing a product; Cohen & Basu, 1987) and those that contribute to the consumers' evaluation of the product.[4] Such *evaluative attributes* are viewed as product benefits when they are positive and as product deficiencies when they are negative. They are likely to be pivotal in consumers' selection of alternative brands and models.

For a significant number of products, socially shared meanings are important to consumers' choices (e.g., jeans conveying youthfulness, beers asserting masculinity, designer labels conveying status). They help convey personal and social identity (both actual and desired) in particular settings and toward various audiences. They may, in addition, buttress or enhance people's feelings about themselves, either directly or by virtue of supportive feedback from others (Schlenker, Britt, & Pennington, 1996). Such products, then, have a social function, in addition to any other benefits they provide. For the most part, however, most of these symbolic attributes are readily understood and easily evoked product and brand associations. In that sense they are quite similar to other product characteristics. They are seldom hidden from view, nor are they necessarily linked to a few generally important life goals and values. Indeed, such products can often be thought of as props, similar to those used by actors to manage particular audiences' impressions (Goffman, 1959; Schlenker, 1985; Solomon, 1983).

The Search for Ultimate Causes

Research procedures associated with laddering — that begin by drawing respondents' attention to distinguishing characteristics of a choice alternative — reflect a commitment to search for underlying reasons for engaging in the behavior. After initially identifying key attributes or features

---

[4]Without unnecessarily complicating the discussion, we note in passing that even descriptive attributes may impact on product evaluations if their presence leads consumers to categorize the products differently. This happens when membership in the alternative categories has different evaluative implications (Cohen, 1982; Sujan, 1985).

desired by consumers, a succession of probes (e.g., "why is that impor-tant?") is used to move up the goal hierarchy. Means–end chain proponents have elected to concentrate on progressively more important goals and val-ues (rather like the hidden desires that characterized the motivation re-search era).

In stressing the importance of higher order values, they continue the motivation research tradition of searching for the ultimate determinants of behavior. Psychologists have long been intrigued with motivational dy-namics, either bubbling up from the wellsprings of desire or as a striving for ideal states. Although very different in innumerable ways (e.g., diver-gent philosophical conceptions of human nature, an emphasis on drives, and tension reduction vs. values and goal attainment), all such concep-tions look for explanations of behavior in terms of more remote causes. Because an attempt to further categorize such approaches would take us far afield, let us simply concede the legitimacy of such analyses to better understand the human condition and to generate greater self-awareness and achieve specific clinical goals. However, whether or not such originat-ing forces may have had some role in shaping our appetites and aversions may be largely irrelevant to the task of predicting and understanding much of everyday behavior.

Do Higher Order Values Guide Consumer Behavior?

The distinction between goals and values, on the one hand, and hidden needs and drives on the other, may be less clear cut than the means–end vocabulary might suggest. When we say that a person is seeking some-thing and we describe the outcome in terms of some type of self-ful-fillment, that puts a positive spin on a behavior that may originate in defi-cit reduction (e.g., lessening of anxiety), compensation (e.g., food cravings), or possibly a reinforced pattern of behavior in childhood (e.g., affiliative tendencies). The shift in terminology tends to suggest contem-poraneous determinants (or mediators, if one prefers) of behavior rather than their historical antecedents.

A compelling argument in favor of focusing on contemporaneous mo-tives was presented by Allport (1955) in defense of the functional auton-omy of motivated behavior and attitudes. In his view, as the individual adapts to his or her environment (e.g., tasks, roles, commonly encoun-tered situations) he or she essentially develops guiding orientations and goals that supplant the more primitive reasons for engaging in a behavior. There is, in other words, a gradual incorporation of central traits, values, self-images, and desires into a more autonomous and salient set of reasons for engaging in the behavior.

Because these more behavior-specific motives are different and greater than the sum of their originating forces, this is a compelling argument for focusing on these guiding motives rather than searching for more remote causes from which they may, in part, have risen. The same argument holds regardless of whether the more remote causes are thought of as impelling forces or a set of instrumental and terminal values. However, it may also be argued that in focusing on functionally autonomous motives, the behavior may be inadequately understood, thus generating fewer useful insights into its determinants and the conditions that may be necessary for change.

The underlying assumption is that by making these terminal values more salient (e.g., through advertising) greater importance will be given to chain-linked product characteristics and resulting consequences, producing the desired effect on behavior. Although this is a theoretically viable approach, its success hinges on the importance of that higher order value in the consumer's choice among competing alternatives. Thus, not only must the value be a potent-driving force, but distinguishing characteristics of the product and the consequences of owning and using it must be seen as consistent with, or furthering, the valued state.

This would appear to be a tall order for most products. Just determining which goals and values are especially potent or salient in a person's life is alone a challenging endeavor. This often involves consideration of perceived discrepancies between ideal or desired states and an assessment of one's current situation, because higher order values that are judged to be important in the abstract are not necessarily active driving forces on a daily basis. Cantor, Marcus, Niedenthal, and Nurius (1986) hypothesized that a working self-concept (i.e., the subset of self-knowledge that is made salient and dominant by contextual factors)—rather than a few generally important self-related values—is likely to guide behavior. Context-recruited self-perceptions (i.e., the working self-concept) help identify intermediate goal regions and influence the means chosen to attain them. Walker and Olson (1991) expressed a similar view; that "central aspects of self" should be related to behavior only when the situation activates these aspects, and that the "particular values that influence behavior may be completely different in different situations" (p. 117).

This position seems to argue for identifying a much broader and more product-specific set of personally important goals, rather than a relatively small number of personally defining values or life goals.

A continuing problem with marketing's search for ultimate determinants of behavior is that one's sense of personal worth and life goals do not seem to hinge very much on the purchase of most of the products we buy and probably even less on the choices we make within product categories. The means–end chain approach not only assumes that psychosocial consequences and even more fundamental instrumental and terminal values are dominant influences on purchasing behavior, but tips the scales empirically to produce such evidence. The key premise is that the critical motivating factors for consumers and marketers alike are person centered rather than product centered and that vital information about reasons for purchase is to be found several steps removed from easily articulated and motivationally salient reasons for the behavior.

THE CASE FOR SALIENT MOTIVES

Expectancy-value approaches stress contemporaneous definition of goals and desires rather than attempting to uncover the historical genesis of a person's motives. As such, they implicitly acknowledge the importance and diversity of behavior (and situationally) specific motivators rather than assigning primary motivational significance to a few deeper explanations. In that sense, expectancy-value approaches enable behavioral scientists to think more broadly about possible reasons for approaching or avoiding objects, and it is a relatively short journey from there to the strategic posture of helping people frame (or reframe) their decision-making relative to such objects (Cohen, 1974; Edwards, Lindman, & Phillips, 1965; Gollwitzer, 1999).

Expectancy-value approaches have been most successful when applied to people's anticipated consequences, so that it is reasonable to expect people to actually take these consequences into account in determining a course of action (see Raynor & McFarlin, 1986). A similar orientation guided early expectancy-value approaches to attitudes (Peak, 1955; Rosenberg, 1956, 1960). [5] The significance of perceived instrumentality relations (i.e., between objects and goals or values) in thinking about more basic motivational functions of attitudes (Katz, 1960; Lutz, 1991; Shavitt, 1989) as underlying sources of value is underscored by the importance of giving people additional insight into the psychodynamics of self-concept based attitudes. Correctly perceiving this relation may be necessary to bring people's attitudes into line with more basic self-related values (Stotland, Katz, & Patchen, 1959). Otherwise these linkages and any potential inconsistencies could well be nonsalient.

Similarly, Rokeach's (1968) conceptualization of *value-attitude systems* builds on the notion of internalized values, which then become standards or criteria for guiding action and developing and maintaining attitudes. Values are either *instrumental* (preferred modes of conduct such as honesty and courage) or *terminal* (preferred end states such as freedom and a meaningful life). Conflict is created when a person cannot behave in a manner congruent with all his or her values. However, this conflict—and subsequent striving for consistency—requires being aware of the implica-

---

[5]For a more detailed comparison of functional theories of attitude and means–ends chains see the accompanying chapter, this volume.

tions of the action for the values. Accordingly, Rokeach used enhanced self-awareness as a means of generating attitude change among participants in his studies.

Probably the most direct examination of the value salience issue in consumer attitude research was carried out by Mazis, Ahtola, and Klippel (1975). Their first experiment compared predictions across four product categories (mouthwash, cigarettes, toothpaste, automobiles) for two versions of Rosenberg's (1956, 1960) means–end based attitude model (as well as several other attitude models). One version used abstract values (e.g., keeping in good health, living a sensible life, associating with the opposite sex, protection against physical harm, recognition as a leader). The other used more immediate product benefits (e.g., pleasant taste, poor gas mileage, rarely needs repairs) as predictors of brand attitude. In the first study the abstract-values version offered the poorest predictability. Their (untested) explanation was that such values may not have been salient. So, although questionnaire responses could easily be elicited, these values probably were not being used to evaluate the products to the same degree as more immediate product benefits. However, it is worth noting that there was no special effort to identify the most appropriate set of abstract values for each product.

Artificially Enhanced Salience

In a follow-up experiment Mazis, Ahtola, and Klippel (1975) used a free-elicitation procedure (e.g., what kinds of things do you look for or take into consideration when you select . . . ?) to identify salient product characteristics and benefits. Because, in their view, it would be extremely difficult to obtain salient abstract values in the same way, they supplied a list of 47 values (Bither & Miller, 1969; Rosenberg, 1956), asking respondents which of these might be responsible for or underlie their choices. Those considered to be important by two thirds of the respondents were designated as "salient", and between three and seven values were used for the three products in the main study. The increase in the predictive power of the Rosenberg value-based model was dramatic. It outperformed the product benefits version. The authors concluded that establishing the salience of beliefs, goals, and values is essential to the success of such models.

Within the means–end chain literature, research establishing the superiority of values (relative to consequences and especially perceptually salient attributes) in predicting preferences has also been reported (see Jolly, Reynolds, & Slocum, 1988; Reynolds, Gutman, & Fiedler, 1984). After laddering is carried out, such researchers obtain ratings of the products or people on the identified attributes, consequences and values. It is important to note that these procedures present respondents with higher level dimensions in order to make such judgments. Doing so, of course, increases their salience. In addition, given approximately equal salience among attributes, consequences and values, people may believe they should use more comprehensive criteria (e.g., values, goals) in order to provide the most significant assessment. Indeed, one virtue of using this procedure in organizational settings is precisely that raters would likely be encouraged to shift to more important criteria — once they had been made salient — to assess a person's actual or probable long-term contributions to the organization.

So, this research does not speak to the question of whether people — without being prompted to do so — would base their preferences and decisions on such higher order dimensions. As with the Mazis et al. (1975) research (which has a similar limitation), these studies document the significance of salient goals and values in guiding judgment and decision-making. Readily perceived and functionally important differences among alternatives are likely to be particularly salient and to dominate consumers' thinking in the absence of such strong outside influences. This seems especially true for preferences that do not require or inspire significant reflection. Although one might argue that, high involvement (whether defined in terms of products or situations) may make higher order goals and values salient, that is an empirical question and should not be assumed. High involvement should typically lead consumers to want to be more confident about their assessments of likely product performance and about tradeoffs among particular features because these are typically the cornerstone of purchase satisfaction.

In summary, the expectancy-value tradition emphasizes the importance of desired or anticipated — and therefore salient — end states and consequences as sources of value that guide preferences and actions. Expectancy-value approaches place particular weight on active cognitive processes involved in problem definition (to determine what needs and goals are relevant), planning, resolving conflicts and making decisions. The means–end chain approach fits within this tradition. Relying on procedures that can make anticipated intermediate and end states salient, researchers have not sufficiently recognized the importance of the accessibility and perceived instrumentality underpinning of means–ends motivational logic. Instead, fairly strong salience assumptions are made about the hierarchical nature of the systems of values and consequences that can be linked to a product.

INFORMATION PROCESSING IMPLICATIONS

At its core, means–end theory's consequences–value definition of *goal regions* appears to assume a conscious striving for these desired ends. Taken in its literal sense, the means–ends hierarchy implies that higher order motivations are essentially the prime movers. Thus, people should actively consider them in constructing and selecting instantiations at lower levels. These lower level indicants of value are derived, and constitute instrumental steps in reaching terminal goals.

Theoretically, the consumer is viewed as a problem solver who starts from a desired end-state or terminal value, and constructs a chain of intermediate steps ending with certain products or product attributes (Miller et al., 1960; Nuttin 1984).

Means–end chain theory has seemingly relaxed this hierarchical assumption. Instead, the chains are conceptualized as associative structures in which the linked elements in the hierarchy are made available selectively through a process akin to semantic activation. The modified assumption would be that these relations (i.e., chains) are activated in memory and made salient each time the product is considered. Consistent with current distinctions in cognitive psychology, means–end researchers could argue that all elements of the chain are available (but not necessarily accessible) to means–end thinking and that their conscious consideration — particularly verbalization — requires heightened reflection, such as when probes are used to explore people's reasons in more depth or when people are prompted to consider the goal or value. Unfortunately, this has the effect of making these higher order elements (and the chains themselves) potential sources of motivational energy. It begs the question of when (i.e., under what naturally occurring conditions) all elements of the chain become salient and affect the purchase outcome. It also questions the degree to which laddering probes distort typical thinking about products. We return to this issue a bit later.

The memory instantiation assumption is not inconsistent per se with the expectancy-value orientation. All that is required is that the network of elements comprising the hierarchy are active, at the time consumers make judgments or decisions about products or actions. As a finesse of hierarchically linked problem-solving steps, relatively automatic transversing of associational pathways in memory works, up to a point. However, the pathways must exist in the first place, and the associations must be strong enough to overcome normal interference (e.g., from other associations and thought processes). Conceptually, then, active-memory approaches may have difficulty dealing with the symbolic aspects of products (e.g., power, femininity, youthfulness) that many feel lie below the surface of most people's conscious awareness. Indeed, much of the marketing appeal of means–end chains probably rests on the tacit assumption that this approach allows researchers to tap into the hidden meanings of products and motivations for purchase that underlie (and are therefore at least one step removed from) consumers' expressed reasons for preferring and buying these products.

Such information processing refinements render means–end chains a far less straightforward conceptualization of consumers' motivational dynamics. The instantiation of any specific chain would become an empirical question, linked to particular conditions (e.g., prompting by advertising, heightened self-examination of behavioral implications). The identification of potentially important underlying motivations (and ruling out others) should still be valuable in its own right, but means–end researchers would need to take the additional step of developing procedures intended to verify the instantiation of these chains, possibly following exposure to particular external influences.

The traditional way of attempting to demonstrate the presence of an instantiated chain would be to conduct effects-oriented experiments in which potential situational influences on the instantiation of a chain are manipulated. For example, experimental groups can be created to reflect differential availability of chain elements, and the potential additive or interactive effects of differential readiness to respond to salience-increasing manipulations (e.g., advertising messages) can be examined (Marcus, 1977; Srull, 1984; Wyer, & Srull, 1986). Another possibility would be to use a research design building on the concepts of heightened perceptual vigilance and selectivity for motivationally relevant stimuli, much as in the "New-Look" tradition of examining top-down effects on perception (Bruner, 1957; Erdelyi, 1974). The activation of a value or higher order goal should increase attention (e.g., reduce response latency) to value relevant information relative to the other information that is perceptually available but that should not be part of the chain. Alternatively a memory-based paradigm could be used because the activation of a goal or value should facilitate the retrieval of related elements from memory over nonchain elements that are equally retrievable (e.g., had been learned to an equivalent level).

Recently, such paradigms have been used to examine how a consumer's active goals affect evaluations of products and advertisements. For example, it has been demonstrated that the provision or activation of a usage goal can direct attention (Huffman & Houston, 1993; Ratneshwar, Mick, Warlop, & Seeger, 1997) or memory retrieval (Hutchinson, Mantrala, & Raman, 1994; Ratneshwar & Shocker, 1991) for goal-consistent information. These successful demonstrations all conceptualize motivation at the very concrete level of product benefits, not at the level of higher order or deeper motives.

In summary, when taking a means–end approach, we believe it is quite important not to be committed to explanations that are too far up or down the motivational ladder. We run the risk of missing what is one step away. In the grand scheme of things, it may be true that even attributes like porcelain (rather than plastic) side panels on a kitchen appliance derive their true value from more basic goals or desires, which are linked more directly to some combination of appearance and performance consequences. Remote controls for home entertainment systems are much in demand, and this can be explained, often in a compelling fashion, in terms of their providing convenience and, perhaps ultimately, some amount of personal freedom or enhanced self-worth.

Explanations of behavior can be at different levels, of course, but most agree that the former determinants are difficult enough to pin down without attempting to trace the circuitous pathways through which the latter might influence product preferences and choices. It is important to distinguish between the picture of the world and the salient concepts carried around by consumers and those invoked by analysts in order to provide more integrative and theoretically provocative explanations.

ASSESSING CONSUMERS' COGNITIVE STRUCTURE

Means–end chains, and laddering research methods in particular, have often been portrayed as a means of assessing consumers' cognitive structure (e.g., Gutman, 1982; Olson & Reynolds, 1983; Reynolds & Gutman, 1988). Resulting hierarchical maps (which summarize the most frequently evoked means–end paths) are then interpreted within an associative-memory framework (Anderson, 1983). Related treatments (Walker & Olson, 1991) adopt an intellectual foundation in cognitive structure conceptualizations of the "self" (Markus, 1977; Markus & Nurius, 1986), as a stored network of interrelated personal constructs and self-knowledge. Core values comprise the most central elements of this self-structure, whereas more peripheral self-knowledge embodies social and psychological goals. Over time and through a variety of consumption experiences, consumer learning is reflected in network structures connecting self-related goals and values with specific products and behaviors that satisfy them (Walker & Olson, 1991). The resulting chains can then be activated as single unitized meanings if the appropriate triggering cues are present in the environment.

Are Memory Models Relevant to Motivational Issues?

Means–end chain approaches are intended to provide insights regarding sources of value that are perceived to be, or could become, motivationally important. This is a significant and ambitious agenda, and no assumptions need to be made about the formal memory representation of these chains to pursue it. How elements comprising such chains and interrelations among them are stored and activated from memory and are integrated with other knowledge is irrelevant to the purpose of the motivational analysis. The latter issues may in fact deflect attention from the richness and complexity of motivational factors. Further, in attempting to incorporate the nuances of models of memory representation and activation, researchers may unwittingly incorporate unnecessary assumptions that redirect or restructure their thinking.

A prime example of this is the adoption of a spreading activation metaphor within a representational model developed for semantic memory research. Means–end chain theory risks being internally inconsistent by simultaneously emphasizing the motivational importance of end-state values as driving forces and the key mediating role of *accessibility* (i.e., activated memory elements) in guiding behavior. Central to the means–end chain approach is the importance of identifying higher order values to explain purchase behavior, over and above the more salient attributes and consequences of the anticipated act. However, now proponents seem to want to have it both ways. They may either have to drop the assumption that a process of spreading activation underlies the influence of more weakly linked values on behavior and judgment, or they should revise the model to incorporate the assumption that values are motivationally relevant only at times and in situations where they are (made) salient.

The importance of information accessibility in consumer decision making and judgement is well documented (Alba, Hutchinson, & Lynch, 1991; Feldman & Lynch, 1988). Further, it is well established that goals can influence which attributes of an object and which potential consequences of behavior will become salient and accessible at any particular point in time. Whether associative network memory theories are the most appropriate way of thinking about such issues is doubtful.

First, these models have been developed originally to represent semantic relations. At this point, however, we do not have well-accepted theories about how to represent anticipated consequences or even product-attribute knowledge in such a network (see, for example, Carlston & Smith, 1996). Of greater importance, whereas contemporaneity is important in theories of motivation (i.e., only currently salient anticipated consequences of behavior need to be considered), the importance of a motive does not reduce to its strength of association with some other concept, as assessed by response time. Spreading activation models examine semantic verification tasks and priming effects in which the salience or accessibility of information is defined within a time span measured in seconds.

Motivational influences on behavior are not limited to rendering information more or less salient or accessible. Beyond enhancing accessibility, goals and values affect processing by influencing which of the accessible information is considered important (for achieving that goal). The consideration of means and ends in any situation is largely an active and conscious process on the part of the individual. Reducing this decision to a pattern of associations in a mechanistic model seems inconsistent with the very nature of a motivational approach.

Inherent Limitations of Laddering

One reason for means–end chain advocates' enthusiasm about the use of the approach to represent cognitive structures seems to be the face validity of a relatively unstructured elicitation task rather than the use of prespecified cognitive categories. However, laddering is far from neutral in the types of responses it elicits (i.e., reasons underlying preferences). Laddering systematically probes for successively higher level goals and values, and therefore cannot be said to reflect how consumers think about products or brands. It is quite likely, for example, that there are many important associations at a given level in the hierarchy — particularly at the attribute or benefit level — that are ignored because of this hierarchical emphasis. In addition, in striving for useful and representative means–end chains, individuals' responses are interpreted, coded, and aggregated, thus necessarily sacrificing a certain degree of accuracy for parsimony. Although such procedures may be sound as a way of focusing on predominant motivational chains, different tradeoffs would be needed if the goal were, in fact, to map consumers' cognitive structures.

A second major issue in the use of laddering to discover how consumers think about products is the leading nature of the procedure. Participants are literally "pushed up" an attribute-consequence-goal-value hierarchy in an effort to discover which of these seem to be linked hierarchically. Whether such a hierarchical arrangement exists (in any form) in the consumer's mind is not investigated; it is assumed. Aside from respondents answering that there was no particular reason why they desired a certain attribute or felt that a certain outcome was beneficial — and risking looking rather foolish — *laddering will produce reasons for preferences.* That is what the technique is designed to do. Unfortunately, it has characteristic features of a problem-solving exercise. In a sense, riddles are posed and solved, proceeding from the shared belief that preferences must have reasons. One can only imagine the thought processes that respondents go through when they realize they have never thought about why a certain outcome is desirable. However, there is ample reason to believe that they will search for a plausible explanation and one that speaks well of themselves (Schlenker, Britt, & Pennington).

LOOKING TOWARD THE FUTURE:
POSSIBLE CONTRIBUTIONS

Means–end chain research has often been portrayed as descriptive of how consumers view products or how they think about them. However, with the laddering method, respondents are more or less "pushed" to come up with answers to questions they may never have thought about (e.g., "why is flavor important to you?") in considering why they prefer a particular product. Therefore, laddering research might best be viewed as a method for enlisting consumers to help analysts better understand the possible and potential sources of value in products. Additionally, laddering might be seen as a way to derive more fundamental and integrative explanations for the sources of value that are found in products.

In planning, executing and interpreting means–end chain research, then, it may be important to differentiate between: (a) typically salient reasons for purchase, (b) potentially important (but not salient) reasons for purchase; (c) nonsalient sources of value underlying reasons for purchase; and, (d) fundamental–theoretically integrative explanations for these sources of value. The contribution of means–end chain research is likely to vary at each of these issue-related segments of the chain. However, there appear to be a number of potentially significant contributions that could be made, especially with some refinements in approach and methodology.

Salient Midlevel Choice Criteria

The initial motivational layer will most often include some mixture of attributes and consequences that together, describe brand- and product-related benefits and deficiencies. Means–end chain researchers can almost certainly make some underappreciated contributions to marketing practice at this level through a better specification of relations between *actionable* elements and *purchase-inducing* (or relationship-maintaining) factors. The latter, by definition, actually drives sales. The former will typically be at the level of product or service ingredients. Often such factors are packaged together to create a more perceptually salient and motivationally important reason for product or firm selection (Hauser & Clausing, 1988).

For example, a bank may institute a number of highly specific customer-service practices that, in combination, consumers perceive as friendly service. The bank might also increase the number of tellers at peak hours, add to its drive-through facilities, and increase the number of money machines it operates around town. When all these steps have been taken customers may regard the bank as *high in convenience*, and this may well be the level at which these marketing actions constitute a meaningful choice criterion. Similar opportunities exist for businesses as diverse as supermarkets and automobile manufacturers.

In all such cases, the actionable elements are one or several levels below the composites consumers use to compare alternatives. Although consumers think about the choice alternatives in terms of the benefits that they provide, businesses need to know which discrete attributes (that may not even be salient on an individual basis) are likely to be bundled together psychologically because of their similarity in function or benefit. Answers to such questions can be pursued through a variety of approaches that essentially look for intercorrelations among attributes and, after establishing meaningful clusters, provide interpretive labels for them. In cases in which consumers are able to verbalize the contribution of discrete attributes to perceived benefits, a laddering-like approach can be very useful to this process, especially if a particular effort is made to begin with entry concepts that are at the level of discrete, actionable elements. The goal, however, is not necessarily to trace the chain to a few truly higher level needs or values but to help management better understand why specific packages of features produce motivationally important composites. This initial exploratory stage of research in new product development should be followed up by quantifying the relation between actionable product or service features and the perceived benefits. Marketing researchers can use the results of an exploratory means–end analysis as an input to the more familiar conjoint-analysis methods or similar techniques developed in engineering or human factors research.

The qualitative nature of the means–end chain approach may help identify important attribute–benefit relations for which the more common quantitative methods are not ideally suited. For example, physical features contributing to automobile safety are clearly complementary in providing a safety benefit, but consumers may perceive some of these features as substitutes rather than complements to safety. For example, a recent study identified the increased availability of airbags as a possible reason for decreasing the use of safety belts (Peterson & Hoffer, 1994). Although the traditional laddering method does not identify differences between substitutable and complementary features (as perceived by the consumer), adaptations of the method might be developed to examine this issue more directly.

Consider the further example of a purchase decision that extends across several traditional product category boundaries, each having a specified set of attributes (e.g., choosing a salty snack from among a number of different types of products). A manufacturer is likely to be in competition with a number of products that, on the surface, have somewhat different characteristics. Finding situationally appropriate higher level criteria that consumers are likely to use in making such a product choice, should have important marketing advantages compared to simply emphasizing attributes in common within one of the narrower product categories (Johnson, 1988). As discussed earlier, however, moving too far up the ladder may not be an advantage because consumers may not think about their decision along those lines.

Unrecognized and Underappreciated Benefits

The second category includes attributes and consequences that might make a difference but have not yet received enough attention or whose advantages were poorly understood. Again, certain automobile safety features might be a good example of these. Other nonsalient attributes and consequences might be important in unanticipated circumstances. Laddering should be particularly useful in identifying underappreciated but potentially important purchase motivators.

Those working within the multiattribute attitude tradition have typically discussed this issue in terms of the attitude (and behavioral) change strategy of increasing attribute value and importance (Cohen, 1974; Lutz, 1975). We do not wish to gloss over the distinction between a lack of attribute–benefit consideration (i.e., the attribute does not come to mind very readily) and consumers' underestimation of its potential value. They are, however, clearly related.

If laddering research can identify important sources of value (e.g., survival in a sideways automobile collision), which are not currently salient, and link these to product attributes (e.g., a horizontal support beam or a side airbag), both the salience and the motivational significance of such an attribute can be enhanced.

Whether the entry point for a laddering research study (i.e., salient attributes) is ideally suited to do this is an open question. However, researchers alerted to this issue may wish to flag intermediate-level consequences and goals (e.g., accident protection, driving safety) whose supporting structure (i.e., lower level attributes and consequences) seems inadequately defined or undifferentiated. It may be possible to work back down the ladder to draw out less salient features as well as opportunities to develop additional links in the chain.

Nonsalient Psychosocial and Higher Level Forces

The third grouping probably includes some combination of psychosocial consequences and values. As an example, consider a means–end chain for men's clothing that culminates in the higher order value, self-esteem. Further, let's assume that when pushed, consumers will say that this is an important reason (several times removed, of course) for them to buy certain suits, shirts, shoes, ties, and so forth. For each of these products, however, consumers have identified more concrete indicants of what they are seeking. They have learned how to categorize desirable articles of clothing in terms of more perceptually salient features, and may anticipate certain favorable judgments by others — and even feeling proud about that — as resulting benefits. Yet the concept of self-esteem may never enter their minds when buying any of these products.

What, then, do we gain by identifying this higher level goal or value? For one thing, it may be useful to understand that this is the glue that holds seemingly diverse clothing attributes and social benefits together. This insight (and laddering research) might help us to identify related midlevel benefits and goals (e.g., being well dressed, having good taste, prestige), any of which could then be emphasized in advertising. However, based on laddering research we might be tempted to recommend that self-esteem be the *driving force* (i.e., the underlying value orientation) in an advertising campaign and that a subset of easily recognized clothing features comprise message elements linked to this overriding theme (see Gengler & Reynolds, 1993; Olson & Reynolds, 1983). One's decisions may depend on whether he or she sees the chain as an integrated unit, with each succeeding link bound to the one above.

Means–end (and Meccas) proponents often treat the above state of affairs as if it were presumptively accurate. However, it is important to emphasize that there is no reason to assume an integrated hierarchical view of purchase motivations. As discussed earlier, functional benefits need not be connected — at least in consumers' minds — to these more abstract or higher level sources of value. Further, building on Allport's (1955) argument, there is no reason to assume that more general (although more central) needs and values will constitute stronger, more important purchase motivations. Unless such a motivational link can be strengthened significantly, there are likely to be other, more obvious, ways for consumers to satisfy the need or achieve the desired state. So, appealing to higher level psychosocial consequences and values may not prove to be as effective a promotional strategy as stressing less important functional consequences.

If the motivational link to a higher order value is tenuous it may be difficult to communicate or be unpersuasive. Consumers may have a difficult time thinking along those lines. It may be argued, of course, that consumers do not have to think about products in terms of higher level consequences and values for these factors to be important. People are often unaware of the effects of contextual factors, moods, and naturally occurring primes on the direction and outcome of mental activity (Ajzen & Sexton, 1999; Bargh & Barndollar, 1996). Semioticians, in particular, emphasize relatively automatic extraction of deeper meaning from a confluence of message elements, subtle cues, texture, and stylistic factors. Part of the meaning is likely to be shared with other recipients as a result of common background and understanding of language and symbols, but much may be personalized depending on the recipient's store of knowledge and experience and mental set (Mick, 1992). Although there are reasonably well-documented instances of consumers' extraction of deeper meanings (e.g., gender, role, and status connotations, inferences about personal attributes), many of the interpretations that are offered are highly speculative, and each case is treated in an ad hoc fashion.

Moreover, means–end chains emphasize the active role of salient consequences and values in guiding choice. It is hard to see how shades of meaning—even if transmitted effectively—would fit directly into this framework, although they may help comprise an associational network for the product or brand. The starting point for means–end chains, we should remember, is the identification of motivationally significant explanations for a person's behavior. Perhaps some low-involvement decision-making can be better explained by models emphasizing readily accessible associations, and in turn by less cognitively demanding encoding and retrieval processes (Bargh & Barndollar, 1996).

Insights Regarding More Fundamental Sources of Value

The fourth category of purchase explanations should be of greater significance to a theoretical conceptualization of consumer motivations (roughly analogous to Rokeach's (1968) work) than to practitioners' needs for actionable insights. Laddering offers an empirically based method for deriving more fundamental sources of value that are represented in consumption alternatives. Meta-analyses of laddering studies might be used to infer the existence and relative importance of values that underlie the consumption experience or perhaps how this varies across major product categories. Among the issues that might be raised in such a context would be the strong reliance on comparatively simple probes and introspection to identify underlying motivations. Each person essentially becomes his or her own analyst. Because the form of the questioning is geared to uncover—or at least generate—positive self-concept linked values and goals, this may well introduce a significant bias in developing a general theory of consumer motivation.

In addition, a theoretically integrative explanation should attempt to explain why the set of terminal values affects particular behaviors (e.g., product choices). A means–end chain is not so much an explanation as it is a statement of a systematic relation among product attributes, consequences, and values that needs to be explained. Such explanations will almost certainly have to take into account the economic, social, and cultural context in which the behavior takes place and their impact on individuals' goals and values.

CONCLUSION

In summary, laddering should be viewed as a method for developing insights about potential means–end chains that underlie purchase decisions. To say that this objective is both important and daunting is a substantial understatement. As emphasized in this chapter, significant conceptual and methodological issues in studying consumer motivations are as yet not adequately addressed by the proponents of means–end chains. To impose the substantial additional burden of mapping consumers' cognitive structures, or even the motivationally relevant parts of such structures, seems unwise. We are asking too much from any single approach for answers to two of the most vexing questions marketers continually ask:

1. Why do consumers buy this product (and how can I influence them to buy more of it)?
2. How do consumers think about this product (and how should I change this perception)?

Laddering seems much better able to provide useful insights about the first of these significant topics, especially as more thought is given to important imbedded assumptions about purchase motivations and the risks and limitations of searching for motives that may have very little bearing on consumers' decisions.

ACKNOWLEDGMENT

We thank Richard J. Lutz for his helpful comments on an earlier version of this chapter.

REFERENCES

Ajzen, I., & Sexton, J. (1999). Depth of processing, belief congruence, and attitude-behavior correspondence. In S. Chaiken & Y. Trope (Eds.), *Dual-process theories in social psychology* (pp. 117–138). London: Guilford Press.

Alba, J. W., Hutchinson, J. W., & Lynch, J. G., Jr. (1991). Memory and decision making. In T. S. Robertson & H. H. Kassarjian (Eds.), *Handbook of Consumer Behavior* (pp. 1–49). Englewood Cliffs, NJ: Prentice Hall.

Allport, G. W. (1955). *Becoming: Basic considerations for a psychology of personality.* New Haven, CT: Yale University Press.

Anderson, J. R. (1983). *The architecture of cognition.* Cambridge, MA: Harvard University Press.

Atkinson, J. W. (1964). *An introduction to motivation.* Princeton, NJ: Van Nostrand.

Bargh, J. A., & Barndollar, K. (1996). Automaticity in action: The unconscious as repository of chronic goals and motives. In P. M. Gollwitzer & J. A. Bargh (Eds.), *The psychology of action: Linking cognition and motivation to behavior* (pp. 457–481). London: Guilford Press.

Bither, S. W., & Miller, S. J. (1969, Fall). A cognitive theory view of brand preference. *Proceedings of the Conference American Marketing Association,* 280–286.

Bruner, J. S. (1957). On perceptual readiness. *Psychological Review, 64,* 123–157.

Cantor, N., Markus, H., Niedenthal, P., & Nurius, P. (1986). On motivation and the self-concept. In R. M. Sorrentino & E. T. Higgins (Eds.), *Handbook of motivation and cognition* (pp. 96–121). New York: The Guilford Press.

Carlson, D. E., & Smith, E. R. (1996). Principles of mental representation. In E. T. Higgins & A. W. Kruglanski (Eds.), *Social psychology: Handbook of basic principles* (pp. 184–210). London: Guilford Press.

Cohen, J. B. (1974). Toward an integrated use of expectancy-value Model. In G. D. Hughes & M. L. Ray (Eds.), *Buyer/Consumer information processing* (pp. 331–346). Chapel Hill: University of North Carolina Press.

Cohen, J. B. (1979). The structure of product attributes: Defining attribute dimensions for planning and evaluation. In A. D. Shocker (Ed.), *Analytic approaches to product and marketing planning* (pp. 54–86). Boston, Marketing Science Institute.

Cohen, J. B. (1982). The role of affect in categorization: Toward a reconsideration of the concept of attitude. In A. Mitchell (Ed.), *Advances in consumer research* (Vol. 9, pp. 94–100), Provo, Utah.

Cohen, J. B., & Basu, K. (1987). Alternative models of categorization: Toward a contingent processing framework. *Journal of Consumer Research, 13,* 455–472.

Edwards, W., Lindman, H., & Phillips, L. D. (1965). Emerging technologies for making decisions. In *New directions in psychology, II* (pp. 259–325). New York: Holt, Rinehart and Winston.

Erdelyi, M. H. (1974, January). A new look at the new look. *Psychological Review, 81,* 1–25.

Feather, N. T. (Ed.). (1982). *Expectations and action: Expectancy-value models in psychology.* Hillsdale, NJ: Lawrence Erlbaum Associates.

Fennel, G. (1975). Motivation research revisited. *Journal of Advertising Research, 15,* 23–28.

Feldman, J. M., & Lynch, J. G., Jr. (1988). Self-generated validity and other effects of measurement on belief, intention, and behavior. *Journal of Applied Psychology, 73,* 421–435.

Gengler, C. E., & Reynolds, T. J. (1993). A structural model of advertising effects. In A. A. Mitchell (Ed.), *Advertising, exposure, memory, and choice* (pp. 283–301). Hillsdale, NJ: Lawrence Erlbaum Associates.

Goffman, I. (1959). *The presentation of self in everyday life.* Garden City, NY: Doubleday/Anchor Books.

Gollwitzer, P. M. (1999). Implementation intentions: Strong effects of simple plans. *American Psychologist, 54,* 493–503.

Greenwald, A. G. (1982). Ego task analysis: An integration of research on ego-involvement and self-awareness. In A. H. Hastdorf & A. M. Isen (Eds.), *Cognitive social psychology* (pp. 109–147). New York: Elsevier/North Holland.

Gutman, J. (1982). A Means–End chain model based on consumer categorization processes. *Journal of Marketing, 46*(1), 60–72.

Gutman, J. (1991, March). Exploring the nature of linkages between consequences and values. *Journal of Business Research, 22,* 143–148.

Hall, C. S., & Lindszey, G. (1957). *Theories of personality.* New York: Wiley.

Hansen, F. (1969). Consumer choice behavior: An experimental approach. *Journal of Marketing Research, 6,* 436–443.

Hauser, J. R., & Clausing, D. (1988). The house of quality. *Harvard Business Review, 66,* 63–73.

Huffman, C., & Houston, M. J. (1993, September). Goal-oriented experiences and the development of knowledge. *Journal of Consumer Research, 20,* 190–207.

Hutchinson, J. W., Raman, K., & Mantrala, M. K. (1994). Finding choice alternatives in memory: probability models of brand name recall. *Journal of Marketing Research, 31,* 441–461.

Johnson, M. D. (1988). Comparability and hierarchical processing in multi-alternative choice. *Journal of Consumer Research, 15,* 303–314.

Jolly, J. P., Reynolds T. J., & Slocum, J. W., Jr. (1988). Application of the means–end theoretic for understanding the cognitive bases of performance appraisal. *Organizational Behavior and Human Decision Processes, 41,* 153–179.

Kassarjian, H. H., & Sheffett, M. J. (1991). Personality and consumer behavior: An update. In H. H. Kassarjian & T. S. Robertson (Eds.), *Perspectives in Consumer Behavior* (pp. 281–303). Englewood Cliffs, NJ: Prentice Hall.

Katz, D. (1960). The functional approach to the study of attitudes. *Public Opinion Quarterly, 24,* 163–204.

Lewin, K. (1951). *Field theory in social science.* Chicago: University of Chicago Press.

Lutz, R. J. (1975). Changing brand attitudes through modification of cognitive structure. *Journal of Consumer Research, 1,* 49–59.

Markus, H. (1977). Self-schemata and processing information about the self. *Journal of Personality and Social Psychology, 35,* 63–78.

Markus, H., & Nurius, P. (1986). Possible selves. *American Psychologist, 41,* 954–969.

Maslow, A. H. (1970). *Motivation and Personality,* 2nd Edition. New York: Harper and Row.

Mazis, M. B., Ahtola, O. T., & Klippel, G. E. (1975, June). A comparison of four multi-attribute models in the prediction of consumer attitudes. *Journal of Consumer Research, 2,* 38–52.

McCracken, G. (1988). *The long interview.* Sage University Paper series on Qualitative Research Methods, Vol. 13. Beverly Hills, CA: Sage.

McGuire, W. J., & Padawer-Singer, A. (1976). Trait salience in the spontaneous self-concept. *Journal of Personality and Social Psychology 36,* 241–244.

Mick, D. G. (1986, September). Consumer research and semiotics: Exploring the morphology of signs, symbols, and significance. *Journal of Consumer Research, 13,* 196–213.

Mick, D. G. (1992, March). Levels of subjective comprehension in advertising processing and their relations to ad perceptions, attitudes and memory. *Journal of Consumer Research, 18,* 411–424.

Miller, G. A., Pribram, E., & Pribram, K. H. (1960). *Plans and the structure of behavior.* New York: Holt.

Nuttin, J. (1984). *Motivation, planning, and action: A relational theory of behavior dynamics.* Hillsdale, NJ: Lawrence Erlbaum Associates.

Olson, J. C., & Reynolds, T. J. (1983). Understanding consumers' cognitive structures: Implications for advertising strategy. In L. Percy & A. G. Woodside (Eds.), *Advertising and consumer psychology* (pp. 77–91). Lexington, MA: Lexington Books.

Peak, H. (1955). Attitude and motivation. In M. R. Jones (Ed.), *Nebraska symposium on motivation* (pp. 148–149). Lincoln: University of Nebraska Press.

Peterson, S. P., & Hoffer, G. E. (1994). The impact of airbag adoption on relative personal injury and absolute collision insurance claims. *Journal of Consumer Research, 20,* 657–662.

Ratneshwar, S., & Shocker, A. D. (1991, August). Substitution in use and the role of usage context in product category structures. *Journal of Marketing Research, 28,* 281–295.

Ratneshwar, S., Warlop, L., Mick, D. G., & Seeger, G. (1997). Benefit salience and consumers' selective attention to product features. *International Journal of Research in Marketing, 14,* 245–259.

Raynor, J. O., & McFarlin, D. B. (1986). Motivation and the self-system. In R. M. Sorrentino & E. T. Higgins (Eds.), *Handbook of motivation and cognition* (pp. 315–349). New York: The Guilford Press.

Reynolds, T. J., & Gutman, J. (1988). Laddering theory, method, analysis, and interpretation. *Journal of Advertising Research, 28,* 11–31.

Reynolds, T. J., Gutman, J., & Fiedler, J. (1984). Understanding consumers' cognitive structures: The relationship of levels of abstraction to judgments of psychological distance and preference. In L. Alwitt & A. A. Mitchell (Eds.), *Psychological processes of advertising effects: Theory, research, and application* (pp. 261–272). Hillsdale, NJ: Lawrence Erlbaum Associates.

Rokeach, M. (1968). *Beliefs, attitudes and values.* San Francisco: Jossey-Bass.

Rosenberg, M. J. (1956). Cognitive structure and attitudinal affect. *Journal of Abnormal and Social Psychology, 53,* 367–372.

Rosenberg, M. J. (1956). Cognitive structure and attitude affects. *Journal of Abnormal and Social Psychology, 53*, 367–372.

Rosenberg, M. J. (1960). An analysis of affective-cognitive consistency. In C. I. Hovland & M. J. Rosenberg (Eds.), *Attitude organization and change* (pp. 15–64). New Haven, CT: Yale University Press.

Rothwell, N. D. (1955). Motivational research revisited. *Journal of Marketing, 20*, 150–154.

Schlenker, B. R., Britt, T. W., & Pennington, J. (1996). Impression regulation and management: Highlights of a theory of self-identification. In R. M. Sorrentino & E. T. Higgins (Eds.), *Handbook of motivation and cognition, Vol. 3, The interpersonal context* (pp. 118–147). London: Guilford Press.

Schlenker, B. R. (1985). Identity and self-identification. In B. R. Schlenker (Ed.), *The self and social life* (pp. 65–99). New York: McGraw-Hill.

Shavitt, S. (1989). Operationalizing functional theories of attitude. In A. R. Pratkanis, S. J. Breckler, & A. G. Greenwald (Eds.), *Attitude structure and function* (pp. 331–337). Hillsdale, NJ: Lawrence Erlbaum Associates.

Sirgy, J. M. (1982). Self-concept in consumer behavior: A critical review. *Journal of Consumer Research, 9*, 287–300.

Solomon, M. R. (1983). The role of products as social stimuli: A symbolic interactionism perspective. *Journal of Consumer Research, 10*, 319–329.

Srull, T. K. (1984). Methodological techniques for the study of person memory and social cognition. In T. S. Wyer & T. K. Srull (Eds.), *Handbook of social cognition*, Vol. 2 (pp. 1–72). Hillsdale, NJ: Lawrence Erlbaum Associates.

Stotland, E., Katz, D., & Patchen, M. (1959). The reduction of prejudice through the arousal of self insight. *Journal of Personality, 27*, 507–531.

Sujan, M. (1985). Consumer knowledge: Effects on evaluation strategies mediating consumers' judgments. *Journal of consumer research, 12*, 31–46.

Tolman, E. C. (1959). Principles of purposive behavior. In S. Koch (Ed.), *Psychology: A study of a science* (pp. 92–157). New York: McGraw-Hill.

Walker, B. A., & Olson, J. C. (1991). Means–End chains: Connecting products with self. *Journal of Business Research, 22*, 111–118.

Wiggins, J. S., & Pincus, A. L. (1992). Personality: Structure and assessment. *Annual Review of Psychology, 43*, 473–504.

Wyer, R. S., Jr., & Srull, T. K. (1986). The role of chronic and temporary goals in social information processing. In R. M. Sorrentino & E. T. Higgins (Eds.), *Handbook of motivation and cognition* (pp. 503–549). New York: Guilford.

A Means–End Conceptualization
of Goal-Directed Consumer Behavior

Rik Pieters
Tilburg University

Doug Allen
Hans Baumgartner
Pennsylvania State University

ABSTRACT

In this chapter we argue that goal-directed consumer behavior is organized hierarchically as a structure of means–end chains, ranging from
concrete, observable motor movements to abstract, personal goals. In a hierarchy of goal-directed behavior, three levels can be distinguished: the
identification (or "what") level, the operation (or "how") level and the
motivation (or "why") level. These levels in the hierarchy can only be determined relative to each other, as why and how a consumer performs a
particular behavior depends on the identification of the behavior. This
identification can change in the course of behavior, which accounts for the
dynamic quality of consumers' actions. We present research illustrating
the usefulness of taking a means–end approach to the study of goal-directed consumer behavior and we discuss some promising avenues for future work.

INTRODUCTION

Consumer behavior researchers have long recognized the value of viewing consumer knowledge as hierarchically structured means–end connections (Gutman, 1982; Olson & Reynolds, 1983). The means–end chain
model is intended to explain the relations between product attributes,

consequences of product use, and consumer values. The approach is based on the assumption that product attributes take on meaning as a result of the consequences they confer. Furthermore, in many cases, these consequences can be found to connect to higher level values. Thus, means–end chains can illustrate whether or not consequences link concrete product attributes to highly self-relevant values. In cases where concrete attributes are judged to lead to consequences that tap into personally relevant values, consumers tend to experience high levels of involvement with a product.

In this chapter, we adapt the means–end chain perspective of product knowledge to goal-directed consumer behavior. It is argued that the behavior of consumers is hierarchically structured and that it can be profitably understood through a means–ends chain approach. Given the presumed centrality of the concept of behavior in the analysis of consumer behavior, it is surprising that researchers have paid so little attention to behavior. Inspection of the extant literature suggests that the term *behavior* is apparently so self-evident that it requires very little explanation. Behavior is simply what people do. But the question is, what do people think they're doing when they engage in observable behavior?

Following Pieters (1993), we suggest that the rather sketchy way in which consumer behavior research has treated behavior precludes a comprehensive understanding of behavior, its antecedents, and consequences. That is, most models treat behavior as either a simplistic response to environmental stimuli or as the mundane consequence of complex cognitive processes that constitute the real focus of interest. In contrast, a hierarchical conceptualization of behavior stresses that consumer behaviors are underdetermined by their overt physical manifestations, and that observable responses must be understood in the hierarchical context of consumers' own phenomenology of what they think they are doing and the higher level goals that underlie their behavior. Just as means–end chains shed light on how concrete product attributes can be personally involving, a means–end approach to goal-directed behavior should be able to provide insights into how concrete motor acts are motivated by abstract, personally relevant goals. By applying the means–end logic to behavior, this chapter develops a hierarchical conceptualization of goal-directed consumer behavior.

A HIERARCHICAL CONCEPTUALIZATION OF GOAL-DIRECTED CONSUMER BEHAVIOR

James (1983) was among the first to stress the importance of studying "the pursuance of future ends and the choice of means for their attainment" (p. 8) in order to understand goal-directed behavior. Since these early days, research on goals has grown steadily (see Pervin, 1989a, for an overview). In this research, it is commonplace to posit a hierarchical structure of goals (e.g., Powers, 1973). In fact, Locke (1991) categorically stated "it is true that people have goal hierarchies" (p. 13), and Bandura (1989) said that "goal systems, of course, usually involve a hierarchical structure" (pp. 48–49). Despite the obviousness of the concept of a goal hierarchy, until recently, few attempts have been undertaken to specify what goal hierarchies look like, which principles and forces shape them, and what role they play in ongoing behavior. In fact, Pervin (1989b), in formulating key issues and questions that should be addressed in research, mentioned that:

> since ordinarily we are considering goal systems rather than single goals, attention must be given to how goals become interrelated and organized in some hierarchical fashion. Thus, there is the task of understanding the developing complexity of the goal system in terms of number of goals, interconnection among goals, and plans and strategies developed to obtain goals. (p. 475)

Interestingly, although the study of the ends that consumers strive toward has attracted substantial interest and has led to in-depth theorizing, the means component has been somewhat neglected. Behavior is often treated as the mundane emission of overt motor responses, as is evidenced by common definitions of consumer behavior that are phrased in terms of observable acts. Pieters (1993) mentioned that the grand models of consumer behavior, such as the Engel, Blackwell, and Kollat model, tend to treat behavior as a bullet that is fired from a gun: The behavioral intention triggers the release of motivational energy into an overt response. Behavior is usually the dependent variable in models that start with environmental stimuli or intra-individual independent variables, and it is treated as an extrapsychic, objective phenomenon, conceptually separated from intrapsychic processes.

In recent years, a different perspective on goal-directed behavior has emerged. In this perspective, goal-directed behavior is conceptualized as a latent construct with both overt and covert, extrapsychic as well as intrapsychic elements.

Hierarchies of Goal-Directed Behavior

Researchers in several subdisciplines of psychology have postulated hierarchies of goal-directed behavior. In the area of social psychology, Carver and Scheier (1981) posited a hierarchy that divides behaviors and goals into three levels—programs, principles, and system concepts. Programs are similar to scripts, principles provide general norms for behavior, and system concepts are the most abstract goals regulating behavior.

In the environmental psychology literature, Little (1983) introduced the idea of personal projects to study human personality. Little (1983) defined a personal project as "a set of interrelated acts extending over time, which is intended to maintain or attain a state of affairs foreseen by the individual" (p. 276). Personal projects serve as the link between concrete acts and overarching values (Little, 1989). Thus, a personal project such as learning to ski can be seen to be the link between concrete acts such as waxing one's skis and high-level goals such as maintaining an active lifestyle. As a final example, in the area of industrial psychology, Hacker (1985) discussed a hierarchy that goes from goals to activities, actions, and operations all the way down to muscle movements. In addition to these three frameworks, other hierarchical approaches to goal-directed behavior have been suggested (e.g., life tasks by Cantor & Kihlstrom, 1987; current concerns by Klinger, 1977; personal strivings by Emmons, 1989). There are many differences in the specifics of each of these perspectives, and some of the approaches even differ in their ontology. However, they all agree that it is useful to think of goal-directed behavior in terms of a hierarchical model of action, and they make specific suggestions as to what the levels in the hierarchy might be. Our own conceptualization is most closely related to the work of Little (1983, 1989) and Vallacher and Wegner's (1985) action identification theory (to be discussed later). We argue that it is most profitable to view a hierarchy of goal-directed behavior as being comprised of three levels. The three levels correspond to the what, why, and how of behavior, or as we also refer to them in the next section, the identification, motivation, and operation levels.

The What, How, and Why of Consumer Behavior

The three levels of goal-directed consumer behavior that we wish to distinguish are presented in Fig. 18.1. A hypothetical hierarchy of goal-directed behavior with respect to weight loss is used as an illustration.

The Identification Level. The "what" of goal-directed behavior refers to how people label or identify what it is that they are doing at any given time. Vallacher and Wegner (1985) offered a conceptualization of the hierarchical organization of goals and behaviors referred to as action identification theory. This theory states that a given behavior can be identified at various levels of abstraction, ranging from very concrete levels in the hierarchy to rather abstract interpretations of the same act. For example, a person may refer to the same action as "picking a box of cereal from the grocery shelf," "purchasing bran cereal," or "getting proper nutrition for breakfast." The level at which a person identifies a behavior is called the *prepotent identification* of the action. The prepotent identification can be viewed as the what of behavior because it represents the typical response

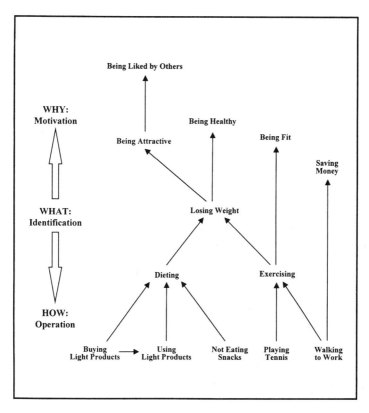

FIG. 18.1. Hypothetical hierarchy of goal-directed behavior for losing weight.

that a person will give when asked the question, "What are you doing at this moment?"

The identification level of a goal-directed behavior hierarchy can be seen to play a role analogous to that of consequences in a product-knowledge hierarchy. In a product-knowledge hierarchy, concrete product attributes have relatively little meaning in and of themselves. Rather, such attributes take on meaning and become involving for a consumer to the extent that they serve as means to consequences that consumers seek from a product. In a similar way, we argue that concrete-level consumer behaviors have relatively little meaning when viewed in isolation. For example, the same overt motor act of raising one's index finger in the air can have very different meanings depending on one's goals (e.g., bidding on an offering at an auction, summoning the waiter at a restaurant, or testing the wind direction on a golf course). Thus, one important role of the identification level of a goal-directed behavior hierarchy is to give meaning to and coordinate concrete acts.

In addition, elements at the identification level of a goal-directed behavior hierarchy can link lower level acts with higher level goals, providing direction and motivation for specific acts. This is similar to cases in means–end chain analysis in which consequences link concrete attributes to abstract values. However, as with product knowledge hierarchies in which product attributes only reach the consequence level, it is probably the case that not all low-level acts connect to high-level goals via elements at the identification level.

In the work of Hacker (1985), a concept called *activities* acts as a bridge between abstract goals and specific acts, similar to the role played by the identification level. As Hacker (1985) stated, "activities are motivated and regulated by higher order goals and are realized through actions that are themselves relatively independent components of each activity"(p. 262). Just as consequences take on motivational efficacy through their relation to higher level values, activities gain their motivational potential from their relation to higher level goals. Similarly, just as consequences define the meaning of lower level attributes, activities give meaning to lower level actions. That is, actions that are identical with respect to their overt physical manifestations are differentiated as a result of their relation to different activities.

In sum, elements at the identification level can be seen to act as a hub in a lattice-like hierarchy of goal-directed behavior. They coordinate and give meaning to a set of more concrete actions and direct these actions to one or more higher level goals.

The Motivation Level.   Levels above the prepotent level of identification in a goal-directed hierarchy of behavior can be viewed as providing insight into the why of behavior. When talking about the why of behavior, we are referring to the upper levels of a hierarchy of goal-directed behavior. This level is composed of personally relevant goals, enduring motivational concerns, or overarching values (Little, 1989). Just as product attributes become personally relevant due to their connection to values, molecular acts become relevant due to their relation to personally relevant goals. As such, this level of the hierarchy consisting of goals provides insight into the motivation behind behavior, or the why of behavior.

In a recent study (Pieters, Baumgartner, & Allen, 1995), we investigated the structure of goals underlying the weight-loss behaviors of university students. The aggregated structure of goals, across 51 subjects, that emerged from the study is presented in Fig. 18.2.

In the goal map in Fig. 18.2, the vertical dimension provides information about the level of abstractness of the goals. With abstractness we do not mean semantic abstractness but abstractness in terms of position in the goal structure. When a goal is perceived to be governing weight-loss be-

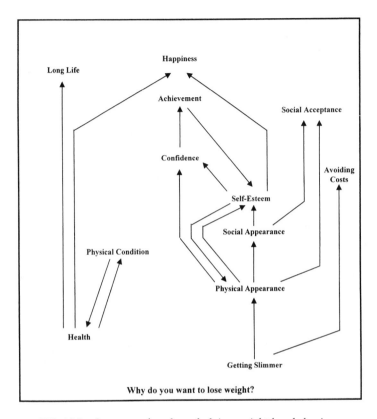

FIG. 18.2. Structure of goals underlying weight-loss behaviors.

havior directly, without any intermediate goals, it is more specific and less abstract than a goal that is perceived to be governing weight-loss behavior indirectly through one or more intermediate goals.

Specific goals are proximal as perceived by the consumers under study. Abstract goals are distal as perceived by the consumers under study. In Fig. 18.2, "pursuing a healthy life" (health) is a relatively specific, proximal goal, whereas "leading a long life" (long life) is a much more abstract, distal goal. The goal "maintain or stimulate self-esteem" (self-esteem) turns out to be an important goal in the goal structure. This is evidenced by the fact that it is connected, either as the sending goal or as the receiving goal, to many other goals. How one feels about oneself is an important goal when trying to lose weight. The most abstract goal, not surprisingly, is to become happy (happiness). Figure 18.2 also shows that there are three distinct parts of the goal structure: health-related goals to the left of the map, achievement- and appearance-related goals in the middle, and cost-related goals to the right. The goals in the middle are well connected.

In another recent study, Bagozzi and Dabholkar (1994) investigated goals that consumers have with respect to recycling their garbage, using the methodological framework described in Pieters, Baumgartner, and Allen (1995). They surveyed 133 consumers by telephone and found that 19 goals were consistently mentioned. Goals included "saving resources," "avoid filling-up landfills," "saving the environment," "providing for future generations" and so forth. Most goals were rather specific to the domain of recycling, and few goals were personal in the sense that they might be goals in other domains of life as well. One such more personal goal, which also emerged in the weight-loss study discussed previously, was "building self-esteem." However, this goal did not occupy a central position in the goal map, and it did not have substantial effects with other variables such as attitude.

In sum, in a hierarchical structure of goal-directed consumer behavior, goals above the level at which a consumer identifies the behavior perform the same function as values do in a means–end structure of product knowledge. Goals give the higher level meanings to specific single acts, and they provide the ultimate motivation for engaging in the behavior.

The Operation Level.   Elements of a hierarchy of goal-directed behavior below the identification level can be viewed as providing insight into the how of behavior. Behaviors at this level deal with the operational aspects of attaining the focal goal, and the operation level is thus concerned with plans of action or actual actions by which a superordinate goal can be attained. One way of thinking about such action plans is in terms of scripts. Script theory (Schank & Abelson, 1977) focuses on the sequential organization of single acts. Scripts are a particular type of schema in which mental representations of prototypical event sequences are stored. According to Abelson (1981), three conditions are necessary for the triggering of scripted behavior: (a) a person must have a cognitive representation of a script; (b) a context that invokes a particular script must be present; and, (c) the person must enter the script. Scripts perform a crucial role in bridging the gap between cognition and behavior because they exist as mental representations and as behaviors. By entering a script, mental representations are transformed into behaviors. Hence, the operational level of a goal hierarchy represents the crucial link between manifest physical acts and mental representations. That is, schemas can be considered to have a double existence—in the form of motor acts and mental representations.

In one of the few instances in which the idea of a hierarchical organization of goal-directed behavior is used explicitly in consumer research, Bettman (1979) conceptualized choice as a person's movement through a goal hierarchy from an initial state to a desired state via intermediate states. Although he mentioned that, depending on the level of analysis chosen, one could look at the basic needs and motives underlying a choice process, Bettman (1979) focused on relatively concrete goals (e.g., purchasing a washing machine). He argued that in order to reach a certain goal a consumer has to attain particular subgoals (e.g., determine which attributes are important, evaluate alternatives on these attributes, and obtain the best alternative). It is apparent that Bettman (1979) dealt mostly with what we call the operation level of a goal hierarchy.

Relations in Hierarchies of Goal-Directed Behavior

Relations between elements *across levels* in a hierarchy of goal-directed behavior are instrumental, with elements at lower levels in the hierarchy serving as means to achieve elements at higher levels as ends. Such vertical relations are of three kinds. Ordinary instrumentality is present when a single element at a lower level is instrumental in attaining a single element at a higher level. Multifinality occurs when a single element at a lower level is instrumental in reaching multiple elements at a higher level. In Fig. 18.1, exercising acts as an instrument of losing weight and staying fit. Equifinality occurs when multiple elements at a lower level are instrumental in accomplishing a single element at a higher level. In Fig. 18.1, both playing tennis and walking to work are instruments of exercising. Due to multifinality and equifinality, the same element may be part of multiple hierarchies of goal-directed behavior, and the meaning of a given element may not be directly obvious or clear. Hacker (1982) called this the *polystructural nature of action*, and Vallacher and Wegner (1985) mentioned that goal-directed behavior is underdetermined by observable responses.

Consumers sometimes do two or more things simultaneously to achieve multiple goals. Consumers may learn a language while driving their car, work while traveling on a plane, discuss business over dinner, and so on. In such cases, consumers perform several behaviors at the same time, each behavior for its own reasons (cf. Heckhausen & Beckmann, 1990). In such cases, consumers are engaged in *parallel finality*, where two or more elements of a lower level are simultaneously involved, each element being instrumental with respect to a different element on a higher level. In a context relevant to consumer behavior, Anderson (1985) noted that viewers engage in a great many activities while watching television. In addition, when visually inattentive, viewers make heavy use of the audio to guide their full attention back to the TV.

The direction of the vertical arrows in Fig. 18.1 denotes instrumental relations between elements, and not causal relations. In the present discussion the main interest is in understanding the hierarchical organization of goal-directed behavior, not in explaining the causation of behavior by goals. If the latter were the case, arrowheads might be reversed. Gutman (1991) made a similar remark with respect to the direction of the arrows in means–end chain models of product knowledge.

Relations between elements *within a particular level* of a hierarchy of goal-directed behavior are conditional, such that a particular behavior can only be performed after another behavior has been performed. The example given by Bettman (1979) about purchasing a washing machine may be used as an illustration. A consumer first has to determine which attributes are important before he or she can evaluate alternatives on these attributes or obtain the best alternative. Although each of these behaviors is instrumental in attaining the final goal, all three need to be performed in a particular sequence in order to attain the goal. Conditionality introduces time into the hierarchy of goal-directed behavior. In Fig. 18.1 "using light products" is conditional on "buying light products." In Fig. 18.1, we have just indicated a single conditional relation, although conditionality may be relevant to other specific behaviors. For example, playing tennis may be conditional on finding someone to play tennis with, making reservations for a tennis court, driving to the court at the appointed time, and so on. Although we have denoted the specific behaviors with a single label, they may in reality be rather complex sequences of behaviors.

It should also be noted that the various levels in the hierarchy of goal-directed behavior can only be defined and determined relative to each other. In other words, why and how consumers perform a particular behavior depends on what they do. For example, a consumer who identifies his or her behavior as exercising may do so by playing tennis in order to stay fit, whereas a consumer who is trying to stay fit may do so by exercising in order to feel better or live longer. The same description may be an identification, a motivation, or an operation. Of course, what a consumer identifies to be doing at any point in time will usually fall within a broad band somewhere in between very concrete acts and very abstract goals. Usually a consumer will not say "I'm contracting my forearm muscle by releasing neurotransmitters in order to pick up the groceries." Also, most consumers will not answer the question, "What are you doing?" with "I'm trying to be happy."

Assessing Hierarchies of Goal-Directed Behavior

Although methodological issues in constructing goal structures are not the focus of this chapter, we want to point out that methods traditionally used for measuring consumers' product knowledge can be adapted to elicit hierarchies of goal-directed behavior. The traditional means–end chain approach measures product knowledge by using laddering techniques that entail a series of "why" questions. Usually the starting point for this line of questioning is a particular product attribute or set of attributes. However, in attempting to obtain a behavior hierarchy, the process must proceed somewhat differently.

First, the researcher must determine the level at which people most commonly identify the behavior (the "what" of behavior). Second, in an attempt to elicit the motivation portion of a goal-directed behavior hierarchy, the researcher would start with the identification level and ladder upward by asking a series of why questions. This approach is similar to the traditional laddering technique used to uncover the connections between product attributes and personally relevant consumer values (Reynolds & Gutman, 1988). Pieters, Baumgartner, and Allen (1995) combined this traditional laddering technique with network analysis (Scott, 1991) to further articulate the goal-level stratum of a goal-directed behavior hierarchy. The additional information provided by network analysis helps one understand the position that individual goals have in the hierarchy. It also allows for an analysis of the relation between the overall structure of the goal-directed behavior hierarchy and other constructs of interest to consumer-behavior researchers (e.g., involvement).

Third, in order to obtain the more concrete-level operations or actions in a hierarchy of goal-directed behavior, the researcher would start with the identification level and ladder downward with a series of how questions. In other words, in addition to asking why a person would engage in a particular behavior, the researcher would also probe into how the person was going to engage in a particular behavior to ascertain the more molecular actions underlying a behavior or goal.

Little (1983) reported implementing a very similar procedure to study the hierarchical nature of people's life projects. He referred to this procedure as act-laddering and value-laddering in which people are asked a series of questions about why they are engaged in a life project, and how they are planning to carry out this life project. Preliminary indications from this work suggest that a similar approach to studying the lower portion of a goal-directed behavior hierarchy may be efficacious.

DYNAMIC ASPECTS OF HIERARCHIES OF GOAL-DIRECTED BEHAVIOR

So far we have mainly considered static aspects of hierarchies of goal-directed behavior. The role that (portions of) hierarchies of goal-directed behavior play in controlling ongoing behavior has not been discussed. In this section such dynamic aspects are introduced.

Specifically, we look at the dynamics of goal-directed behavior in two senses. First, ongoing behavior is not always monitored from the same vantage point in the hierarchy. Although the assumption that behavior is generally controlled by goals at an intermediate level is reasonable as a first approximation, control may shift to lower or higher levels as the behavior unfolds and, as we see in the following, these shifts are systematically related to certain factors. Second, components of any particular goal hierarchy (especially lower level components) can also be elements of other goal hierarchies (e.g., a person may exercise to lose weight, but exercising may also serve to lead an active life, etc.). Therefore, an initial move toward a lower level and a subsequent move toward a higher level of action control may result in a different identification of the behavior. In this way the higher level meanings associated with particular behaviors may change and new actions may emerge. Both ideas are based on action identification theory (Vallacher & Wegner, 1985) and we draw heavily on that framework in this section.

Level of Identification and the Control of Action

Although complete hierarchies of goal-directed behavior can be elicited on prompting, it is unreasonable to expect that all levels will be consciously represented in memory at all times. This leads to questions such as: Which parts of the hierarchy of goal-directed behavior will be activated at any particular point in time?; At which level will behavior be monitored? Are there factors that systematically influence the level at which behavior is identified and controlled?

Vallacher and Wegner (1985) contributed answers to these questions based on their theory of action identification. According to their theory, behavior is controlled at the level at which it is identified, and people have a tendency to control their behavior at the most abstract level possible. Moreover, if behavior can no longer be maintained at the current level, there is a tendency to shift to a lower level. This leads to the suggestion that there is an optimal identification level at which behavior can be controlled most effectively and efficiently. Both identifications above and below the optimal level may be counterproductive. For example, imagine a consumer who wants to get money from an ATM in order to buy a gift for her boyfriend. The initial identification for the behavior might be "getting money so I can buy a gift." However, suppose that the consumer encounters a problem while trying to withdraw the money. In that case she may have to focus on the exact sequence of specific actions such as inserting the MAC card into the slot, typing in the personal identification number, indicating the amount to be withdrawn, and so forth.

Several factors have been shown to affect the level at which behavior is identified. These factors can be classified as characteristics of the actor, characteristics of the action, and characteristics of the context in which the action takes place. Characteristics of the actor include a person's previous experience with the action and individual differences in action identification. With regard to the first factor, the more familiar someone is with an action, the more automatic the individual action components become and the higher the identification level will be at which the behavior can be controlled (Vallacher & Wegner, 1987). Individual differences in the level at which people tend to identify their behavior across situations have been observed as well. Vallacher and Wegner (1989) referred to this dimension of personality as a person's *level of personal agency* (LOPA). People low in LOPA tend to be concerned with the details of action, having the mechanics or operational aspects of behavior in mind, whereas people high in LOPA tend to think of their actions in terms of consequences, behaving more with their goals and motivations in mind. Vallacher and Wegner (1989) developed an instrument to assess such individual differences in level of personal agency in which people have to indicate whether a low-level (e.g., chewing and swallowing) or a high-level (e.g., getting nutrition) identification seems more appropriate for a given behavior (e.g., eating). Compared to those scoring low, people scoring high on the LOPA scale were shown to have greater action effectiveness, to engage in more action planning, and to possess a more well-developed self-understanding.

In addition to personal factors, there are also characteristics of the action that influence at what level behavior is identified. One important factor, somewhat related to action experience, is the difficulty of the behavior. Vallacher and Wegner (1987) showed that the more difficult the action, the more complex in terms of subacts, and the longer the enactment and learning time, the lower the level at which the action is identified. A somewhat similar point was also made by Heckhausen and Beckmann (1990). They distinguish wide-spanned goals from narrow-spanned goals. Very abstract goals span several clusters of activities, or even whole domains of life, whereas very specific goals are closely tied to a small set of single acts. Heckhausen and Beckmann (1990) argued that wide-spanned goals are appropriate when the attainment of the goal is conditional on enactment of simple, easily managed behaviors that need little conscious attention.

Finally, there are contextual factors that influence how behavior is identified. Research has shown that when the normal stream of behavior is interrupted, or when something unexpected occurs, people will lower the level at which they identify what they or other actors are doing, in an attempt to deal with the situation properly. For example, Newtson (1973) asked subjects to code behavior units in the performance of an actor on videotape. Two groups of subjects saw the same tape, except for a small segment in the middle. On one tape, the actor continued his normal routine in the segment. On the other tape, the actor performed an unexpected sequence of behaviors, that is, he removed a shoe, put it on the table, and rolled his other pant leg up to the knee. The dependent variable was the number and size of the behavior units that observers identified before and after the unexpected segment on the tapes. Not surprisingly, the number and size of behavior units that subjects identified before the target segment did not differ between tapes. However, subjects who had viewed the unexpected scene employed significantly more behavior units after that scene than subjects who had viewed the expected sequence of events. Hence, an unexpected contextual event led to a relatively fine-grained analysis of another person's behavior. Other research finds similar results for the identification of one's own behavior (e.g., Wegner, Vallacher, Macomber, Wood, and Arps, 1984).

The effects of level of personal agency and past experience on the identification of weight-loss behaviors were explored in the weight-loss study mentioned previously. Subjects were asked to list "things you would do if you wanted to lose weight." A maximum of 10 behaviors could be listed, each on a separate line. Behaviors were content-analyzed into 13 categories. Ten categories concerned specific, relatively low-level dieting (e.g., avoid snacking after dinner), exercising (e.g., play tennis twice a week) and behavioral control activities (e.g., join a Weight Watchers program). Three categories dealt with dieting, exercising, and behavioral control more generally. For example, if a subject mentioned that he or she would "change my eating habits," this was coded as a general dieting behavior. In a separate section of the questionnaire, past behavior with respect to weight loss and LOPA were assessed. It was expected that people with extensive weight-loss experience would not only list more behaviors, due to their familiarity and expertise, but that they would also list more abstract, general behaviors, as compared to people with limited or no weight-loss experience. In addition, we expected that after controlling for past behavior, people high in LOPA would produce a higher proportion of general, abstract behaviors than people low in LOPA.

On average, subjects listed 6.7 weight-loss behaviors, of which 1.6 were at a general level and 5.1 were at a specific level. As expected, the frequency of past weight-loss attempts positively affected the number of behaviors listed ($r = .50$, $n = 49$, $p < .01$), the number of general-level behaviors mentioned ($r = .35$, $n = 49$, $p = .02$), and the proportion of general-level to total behaviors provided ($r = .3007$, $n = 49$, $p = .04$). LOPA did not affect any of these measures directly. However, when the sample was split into two groups depending on whether subjects sometimes, often, or always versus seldom or never tried to lose weight, some interesting results emerged. For the first, experienced group, LOPA was unrelated to the three dependent variables (correlations of .21, −.05, and −.03 for total number of behaviors listed, number of general-level behaviors mentioned, and proportion of general-level to total behaviors provided, n = 28). On the other hand, for the second, inexperienced group, LOPA was significantly correlated with the number of general-level behaviors listed (r = .50, n = 21, p = .02) and the proportion of general-level to total behaviors provided (r = .45, n = 21, p = .04). The correlation with the total number of behaviors provided was nonsignificant (r = .05, n = 21). Thus, whereas the effects of past weight-loss behavior dominated the results, LOPA did have the expected effect for people who had no or limited experience with weight loss. Given the limited range of levels in the weight-loss hierarchy that we elicited in this task (i.e., by asking what subjects would do in order to lose weight we didn't tap higher level meanings), these results are encouraging. They confirm the influence of personal factors on the level in the behavioral hierarchy that an individual focuses upon.

The Emergence of New Identifications and Action Change

The level at which behavior is identified affects evaluation processes and the emergence of subsequent behavior. Research indicates that when people monitor the specific, concrete mechanics and operations of behavior, they tend to reflect on the costs or sacrifices of behavior. Vallacher and Wegner (1985) found that people who performed a potentially painful task (turning nuts and bolts while having one's hands submerged in ice water) experienced more pain when they identified their behavior at a low level than when they identified their behavior at a high level. In addition, people who identified their behavior at a low level performed worse. Hacker (1985) found that employees who were trained in the specific skills and in the abstract rules and heuristics necessary for a job showed superior performance without increased fatigue, compared to employees who were trained in the specific skills only. It is likely that in these situations people who monitor behavior at a high level of abstraction tend to reflect more on the benefits or advantages of behavior. This might also be a reason why people have a tendency to control their behavior at the most abstract level possible.

A specific behavior may lead to multiple goals, and it may be part of several larger units of behavior. Therefore, the same specific behavior may lead to different subsequent behaviors, depending on the goal that people perceive to govern the behavior. Research by Wegner et al. (1984) illustrated this. They gave two groups of subjects a cup of coffee to drink and asked them to describe what they were doing. One of the groups drank the coffee from normal cups. The other group drank the coffee from heavy, tall, and unwieldy cups. Half of each group received information that they drank the coffee to seek stimulation, the other half that they drank the coffee to avoid stimulation. Next, all subjects listened to music, and they were allowed to control the volume of the music. It was expected that subjects who drank from the unwieldy cups would identify their behavior at a lower level than the other subjects and that, as a consequence of this, they would be more susceptible to information concerning the reasons for doing this. Thus, people given the "seek stimulation" goal were expected to turn up the volume, and people given the "avoid stimulation" goal were hypothesized to turn down the volume. On the other hand, subjects who drank the coffee from normal cups should be less open to suggestions about what they were doing. The results showed that subjects in the "unwieldy cup, seek stimulation" condition indeed turned up the volume of the music, whereas subjects in the "unwieldy cup, avoid stimulation" condition turned down the volume. Only slight effects (in the opposite direction) emerged in the normal-cup condition. These results are consistent with the hypothesis that behaviors identified at a relatively low level are more changeable, and they suggest that getting consumers to think of their behaviors in operational terms may make it easier to influence their behavior.

IMPLICATIONS AND DIRECTIONS FOR FUTURE RESEARCH

The central argument of this chapter is that in order to fully understand goal-directed consumer behavior, it is necessary to study the means–end connections across all levels of the behavioral hierarchy, ranging from the relatively concrete level of specific action plans (the how of behavior) to the more abstract level of personal goals (the why of behavior). This basic idea is quite similar to the notion of means–end chain analysis that, in order to understand what makes products personally relevant, one has to model the perceived relations between a product (defined as a collection of attributes) and a consumer (regarded as a holder of values). Means–end chain analysis yields a hierarchical value map (also called a consumer decision map) that shows the salient linkages between attributes, consequences, and values for a particular product class, and this information represents the motivationally-relevant meanings associated with a product (Reynolds, Westberg, & Olson, 1994). A hierarchical structure of goal-directed behavior, on the other hand, provides insights into consumers' subjective understanding of their actions and indicates both the means by which something can be achieved and the ends to which it is ultimately directed.

The hierarchical model of goal-directed behavior proposed in this article is based on the assumption that, on prompting, consumers can verbalize linked sequences of means–end connections between behaviors and goals at different levels. However, the approach does not imply that complete goal hierarchies are consciously represented in memory at all times. Following action identification theory, it is assumed that behavior is controlled at the level at which it is identified and that consumers do not concern themselves with levels much below or above the identification level. However, the identification level may shift in the course of ongoing behavior. In the interest of gaining a more comprehensive understanding of their actions, people may try to identify a behavior more broadly. However, when difficulties arise, it might be necessary to shift toward a lower identification. Little (1989) called this the struggle to find a balance between the meaningfulness and manageability of projects.

It appears that some of the ideas about the dynamic nature of goal hierarchies and action control may also be applicable to means–end chain structures of consumers' product knowledge. Analogous to the issue of action identification, one might ask at what level a consumer thinks about a product (in terms of attributes, consequences, or values). In general, it seems likely that consumers will focus on the functional consequences of product use (i.e., the tangible benefits that a product confers). However, this focus may vary as a function of characteristics of the consumer, characteristics of the product, and characteristics of the context in which the consumer thinks about the product. For example, there are probably individual differences in the way a person characteristically views a product. If the LOPA scale, discussed previously, is too domain-specific and other conceptually related scales are too general (e.g., measures of cognitive style), it should be straightforward to construct an instrument in which consumers are asked whether given products are best thought of as bundles of attributes, providers of benefits, or satisfiers of values. With respect to product characteristics, one obvious distinction that should affect at what level a consumer thinks about a product is between functional, symbolic, and experiential brands (Park, Jaworski, & MacInnis, 1986). Products that serve symbolic and experiential purposes are more closely linked to the self and should thus tap higher level meanings in a hierarchy of product knowledge than functional products. Finally, as an example of a situational factor, the choice context may influence whether the focus is on attributes, consequences, or values. If a consumer makes a choice based on *Consumer Reports* ratings, lower levels in the hierarchy of product knowledge will likely figure more prominently, whereas when the alternatives are noncomparable, choice will probably have to be based on more abstract considerations. The factors that influence at what level consumers think about products could be used as segmentation variables and in product positioning.

A hierarchical model of goal-directed behavior may provide a useful framework for investigations in several important areas of consumer research. One application would be to work on the motivations that underlie broad classes of behaviors that have been of particular interest to consumer researchers (e.g., shopping behavior, gift giving, weight control, blood donation, aesthetic consumption, etc.). The objective would be to compile, for each of these categories of behavior, a listing of domain-specific, middle-range goals and to relate these to both the specific behaviors that are instrumental to their attainment and the more abstract personal goals that span different life domains. The various goals could be rated in terms of different dimensions such as importance, difficulty, desirability, and so on (cf. Emmons, 1989; Little, 1983). Then, these ratings could be used to characterize consumers' goal structures and to study the relation between aspects of the goal hierarchy and other variables of interest. Furthermore, the analysis could be extended to include measures of the compatibility or conflict between an individual's goals. Both Emmons (1989) and Little (1989) described methods for analyzing the extent to which a person's goals are compatible or in conflict and what effects this has on other variables such as measures of subjective well-being.

A hierarchical perspective on goal-directed behavior may also provide a useful conceptual framework for investigations of the process of goal striving. Traditionally, research dealing with the antecedents of action (e.g., Fishbein & Ajzen's, 1975, theory of reasoned action and its various extensions) focused on the issue of intention formation and goal setting. We believe that much is to be learned about the way abstract goals are translated into specific action plans and how these plans are enacted in the face of temptations and obstacles. Consumers are often confronted with conflicting goals, and frequently repeated attempts are required to attain a goal. It is important to understand how consumers manage to attain such goals. A hierarchical model of goal-directed consumer behavior can help to understand which portions of the hierarchy are activated before and during actual goal-directed behavior, which conflicts between goals consumers perceive, and how these conflicts can be resolved. It can also explicate which knowledge consumers have about the specific means to achieve goals and whether this knowledge is correct.

The notion of a hierarchical model of goal-directed behavior should also have useful implications for changing consumer behavior. There is evidence that the activation of behavioral scripts influences people's intention to engage in behavior and ultimately actual behavior (cf. Anderson, 1983). Because a behavioral hierarchy represents script-like action plans for attaining the goal of interest, this information can be used to formulate influence strategies aimed at inviting consumers to enter into the script (Abelson, 1981) and enact the sequence of behaviors necessary to reach the desired goal. Furthermore, the higher level goals underlying the focal goal can be used to imbue the lower level behaviors with incentive value, thus further increasing the probability that consumers will engage in the behavior of interest (Markus & Ruvolo, 1989). Such a perspective on behavioral change is quite different from traditional views such as expectancy-value attitude theory, where changes in behavior depend on changes in attitudes and beliefs about the consequences of behavior. However, by focusing more directly on sequences of behaviors instrumental in reaching the focal goal and on the personal goals that make the focal goal self-relevant, it is likely that influence strategies based on knowing consumers' goal hierarchies will be more successful than traditional approaches in bringing about desired behavioral changes.

In sum, a hierarchical model of goal-directed consumer behavior promises to stimulate future research into a variety of important issues, and it has the potential to contribute to theory building about the essence of consumer behavior, the behavior itself.

REFERENCES

Abelson, R. P. (1981). Psychological status of the script concept. *American Psychologist, 36,* 715–729.

Anderson, C. A. (1983). Imagination and expectation: The effect of imagining behavioral scripts on personal intentions. *Journal of Personality and Social Psychology, 45,* 293–305.

Anderson, D. R. (1985). Online cognitive processing of television. In L. F. Alwitt & A. A. Mitchell (Eds.), *Psychological processes and advertising effects: Theory, research and applications* (pp. 177–199). Hillsdale, NJ: Lawrence Erlbaum Associates.

Bagozzi, R. P., & Dabholkar, P. A. (1994). Consumer recycling goals and their effects on decisions to recycle: A means–end chain analysis. *Psychology and Marketing, 11,* 313–340.

Bagozzi, R. P., & Warshaw, P. R. (1990). Trying to consume. *Journal of Consumer Research, 17,* 127–140.

Bandura, A. (1989). Self-Regulation of motivation and action through internal standards and goal systems. In L. A. Pervin (Ed.), *Goal concepts in personality and social psychology* (pp. 19–85). Hillsdale, NJ: Lawrence Erlbaum Associates.

Bettman, J. R. (1979). *An information processing theory of consumer choice.* Reading, MA: Addison-Wesley.

Cantor, N., & Kihlstrom, J. F. (1987). *Personality and social intelligence.* Englewood Cliffs, NJ: Prentice Hall.

Carver, C. S., & Scheier, M. F. (1981). *Attention and self-regulation: A control theory approach to human behavior.* New York: Springer-Verlag.

Emmons, R. A. (1989). The personal striving approach to personality. In L. A. Pervin (Ed.), *Goal concepts in personality and social psychology* (pp. 87–126). Hillsdale, NJ: Lawrence Erlbaum Associates.

Fishbein, M., & Ajzen, I. (1975). *Belief, attitude, intention, and behavior: An introduction to theory and research.* Reading, MA: Addison-Wesley.

Gutman, J. (1982). A means–end chain model based on consumer categorization processes. *Journal of Marketing, 46,* 60–72.

Gutman, J. (1991). Exploring the nature of linkages between consequences and values. *Journal of Business Research, 22*, 143–148.

Hacker, W. (1982). Wanted: A grammar of actions? Cognitive control of goal-directed actions (Review II). In W. Hacker, W. Volpert, & M. von Cranach (Eds.), *Cognitive and motivational aspects of action* (pp. 226–283). Amsterdam: North-Holland.

Hacker, W. (1985). Activity: A fruitful concept in industrial psychology. In M. Frese & J. Sabini (Eds.), *Goal-directed behavior: The concept of action in psychology* (pp. 262–283). Hillsdale, NJ: Lawrence Erlbaum Associates.

Heckhausen, H., & Beckmann, J. (1990). Intentional action and action slips. *Psychological Review, 97*, 36–48.

James, W. (1983). *Principles of Psychology*. Cambridge, MA: Harvard University Press. (Original work published in 1890)

Klinger, E. (1977). *Meaning and void: Inner experience and the incentives in people's lives*. Minneapolis: University of Minnesota Press.

Little, B. R. (1983). Personal projects: A rationale and method for investigation. *Environment and Behavior, 15*, 273–309.

Little, B. R. (1989). Personal projects analysis: Trivial pursuits, magnificent obsessions, and the search for coherence. In D. M. Buss & N. Cantor (Eds.), *Personality psychology: Recent trends and emerging directions* (pp. 15–31). New York: Springer-Verlag.

Locke, E. A. (1991). Goal theory vs. control theory: Contrasting approaches to understanding work motivation. *Motivation and Emotion, 15*, 9–27.

Markus, H., & Ruvolo, A. (1989). Possible selves: Personalized representations of goals. In L. A. Pervin (Ed.), *Goal concepts in personality and social psychology* (pp. 211–241). Hillsdale, NJ: Lawrence Erlbaum Associates.

Newtson, D. (1973). Attribution and the unit of perception of ongoing behavior. *Journal of Personality and Social Psychology, 28*, 28–38.

Olson, J. C., & Reynolds, T. J. (1983). Understanding consumers' cognitive structures: Implications for marketing strategy. In L. Percy & A. G. Woodside (Eds.), *Advertising and consumer psychology* (pp. 77–90). Lexington, MA: Lexington Books.

Park, C. W., Jaworski, B. J., & MacInnis, D. J. (1986). Strategic brand concept-image management. *Journal of Marketing, 50*, 135–145.

Pervin, L. A. (1989a). Goal concepts in personality and social psychology: A historical perspective. In L. A. Pervin (Ed.), *Goal concepts in personality and social psychology* (pp. 1–17). Hillsdale, NJ: Lawrence Erlbaum Associates.

Pervin, L. A. (1989b). Goal concepts: Themes, issues, and questions. In L. A. Pervin (Ed.), *Goal concepts in personality and social psychology* (pp. 473–479). Hillsdale, NJ: Lawrence Erlbaum Associates.

Pieters, R. G. M. (1993). A control view on the behavior of consumers: Turning the triangle. In G. J. Bamossy & W. F. van Raaij (Eds.), *European advances in consumer research* (pp. 507–512). Provo, UT: Association for Consumer Research.

Pieters, R. G. M., Baumgartner, H., & Allen, D. (1995). A means–end chain approach to consumer goal structures. *International Journal of Research in Marketing, 12*, 227–244.

Powers, W. T. (1973). *Behavior: The control of perception*. Chicago: Aldine.

Reynolds, T. J., & Gutman, J. (1988). Laddering theory, method, analysis, and interpretation. *Journal of Advertising Research, 28*, 11–31.

Reynolds, T. J., Westberg, S. J., & Olson, J. C. (1994). A strategic framework for developing and assessing political, social issue and corporate image advertising. In L. Kahle (Ed.), *Advertising and consumer psychology* (pp. 3–23). Lexington, MA: Lexington Books.

Schank, R. C., & Abelson, R. P. (1977). *Scripts, plans, goals, and understanding*. Hillsdale, NJ: Lawrence Erlbaum Associates.

Scott, J. (1991). *Social network analysis: A Handbook*. London: Sage.

Vallacher, R. R., & Wegner, D. M. (1985). *A theory of action identification*. Hillsdale, NJ: Lawrence Erlbaum Associates.

Vallacher, R. R., & Wegner, D. M. (1987). What do people think they're doing? Action identification and human behavior. *Psychological Review, 94*, 3–15.

Vallacher, R. R., & Wegner, D. M. (1989). Levels of personal agency: Individual variation in action identification. *Journal of Personality and Social Psychology, 57*, 660–671.

Wegner, D. M., Vallacher, R. R., Macomber, G., Wood, R., and Arps, K. (1984). The emergence of action. *Journal of Personality and Social Psychology, 46*, 269–279.

Author Index

Subject Index

A

a-b-e (attribute-benefit-emotion) model, 184, 187–190
  attribute focus of, 196–200
  benefit focus of, 200–203
  compared to the means–end model, 190–196, 210
  emotional focus of, 203–209
  summary of conditions for, 209–210
Acquisition strategy, 342–343, 353
Advertising, 145, 183–184, 283, 344
  and motivation, 395, 400, 407
  and socially negative products, 187
  and the a-b-e (attribute-benefit-emotion) model, 188–190, 196–209
  content analysis of, 184–187
  emotional effects of, 203–209
  evaluation of, 55–56, 172–176, 178–180, 239–242, 247–249, 252–261
  examples of effective, 205, 219, 222, 224–230, 235–239
  expenditures, 247
  fear appeals in, 208
  for new products, 237
  informational, 201–202
  multicultural, 235–236
  sexual imagery in, 205–207
  targeted to different market segments, 293–296
Advertising strategy
  definition of, 249
  development of, 56–58, 133–139, 153–154, 159–160, 163, 223–232, 293–296
  execution of, 236–241
  specification of, 232–236, 250
American Express, 208
American Plastics Council, 227–228
Animatics, 249, 254, 262
  using MECCAS and strata to test effectiveness of, 254–261
Arm and Hammer, 326, 337
Arthur S. DeMoss Foundation, 231–232
Association Pattern Technique, 86
Attitude models, 150–151
Attributes, 92, 114, 124, 149, 154–156, 184, 188, 190–191, 223, 287, 404–405
  and involvement, 375–376
  and meaning, 249–250
  as focus of the a-b-e model, 196–200
  in means–end research, 219, 363
  evaluative, 393
  salience of, 186
Avon, 341